D1288548

504

Selling the People's Cadillac

# Selling the People's Cadillac

## The Edsel

## and Corporate Responsibility

**Jan G. Deutsch**

New Haven and London
Yale University Press
1976

Copyright © 1976 by Yale University. All rights
reserved. This book may not be reproduced, in whole or
in part, in any form (except by reviewers for the public
press), without written permission from the publishers.
Library of Congress catalog card number: 75–37292.
International Standard book number:
   cloth: 0–300–01950–5
   paper: 0–300–02014–7

*HD
60.5
U5
S44*

Printed in the United States of America by
The Alpine Press, Inc.
Published in Great Britain, Europe, and Africa by Yale
University Press, Ltd., London.
Distributed in Latin America by Kaiman & Polon, Inc.,
New York City; in Australasia by Book & Film Services,
Artarmon, N.S.W., Australia; in Japan by John
Weatherhill, Inc., Tokyo.

The author wishes to thank those mentioned below for permission to
quote the following:

Robert J. Art, *The TFX Decision,* © 1968, by Little Brown and Company
Inc. Permission granted by the author.

George E. Berkeley, *The Administrative Revolution: Notes on the Passing
of Organization Man.* © 1971, p. 135–137. Reprinted by permission of
Prentice-Hall, Inc., Englewood Cliffs, New Jersey.

John Brooks, *The Fate of the Edsel.* From *Business Adventure* (Weybright
& Talley). Reprinted by permission; © 1960 John Brooks. Originally
in *The New Yorker.*

Reprinted from the issues of *Business Week* by special permission.
©1956, 1957, 1959 by McGraw-Hill, Inc. Nov. 24, 1956; June 8, 1957;
Dec. 7, 1957; Sept. 26, 1959; Nov. 28, 1959.

*Consumer Reports,* "The Edsel Story." Copyright © 1958 by Consumers
Union of United States, Inc. Mount Vernon, N.Y. 10550. Reprinted by
permission from *Consumer Reports,* April 1958.

Jan G. Deutsch, "Neutrality, Legitimacy, and the Supreme Court."
Copyright © 1968 by the Board of Trustees of the Leland Stanford
Junior University; first published in the *Stanford Law Review,* Volume
20, page 169.

Jan G. Deutsch, "The Responsibility of a Corporation: An Attempt at
Implementation," *The Villanova Law Review,* June 1975. Copyright ©
1975 by Villanova University, Villanova, Pennsylvania.

J. K. Galbraith, *The New Industrial State,* rev. ed. © 1967, 1971 by John
Kenneth Galbraith. Reprinted by permission from Houghton Mifflin
Company.

Howard Gardner, *The Shattered Mind,* p. 315. Copyright © 1974 by
Howard Gardner. Reprinted by permission.

*The Best and the Brightest,* by David Halberstam. Copyright © 1969,
1971, 1972 by David Halberstam. Reprinted by permission of Random
House.

Booton Herndon, *Ford: An Unconventional Biography of the Men and
Their Times,* pp. 14–15, 167, 219–25. Copyright © 1969, 1970 by
Booton Herndon. Reprinted by permission of Weybright and Talley, Inc.

Eric Larrabee, "The Edsel and How It Got That Way," in *Harper's
Magazine,* Sept. 1957. Copyright © 1957 by Harper's Magazine.

Simon Lazarus, "Galbraith Revisiting Galbraith." Reprinted by
permission of *The New Republic,* © 1971, The New Republic, Inc.

Eugene J. McCarthy, "Pentagon Papers." Reprinted by permission of
*The New Republic,* © 1971, The New Republic, Inc.

Robin Marris, "Galbraith, Solow, and the Truth about Corporations."
*The Public Interest,* Number 11 (Spring 1968). © 1968 by National
Affairs.

John Montgomery, *History and Christianity,* p. 12. Taken from *History
and Christianity* by John Warwick Montgomery. © 1964 and 1965 by
Inter-Varsity Christian Fellowship of the U.S.A. Used by permission of
Intervarsity Press.

Allen Nevins and Frank Hill, *Ford: Decline and Rebirth,* pp. 380–81.
Copyright © 1962, 1963 Columbia University. Reprinted by permission
of Charles Scribner's Sons.

Nelson B. Polsby, "On the Intersections Between Law and Political
Science." Copyright © 1968 by the Board of Trustees of the Leland
Stanford Junior University; first published in the *Stanford Law Review,*
Volume 21, p. 142.

*The New York Times.* "Soviet Art," by John Russell, Sept. 22, 1974.
"The Bow and the Lyre," by Helen Vendler, June 30, 1974. "The World
As An Audience," by Gian Carlo Menotti, Oct. 14, 1973. Anthony
Burgess, in the Sunday Magazine, Nov. 7, 1971. © 1974/1973/1971 by
the New York Times Company. Reprinted by permission.

*Newsweek,* "Now Comes the Edsel." Copyright © 1965 by Newsweek,
Inc. All rights reserved. Reprinted by permission.

John B. Rae, *The American Automobile: A Brief History,* pp. 205–206.
Copyright © 1965 by the University of Chicago. Reprinted by permission.

Andrew Shonfield, *Modern Capitalism,* pp. 341–342. © Royal Institute
of International Affairs 1965.

Robert M. Solow, "The Truth Further Refined: A Comment on Marris"
*The Public Interest* Number 11 (Spring 1968), pp. 47–52. Copyright ©
1968 by National Affairs, Inc.

Stavins, Barnet, and Raskin, *Washington Plans an Aggressive War.*
Copyright © 1971 by Ralph Stavins, Richard J. Barnet, and Marcus G.
Raskin. Reprinted by permission of Random House, Inc.

*Time,* "The $250 Million Flop," Nov. 30, 1959. Reprinted by permission
from Time, The Weekly News-Magazine; Copyright 1959 Time, Inc.

Henry L. Trewhitt, *McNamara: His Ordeal in the Pentagon.* Copyright ©
1971 by Henry L. Trewhitt. Reprinted by permission of Harper & Row,
Publishers, Inc.

*The Wall Street Journal,* "General Dynamics F-111 Output to Be Ended
By Pentagon," Notes on the Yom Kippur War." Reprinted with
permission of the *Wall Street Journal,* © Dow Jones & Company, Inc.
1973. All Rights Reserved.

*The Washington Post,* Nov. 2, 1971. © 1971 The Washington Post.

*The author wishes also to acknowledge:
Jane Isay, the editor who taught me the meaning of the
book I compiled, but did not articulate;
and Tom Strong, the artist who made the articulation
meaningful.*

251762

*For Barbara*
*helpmate and spur*
*with love and thanks*

251762

# Preface

If this book is more successful than its subject, the reader will find herein a multi-disciplinary analysis of a relatively rare phenomenon in American corporate history—utter failure. By weaving through the various perspectives of economics, philosophy, and sociology, it is hoped one can travel the path forged by Galbraith into understanding corporate America and, perhaps, more importantly, corporate psychology—particularly in terms of behavioral notions of organization, culture, and personality.

Beginning with a set of popular and fundamental premises about the economy, the selections attempt to demonstrate that in order to ponder such imponderables, one must become fully and simultaneously aware of both the complex interdependent nature of domestic commercial activity, and the enormous role of the corporation in American history, while keeping a constant eye on the human aspects which account for the complexity of both business and history. It is that task to which this book is devoted.

unpublished book review

# John Kenneth Galbraith and his Critics

by Charles H. Hession
240 pp. New York: New American Library $6.95

Hession's title indicates the importance he assigns to John Kenneth Galbraith, the president of the American Economic Association. The structure and organization of this book demonstrate Hession's acceptance of Galbraith's thesis that the academic—a member of the "educational estate"—has achieved enhanced status in the current *New Industrial State.* Thus, a volume whose preface notes that it is written "mainly for the nonprofessional reader" not only analyzes in detail the content of the Galbraithian trilogy of *American Capitalism, The Affluent Society*, and *The New Industrial State*, and provides a biographical sketch delineating the factors that engendered Galbraith's social criticism, but also attempts to analyze the social and cultural factors that produced those works and the reception they received. The academic emphasis is perhaps most clear in the concluding chapter, where Galbraith's views concerning economic reality are compared with those of earlier economic theorists (said by critics to have originated concepts borrowed,without acknowledgement, by Galbaith), and in the fact that so much of the book is devoted to a review of academic debates.

In his Introduction to this volume, Robert Lekachman notes that, on the basis of the "well-known attributes of academic gamesmanship," which "come to mind because the hero of Professor Hession's judicious evaluation is so conspicuous a violator of his trade union's code. . . . [Galbraith] is a disgrace to his profession." Hession's volume is characterized by adherence to such academic virtues as modesty, balance, openness to contrasting viewpoints, and wide acquaintance with the literature embodying relevant empirical research. Given those virtues, it seems not unfair to criticize Hession for having failed to take Lekachman's accusation seriously: to regret—in so wide-ranging and analytical a volume —the absence of any attempt to explore the significance of Galbraith's professional iconoclasm.

In a review of *The New Industrial State* quoted by Hession, for example, Irving Kristol pointed out that it was precisely Galbraith's status as an economist that gave

good tidings to the entire spectrum of dissenters—to the socialist squares and those who are far out, to individualists who despise "the power structure" and embryonic central planners. Professor Galbraith patiently explains to them all that they are right in attacking the system, though not always for the right reasons. It is predictable that his book will become one of their sacred texts.

Kristol's "intuition" concerning sacred texts, agrees Hession:

was strikingly borne out three years later by the publication of Charles A. Reich's *The Greening of America* [which] explicitly cited Galbraith's book as providing the factual foundation for part of its severely critical analysis and condemnation of the American corporate state.

Later in the same chapter, however, Hession characterizes *The Greening of America* as an example of transmutation of Galbraith's theoretical construct of partial producer—as opposed to consumer—sovereignty into "the simple notion that the large corporations absolutely control demand." Hession's defense, of an economic concept basic to Galbraith's social criticism, against the oversimplification represented by *The Greening of America* would be considerably more impressive if, in his concluding chapter, Hession did not criticize Galbraith for "fail[ing] to stress the need for a new type of man, a new consciousness that would make . . . a [Galbraithian] standard operative and practicable"; and, more generally, if Hession did not attribute Galbraith's importance as a social critic precisely to the facts that he wrote for a general public rather than for academic economists, and that he dealt with aspects of reality not generally regarded as falling within that discipline.

This is not to deny that Galbraith's economics are far more rigorous than those espoused by Reich. It is to point out only that it seems somewhat lacking in scholarly rigor for Hession to criticize Reich for oversimplifying Galbraith and then to criticize Galbraith for failing to stress an aspect of reality that was the focus of the work that had been found guilty of oversimplification.

Analogous questions arise in connection with the earlier two works in the Galbraithian trilogy. Once we accept Hession's postulate that Galbraith's social criticism is not to be judged in terms of academic standards of empirical accuracy, theoretical rigor, or mathematical sophistication—but rather in terms of impact on the general public—we must face the issue of the extent to which these works reflected rather than influenced their times, and followed (or anticipated) fashions, rather than promulgating new insights. The question that must be confronted is the extent to which the concept of countervailing power—that the existence of large business organizations automatically produced organizations that represented rival interests, and thus limited the exercise of business power—reflected rather than influenced the beliefs of the America of 1952 (the year *American Capitalism* was published), when it is remembered that that year also witnessed the beginning of an era in American history which saw the development of consensus as the central concept in political theory, senators such as Lyndon Johnson and Robert Kerr with significant business interests, and George Humphrey as Secretary of the Treasury. Similarly, in connection with *The Affluent Society* (published in 1958), the question that must be asked is whether the insights being presented had a value independent of the sense in which they clearly anticipated the political mood to which President Kennedy responded by suggesting that one ask not what society can do, but what one can do for society.

One answer to these questions—one that Lekachman gives in the Introduction—is to stress the extent to which Galbraith's views on contemporary economic policy questions seem to be preferable to those presently being implemented: In Lekachman's words, to stress the extent to which "Galbraith is relevant and most of official economics increasingly irrelevant to the major public issues of the 1970s." If sensitivity to public mood and sophisticated awareness of the causes of economic behavior are the standards to be applied, however, Lekachman's case is far from evident. Assuming Arthur Burns is representative of "official economics," it seems to me his recent testimony concerning the extent to which foreign and domestic troubles had created a mood of uncertainty that led to a decline in consumer purchasing represented a model of "relevant" insight. Even if the stress is less on insights than on specific policy proposals, moreover, the case is far from clear.

Thus, three days after the publication of the *New Industrial State*, Galbraith assembled with three other men who had engaged in economic analysis to discuss the question, "Are planning and regulation replacing competition in the new industrial state?" before two subcommittees of the Senate.

Citing the market power which the other participants had condemned in their published work, [Galbraith] challenged them to ask for "all-out dissolution proceedings" against General Motors and a roster of other corporate giants. Only

such an onslaught, he declared, would legitimize the objections to his position. If such a crusade is not to be launched, then his colleagues in the seminar had no alternative but to agree with him. The antitrust laws are simply part of American folklore; we should allow them quietly to atrophy.

The question of whether or not the antitrust laws should automatically be applied once certain levels of magnitude are achieved by business organizations is, of course, a complex and delicate policy issue on which Galbraith's view may well be correct. Only an economic scholar whose view of reality is wholly one-dimensional, however, who believes that national folklore has no effect whatsoever on the actions of business organizations, could argue that a failure to apply antitrust policy to existing structures automatically justifies the conclusion that antitrust enforcement should quietly be allowed to atrophy. The fact is—and it is a fact that public policy should take into account—that the application of antitrust policy to present business practices (the fact that that policy is a living part of American folklore) serves to slow the potential rate of growth of certain existing business structures by foreclosing routes of expansion.

Finally, it seems to me an indication of the thoroughness and sensitivity with which this volume has been organized that it provides a biographical insight into the iconoclastic techniques employed by Galbraith in connection with his trilogy of social criticism. Thus, in 1951 (the year before the publication of the first volume in the trilogy) Galbraith rewrote two of his earlier articles on price-fixing—based on his experiences as deputy administrator of the Office of Price Administration—and included them with much new material in a book entitled *The Theory of Price Control*. Galbraith's reaction to the general lack of attention this book received was carried in *The New York Times Book Review* of June 25, 1967, and is quoted by Hession as follows:

I think most people who have read it would say that it is the best book I have ever written. The only difficulty is that five people read it. Maybe ten. I made up my mind that I would never again place myself at the mercy of the technical economists who had the enormous power to ignore what I had written. I set out to involve a larger community. I would involve economists by having the larger public say to them, "Where do you stand on Galbraith's idea of price control?" They would *have* to confront what I said.

That John Kenneth Galbraith has succeeded in involving a larger public is clear. The question remains whether the techniques he has employed should be approved by his scholarly peers.

*April 1972*

# The argument being made

is that we do not pay sufficient attention to the Edsel event.[1]

If we assume that psychoanalytic technique is based on an accurate description of the mechanisms in terms of which we perceive reality, the argument would be that we are "repressing" the Edsel event, and that the basis for that repression is the desperate attempt to keep from consciousness what it is the Edsel means.

Continuing in the psychoanalytic mode, the fact is that simply calling something repressed does not bring it to consciousness. But the hope is—and psychoanalysts have had a fair measure of success in making their patients aware—that something that has been repressed will be brought to consciousness by spending time focusing upon it: describing it, examining it, and searching for its historical roots.

1. From John B. Rae, *The American Automobile: A Brief History* (1965), 205–06, a volume in the Chicago History of American Civilization series: The 1950's saw the Ford Motor Company firmly and profitably reestablished in second place among automobile manufacturers and energetically but unavailingly trying to narrow the gap between it and General Motors. The Ford weakness was, or seemed to be, in the middle price range, where the Mercury had to compete with General Motors' Buick, Oldsmobile, and Pontiac and Chrysler's Dodge and DeSoto. The Ford firm did not arrive at its conclusion hastily; if anything, it took too long. In the face of suggestions that what was really wanted was a smaller and cheaper car than was being offered, the company conducted an extensive market research, which concluded that there was insufficient demand for a small car but a bright prospect for one in the range between the Lincoln and the Mercury. The result was the Edsel, in which the Ford Motor Company invested $250 million, including whatever it paid the poet Marianne Moore to think up names for it that were never used. It was a well-engineered but rather awkwardly styled car, and it lasted just two years after it was put on the market in 1958. Its failure was due fundamentally to its timing: 1958 was a recession year, when the prospect for a new high-priced automobile was poor in any event, and somewhere between the planning and the unveiling of the Edsel public preference turned away from the big, ornate cars that had dominated the scene for several years. The experiment served to provide a vivid explanation of why the automobile industry had evolved into its pattern of domination by a few very large firms; only a big company could make a mistake costing a quarter of a billion dollars and live.

# What it is we are repressing

was succinctly put by Walker Percy in his 1966 novel, *The Last Gentleman:*

But he saw no more than the car, a faded green Edsel which swung out of the steep driveway and disappeared down the links road. Jamie told him that Sutter drove an Edsel to remind him of the debacle of the Ford Motor Company and to commemorate the last victory of the American people over marketing research and opinion polls. (p. 188)

The extent to which this meaning has entered our language is also indicated by a *New York Times* news story of April 11, 1971, headlined:

DuPont's $100-Million Edsel: Market Research Doomed Corfam

Similarly, given the crucial role of the academic intellectual in the materials in later sections, it seems significant that a book concerning the life of a man who is located at a United States university and who considers himself a failure—a book written by the poet Karl Shapiro in 1971—should be entitled *Edsel*.

The question arises, however, why any of these facts should be accepted as significant or meaningful: why should we turn to literature for insights concerning a reality involving corporations and consumers?

A relevant and persuasive answer to that question was given in an article entitled "Is America Falling Apart?" in *The New York Times Magazine* of November 7, 1971, by Anthony Burgess, the British novelist, who had spent the prior academic year teaching at Princeton. The article consists of attempts to delineate the meaning of a series of personal impressions of life in the United States. The extent to which the reactions are personal is made clear by the opening of the piece:

I am back in Bracciano, a castellated town about 13 miles north of Rome, after a year in New Jersey. I find the Italian Government still unstable, gasoline more expensive than anywhere in the world, butchers and bank clerks and tobacconists (which also means salt-sellers) ready to go on strike at the drop of a *cappello* . . .

Nevertheless, it's delightful to be back. (p. 99)

How these impressions relate to corporations and consumers is made clear by what Burgess says about life both in Italy:

Manifold consumption isn't important here. The quality of life has nothing to do with the quantity of brand names. What matters is talk, family, cheap wine in the open air, the wresting of minimal sweetness out of the long-known bitterness of living. (p. 99)

and in the United States:

Americans are admirable in their distrust of the corporate state—they have fought both Fascism and Communism—but they forget that there is a use for everything, even the loathesome bureaucratic machine. America needs a measure of socialization, as Britain needed it. Things—especially those we need most—don't always pay their way and it is here that the state must enter, dismissing the profit element. (p. 101)

Of course, America was built on a rejection of the past. Even the basic christianity which was brought to the continent in 1620 was of a novel and bizarre kind that would have nothing to do with the great rank river of belief that produced Dante and Michelangelo. America as a nation has never been able to settle to a common belief more sophisticated than the dangerous naiveté of the Declaration of Independence. "Life, liberty and the pursuit of happiness," indeed. And now America, filling in the vacuum left by the liquefied British Empire, has the task of telling the rest of the world that there's something better than Communism. The something better can only be money-making and consumption for its own sake. In the name of this ghastly creed the jungles must be defoliated. (p. 102)

In terms of a solution, notes Burgess:

The guides, as always, lie among the writers and artists. And Americans ought to note that, however things may seem to be falling apart, arts and the humane scholarship are flourishing here, as they are not, for instance, in England. I'm not suggesting that Bellow, Mailer, Roth and the rest have the task of finding a solution to the American mess, but they can at least clarify its nature and show how it relates to the human condition in general. Literature, that most directly human of the arts, often reacts magnificently to an ambience of unease or apparent breakdown. The Elizabethans, to whose era we look back as to an irrecoverable Golden Age, were far more conscious than modern Americans of the chaos and corruption and incompetence of the state. Shakespeare's period was one of poverty, unemployment, ghastly inflation, violence in the streets. Twenty-six years after his death there was a bloody civil war, followed by a dictatorship of religious fanatics, followed by a calm respite in which the seeds of a revolution were sown. England survived. America will survive. (pp. 103–04)

Certainly I am not proposing that, in the role of guides, we accept writers and artists to the exclusion of psychoanalysts, lawyers, or historians. If we accept the greatness of Shakespeare, however, it seems to me difficult to deny the relevance of the argument made by Burgess.

Like all systems, nevertheless, a literary personage or work represents a set of correlations that may or may not be relevant, meaningful, or significant in any given situation. The task, therefore, is to identify the specific nature of the failures that the Edsel event signifies.

*New York Times Book Review*, June 30, 1974

# The Bow and the Lyre

*By Octavio Paz.*
*Translated by Ruth L. C. Simms.*
*281 pp. Austin: The University of*
*Texas Press. $8.50.*

## *By HELEN VENDLER*

Is not this to say that poetry and comedy are mutually exclusive? But we know, from Shakespeare, that they are not. And yet Paz, more temperamentally akin to Greek tragedy with its divine inperatives and prohibitions, or to the tragic debates of Racine, or to the high dramatic plane of the *autos sacramentales*, is uneasy in the presence of Shakespeare.

"In Shakespeare's world, chance replaces necessity. At the same time, innocence and guilt turn into words with no value. The dialectical equilibrium is broken, the tragic tension is relaxed. Despite their devastating passions and their cries that cause the earth to tremble, the characters in the Elizabethan theater are not heroic. There is something childish in them all. Childish and barbarous. Violent or gentle, candid or treacherous, brave or cowardly, they are a heap of bones, blood, and nerves doomed to calm for an instant the appetite of a deified nature. Sated, the tiger withdraws from the stage and leaves the theater covered with bloody traces: men. And what is the meaning of all that residue? Life is a tale told by an idiot. . . .

"Freedom is the foundation of being. If man renounces freedom, chaos irrupts and being is lost. In Shakespeare's world we witness the return of chaos. The limits between things and beings disappear, crime can be virtue, and innocence, guilt. The loss of legality causes the world to vacillate. Reality is a dream, a nightmare. And again we move among ghosts."

Like the passage on the novel, this paragraph provokes, and intends to provoke. Paz's remarks on Shakespeare rest on a belief that "as soon as the human happening loses its former sacred references [whether Greek or Christian] it turns into a succession of meaningless acts, which also lose connection with one another. Man becomes a plaything of chance."

# Facts

J. K. Galbraith, *The New Industrial State*

With the rise of the modern corporation, the emergence of the organization required by modern technology and planning and the divorce of the owner of the capital from control of the enterprise, the entrepreneur no longer exists as an individual person in the mature industrial enterprise. Everyday discourse, except in the economics textbooks, recognizes this change. It replaces the entrepreneur, as the directing force of the enterprise, with management. This is a collective and imperfectly defined entity; in the large corporation it embraces chairman, president, those vice presidents with important staff or departmental responsibility, occupants of other major staff positions and, perhaps, division or department heads not included above. It includes, however, only a small proportion of those who, as participants, contribute information to group decisions. This latter group is very large; it extends from the most senior officials of the corporation to where it meets, at the outer perimeter, the white and blue collar workers whose function is to conform more or less mechanically to instruction or routine. It embraces all who bring specialized knowledge, talent or experience to group decision-making. This, not the management, is the guiding intelligence — the brain — of the enterprise. There is no name for all who participate in group decision-making or the organization which they form. I propose to call this organization the Technostructure.

★    ★    ★

## The Imperatives of Technology

ON JUNE 16, 1903, after some months of preparation which included negotiation of contracts for various components, the Ford Motor Company was formed for the manufacture of automobiles. Production was to be whatever number could be sold. The first car reached the market that October. The firm had an authorized capital of $150,000. However, only $100,000 worth of stock was issued, and only $28,500 of this was for cash. Although it does not bear on the present discussion, the company made a handsome profit that year and did not fail to do so for many years thereafter. Employment in 1903 averaged 125 men.

In the spring of 1964, the Ford Motor Company introduced what is now called a new automobile. In accordance with current fashion in automobile nomenclature, it was called, one trusts inappropriately, a Mustang. The public was well prepared for the new vehicle. Plans carefully specified prospective output and sales; they erred, as plans do, and in this case by being too modest. These preparations required three and a half years. From late in the autumn of 1962, when the design was settled, until the spring of 1964, there was a fairly firm commitment to the particular car that eventually emerged. Engineering and "styling" costs were nine million dollars; the cost of tooling up for the production of the Mustang was fifty million dollars.[2] In 1964 employment in the Ford Motor Company averaged 317,000. Assets were approximately six billion dollars.

Virtually all of the effects of increased use of technology are revealed by these comparisons. We may pass them in preliminary review.

[2] I am grateful to Mr. Walter T. Murphy of the Ford Motor Company for providing these details. In this and subsequent chapters, I have also drawn on earlier help of Robert McNamara which he gave when he was still an executive of Ford. I wish here, at the outset, not only to concede but to emphasize that one may have planning without precision of result and that there will also be occasional failures. Accordingly, to cite a failure — another Ford creation, the Edsel, comes automatically to the mind of the more impulsive critics — is not to disprove this argument.

★     ★     ★

From the time and capital that must be committed, the inflexibility of this commitment, the needs of large organization and the problems of market performance under conditions of advanced technology, comes the necessity for planning. Tasks must be performed so that they are right not for the present but for that time in the future when, companion and related work having also been done, the whole job is completed. And the amount of capital that, meanwhile, will have been committed adds urgency to this need to be right. So conditions at the time of completion of the whole task must be foreseen as must developments along the way. And steps must be taken to prevent, offset or otherwise neutralize the effect of adverse developments, and to insure that what is ultimately foreseen eventuates in fact.

In the early days of Ford, the future was very near at hand. Only days elapsed between the commitment of machinery and materials to production and their appearance as a car. If the future is near at hand, it can be assumed that it will be very much like the present. If the car did not meet the approval of the customers, it could quickly be changed. The briefness of the time in process allowed this; so did the unspecialized character of manpower, materials and machinery.

Changes were needed. The earliest cars, as they came on the market, did not meet with complete customer approval: there were complaints that the cooling system did not cool, the brakes did not brake, the carburetor did not feed fuel to the engine, and a Los Angeles dealer reported the disconcerting discovery that, when steered, "Front wheels turn wrong." These defects were promptly remedied. They did the reputation of the car no lasting harm.

Such shortcomings in the Mustang would have been unpleasant. And they would have been subject to no such quick, simple and inexpensive remedy. The machinery, materials, manpower and components of the original Ford, being all unspecialized, could be quickly procured on the open market. Accordingly, there was no need to anticipate possible shortage of these requirements and take steps to prevent them. For the more highly specialized requirements of the Mustang, foresight and associated action were indispensable. In Detroit, when the first Ford was projected, anything on wheels that was connected with a motor was assured of acceptance. Acceptance of the Mustang could not be so assumed. The prospect had to be carefully appraised. And customers had to be carefully conditioned to want this blessing. Thus the need for planning.

★    ★    ★

When a firm is enjoying steady patronage by its existing customers and recruiting new ones, the existing sales strategy, broadly defined, will usually be considered satisfactory. The firm will not quarrel with success. If sales are stationary or slipping, a change in selling methods, advertising strategy, product design or even in the product itself is called for. Testing and experiment are possible. Sooner or later, a new formula that wins a suitable response is obtained. This brings a countering action by the firms that are then failing to make gains.

This process of action and response, which belongs to the field of knowledge known as game theory, leads to a rough equilibrium between the participating firms. Each may win for a time or lose for a time, but the game is played within a narrow range of such gain or loss. As in the case of Packard or Studebaker (as a producer of cars), firms that do not have the resources to play — particularly to stand the very large costs of product design and redesign — will lose out and disappear. And the firms that can play the game will, on occasion, find customers adamant in their resistance to a particular product; no response can be obtained at tolerable cost by any strategy that can be devised.[8]

---

[8] As in the case of the Edsel. I mention this again for, to a quite remarkable extent, this disaster is cited (by those who are made unhappy by these ideas) to prove that planning will not work. It proves what I unhesitatingly concede, which is that it doesn't work perfectly. Its notoriety owes much to its being exceptional.

# Galbraith and His Technostructure: A Second Look

*THE NEW INDUSTRIAL STATE: Second Edition, Revised. By John Kenneth Galbraith.*

(Houghton Mifflin, 423 pp., $8.95)

### Reviewed by Bernard D. Nossiter

*The reviewer is The Washington Post's London correspondent and is author of The Mythmakers: An Essay on Power and Wealth, a 1964 study of corporate pricing and political power.*

When "The New Industrial State" first appeared in 1967, Life Magazine commissioned but did not print a review. The review, largely favorable, gave Prof. Galbraith high marks for abandoning his earlier notion that big unions and big government countervailed big business, and for insisting on the economic primacy and near autonomy of the giant corporations. Life substituted for the review an editorial that argued Galbraith had it all wrong, in effect that General Motors, like a Wisconsin dairy farmer, was subject to rigorous competition and the imperatives of a generally unfettered market.

It is a measure of how far and fast we have come that a nationally right-wing Republican President and his conservative Democratic Treasury Secretary have implicitly endorsed the notion of the corporations' power and felt compelled to control prices and wages on their behalf.

Today, a popular view holds that Galbraith's enormously successful book inspired the new thinking about corporations. His influence is undeniable, but the claims for priority belong elsewhere. There is a belief, too, that Galbraith is some kind of radical. In fact, as a close reading of

"The New Industrial State" makes clear, Galbraith is a fatalistic conservative, an unrecognized defender of things more or less as they are. For he insists that giant corporations are the inevitable consequence of sophisticated technology and industrialization. Give up one, he contends, and you lose the other.

The Galbraithian argument runs along these rails: the modern economy is dominated by a few hundred massive concerns, largely free from competition because so few control each industry. Their primary goal is security, the avoidance of risk, not, as the conventional textbooks have it, the maximization of profit.

To achieve security and reduce risk, the large corporations control prices through their power in concentrated markets; control materials' costs by owning or dominating suppliers, or through long term deals with corporate peers; fix labor costs through collaboration with unions; control capital needs by raising investment funds through the prices they set rather than purchasing them from lenders or new investors; and control the demand for their products through a ceaseless manipulation of consumer desires. The system requires only one other element, an assured total demand. This is supplied by the Keynesian economic policies of the modern state.

Although corporations as organizations are powerful, power inside their bureaucracies is diffused. It does not lie with stockholders; typically, they are many and dispersed. It does not lie with self-perpetuating exec-

utives; they reign but do not rule.

Instead, power to make decisions is lodged with groups or committees of specialists — engineers, scientists, marketing experts, computer teams and the like. Galbraith invents an uncharacteristically awkward term for these people, the technostructure. In his view, this power group embraces virtually everyone above the blue collar and routinized white collar level.

Since talent, in this scheme, has become the decisive factor of production, the academic community or educational and scientific estate, occupies a strategic role. This community, training and supplying the talent, is potentially the most powerful in a modern society. It must throw off its financial chains to the corporations and their allied state and modify corporate goals to allow for the things that make life richer — aesthetic concerns, regard for the environment, a peaceful rather than a militant foreign policy.

As a description of what is, much of this will rightly be recognized as unimpeachable. But as a model of what must be or even what can be, we are entitled to skepticism.

Galbraith's a r g u m e n t rests on the central assumption that technology, with its demands for large capital investment, technical virtuosity a n d the coordination of committees of talents requires huge organizations. But it is far from clear that technological virtuosity goes hand in hand with corporations of the size we now enjoy.

General Dynamics, North

American Rockwell and Lockheed Aircraft are examples of Galbraith's technostructure carried to the limiting point. They boast a remarkable record of planes with cracked wings or falling engines, misfiring missiles, of ordnance that regularly fails to meet promised specifications. Indeed, this may be their secret contribution to peace. What military, no matter how adventurous, could engage an advanced power equipped with weapons like these? In any case, their producers are hardly an argument for the present scale of the technostructured corporation.

Again, hundreds of thousands of automobiles are recalled for structural defects. This suggests that Detroit's four firms may not constitute an ideal arrangement from a technological standpoint. The slow but steady erosion in telephone service has even raised questions about AT and T, once regarded, along with the Catholic Church and Jersey Standard, as the summit of managed excellence.

It is even harder to accept Galbraith's notion that giant firms spur innovation. The American steel industry's tardy adoption of Europe's efficient oxygenation process, and the American auto makers' coolness towards the rotary engine and a non-polluting power mechanism both argue that the giants' quest for security inhibits rather than encourages innovation. We lack conclusive evidence here. But "The Sources of Invention," a suggestive study by John Jewkes of Oxford, indicates that more industrial invention flows from independent individuals or small firms than from the labora-

review of Galbraith's *The New Industrial State*

tories of the large corporations.

It is one thing to argue, as does Galbraith, that the capital, manpower and technical requirements of modern industry require organizations of size. Galbraith, however, slips from this to the implied conclusion that the size of GM, US Steel, GE and Jersey Standard is a natural expression of this requirement, that they have reached an optimum and necessary size.

Buried in the files of the Justice Department's antitrust division and at the Federal Trade Commission are plans for dismembering GM and US Steel. These careful studies conclude that the auto giant could be broken into separate and economically viable firms named Chevrolet, Buick, Oldsmobile and the like: that US Steel derives no discernible advantage save power from enfolding a group of large plants, each of which could stand on its own. If such a breakup were ordered — admittedly an event of low political probability — it would still leave companies of size. And the pricing, investment and innovative behavior in an industry of 20 or 30 firms is likely to be quite different and possibly more satisfactory than one dominated by three or four.

In other words, those who have looked at the problem closely agree that size is necessary but hardly its present dimensions. They flow from a will to power rather than any technological imperative.

Galbraith's treatment of power within the corporation may comfort some of these institutions but it too is far from convincing. There is no reason to think the hierarchal arrangement in large corporations, with authority flowing upward to an ever narrowing apex, is merely an abstract design that does not picture reality. Certainly committees of specialists exist. But their goals, their funds, their existence is fixed by those on top of them. Presidents and executive vice presidents may like to avoid decision or give the appearance of powerlessness. But there is no reason, other than Galbraith's assertion, to think that top managers do not make or at least transmit, key decisions about the appropriate target rate of return (which fixes prices), about major investments, acquisitions, mergers and the other central elements of corporate life.

Just as dubious is Galbraith's unquestioning acceptance of the A. A. Berle-Gardiner Means thesis that the legal owners, the stockholders, play no decisive role in large corporations. Galbraith acknowledges the obvious exceptions, the Ford and Du Pont families. He passes over the less obvious but equally real instances of Rockefellers and Mellons. Beyond these, is it right to assume that the single holder of say five per cent of the shares in a firm with widely scattered holdings never intrudes on managers' crucial decisions, passively accepting all that managers do? The uncomfortable fact is that we know very little about decision-making in the giants and we need to know more.

Even if we are uncertain whether leading stockholders, managers or a combination of both are top dog, Galbraith's candidate, the technostructure, is unlikely. If this is so, then his educational and scientific estate is far less consequential and fills the role conventionally assigned to it, supplier of tools or hired hands for corporate needs. No doubt, if all the technically trained people in some corporation withheld their labor to induce support for an arts council or respect for the environment, they might succeed. But the prospects for this happening are not very bright.

As almost his sole specific evidence for the power of the academic community, Galbraith cites the Vietnamese War. He asserts that the educational and scientific estate toppled Johnson from power and reversed the course of the conflict. In fact, hired academics supplied much of the rationale for the war (Galbraith was a notable and honorable exception) as well as its instruments. Many who have since changed their minds did so after considerable prompting from the young men and women who are their customers in the universities. If, as Galbraith says, "For goals that are now important, there are no other saviors" outside the educational and scientific estate, we may all very well be damned.

Galbraith likes to pose in public as vain and immodest. In fact, he is an exceptionally large spirited and generous man, usually quick to credit others and not at all troubled about changing his mind, as he did in surrendering countervailing power. This makes all the more curious his failure to point out that the theory of corporate pricing power, administered prices, was developed by Gardiner Means in the 1930s and demonstrated empirically in the remarkable hearings held by Sen. Estes Kefauver 20 years later. These hearings, directed by John Blair, and particularly those on steel, autos and drugs, led directly to what Galbraith properly calls the most innovative feature of Kennedy economics — wage-price guideposts. This was the first, tentative effort at controls and the first federal acknowledgement that the pricing power of large corporations makes impossible stable prices at high levels of employment. Galbraith's slighting of Means and Kefauver is not in character.

To put Galbraith's work in perspective, to question some of his assumptions and assertions in no way diminishes his role or "The New Industrial State." Its central theme, the far ranging powers of the huge corporations and their intimate collaboration with a state that adopts and furthers their goals, touches on crucial problems in modern societies. Galbraith writes with the elegance and irony of a Thorstein Veblen and he has helped educate a vast audience to some of the realities of contemporary political economy. For this, we owe him much.

Simon Lazarus, *The New Republic*, Oct. 16, 1971

# Galbraith Revising Galbraith

## The New Industrial State
## by John Kenneth Galbraith

(Houghton Mifflin; $8.95)

Galbraith's first major work, *American Capitalism: the Concept of Countervailing Power*, which appeared in 1952, was drastically – though tacitly – qualified six years later by *The Affluent Society*, and both are in significant respects repudiated by *The New Industrial State* (first published in 1967; now revised). The thesis of the first of these was that even though the New Deal had failed to impose either strong regulatory or antitrust restraints on the great corporations, there was no need for concern; their power, Galbraith said, was offset by "countervailing" centers of power held by their equally well-organized customers and suppliers, whether the latter were unionized workers, agricultural cooperatives, or simply other oligopolies. Therefore, each industry's monopoly profits would be bargained away while goods were in the process of being produced and distributed and before reaching the consumer.

This reassuring message, well-tailored to the complacency of the early Eisenhower years, was almost wholly wrong. GM may bargain hard when shopping at US Steel; the result, however, is not lower auto prices but higher GM dividends, profits and salaries. If big retailers like Sears do seem to pass on the cost-savings won by their buying power, it is only because they are obliged to do so by competition, which Galbraith has always been at pains to deride.

In due course Galbraith recanted his initial optimistic account of the effects of corporate power and in *The Affluent Society* counseled that corporate propaganda for private consumption diverted society's attention from other economic needs such as education, health, and transportation – all of them essential for the corporate system itself and its affluent middle-class clientele. To counter these distortive pressures, Galbraith recommended more government spend-

ing. Liberal opinion, several powerful lobbies, and the Kennedy and Johnson administrations concurred.

But the Great Society turned out to be almost as unsatisfactory as the Affluent Society of the fifties. In 1967 Galbraith was ready with *The New Industrial State* to explain why. Corporate power had not, after all, been offset by big government. Indeed, activist stabilization policies, federal aid to higher education, and other measures which Galbraith and his colleagues had fought for (against, it was often believed at the time, the opposition of business) turned out to provide vital services to the new, "mature" corporate bureaucracies; viewed from this perspective, they became part of a piece with the even more vital services provided by the space and defense programs to the aerospace, electronics, weapons, and allied industries. "The state as here envisaged," Galbraith conceded in a more recent essay expanding on the central themes of the book, "comes close to being the executive committee of the large producing organization – of the technostructure." This picture of modern society is quite different – and far more grim – than that of 1952 or even 1958.

What gives rise to question in Galbraith's most recent work is not that his views have changed, but that his revision of old verities appears to have reached an abrupt and illogical halt. Despite his new-found suspicion of the modern state, Galbraith still seems to stand four-square with the New Deal statist tradition, and against the grain of the decentralist emphasis which Ralph Nader and others have more recently advanced. They have tended to look toward antitrust action to break up monopolistic and oligopolistic combines, to active judicial restraints on both private and public bureaucratic

power, and even to *de*regulation and an enlarged role for the private market.

*The New Industrial State*, however, affirms Galbraith's distaste for antitrust, which he calls "obscurantist." He comes close to saying that everything from computers to corn flakes is produced with maximum efficiency under conditions of tight oligopoly – where four or fewer huge firms, each selling perhaps $1 billion per year, dominate the market.

More remarkable than his support for corporate giantism is his loyalty to big government. "The Democratic Party," he has said recently, "must henceforth use the word socialism, it describes what is needed" – needed to lift urban and interurban transportation and housing, among other things, from their present squalid state. His suggestion for a "consolidated regulatory body for all regulated industries" is similar; it is based on the principle that "it takes a large public bureaucracy to police powerful private bureaucracy."

Such sentiments seem to me remarkable, given the anatomy of power sketched in *The New Industrial State*. If business has captured the state and turned it into an executive committee to serve its needs, why will not the same fate befall all the agencies which Professor Galbraith would like to build? The difficulty is not merely theoretical. There are few better examples of industries with a track record of controlling their regulators than those for which he dreams of streamlined socialist solutions. What, after all, are the precedents he has in mind – the ICC? the CAB? FHA? the Port of New York Authority?

The problem is not much different in the case of wage and price controls. Given business and labor influence within the federal government, why should their power to extort excessive prices from the public diminish or disappear just because the formal locus of wage and price decisions shifts from board rooms and collective bargaining sessions to the Executive Office Building? In the short run, when business, labor, and the public want to stop inflation, controls can work. In the long run, it seems difficult to dismiss, as Galbraith does, the case for using anti-

review of Galbraith's *The New Industrial State*

trust laws against strategic bastions of market power, as part of any program to reduce fundamental inflationary pressures.

If the new edition has not come to terms with its predecessor's schizophrenia about the beneficence of state power, a more unfortunate default is the author's refusal to qualify his assertion that the composition of consumer demand is dictated by business needs, not consumer wants. Some critics have charged that this dogmatism is mainly a slick cover for his own class prejudices against middle-class tastes. The charge is correct. He revealed his feelings on the matter two decades ago in *American Capitalism*, when he attacked the "Unseemly Economics of Opulence," and told economists to stop worrying "about partially monopolized prices or excessive advertising and selling costs for tobacco, liquor, chocolates, automobiles and soap in a land which is already suffering from nicotine poisoning and alcoholism, which is nutritionally gorged with sugar, which is filling its hospitals and cemeteries with those who have been maimed or murdered on its highways and which is dangerously neurotic about normal body odors." Then Galbraith was saying, "If that's what the people want, well let the fools go ahead and pay a little extra for it." Now he blames it all on Madison Avenue and says that the people do not really "want" these vulgar things, after all.

**Simon Lazarus**

If the old-time salesman is going the way of the vaudevillian whom he so often resembled, another form of hucksterism appears to have taken his place. Expenditures on advertising have risen rapidly in recent years and many regard the members of the industry as the master manipulators of all time. The alarm was first sounded, or at least loudly sounded, by Vance Packard in his book *The Hidden Persuaders*. The theme has since been taken up by others, among them John Kenneth Galbraith.

In his best selling book, *The New Industrial State,* Galbraith showed that he had swallowed Packard's thesis and swallowed it whole. Advertising and its related techniques have become for Galbraith the major molds in which the supposedly omnipotent business organization of today shapes the consumer's taste to its own will and whim. Thanks to advertising, he argues, today's consumer doesn't stand a chance. Furthermore, Galbraith appears to feel that this is the natural course of events in our modern age. "In the more technological and more complex society, the sovereignty of the individual gives way to the producing organization," he has since said (in a speech at Northeastern University, in 1970).

The idea has struck a responsive cord in the minds and hearts of many socially-concerned citizens. It is quite understandable why it should. Certainly, the commercials which disrupt our TV shows and the billboards which litter our landscape offer cause for dismay if not despair. Certainly, advertising seems more extensive and more oppressive now than it did years ago. Certainly, the gamut of social horrors ranging from cigarette smoking to tailfins which characterize our society would seem to have been encouraged if not fostered by advertising.

However, as with most social phenomena, the function and impact of advertising is much more complex than appearances indicate. One of the first things to note is that advertising bases itself on market research. And market research bases itself on finding out what the consumer wants and what he will respond to. Over 20,000 people in the United States today are engaged in trying to discover just what the felt needs of the buying public are, and it is upon their discoveries that new products are usually created and advertised. Contrary to the Packard-Galbraithian thesis, products are not just hatched at will by the producing company and palmed off to the public through clever commercials. Whenever this has been attempted, disaster has often ensued.

The classic case that is frequently referred to in this connection is the Edsel, the brainchild of the Ford Motor Company that burst on the scene in the late 1950s in a blaze of souped-up salesmanship and soon disappeared. This, however, was not the first time the giant motor company experienced a marketing setback. A few years prior to the Edsel, Ford had sought to introduce seat belts and other safety features in its cars. Failing to get the American public to buy them, it had to retreat.

Robin Marris, *The Public Interest*, Spring 1968

# Galbraith,
# Solow,
# and the truth about
# corporations

## ROBIN MARRIS

I have volunteered to intervene in the Solow-Galbraith controversy, which began in the Fall issue of this journal, because I have some doubts whether, at the end of the day, the lay reader was left clear about the basic issues. I am not concerned with the scores in the personal exchange: both protagonists are especially brilliant in polemic, and the reader certainly got his money's worth in style. The reader also got from Professor Solow an excellent summary of *The New Industrial State*, almost as skillful as his attempt to destroy it. For the record, I will only say that I do not think either protagonist has a Beautiful Appearance: both are imposingly tall, and both have very craggy faces that seem, in their different ways, to express so much of what has made this country what it is. As will become apparent, however, I am politically biased in favor of Galbraith and will probably be unfair to Solow.

It is true that Galbraith relies largely on assertion (or, shall we say,

------

*Dr. Marris is the author of* The Economic Theory of "Managerial" Capitalism *(New York, 1964) which was referred to by both Professors Robert Solow and John Kenneth Galbraith in their discussion. He teaches economics at King's College, Cambridge, England, and is currently a visiting professor at Harvard University.*

Robin Marris, *The Public Interest*, Spring 1968

on persuasive writing) in contrast to large-scale evidence to make his case — especially his case about advertising. It is also true that, by a great deal of hard work and by painstaking development of mathematical and statistical methods, economists over the last twenty years have learned to work more scientifically. But, for reasons which seem to be as much cultural as technical, the leading exponents of the new methods have chosen largely to confine themselves within the framework of the traditional assumptions. The form of their experiments has tended to preclude answering many of the questions here in debate. The influence of advertising, for example, has not been tested, but when the question arises it is customary to say that the traditional framework, now endowed with statistical flesh, provides a reasonable explanation of observed behavior, so that it is probably unnecessary to worry about Madison Avenue. If asked for a further opinion, exponents of this school usually themselves resort to assertions: specifically, they assert that the effects of large-scale advertising largely cancel themselves out, leaving the broad pattern of consumer expenditure undisturbed. Solow's review of Galbraith followed this line of argument almost precisely.

### The question of advertising

The statistical studies which are said to support the argument are not referred to in detail. But I think I know the literature Solow has in mind (even if Galbraith does not!), and I would suggest that, when it is carefully examined, the implications change considerably. When econometric studies look at the problem from the producers' side (i.e., when they test the hypothesis that variations in selling prices and profits can be explained, in Solow's words, by "supply and demand"), the results in fact leave a great deal of variation unexplained. When they start from the consumer end, they succeed in explaining a good deal of the observed variations in demand for individual commodities only by introducing factors other than conventional economic variables. These other factors, however, are not directly observable; they have to be inferred from the statistical results[1] and described as the trend of tastes, rate of habit formation, reaction to existing stocks of consumer durables, and so on. It is by no means unlikely that advertising has significant net effects on the strength of these relationships. But at present we cannot say whether this is so or not, because, after a quarter-century during which advertising has become one of the outstanding features of our economic life, and scientific economics has been intensively developed, the relevant experiments have never been tried.

---

[1] I should make it clear that like most of my colleagues I regard these methods as not only valid, but often brilliantly conceived.

Robin Marris, *The Public Interest*, Spring 1968

There is substantial technical justification for the situation, since the experiments required would stretch our capacity for rigorous testing to the limit. On the other hand, if the great majority of applied economists in this country are really so sure that they already know the answer, i.e., they are sure that most advertising results in a stand-off, the profession has clearly been guilty of a grave dereliction of duty to the public. They should have been shouting loudly and with one voice, "Here is an activity that has no significant net economic effect, good or bad; it is a total waste; it should be prohibited like arson." The discussion would then be thrown back into the sociological arena. I personally regard the cultural effects of advertising as debasing to language, to truth, and to logic, and as especially despicable because advertising is known to be most effective where the consumer has the least capacity to obtain the information necessary to evaluate products. There are sociologists who argue that the modern style of advertising (especially television) has a function in integrating the working class into the mass society and that the less well-educated obtain satisfaction from being wooed by advertisers. It is true that it is mostly the educated who scoff at advertising. We know from British experience that the working class positively prefers commercial programs and that BBC's audience is largely confined to the better educated. On the other hand, one has to count the cost of the recent effects in the United States of parading television commercials before people living in squalid conditions who can see no hope of buying many of the goods displayed. These are sorts of questions which economists have not equipped themselves to judge, and here I would align myself with Galbraith (in his rejoinder) in a plea for the broadening of both economics and sociology.

### The myth of "consumers' sovereignty"

This said, I must confess that the picture which, in my book, I drew in support of my own theory was more complex than Galbraith's and put considerably less emphasis on the effects of advertising as such. The picture was not strictly confirmed by "hard" evidence, although it is considerably supported by evidence drawn from the work of sociologists and market researchers. I saw the process by which consumer tastes develop as a complicated interaction of personal influence (meaning the influence of consumers on other consumers), greatly helped at critical points by advertising and marketing efforts generally. Sociologists have shown, in rather carefully designed experiments, that consumption decisions are effectly influenced, on the one hand, by a variety of advertising media and, on the other, by the recommendations of other persons known to the individual consumer. Each factor — advertising and personal recommendation — is responsible, very broadly, for about an equal share of the total result.

The experiments cannot contribute directly to the present controversy, because they relate to decisions between alternative brands of the same product at given prices; but they remain suggestive.

The implications for the "affluent society" thesis, and for economic theory, are also clear. A complex, dynamic, socio-economic system of this kind must be considered to be something like a biological phenomenon. Chance constellations of small individual factors at a particular time can have a considerable influence on the future direction of a plant's development. The needs, interests, and performance of producers are a particularly potent example of such influence, and one way of reading Galbraith is to take "advertising" as a portmanteau word for all these kinds of effects. In any event, once we accept this kind of picture, the notion of "consumers' sovereignty" becomes vague, to say the least, and we are provided with a virtually complete justification for a wide range of political action to impose social value judgments in the direction of consumption patterns. Here, quite likely, Solow would want to raise his hand and say, "I do not disagree." But the fact remains that the notion of consumers' sovereignty, essentially an *economic* theory, retains very considerable political force in defense of the status quo. Anyone who doubts the close political relationship should take a look at an advertisement in the January 1968 issue of *Fortune* magazine,[2] paid for by the Magazine Publishers' Association. This advertisement pointed to the alleged relative economic failure of East Germany, as compared with West Germany, in a defense of the activity of United States mass media in fostering demand for a wide range of, and variety among, individual consumers' goods (using the example of stuffed olives). A dramatic juxtaposition of a representation of the Berlin Wall was clearly intended to create a mental association between political repression and government intervention in the pattern of consumption.

### The large corporation

The other basic issue between Galbraith and Solow concerned the role of the large corporations. Of course it is true that important sectors of the American economy are still traditionally organized. Supermarkets were an important social innovation, and still more important was the discovery that they can be operated successfully by quite small businesses. But does Solow or anyone else *really* believe that these small-business sectors have a significant influence on the speed and pattern of economic development? The drive of our system comes manifestly from the large-scale sector, now increasingly including the government as well as the large "profit-making" corporations.

And there is a major exception that marvelously tests the rule. The

---

[2] Page 228. Ironically the issue was devoted to the United States Urban Crisis.

Robin Marris, *The Public Interest*, Spring 1968

temporary visitor to this country cannot help being impressed by the apparently general dissatisfaction with the economic and social performance in the field of urban development, dissatisfaction which ranges from the fact of the existence of slums (and the associated difficulty in providing low-cost housing) to the more general question of the adequacy of city planning, the development of the suburbs, and so on. From overseas, the United States appears so prosperous that the "urban" problem is widely assumed to be no more than a euphemism for the race problem. But is it a coincidence that the production sector most closely concerned (namely the construction industries and the real estate business) happens to represent the most prominent exception to the rule of "managerial" capitalism? In this sector, medium-scale organization is typical, and large-scale organizations are usually owned by traditional capitalists. In particular, the free market in urban land (which is at the bed of this whole sea of troubles) displays one of the purest forms of traditional capitalism still surviving. And the cream of the joke is that most qualified observers of the scene other than economists are asking that the great managerial corporations come to the rescue.

Galbraith, on the other hand, thinks that the "Technostructure" cannot or will not undertake the task, because its performance would lack technical virtuosity.[3] I am not convinced. Although put across with characteristic force, the argument is not in fact very strong. There is not firm evidence that, if money were provided for massive urban projects on a scale comparable with current military and space programs, opportunities for exercising technical virtuosity would not be found or would be rejected, especially if the new programs made liberal use of such labels as "Componentization Research" and "Systems Analysis." Galbraith's later argument (in his chapter on the Cold War), that one reason why this kind of money is not in practice available is the indirect political (and indirectly bellicose) influence of the existing Technostructure, is much more convincing, but was not referred to by Solow.

### The real world of the firm

When we reach the core of the debate — i.e., the economic theory of corporate behavior — the truth is that Solow was disingenuous, but that Galbraith had left out vital elements and laid himself open to legitimate attack. What Solow omitted to tell was that my theory implies that *in spite* of the existence of "an important discipline in the capital market," the real-world system almost certainly behaves

---

[3] "[W]e find technological *advance*, as significantly it is called, solidly enshrined as a social good ... [15 lines omitted] There is no need to measure the advantage of space achievements against help to the poor. In the nature of successful adaptation the absolute virtue of technological advance is again assumed" (p. 175).

Robin Marris, *The Public Interest*, Spring 1968

very differently from the way implied in the conventional theory: the conventional theory would imply that corporations would choose to grow considerably more slowly and reward stockholders significantly better. Galbraith, however, in failing to meet the argument that profits are needed for growth, failed to explain how this divergence can occur. In offering to put the record straight, I am motivated not only by vanity, but also by the conviction that an accurate theory about corporate growth is essential for a correct understanding of a wide range of contemporary problems of economic and social policy. The theory cannot be made simple, but can be summarized as follows.

A growing corporation faces two problems: the problem of creating a growing demand for its products, and the problem of financing the necessary growth of capacity. The corporation may strive to be as efficient as possible, in the sense of squeezing the maximum profit from its existing markets; but the search for (or creation of) *new* markets inevitably costs money (in research, marketing, and losses from failures), and so, as the growth process is accelerated, the average return realized on the *total* assets of the corporation must be adversely affected (even if the development expenditure is deployed as efficiently as possible). In theoretical language, we say there is consequently a "functional relationship" between the rate of return and the rate of growth of saleable output, which varies from corporation to corporation (in the sense that some can get a better return with a given growth rate than others) and from time to time, but that at a given phase in a particular corporation's history, when all the facts are known, the relationship is unique. At the same time, any given growth rate of sales must be supported by a corresponding growth rate of production capacity and hence requires an adequate supply of financial capital. If the main source of finance is internal, the existing level of profits is obviously a major factor governing the sums available, so we get a "feed-back" loop in which the rate of growth both influences and is influenced by the rate of profit. In fact, it is not difficult to see that if retained earnings were the only source of finance, and if the *proportion* retained were arbitrarily fixed by law or convention, we would already have what is called a "closed model": given the relationships described, for each individual corporation there would be only one rate of growth which could satisfy both conditions simultaneously (the unique value would, however, vary *between* corporations). This would be an "equilibrium" relationship between growth rate and profit rate, in the sense that the profit rate was at the same time just *low* enough to be consistent with the growth rate of sales and just *high* enough to provide adequate finance. This is about the simplest and neatest "theory of the growth of the corporation" one can conceive. To the best of my knowledge it was invented by Carl Kaysen, now Director of the Institute for

Robin Marris, *The Public Interest*, Spring 1968

Advanced Studies at Princeton, New Jersey, in an unpublished seminar paper given in England about ten years ago. It is not difficult
to make the theory more realistic by allowing for flexibility in the
retention/pay-out decisions and by bringing in outside finance. In
my earlier work I put considerable emphasis on the role of internal
finance, and more particularly on the balance between internal and
external finance in "closing" a more realistic model. More recently, I
have become increasingly impressed by the theoretical work of other
economists which suggests that the basic implications are much the
same whether one assumes finance to be all internal, all external, or
a mixture of the two. In other words, I now think it may not matter
too much whether Galbraith or Solow was most right in their con-
frontation on this point. But to explain the next step in the argument
most easily (and for that reason only), it is convenient to write as
if all finance were internal.

If we accept that, within very wide limits, the retention ratio is
effectively decided by the management, the basic structure of the
theory remains unchanged — but it is turned around. If the management chooses to go for a certain growth rate, this will determine the
profit rate, so there is now only one value of the retention ratio which
will provide the continuous finance required. Once the management
has decided its target growth rate, it *must* adopt a corresponding
retention ratio; if not, the corporation will either (1) run out of money
or (2) fail to achieve its target. Of course, Boards of Directors do not
see their problems in these precise terms; but there is considerable
evidence that they feel and understand the essential structure of the
problem in this way.

### Profits and/or growth

If the process of growth were steady and continuous, and if the
numerical values of the relations involved remained unchanged
(neither conditions, of course, being satisfied in real life), a decision
by the management to grow at a certain rate, and to choose the consistent retention ratio, must also evidently imply a unique level and
expected rate of growth of the dividend; and so, in a rational stock
market, the decision must imply a unique current price and prospective capital gain in the corporation's stock. Up to a point, actual or
potential stockholders may be content to see increased growth creating prospects of future gain at the expense of current dividends;
beyond this point, any further increase in the growth rate chosen by
the management must have a depressing effect on the stock price.
There is no reason to suppose that a growth-oriented management
will always refrain from accelerating beyond this point; and if they
go too far they will undoubtedly lay themselves open to a variety of
dangers (e.g., a take-over raid). I suggested in my theory that we

Robin Marris, *The Public Interest*, Spring 1968

might describe a typical "managerial" objective as maximum growth subject to a *minimum* on the stock price.

Solow said that my theory, in recognizing the minimum stock-price constraint, "came closer to the conventional view." On the contrary, in the conventional view management exists only to serve stockholders, and the essential technical problem is to find decision rules that would establish the policy which will, in fact, *maximize* the price of the stock. The two theories become "similar" only in the special conditions where the minimum and maximum position lie close together. These conditions are most improbable; in other words, the traditional theory is literally a "special case."

Because large-scale, professional management, not personally owning large supplies of finance, has such predominant technical advantages in the modern economy; because, although it may *use* stock-market investors and bankers, it no longer *depends* on them; because the (not insubstantial) true capitalists who remain in our system avoid speculating in large manufacturing businesses unless these are going very cheap (they prefer real estate); because the other potential take-over raiders are typically themselves management-controlled — because of all this and much more, it is inevitable that the safe minimum level of the price of a corporation's stock will be significantly lower, and the safe maximum growth rate correspondingly higher, than the values which would be chosen by a management that really did care only for the welfare of the stockholders. Numerical calculations based on statistical observation suggest that a rather growth-conscious management could typically grow almost twice as fast, setting the stock market value at all times about one-third lower, as compared to the values which would be obtained in an otherwise comparable corporation dominated by stockholders who knew all the facts. Furthermore, the growth-oriented management could safely continue the policy indefinitely, even if there were quite a number of others who chose to behave otherwise. Since the growth-oriented managements will by definition be located in the faster growing corporations, this type of behavior must in time drive out other types — a process which, I suggest, has been going on for some time. The further the process goes, the weaker is the power of the stock market to resist. Since the growth-oriented firms are technically efficient, they display not unattractive levels and growth rates of dividends, the incentive to resistance is dampened, and the latent preference for slower growth and higher current dividends remains unrecognized.

Furthermore, because managements, in fostering growth, also create technical progress, new wants, new goods, and a generally different dynamic environment, the implications of the two types of theory cannot easily be compared. We cannot possibly assert that it would necessarily be in the public interest to compel managements to conform to the traditional norm; we might very likely make many

Robin Marris, *The Public Interest*, Spring 1968

people worse off and few better off. Galbraith, however, imposed the value judgment (the "affluent-society" thesis) that the higher rate of consumer innovation resulting from "managerial" behavior by the corporations is undesirable, because it is biased against the expression of leisure preferences and against the development of "public" goods. He does not, however (as maybe does Solow in saying "it might perhaps be better if companies were forced more often into the capital market") suggest that the remedies lie in the direction of the traditional model.

The conclusion I draw (and it is an implication which I suspect to be one of the causes of the considerable ideological drive of "neo-classical" economics in the United States) would probably be disliked by both parties: namely, that once the classical idealization of capitalism is thus destroyed, there is no *economic* case for its superiority over socialism. Consequently, the attempt to impose capitalism all around the world, in some cases virtually by force, can only be justified on political grounds. The latter, however, seem to get thinner every day. In the miserable developing countries of the "free" world, where we cheerfully give aid to almost any form of dictatorship provided no industries are nationalized (the case of Tito being a historical freak, much disliked by the Congress, I understand), there is no dearth of greedy *profit* maximizers, many living in considerable luxury. What the nonaffluent majority of the world's population so badly needs is a much greater number of *growth* maximizers.

### The need for "restructuring"

More domestic and less inflammatory implications of the truth about the corporations are varied and pervasive. I will conclude with an example which may be of some topical interest. Suppose it is desired to get the corporations interested in replacing slums with wholesome low-rental dwellings, and suppose that the political conditions for the necessary diversion of national resources have already been created. Suppose federal contracts provide a massive injection of technical stimulus into the construction sector. We would still face the difficulty that low-income housing is an unprofitable line of business. This keeps out the traditionally motivated corporation and also discourages the growth-motivated corporation, because it means growing in directions that offer a particularly unfavorable relationship between growth and profitability, and consequently, means low "equilibrium" rates of growth in accordance with the theory. Under present conditions, therefore, a growth-oriented management undertaking these desirable activities *will be penalized in terms of its own motives* — a point which, once seen, appears rather obvious, but is not in fact generally well understood, and seems to have been missed by Galbraith.

Robin Marris, *The Public Interest*, Spring 1968

Solow and many of his colleagues would then say, of course, that here is a perfect example of the traditional assumptions being good enough for policy purposes. On the contrary, it provides an excellent example of the serious practical errors which can result from that attitude. Suppose a certain senator, who may be nameless, proposes a scheme of tax credits to firms which will undertake socially oriented urban renewal projects. On the traditional assumptions, the function of the subsidy is simply to compensate stockholders for a reduced pre-tax rate of return. In my kind of model, the function is to compensate the management for lost growth-opportunity by offsetting the reduction in cash flow. If we follow this through, we will find that the size of the tax credit needed to obtain a given amount of housing would be substantially smaller, and the general political appeal of the project consequently more attractive.

Finally, I would suggest, if we were to "restructure" our economic system so that the units of production were endowed with the social norm of growth maximization (subject to financial constraints), and were freed from the embarrassments of stockholders and other trappings of private property, manipulation of the financial rules to offset various kinds of built-in bias, and generally to foster a good society, would be much easier. We would be freed from the inhibitions and costs resulting from our archaic but powerful custom of assigning a private owner or part owner to most of our means of production. We should be able to concentrate on the task of finding the most efficient ways of organizing all the things we want to do, and to stop wasting our time discussing whether the old corporations did, or were supposed to, "maximize profits." But that is a longer story.

Robert M. Solow, *The Public Interest*, Spring 1968

# The truth
# further refined:
# A comment on Marris

## ROBERT M. SOLOW

I want to welcome Robin Marris to this performance of Our Gang. Since you cannot tell the players without a scorecard, perhaps I should explain to readers of this magazine that Marris is shorter than I am, but not nearly by so much as I am shorter than Galbraith. I will not pass on his beauty, but he has an attractive air of distraction that is really quite deceptive (witness that he is a better skier than I am, though I have not had the opportunity to compare him with Galbraith in this respect). Nor can I say whether his face, which is only moderately weatherbeaten, expresses much of what has made England what it is today. Indeed, the low music you hear may well be Galbraith whistling a few bars of "The Maple Leaf Forever." Since I, too, am politically biased in favor of Galbraith, I do not see why this fact should cause Marris to be unfair to an old friend. Actually, he is not. (I will return to this matter of politics later.)

Marris comments at length on the influence of advertising in the management of consumer demand, and on the theory of corporate behavior. On the first, he does not endorse Galbraith's view of the utter helplessness of the consumer, but he does agree that the success of salesmanship undermines conventional presumptions about the beneficence of market processes. On the second, he presents a theory which corresponds roughly with Galbraith's more impressionistic sketch, but which, because of its greater precision, offers less freedom

Robert M. Solow, *The Public Interest*, Spring 1968

to draw picturesque implications. I shall say a word about each subject.

### On advertising

Here one must be clear what the question is. No one who believes, as I do, that profit is an important business motive could argue that advertising has no influence on the willingness of consumers to buy a given product at a given price. After all, how could I then account for the fact that profit-seeking corporations regularly spend billions of dollars on advertising? Nor did I exactly "resort to assertion." What I said was: "I have no great confidence in my own casual observations either. But I should think a case could be made that much advertising serves only to cancel other advertising, and is therefore merely wasteful." I should think it obvious that this almost *has* to be true — i.e., that much advertising merely cancels other advertising — for otherwise there would be nothing to stop both the cigarette industry and the detergent industry from expanding their sales to their hearts' desire and to the limits of consumers' capacity to carry debt. And what would stop each individual manufacturer of cigarettes and detergents from doing the same?

No, that is hardly the issue. I have no wish to deny that an individual seller can shift the relation between his sales and the price he charges by incurring advertising or other selling costs. There is even a lot of conventional theory about that. It is important that the evidence Marris cites relates, as he admits, to consumers' "decisions between alternative brands of the same product at given prices." I suppose, on common sense grounds, that it must be relatively easy to affect such decisions by advertising. That is why essentially all tobacco companies advertise — because each is forced to offset the advertising of any one of their number, or lose sales. It must be harder to influence the consumer's choice between purchases of cigarettes and purchases of beer, and much harder still to influence his distribution of expenditures among such broad categories as food, clothing, automobiles, housing. It is open to legitimate doubt that advertising has any detectable effect at all on the sum total of consumer spending or, in other words, on the choice between spending and saving.

My remarks on page 105 of my original review were directed primarily to this last proposition. I wanted to show how shaky the foundations are for the naïve belief that not only the fortunes of individual companies, but also the viability of capitalism, rests on the success of the Madison Avenue shock troops, because without them the flow of consumer spending would dry up.

I suspect Marris would agree with me on this point. He goes on to ask why, if much advertising is merely wasteful, economists are

Robert M. Solow, *The Public Interest*, Spring 1968

not in favor of prohibiting it. Well, as a principle, that does seem to
border on the tyrannical. But it has sometimes occurred to me that
there might be some point in taxing advertising expenditure, and I
gather from conversation with other economists that they have had
the same thought. If we do not push it very hard, that is perhaps
because up to now there have been more important causes to promote,
with a considerably greater chance of success.

That leaves the difficult question of the status of the notion of
consumers' sovereignty. Once sellers of commodities can influence,
even if not control, consumers' preferences among commodities, it
becomes a much less persuasive defense of laissez-faire to say that
the system caters to consumers' preferences. Since I am not much of a
believer in laissez-faire anyway, that doesn't disturb me. But I am
not, for a number of reasons, prepared to accept Marris' leap to
apparently wholesale political steering of the direction of consumption. In the first place, to the extent that competition induces sellers
to offset one another's advertising campaigns, the seriousness of the
problem is tempered and we are back again to waste (and the possibility of taxation as a remedy). Second, there is already piecemeal
political intervention in the direction of consumption, beginning with
pure-food-and-drug legislation, the mild policing of deception in
labeling and advertising, and the various other consumer-protection
laws recently proposed or enacted. There would seem to be plenty
of room for strengthening and extending such devices. Moreover,
just because the formation of consumer preferences is inescapably a
social process, it is not clear by what standard Marris' proposal is
superior to what we have now. Indeed, "collective political action . . .
to steer the direction of consumption" might simply centralize taste-
making powers in the hands of a government certainly more powerful
and probably more nearly monolithic than even the world of large
corporations. I am not sure I want exclusive access to the formation
of my tastes to rest with the government of an Eisenhower or a
Johnson (or a Douglas-Home or a Wilson). Probably neither does
Marris, and in practice we might accept the same sort of policies.

### On corporate behavior

Marris has summarized, with quite wonderful economy, his own
theory of corporate behavior. It is a self-contained determinate theory,
with implications that are testable at least in principle. Like any
theory, this one raises two questions. Does it tell a true story? And,
if it does, what are its larger implications about economic life?

As I mentioned in my review of Galbraith, it is not easy to invent a
clear-cut statistical test of the Marris theory of corporate growth
against the more standard model of long-run profit maximization
anchored by a target rate of return. I suggested that this is because

Robert M. Solow, *The Public Interest*, Spring 1968

the two theories do not have drastically different implications. Marris objects; like any student of advertising, he would like to stress the differences between his own product and Brand X. I should have been more precise. The two theories need not have very different implications, but they may. Whether they do depends on the height of the minimum acceptable-rate-of-return (or stock price) in Marris' model. The higher it is, or the closer to the target rate of return, the more similar a Marris economy will be to mine. I am uncertain about the source of Marris' conviction that the differences are in fact large, since so far as I know his theory has not yet been given a large-scale run against the facts. One would like to know, for example, how well it does as a predictor of plant and equipment spending.

In the meanwhile, we are reduced to casual empiricism about the assumptions and implications of the Marris theory. This is hardly the place to discuss the matter in detail. I will simply say that the theory, interesting and attractive as it is, seems to me to rest on two fairly weak assumptions. The first is that for a given corporation in a given environment there must be a well-defined relation between its rate of growth (of output) and its rate of return on capital, independent of the absolute size of the corporation. It is not enough for the theory that, with everything else momentarily given, a corporation's profitability should depend on how rapidly it is trying to expand its sales and its capacity. What is required is that this relation hold for long intervals of time during which the corporation is actually growing. Both at the beginning of the period, when the company is small, and at the end, when it is large, it has to be true that to a particular, more or less steady rate of growth of x per cent a year corresponds the same more or less steady rate of profit of y per cent a year. This is not outlandish, but I think the assumption rests on too simple a view of the business of sales promotion, and on insufficient attention to the production-cost side of the problem.

The second dubious assumption is the one that names growth of sales as the prime object of the corporation. Marris does not simply assert this; he argues it with care and sociological circumstance in his book. He gives two versions: a management may "choose to go for a certain growth rate," or else it may seek "maximum growth subject to a minimum on the stock price." In a more technical statement of the theory he can allow profits and growth to be two separate objectives which have to be weighed against each other. The more weight a corporation attaches to profits and the less to growth, the more nearly it will behave according to the conventional theory.

There is certainly a lot of talk in the business press about growth and expansion. But this, by itself, is hardly support for the Marris-Galbraith doctrine. In the first place, the alternative theory — that corporations maximize long-run profits more or less, and expand whenever they earn more than a target rate of return — also entails

Robert M. Solow, *The Public Interest*, Spring 1968

that successful companies will be growing most of the time, and will no doubt be talking about it. In the second place, one must keep in mind that the federal government taxes long-term capital gains only half as heavily as dividends, and under some circumstances considerably less than that. Retention and reinvestment of earnings — i.e., internally financed growth — is the obvious way for a corporation to convert dividends into capital gains for its shareholders, including its officers. So devotion to growth is quite consistent with profit-maximization if profit is interpreted as the after-tax return to the stockholder.

Theories that emphasize the separation of ownership and control tend to ignore the fact that, if the common stockholder cannot control the policy of the corporation he owns, he can arrange to own a different corporation by merely telephoning his broker. He can even buy shares in a mutual fund that will tailor a portfolio to his expressed preferences between current dividends and capital gains. Indeed, such theories generally tend to ignore the large-scale institutional investors, whose presence on the other side of the market makes the balance of power between management and owner look a little different.

This would seem to be important, even within the framework of Marris' theory. He admits that some corporations can be more growth-oriented and less profit-oriented than others. If any substantial number of stockholders strongly favors immediate profits over growth, their demands can be mobilized by institutional investors. Corporate managements are sure to be found or created who will be prepared to get their kicks by catering to these demands.

I realize that these casual remarks about the plausibility of assumptions can never be decisive. For that we will have to wait for serious empirical testing. And if I am right that the two theories could turn out to have similar implications, we may have to wait even longer — but of course it will matter less. By the way, Marris' discussion of the problem of getting private firms interested in the construction of low-rent housing seems to me to favor my view of the matter at least as much as it does his. It turns out that low-income housing is now an unattractive business to be in, on the assumptions of either theory. When you get right down to the nitty-gritty, the difference is merely the size of the subsidy needed to obtain a given amount of housing, and there is probably room for more than one opinion about that, too.

### On ideology

Marris considers his theory to be subversive of the existing order. Since the consumer is presumably manipulated and the stockholder presumably ignored, no intellectual case remains for capitalism as an efficient economic system. Even leaving aside the question whether

Robert M. Solow, *The Public Interest*, Spring 1968

this argument applies to the regulated mixed economy of today, it is the damnedest argument for socialism I ever heard. Who would storm the Winter Palace so that units of production could be "endowed with the social norm of growth maximization (subject to financial constraints)" even if "manipulation of the financial rules to offset various kinds of built-in bias . . . would be much easier"?

Marris also suspects that only an ideological drive can explain the persistence with which economists in the United States cling to some (incomplete) confidence in market mechanisms. I would not deny that some academic disputes have a genuine ideological content. But I would also assert that there is far less ideology wrapped up in academic economics in the United States than a man from Cambridge, England, can possibly realize. (One of Cambridge's most distinguished economists, with whom I had been carrying on a rather abstract controversy, once said to me at a party: "You're not a reactionary; so why don't you agree with me?" I thought it was a good question.) In fact, I don't think that my argument with Galbraith and Marris is really ideological in character. My own view is that any economic system can be made to work, if you go at it cleverly. But to do that, you have to get the analysis right. If Marris' theory of the firm turns out to work better, which is conceivable, I will buy it cheerfully.

J. K. Galbraith, *The New Industrial State*

A further line of criticism has been heavily concerned with my case that the large industrial corporation can manage its consumers — and by inference that the defense establishment (the weapons producers and the Pentagon) instructs the public on the defense needs and not the reverse. The critics hold that no such power can be proven. This is a vital point. If it can be shown that the consumer and the citizen can be managed by those who, nominally, exist to serve him, then the revised sequence — a tendency toward producer instead of consumer sovereignty — becomes possible. If the consumer and citizen cannot be so managed then the established system is secure. Production responds to his unmanaged decision. I would not suggest that my critics, in rallying to the defense of the independent power of the consumer and citizen — to his immunity to persuasion and to his power in the democratic process — are being tendentious. But there is also no doubt that they are seeking to shore up the established structure of economics at its most vulnerable point. Their effort reflects an extremely happy coincidence between scientific conviction and the defense of intellectual vested interest.

I have no recourse here but to stand on my argument — and appeal among other things to the evidence of the eye. And the evidence of the eye is assuredly there. The eye sees a vast advertising and sales effort employing elaborate science and art to influence the customer. It sees huge sums expended for this effort, an estimated $19.6 billion for advertising in 1969. It senses great and subtle effort by the aerospace and like industries to persuade the armed services to want what they can supply. It sees a wholly unsubtle process by which the Pentagon instructs the Congress on what it wishes to have. Those who say that what is so seen cannot be proven are, in effect, saying that nothing can be proven. They are using a pseudoscientific syllogism to avert attention from reality.

*The Detroit Free Press*, May 19, 1955

# *Galloping Guess Supplanted*

LEWIS D. CRUSOE, executive vice president, Ford Motor Co., told the San Jose (Calif.) Chamber of Commerce that the "rail-fence galloping guess" has been supplanted by accurate business forecasting based on market research.

The application of scientific forward planning provided the information that led Ford to add 625 million dollars to its $1,700,000,000 expansion program, he said.

"We feel that our business is too valuable to the national economy to be jeopardized by individuals who volunteer to run it on the basis of their opinions, or to guide its course by seaman's eye," he said.

"We feel also that market research has reached a stage where if we neglect the use of the information it provides, we would be violating our responsibility."

*Business Week*, Nov. 24, 1956

# The New Sales Race

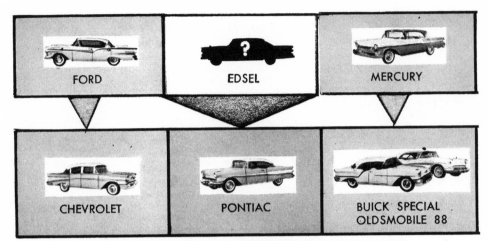

| FORD | EDSEL | MERCURY |
| CHEVROLET | PONTIAC | BUICK SPECIAL OLDSMOBILE 88 |

## Ford Motor Co. Adds Its Edsel Line...To Match the General Motors Line-Up

# Ford vs. GM: New

The drawing above shows the way a new competitive battle shapes up in Detroit, now that Ford Motor Co. has admitted that it is tooling up for an additional line of cars.

Ford confirmed that it is planning a new line to be named the "Edsel," in honor of the father of Henry II, Benson, and William Ford. The new line will be introduced in late 1957 as 1958 models and will be sold through a completely new dealer organization. The Edsel will be in the medium-price field, which is another point that has long been understood (BW—Apr.23'55,p28).

Pres. Henry Ford II spoke guardedly this week about the car itself, where it would fit into the market, and how it would be sold. But Detroit observers, after years of studying the case of Ford vs. General Motors, could read names between the few lines in which Henry Ford discussed the reasons for a new line of cars.

## I. Balancing the Line

GM's Buick is the key to understanding what Ford is up to. "We have been growing customers for General Motors," Ford Executive Vice-Pres. Lewis D. Crusoe is quoted as saying in a recent study of Ford by Lehman Bros. When a Ford-car customer is ready to step up to a bigger, more expensive car, he has one Ford line to choose: Mercury. He has three GM lines to pick from (including a line of three Buicks), and three at Chrysler.

• **Medium-Price Field**—This has been

a terrific handicap to Ford's growth. Top people at Ford talk seriously about someday meeting or beating GM's share of the market, which is now roughly 50%. But the Lehman study sharply illuminates Ford's problem:

• At GM, 45% of new car registrations are in the medium-price field.

• At Chrysler, 47% are in the medium-price field.

• At Ford, only 17% of registrations are in the medium-price field.

To put it another way, while only 50% of GM's volume rests on Chevrolet, 80% of Ford's volume comes from the Ford car. That makes Ford an extremely unbalanced motor company, with its success and profitability depending on the Ford Div. alone.

Naturally, this imbalance shows in the market-place. GM has 67% of the medium-low market, Ford 16%, and Chrysler 14%. In the upper-medium bracket, GM has 56%, Chrysler 29%, and Ford 3%—and that only by including the Thunderbird.

• **A Better Choice**—These are the kind of figures that Henry Ford II referred to when he said: "Studies conclusively prove that when a company has two or more entries in the medium-priced field, the result is to strengthen the sales of all its car lines."

The company wants to have some place for its Ford-car customers to go when they are ready to step up.

As Crusoe said on another occasion, "I don't want a man to leave my store to go down the street to Mercury but have Buick grab him on the way."

The Ford Div. customer eventually will have plenty of other Ford products to choose from when he is ready to move up. Not all three of the Edsels may appear in the 1958 selling year; reports of a "Super-Mercury" have been published, but its place in the market is still problematical.

The exact place of the new Edsels in the price groups and whether two or three will be offered for 1958, depend largely upon two other factors—dealers and manufacturing facilities.

## II. Who Will Sell It?

"The new Edsel line will be introduced and marketed by a completely new dealer organization," Henry Ford II said this week. But in the auto industry, dealers right now are more precious than steel. How the company plans to find new ones was hinted by Henry Ford in a letter to existing dealers: "As in the past, full consideration will be given, individually, to the qualifications of any Ford, Mercury, or Lincoln dealer who, in addition to his present franchise, might also be interested in an Edsel franchise."

This indicates that Ford's main approach will be to persuade present Ford Co. dealers to invest some of their profits in new dealerships for the Edsel. This is a fairly routine endeavor in Detroit. Whenever an auto company wishes to obtain new dealers, it thinks first about successful existing dealers, either of its own or of competing lines. A successful dealer doesn't necessarily

*Business Week*, Nov. 24, 1956

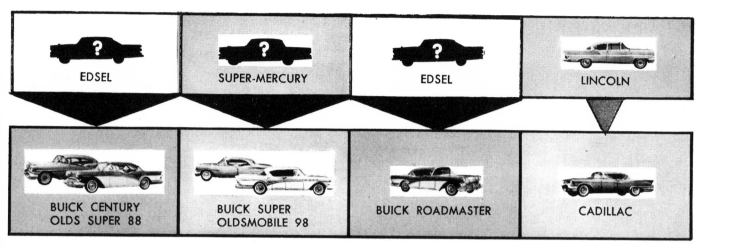

# Line Makes It a Car-for-Car Battle

have to have all the required capital for another dealership—all three of the big auto companies have programs to lend dealers money.

• **Sales Core**—The Edsel Div.—which is the name given this week to the former Special Products Div.—has already set up regional sales offices in five cities.

Meanwhile, J. C. Doyle, general sales and marketing manager of the Edsel Div., will begin to recruit 1,200 dealers from among the company's existing 9,000 retailers and others. The dealer and sales program will be fully disclosed in a closed-circuit television announcement on Feb. 4.

• **Reshuffle**—Along with the recruitment of Edsel dealers will go a sweeping realignment of the Ford retail network. This was forecast as long ago as the spring of 1955, when the Lincoln-Mercury Div. was split into two organizations. This week Ford Chmn. Ernest R. Breech said: "Ford is setting out to have four complete lines of dealers." Since Lincoln and Mercury still have the same dealer organization, this is confirmation that there now will be separate Lincoln and Mercury dealers, as well as Edsel and Ford dealers.

Breech added, however, that the introduction of the Edsel will give the company an opportunity to do more dualing of cars. Lincoln volume alone could not support all its dealers, so it is likely that most Lincoln dealers will need another volume car to sell. This will most probably be the Edsel. Breech says the company is budgeting the Edsel for sales of 200,000 cars in the

first year—too great a volume for Mercury dealers to absorb along with a Super-Mercury, but enough to enable a high-priced line of dealers such as Lincoln's to operate at a profit.

## III. How It Comes About

Ford plans no new assembly plants for the Edsel. Richard E. Krafve, company vice-president and general manager of the new division, said this week that his cars will be built "in the existing Ford network of plants"—specifically in Ford and Mercury assembly plants. One version may later be built in Lincoln's new assembly plant, now being constructed at Novi, Mich.

This could give some indication of what kind of car the Edsel will be. Breech said that some sheet metal will be interchangeable with the Ford and Mercury. If the Edsel is to roll down the same lines as the Ford and Mercury, it could mean that the new car will have the same basic body shells and wheelbases as the Ford and Mercury. This would follow the GM practice, where the Buick Roadmaster and Super use the same shell as the Cadillac, while the Buick Century and Special and the Olds use a different common shell.

• **Long in Coming**—Across-the-board competition with GM has been a Ford goal almost from the time that Henry Ford II, Ernest R. Breech, and Lewis D. Crusoe set out to rebuild the company in 1946. This week, Ford said planning for the Edsel began in 1948,

then was interrupted by the Korean War.

Meanwhile, a Special Products Div. was created, becoming the Continental Div. with the advent of that car. A new Special Products Div. was established in April, 1955, with Richard E. Krafve at its head. A few weeks ago, Krafve was elected a company vice-president and continues to head the new Edsel Div. His staff, ironically, is taking over the former Continental Div. offices, since that division has been abolished and the Continental car restored to the Lincoln line, where it was originated by Edsel Ford before World War II.

*Newsweek*, Nov. 26, 1956

AUTOS:

# Now Comes the Edsel

One of the most publicized "secrets" in the auto industry became open and official knowledge this week. The Ford Motor Co.'s new medium-priced line, due next year, president Henry Ford II announced, will be called the "Edsel," in honor of his late father, Ford president for 24 years. The new tag actually was the first suggested for the new car, but the company sifted 18,000 others (samples: Mars, Jupiter, Apollo, Henry, Benson, Cavalier, and Drof—Ford spelled backwards) before deciding its first choice was best. Heading up the new

Ford's new E for Edsel

Edsel Division, which will have its own dealer organization, is Richard E. Krafve, a Minnesota-born engineer who came to Ford in 1947 as assistant to the purchasing vice president and who has been handling the new line (as head of the "Special Products Division") since its formation in April 1955.

More important to the auto trade is the price field in which the Edsel will compete. The car will blanket the middle range, the way General Motors' Buicks are priced all the way from Chevrolet's level up to Cadillac's. So far Ford has had but one contender, Mercury, in this spread.

**Price Tags:** Best Detroit guess now is that one Edsel series, built on a Ford shell, will be factory-priced from about $2,200 to $2,700 (customers will, of course, pay several hundred dollars more). A second series, on a Mercury shell, will be tagged from $3,000 to $3,500. Thus the new line will run from the Ford bracket almost into the Lincoln class. (Ford had also been thinking of a still higher line, on a Lincoln shell, but discarded it in favor of a bigger and more expensive Mercury due probably in 1958.)

In looks, the Edsels will, of course, be different—front and rear—from other Ford lines, featuring horizontally mounted dual headlamps and a rather modest oval grille (reflecting the splendidly simple lines of the $10,000 Continental). The lower series will run 118 inches in wheel base, industry guessers figure; the top series, 124 inches.

*Business Week*, June 8, 1957

## The Role of the Edsel Line
## In Loyalty to Ford Products

In a somewhat unusual way, Ford Motor Co. has disclosed a few more facts about its closely guarded line of Edsel cars that go on the market in the fall (BW—Nov.24'56,p30). Since 1948, when fundamental research began, Ford has invested $250-million in research and marketing activities.

This fact emerged when J. Emmet Judge, Merchandising and Product Planning Manager of Ford's Edsel Div. spoke to a research conference held by the National Cotton Council of America. Judge used Ford's experience with the Edsel as a case history in market research.

**In long-range planning, Ford projects a car market that looks something like this:** Ford estimates the 1965 GNP at $535-billion. In that year, it expects new car sales to reach $26-billion, compared with $19-billion in 1955. And with a 1956 car population of 50-million cars, Ford sees 70-million cars in use in 1965.

Judge cited some figures that show why Ford decided to put its Edsel line in the medium price range. **Basically, Ford wants a larger line of cars to compete with General Motors' and Chrysler's middle-price lines.** In addition to swelling sales in the middle price range, an important factor is to keep consumer loyalty with Ford. Judge pointed out that 40% of new car buyers switch makes, either sticking with the over-all manufacturer of their old model or going to a rival company. According to Judge, for example, 87% of Chevrolet owners stay in the GM family when they move to a higher price car—they buy Pontiacs, Oldsmobiles, Buicks, even Cadillacs. But only 26% of Ford owners move up to a Mercury. About 69% stick with one of the Ford Motor Co. cars. Ford expects to boost this holding power to 74% through addition of the Edsel line.

*Business Week*, Dec. 7, 1957

# Edsel Gets a Frantic Push

⬤ Sales of the new car have been disappointing—to Ford as well as to dealers.

⬤ So the company is initiating a big promotional campaign to counteract waning interest in the car.

⬤ The program is designed to meet complaints of many dealers, who, by and large, still hope to put Edsel over.

This week the first of nearly 1.5-million letters to owners of medium-priced automobiles cascaded through the Detroit Postoffice to start a hard-sell campaign by an auto maker who discovered that novelty appeal wears off quickly.

The letters are signed by Richard E. Krafve, a Ford Motor Co. vice-president and general manager of its Edsel Div., and they ask the readers please to stop by an Edsel dealership and test-drive the industry's newest car.

Those who do, get a scale-model of the Edsel. The model, the letters, and promotional material for use directly by the dealers, all are paid for by the Edsel Div.—a departure from the auto industry's long-standing practice.

In this way, the Edsel Div. is trying to meet a major complaint of its dealers—that sales promotion has been lacking and national advertising poor; showroom traffic in September was fabulous, but few people have come back actually to try the car; and interest in Ford's quarter-of-a-billion-dollar baby has waned.

• **Disappointing Sales**—These complaints mask the real gripe: Sales have been greatly disappointing. Krafve last week said sales are about where he expected them to be, but not where he had hoped they would be.

In September, the month the new car went on sale, 11,544 Edsels were delivered to dealers. The October deliveries backed down to 7,601. November figures are expected to look only a little better than October.

This has been a less-than-satisfactory performance to practically everyone, and particularly to a veteran—and vocal —New York City dealer named Charles Kreisler. Last summer, in a blare of publicity, Kreisler threw in his Oldsmobile franchise and signed up for Edsel. Last week, Kreisler gave up his Edsel deal (having meanwhile signed on with American Motors). Ford Motor Co., Kreisler says succinctly, "laid an egg." His opinion is widely shared.

• **"Here to Stay"**—As an answer, Henry Ford, II, in a closed-circuit TV meeting for all Edsel dealers, said: "The Edsel is here to stay." He added that the company would give all the support necessary to the division and its dealers to put the Edsel over.

No one believes it's going to be easy. The Edsel encountered almost every imaginable problem connected with launching a new product.

## I. The Dealers' Story

Talking to dealers this week, BUSINESS WEEK reporters had a rundown of the Edsel's problems.

• **Design**—In pondering what the Edsel people have been faced with in trying to break into the auto market, you can start with the design. Says a St. Louis dealer: "The Edsel design shocks some people. It did me, too, but the design grows on you. I have found that once I get a man in the car I can sell him." A dealer in Washington mournfully hopes the design "will grow on people."

But, conversely, a Texas dealer says: "People are talking about the Edsel. They like its distinctive styling—a restrained, classic look without extremes." In San Francisco, a dealer claims the design is his main sales pitch.

• **Dealer Setup**—After designing a new car, you have to find people to sell it. Edsel Div. lined up nearly 1,100 dealers by introduction day (BW—Jun.22'57, p52). Since then, it has added 105 dealers, and had lost 19 up to last week. Competitors say other dealers are quitting, but only a few Edsel dealers interviewed admitted any such thought. On the other hand, a number of dealers want to take on a second line of smaller, cheaper cars. Several dealers declared that Edsel should be dualed with Ford, which actually was discussed in the company at one stage of the Edsel planning.

One dealer who did give up his franchise, Theodore C. Truden, Bristol, Conn., thinks styling was an indirect cause of his slow sales. He feels the styling appeals to the younger set, but the price does not. The Edsel "will come along," he says. "It's not going to flop." But he added that he just didn't have the financial strength to take the long pull.

• **Too Little, Too Soon?**—Once you get dealers for your car, you have to bring it to market. On this score, BUSINESS WEEK reporters ran into a blizzard of complaints. The Edsel was introduced too early, the opinion runs, and the factory's follow-up was poor.

In Columbus, a dealer complains: "We've been selling against the clean-up of '57 models. We were too far ahead of the 1958 market. Our big job is to get our original lookers back into the showroom." In Minneapolis, the complaint gets sharper: "Damn poor promotion, damn poor advertising —some people didn't even know it was a '58."

• **Volatile Market**—Next, in introducing a new car, you have to find your market. This is where Edsel has had its biggest problem. A competitive dealer in San Francisco sums up the situation quickly: "The medium-priced market is extremely healthy in good times, but it is also the first market to be hurt when we tighten our belts during depression . . . When they dreamed up the Edsel, medium-priced cars were a big market, but by the time the baby was born that market had gone helter-skelter."

Despite this, dealers in widely scattered cities reported their sales were fair to good. No particular type of buyer has yet emerged, although dealers report many are middle-aged, middle-income and trade in a three-year-old Mercury or General Motors car.

There is widespread unhappiness among Edsel dealers—about the market, not the car—but grim determination, too. A Portland (Ore.) dealer who switched from Dodge, sounds a common note: "Edsel is tougher than we thought it would be. I think I'd have the same problems if I hadn't changed to Edsel."

## II. The Division's Story

Edsel Div. people have a simple way to spotlight the whole problem of the car. There are 20,000-odd Edsels on

*Business Week*, Dec. 7, 1957

the road, compared with more than 56-million other cars. Say Edsel people, "We just lack visibility."

• **Major Task**—Gen. Mgr. Krafve divides his division's initial task into three parts: First, "we had to get people to look at it." Second, people have to recognize they can buy an Edsel at a price they can afford. Third job is to get people behind the wheel.

Krafve thinks the first job was accomplished with the introduction on Sept. 4.

• **The Strategy**—Krafve doesn't think the car was introduced too early. Right about now is when the Edsel Div. people have thought the industry-wide sales push would come, and they figured their new dealer body would need a long shakedown period.

That also accounts for the lack of promotion, and the institutional-type of advertising since September. While all the other new models were being introduced in October and November, Edsel people say, they saw little point in trying to steal attention normally centered on new models.

Now, Edsel Div. has started simultaneously on Krafve's No. 2 and No. 3 jobs. You can see now Edsel's new advertising theme: "The car that's really new is the lowest-priced, too."

• **Price**—This should make dealers happy. There is widespread dealer opinion that the car is priced too high —even though Edsel's Ranger is the least expensive of what is generally called the "medium-priced field," and the Pacer, Corsair, and Citation, in both price and features, are competitive across the board, as shown in BUSINESS WEEK's price chart (Nov.30'57, p30). (Automatic transmission is standard on the Corsair and Citation, as it is on competitive cars, not optional.)

The dealers' views on price apparently are conditioned by three factors. One is the sluggishness of all medium-priced cars. A second factor is the still-green memory of selling against the severely discounted 1957 models during the clean-up period. Thirdly, most of the dealers, while complaining about sales, say Edsel profits are good. J. C. Doyle, Edsel sales manager, says 46% of his dealers made a profit in September, even including their launching costs.

• **New Effort**—The letters now being mailed to competitive owners are part of Krafve's third job—getting people behind the wheel of an Edsel. Right now, Krafve—and a lot of the dealers, too—

believes this is the best way to boost Edsel sales.

The division also is striking at another source of dealer unhappiness: little service business. Ordinarily an automobile dealer counts on his service shop to meet 60% or more of his gross operating costs. Most Edsel dealers thought they would have no problem getting service business because they switched from another make of car, and so had a service list to build on.

But many people apparently are taking their service business to dealers handling their make of car. So the Edsel Div. has prepared sample letters for dealers. Addressed, for example, "Dear Mr. Buick Owner," the letters point out: "We have the same mechanics who have given you the service that has merited your confidence and who know your car so well." And the letter ends with a suggestion to "try an Edsel."

With these direct mail campaigns, the new advertising, radio and TV spots and shows, the Edsel Div. is trying to stir up the interest the car had last September and then—from what dealers say—lost. Apparently by coincidence, Edsel Div. also has new directors of public relations and of sales promotion —one of the ex-directors left for another job and the other transferred within the company for reasons of health.

Krafve is completely undismayed by Edsel's sales record to date. He emphasizes that everyone knew it would be a long, hard pull and every sale is "conquest business," taken from someone else because Edsel has no "loyal owners" to draw from. "We build cars by the thousands," Krafve likes to say, "but they're sold one by one."

*Consumer Reports*, April 1958

## economics for consumers

# The Edsel Story

*Behind the scenes of*

*the automobile extravaganza*

*that excited Detroit*

*but left consumers apathetic*

It took a reported $250 million to conceive, publicize, design, produce, distribute and advertise the *Edsel*, the new car added this year to the Ford Motor Company's family line of *Ford, Mercury* and *Lincoln*. All the publicity resources of the world's second largest auto manufacturer were tapped to glamorize the birth of this commercial prince. The *Edsel* was heralded as the heir to the accumulated engineering know-how of the past plus the latest wisdom to be gleaned from the new research techniques in the consumer-motivation field. The *Edsel*, so the mountainous publicity ran, was therefore doubly designed for success: It was to be more than the best and newest car in reality; it was to be the embodiment of a dream of a car as well—a dream already existing in the minds of prospective buyers.

On September 4, 1957, after a year of intensive and elaborate build-up (in which no detail of the car was revealed) and better than a month before any other 1958 models were out, the public was finally invited in to see the dream made real. During that first month crowds flocked to the showrooms of the approximately 1160 newly recruited *Edsel* dealers. The long-drawn-out publicity had paid off; people were curious.

★    ★    ★

It takes years to plan a new car these days. And once the plan is set and action is under way, it takes at least a year to translate all the paper work into an inventory of raw

materials, a network of contracts with parts suppliers, a production line, a dealer organization for distribution, and so on. So, fairly early in 1956, a full year before the *Edsel* appeared, the Ford Motor Company was already well along on its irreversible road toward September 4, 1957, guided by directives that were based on market data from 1955, the year when more than 7,000,000 U.S. passenger cars were sold—the biggest year, by far, in history.

It has frequently been said that market statistics are tricky because the best they can do is tell you where you have been, not where you are going. On the basis of detailed market analyses of the years up through 1955, the Ford Motor Company became convinced that consumers were in a long term trade-up mood, determined to live more expensively and elaborately each year, to buy bigger and bigger cars every two years. Some of the market data also indicated that when *Ford* owners wanted to enhance their social status by trading up into the middle-price bracket, some 70% of them left the Ford family to buy *Oldsmobiles, Buicks* and *Dodges* instead of *Mercurys*, Ford's middle-bracket car.

Here is where the idea for the *Edsel* was actually germinated. This latest addition to the Ford line was not originally conceived of as a consumer dream nor guided into being via consumer-motivation engineering. Such studies were certainly launched. But for all practical purposes, they came *after* the decision was made to put a second car in the middle-bracket price class, one which would lure more *Ford* trade-ins back to the Ford family line. The *Edsel* was

*Consumer Reports*, April 1958

designed first and foremost because the Ford Motor Company was avid for a greater share of the consumer's automobile dollar.

## How the stage was set

There is almost no seller these days who believes that he is getting "his share" of the market. Few sellers, however, have the gigantic resources with which to gamble for the bigger share they covet on the scale that the Ford Company did with the *Edsel*. And had the *Edsel* made its appearance in 1953, 1954, or even in 1955, chances are its fate might have been different; certainly it would have been less disastrous. But the *Edsel* and the current economic recession hit the market at almost precisely the same time.

During that first month of the *Edsel*'s showings, September 1957, when it stood alone in the limelight as the first 1958 model, the stage it dominated was wobbly. The stock market was in a trough. And most important to *Edsel*'s fate, other car dealers were slashing prices on their 1957s in an attempt to clear out stocks to make ready for their own 1958 models not yet on the market. *Edsel* with its high 1958 prices looked very expensive, indeed, compared with the heavily discounted 1957s.

Thus, the limelight that *Edsel* sought by its early introduction narrowed into a sharp spotlight on its price tag. All the smoldering resentment against high auto prices on the part of consumers, dealers and bankers seemed to spark into flame. When the other 1958s came out, they, too, had high price tags. Motor manufacturers have raised prices with maddening regularity for 12 years now. But *Edsel* had maneuvered itself into a fall guy's position by its publicity clamor and its publicity-dictated early introduction.

Furthermore, the car itself, as well as its price, seemed to epitomize the many excesses which, despite sales volume, were repulsing more and more potential car buyers. *Edsel* was longer, more uselessly overpowered, more chrome laden, more gadget bedecked, more hung with expensive accessories than any car in its price class. To be sure, the market and sales statistics studied by the Ford Motor Company had seemed to indicate that this was precisely what consumers wanted in a car, or at least *had* wanted up through 1955.

## What consumers know

But what about those consumer-motivation studies—those vaunted new techniques with which researchers claim to be able to learn from consumers what they (the consumers) really know and feel but do not yet know that they know and feel? Those studies sponsored by the Ford Motor Company continued through 1955, 1956, and 1957; and they are still in process. Surely such a probe should have touched the live nerve in consumer reactions which was inaccessible through any statistical analysis based on old market data.

The trouble here seems to have been the elemental mistake on which research can founder—failure to ask questions which elicit meaningful replies. For example, the

Ford Motor Company asked no questions at all about: car prices, cost of upkeep, cost of operation, rising insurance rates, growing difficulty in parking, irritation at cars too long for garages, etc. In fact, the consumer research program conducted in behalf of the motor company completely ignored automobiles as functioning machines of transportation. It centered instead on cars as status symbols, as extensions of ego. The questions were all about the feelings of car owners and none was about comparative car performances. And the feelings probed were those about personality identification—car personality vis-a-vis owner social status; product snobbery, to put it simply.

There has been some talk in advertising circles to the effect that *Edsel*'s woeful failure to find the profitable image in the consumer mind would set back motivation research for a decade or more. But the Ford Motor Company, it appears, is not yet disenchanted with attempts to mine gold out of the consumer psyche. In the latter part of last year, after the *Edsel* egg was freshly laid, the following note appeared in the *Wall Street Journal*: "Ford Motor has called on the Institute of Motivational Research to find out why Americans buy foreign economy cars."

As for the *Edsel* itself, the following item appeared in *Newsweek* magazine just a little more than a month ago: "*Edsel* cars, a sharp disappointment to Ford this year, will be drastically restyled and cheaper when the 1959 models come out."

John Brooks, *The New Yorker*, Nov. 26, 1960

By a preliminary program of promotion and advertising, the Ford company had built up an overwhelming head of public interest in the Edsel, causing its arrival to be anticipated and the car itself to be gawked at with more eagerness than had ever greeted any automobile before it. After all that, it seemed, the car didn't quite work. Within a few weeks after the Edsel was introduced, its pratfalls were the talk of the land. Edsels were delivered with oil leaks, sticking hoods, trunks that wouldn't open, and push buttons that, far from yielding to a toothpick, couldn't be budged with a hammer. *Automotive News* reported that in general the earliest Edsels suffered from poor paint, inferior sheet metal, and faulty accessories, and quoted the lament of a dealer about one of the first Edsel convertibles he received: "The top was badly set, doors cockeyed, the header bar trimmed at the wrong angle, and the front springs sagged." The Ford company had the particular bad luck to sell to Consumers Union— which buys its test cars in the open market, as a precaution against being favored with specially doctored samples—an Edsel in which the axle ratio was wrong, an expansion plug in the cooling system blew out, the power-steering pump leaked, the rear-axle gears were noisy, and the heater emitted blasts of hot air when it was turned off. A former executive of the Edsel Division has estimated that only about half of the first Edsels really performed properly.

A layman cannot help wondering how the Ford company, in all its power and glory, could have been guilty of such a Mack Sennett routine of build-up and anticlimax. Krafve, the wan, hard-working boss of the Edsel operation, explains gamely that when a company brings out a new model of any make—even an old and tested one— the first cars often have bugs in them. A more startling theory—though only a theory—is that there may have been sabotage in some of the four plants that assembled the Edsel, all but one of which had previously been, and currently also were, assembling Fords or Mercurys. In marketing the Edsel, the Ford company took a leaf out of the book of General Motors, which for years had successfully been permitting, and even encouraging, the makers and sellers of its Oldsmobiles, Buicks, Pontiacs, and the higher-priced models of its Chevrolet to fight for customers with no quarter given; faced with the same sort of intramural competition, some members of the Ford and Lincoln-Mercury Divisions of the Ford company openly hoped from the start for the Edsel's downfall. (Krafve, realizing what might happen, asked that the Edsel be assembled in plants of its own, but his superiors turned him down.) However, J. C. Doyle, a forty-two-year veteran of the automobile business who was Krafve's second-in-command, pooh-poohs the notion that the Edsel was the victim of dirty work at the plants. "Of course the Ford and Lincoln-Mercury Divisions didn't want to see another Ford-company car in the field," he says, "but as far as I know, anything they did at the executive and plant levels was in competitive good taste. On the other hand, at the distribution and dealer level, you got some rough infighting in terms of whispering and propaganda. If I'd been in one of the other divisions, I'd have done the same thing." No proud defeated general of the old school ever spoke more nobly.

*Time,* Nov. 30, 1959

## AUTOS
### The $250 Million Flop

Detroit had expected it for months; last week Ford Motor Co. finally had to make it official. The company dropped its medium-priced Edsel, introduced only two years ago. Said Ford, in a pained announcement: "Retail sales have been particularly disappointing, and continued production of the Edsel is not justified, especially in view of the shortage of steel."

Ford's hand was forced by a stock prospectus issued by the Ford Foundation, which plans to sell another 2,000,000 shares of Ford stock (worth some $155 million) in order to diversify its holdings. Included in a list of company products was a footnote on Edsel: "Introduced in September 1957 and discontinued in November 1959." Once that got out, Ford had to speak out, though it had planned to hold off until all Edsels in dealers' inventories were sold. It really did not make much difference. As of last week, only about 2,800 of the "all-new" 1960 Edsels had been made. To mollify those few customers whose cars are now orphans with low trade-in value, Ford offered a $300 certificate to be applied against the purchase of any other Ford product.

**Right "Personality."** What happened? As it turned out, the Edsel was a classic case of the wrong car for the wrong market at the wrong time. It was also a prime example of the limitations of market research, with its "depth interviews" and "motivational" mumbo-jumbo. On the research, Ford had an airtight case for a new medium-priced car to compete with Chrysler's Dodge and DeSoto, General Motors' Pontiac, Oldsmobile and Buick. Studies showed that by 1965 half of all U.S. families would be in the $5,000-and-up bracket, would be buying more cars in the medium-priced field, which already had 60% of the market. Edsel could sell up to 400,000 cars a year.

After the decision was made in 1955, Ford ran more studies to make sure the new car had precisely the right "personality." Research showed that Mercury buyers were generally young and hot-rod-inclined, while Pontiac, Dodge and Buick appealed to middle-aged people. Edsel was to strike a happy medium. As one researcher said, it would be "the smart car for the younger executive or professional family on its way up." To get this image across, Ford even went to the trouble of putting out a 60-page memo on the procedural steps in the selection of an advertising agency, turned down 19 applicants before choosing Manhattan's Foote, Cone & Belding. Total cost of research, design, tooling, expansion of production facilities: $250 million.

**A Taste of Lemon.** The flaw in all the research was that by 1957, when Edsel appeared, the bloom was gone from the medium-priced field, and a new boom was starting in the compact field, an area the **Edsel research had overlooked completely. Edsel's styling, in particular the grille, which resembled an Oldsmobile sucking a lemon, was not much help, even after the lemon was removed. In its first six months Edsel made 54,600 cars, and then went steadily downward: 26,500 cars in 1958, fewer than 30,000 cars so far in boom-time 1959.**

Actually, Ford will not lose its entire investment. Of the total, $100 million went for production facilities, which will be used to produce Ford's second entry into the compact-car field next spring. As a running mate for the Falcon, Ford plans a slightly larger, more luxurious compact model that it originally thought of calling the Edsel Comet. Now the new car will just be called the Comet.

• • •

As the Edsel died, Ford got ready to put more pep into the Ford line. Next month Ford will begin deliveries of a 360-h.p. engine that is topped among U.S. stock cars only by the 380 h.p. in the Chrysler 300-E. Ford's aim is to outdo both Plymouth (330-h.p. top) and Chevrolet (335-h. top) with its new engine.

Associated Press

LAST EDSEL OFF THE LINE (1960)

*Business Week*, Nov. 28, 1959

# The Edsel Dies, and

**1958: COMING . . .**

**. . . GOING . . .**

**. . . GONE**

**Its $450-million mistake in the past, Ford is strengthening the Ford Div. in a return to its pre-1955 centralization.**

Ford Motor Co. last week admitted for all to know that its Edsel car was one of the most expensive mistakes a U.S. corporation has ever made. After costing Ford $250-million to bring to market, the Edsel lost an estimated $200-million more during the nearly 2½ years it was in production.

At the same time that Ford scuttled this first try for bigger sales in the medium-price bracket, it also retreated from its 1955 plan for separate car divisions to compete line-by-line with General Motors.

• **Erosion**—Within four years, Ford brought out two completely new car lines—the Continental Mark II and the Edsel—and then abandoned both because of poor sales. In the same period it created four new car divisions—Continental, Lincoln, Mercury, Edsel—and junked them because sales weren't robust enough to carry the overhead.

In 1957 and 1958, Mercury, Edsel, and Lincoln were combined into one division, and about 6,000 salaried employees were discharged. Now Ford has transferred the Lincoln-Mercury Div.'s assembly, purchasing, and production engineering operations to the Ford Div., and about 600 more salaried personnel at L-M will be out of work. In the future, the Lincoln-Mercury Div. will be essentially a sales organization.

Luckily for Ford, these management miscalculations were offset by the smashing success of four new lines added by the Ford Div. over the same period—the Fairlane, the two-place Thunderbird, the four-place T-Bird, and last year the Galaxie. Since the Ford Div. was established as a separate entity in 1949, it has been accounting for 80% or more of company income. But in making sure that the division could always contribute so generously to revenues, the company had cut into the sales potential of both Edsel and Mercury.

## I. How to Defeat Yourself

The Continental, a luxurious $10,-000 two-door, was never a large operation at Ford. Some members of company management will argue that the money lost on Continental was a cheap price to pay for the prestige it

gave to all Ford products.

But Edsel's story came to a sad ending for a complex of reasons—understandable misinterpretation of the auto market, for one thing. In addition, there were some factors difficult for management to control—and others management might have been able to control but didn't.

• **Long Buildup**—Ford has always traced its planning of additional car lines back to 1948. The preparations were interrupted first by the Korean War and then by the grooming of the Continental, introduced in 1955 as a 1956 model. In April, 1955, Ford organized a Special Products Div. to develop a new medium-priced auto. At the same time, it set up the separate Lincoln and Mercury Divs.

Meanwhile, in the fall of 1954, Lewis D. Crusoe, vice-president and general manager of the Ford Div., had unveiled the 1955 Ford Fairlane in an admitted attempt to vie with Buick and other medium-priced makes. At the time, the company's Mercury was its only entry in the middle range served by six GM and Chrysler cars. Said Crusoe: "I don't want to drive a man out of my store because he wants something better."

• **Wrong Reading**—In 1955, it looked smart to sponsor a new and separate line of medium-priced cars. That bracket was taking more than 40% of all sales. Inside the bracket, GM had 60% of the gravy—and Ford was envious. Besides, the higher a car's price, the more profit there is in it.

But by September, 1957, when Edsel bowed as a 1958 model, nearly every medium-priced brand was in trouble. The U.S. was in a recession, and customers were screaming for small economy cars of the sort that were arriving from abroad. Crusoe's 1955 Fairlane had forced Chevrolet to come up with a super-duper model, too; price tags and features enabled them both, with some help from Plymouth, to bite deeply into what was traditionally the medium price range.

Ford Div. pushed into the medium-price area again with 1958's four-place Thunderbird. Meantime, F. C. Reith, a Crusoe protege who headed the independent Mercury Div., had broadened his Mercury line with restyled cars for 1957 and the big, luxurious Park Lane for 1958. By the time Richard E. Krafve, Edsel Div. general manager, rolled his car out, the field was full of booby traps.

*Business Week*, Nov. 28, 1959

# Ford Regroups Survivors

## II. Too Late to Turn Back

The perils were obvious to Ford officials. At Edsel's press showing in the summer of 1957, a reporter said to a Ford executive: "It all sounds good . . . provided there's still a market for medium-priced cars." The Ford man gloomily agreed and added that if the company weren't in so deep, "we never would have brought it out now."

The car had been named for the late Edsel Ford, father of company Pres. Henry Ford II and his brothers Benson and William. A new plant had been built for Edsel engines. A separate dealer force of some 1,400 had been lined up, and a fully staffed operating division had been organized.

• **Market Studies**—Conventional market research never went into the Edsel. Instead, Ford used a type of motivational research called "imagery studies," based on the premise that a customer can describe what kind of product will best reflect his image of himself—and be most acceptable to him.

In the more conventional approach to market studies, economic and social factors are sifted to seek out a chink in the product line—a group of consumers inadequately served. Such an analysis, even in 1955, probably would have revealed no chink in the medium-priced auto field. This would have led to the conclusion that Edsel would have to wrest customers away from its well-established rivals.

Of course, it's not impossible for a new product to do this, even in the auto business. But Edsel's product turned out to be a nightmare, complete with collar. The original front end design by Ford's top styling people, strikingly similar to the 1959 Pontiac and 1960 Edsel, was discarded in favor of a design by the Edsel Div.'s own stylist. The tricky push-button shift in the center of the steering post turned out to be too tricky.

• **More Models**—When the idea first arose, Ford had contemplated only two new models, one in the low-medium bracket, another in the high-medium; Mercury could serve the area in between. Edsel was to have been handled by Lincoln dealers (who would be asked to drop Mercury) and by some Mercury outlets—but there were to be only a few exclusive dealers.

Instead, the final decision was to offer four models, blanketing Mercury as well as the GM and Chrysler competition, and to build a completely new and separate dealer network. This is something no auto company has done successfully since the 1920s.

In retrospect, these two decisions look like the biggest blunders of all, but you can't find a villain in Ford to blame. Ford's committee system thoroughly disguises individual responsibility at the top level. Besides, Crusoe, Krafve, and Reith all have left the company. By the time Robert S. McNamara (BW—Sep.26'59,p74) became group vice-president for the car divisions, the Edsel program had reached the point of no return.

• **Action, Too Late**—Ford rectified some of its mistakes, but too late to help. The 1959 Edsel was in only two series, both of them at the low end of the medium-price bracket. The Lincoln-Mercury and Edsel dealers were combined and given the small British and German Ford cars to sell, too.

A year ago, a Ford study recommended death for Edsel, but top management feared dealer reaction. The final decision to discontinue was made last summer, before the 1960 model's debut. The timing was advanced because the prospectus filed last week by the Ford Foundation, in preparation for selling more of its Ford stock, would have to include a statement on the planned cancellation.

## III. Centralizing Again

The advent of compact cars unquestionably is the dominant reason for giving up on Edsel after production of 110,000 cars. Ford already has announced a 114-in.-wheelbase auto, the Comet, for sale in the spring of 1960, in addition to the Falcon on the market now. At the time of the announcement, the company said Comet would be handled by the M-E-L Div., now the Lincoln-Mercury Div.

Reportedly, Ford planned Comet in late 1958 with the idea of scaling the Edsel down to compact size. Then the big Edsel could quietly have been junked. Then the thinking apparently changed; last summer Edsel sales picked up, and Detroit betting was that Ford would bring out the new compact and retain the big Edsel, too. Such hopes might account for giving the compact a different name, but the ultimate reason was doubtless a feeling that the Edsel label would be too much of a handicap for the new line.

With increased centralization, Ford returns to where it was organizationally in the spring of 1955—with a difference. This time, its two divisions both have nearly full lines of cars to sell. Lincoln-Mercury has the imports, the Comet, Mercury, and Lincoln; Ford Div. the Falcon, standard Ford, Galaxie, and T-Bird.

One management consultant thoroughly versed in Ford ways wonders if the trend back to centralization means Ford is working toward the use of data collecting and processing machines to replace layer on layer of office workers. Whether or not there's anything to this theory, it's obvious that past decentralization has cost Ford more money than the company thinks it can justify in the future to its growing number of public partners.

John Brooks, *The New Yorker*, Nov. 26, 1960

An article by
S. I. Hayakawa, the semanticist, that
was published in the spring of 1958 in
*ETC: A Review of General Semantics*,
a quarterly magazine, under the title
"Why the Edsel Laid an Egg." Hayakawa, who is both the founder and the
editor of *ETC*, explained in an introductory note that he considered the subject within the purview of general semantics because automobiles, like words,
are "important . . . symbols in American culture," and went on to argue that
the Edsel's flop could be attributed to
Ford-company executives who had been
"listening too long to the motivation-re-
search people" and who, in their efforts
to turn out a car that would satisfy customers' sexual fantasies and the like,
had failed to supply reasonable and practical transportation, thereby neglecting
"the reality principle." "What the motivation researchers failed to tell their
clients . . . is that *only* the psychotic and
the gravely neurotic *act out* their irra-
tionalities and their compensatory fantasies," Hayakawa admonished Detroit
briskly, and added, "The trouble with
selling symbolic gratification via such
expensive items as . . . the Edsel Her-
maphrodite . . . is the competition offered by much cheaper forms of symbolic gratification, such as *Playboy* (fifty
cents a copy), *Astounding Science Fiction* (thirty-five cents a copy), and television (free)."

John Brooks, *The New Yorker*, Nov. 26, 1960

Wallace clearly recalls the reasoning—candid enough—that guided him and his assistants as they sought just the right personality for the E-Car. "We said to ourselves, 'Let's face it—there is no great difference in basic mechanism between a two-thousand-dollar Chevrolet and a six-thousand-dollar Cadillac,'" he says. "'Forget about all the ballyhoo,' we said, 'and you'll see that they are really pretty much the same thing. Nevertheless, there's something—there's *got* to be something—in the makeup of a certain number of people that gives them a yen for a Cadillac, in spite of its high price, or maybe because of it.' We concluded that cars are the means to a sort of dream fulfillment. There's some irrational factor in people that makes them want one kind of car rather than another—something that has nothing to do with the mechanism at all but with the car's personality, as the customer imagines it. What we wanted to do, naturally, was to give the E-Car the personality that would make the greatest number of people want it. We figured we had a big advantage over the other manufacturers of medium-priced cars, because we didn't have to worry about changing a preëxistent, perhaps somewhat obnoxious personality. All we had to do was create the exact one we wanted—from scratch."

As the first step in determining what the E-Car's exact personality should be, Wallace decided to assess the personalities of the medium-priced cars already on the market, and those of the so-called low-priced cars as well, since the cost of some of the cheap cars' 1955 models had risen well up into the medium-price range. To this end, he engaged the Columbia University Bureau of Applied Social Research to interview eight hundred recent car buyers in Peoria, Illinois, and another eight hundred in San Bernardino, California, on the mental images they had of the various automobile makes concerned. (In undertaking this commercial enterprise, Columbia maintained its academic independence by reserving the right to publish its findings. It hasn't published them yet, but has made them available to researchers.) "Our idea was to get the reaction in cities, among clusters of people," Wallace says. "We didn't want a cross-section. What we wanted was something that would show interpersonal factors. We picked Peoria as a place that is Midwestern, stereotyped, and not loaded with extraneous factors—like a General Motors glass plant, say. We picked San Bernardino because the West Coast is very important in the automobile business, and because the market there is quite different—people tend to buy flashier cars."

The questions that the Columbia researchers fared forth to ask in Peoria and San Bernardino dealt exhaustively with practically everything having to do with automobiles except such matters as how much they cost, how safe they were, and whether they ran.

Very early in its history, Krafve had suggested to members of the Ford family that the new car be named for Edsel Ford, who was the only son of old Henry; the president of the Ford Motor Company from 1918 until his death, in 1943; and the father of the new generation of Fords—Henry II, Benson, and William Clay. The three brothers had let Krafve know that their father might not have cared to have his name spinning on a million hubcaps, and they had consequently suggested that the Special Products Division start looking around for a substitute. This it did, with a zeal no less emphatic than it displayed in the personality crusade. In the late summer and early fall of 1955, Wallace hired the services of several research outfits, which sent interviewers, armed with a list of two thousand possible names, to canvass sidewalk crowds in New York, Chicago, Willow Run, and Ann Arbor. The interviewers did not ask simply what the respondent thought of some such name as Mars, Jupiter, Rover, Ariel, Arrow, Dart, or Ovation. They asked what free associations each name brought to mind, and having got an answer to this one, they asked what word or words was considered the opposite of each name, on the theory that, subliminally speaking, the opposite is as much a part of a name as the tail is of a penny. The results of all this, the Special Products Division eventually decided, were inconclusive.

It was at this stage of the game that Wallace, resolving to try and wring from genius what the common mind had failed to yield, entered into a car-naming correspondence with the poet Marianne Moore, which was later published in this magazine and still later, in book form, by the Morgan Library. "We should like this name . . . to convey, through association or other conjuration, some visceral feeling of elegance, fleetness, advanced features and design," Wallace wrote to Miss Moore, achieving a certain feeling of elegance himself. If it is asked who among the gods of Dearborn had the inspired and inspiriting idea of enlisting Miss Moore's services in this cause, the answer, according to Wallace, is that it was no god but the wife of one of his junior assistants—a young lady who had recently graduated from Mount Holyoke, where she had heard Miss Moore lecture. Had her husband's superiors gone a step further and actually adopted one of Miss Moore's many suggestions—Intelligent Bullet, for instance, or Utopian Turtletop, or Bullet Cloisonné, or Pastelogram, or Mongoose Civique, or Andante con Moto ("Description of a good motor?" Miss Moore queried in regard to this last)—there is no telling to what heights the E-Car might have risen, but the fact is that they didn't. Dissatisfied with both the poet's ideas and their own, the executives in the Special Products Division next called in Foote, Cone & Belding, the advertising agency that had lately been signed up to handle the E-Car account. With characteristic Madison Avenue vigor, Foote, Cone & Belding organized a competition among the employees of its New York, London, and Chicago offices, offering nothing less than one of the brand-new cars as a prize to whoever thought up an acceptable name. In no time at all, Foote, Cone & Belding had eighteen thousand names in hand, including Zoom, Zip, Benson, Henry, and Drof (if in doubt, spell it backward). Suspecting that the bosses

John Brooks, *The New Yorker*, Nov. 26, 1960

of the Special Products Division might regard this list as a trifle unwieldy, the agency got to work and cut it down to six thousand names, which it presented to them in executive session. "There you are," a Foote, Cone man said triumphantly, flopping a sheaf of papers on the table. "Six thousand names, all alphabetized and cross-referenced."

A gasp escaped Krafve. "But we don't want six thousand names," he said. "We only want one."

The situation was critical, because the making of dies for the new car was about to begin and some of them would have to bear its name. On a Thursday, Foote, Cone & Belding cancelled all leaves and instituted what it called a crash program, instructing its New York and Chicago offices to set about independently cutting down the list of six thousand names to ten and to have the job done by the end of the weekend. Before the weekend was over, the two Foote, Cone offices presented their separate lists of ten to the Special Products Division, and by an almost incredible coincidence, which all hands insist was no more than that, four of the names on the two lists were the same; Corsair, Citation, Pacer, and Ranger had miraculously survived the dual scrutiny. "Corsair seemed to be head and shoulders above everything else," Wallace says. "Along with other factors in its favor, it had done splendidly in the sidewalk interviews. The free associations with Corsair were rather romantic—'pirate,' 'swashbuckler,' things like that. For its opposite, we got 'princess,' or something else attractive on that order. Just what we wanted."

Corsair or no Corsair, the E-Car was named the Edsel in the early spring of 1956, though the public was not informed until the following autumn. The epochal decision was reached at a meeting of the Ford executive committee held at a time when, as it happened, all three Ford brothers were away. In President Ford's absence, the meeting was conducted by Breech, who had become chairman of the board in 1955, and his mood that day was brusque, and not one to linger long over swashbucklers and princesses. After hearing the final choices, he said, "I don't like any

of them. Let's take another look at some of the others." So they took another look at the favored rejects, among them the name Edsel, which, in spite of the three Ford brothers' expressed interpretation of their father's probable wishes, had been retained as a sort of anchor to windward. Breech led his associates in a patient scrutiny of the list until they came to "Edsel." "Let's call it that," Breech said with calm finality. There were to be four main models of the E-Car, with variations on each one, and Breech soothed some of his colleagues by adding that the magic four—Corsair, Citation, Pacer, and Ranger—might be used, if anybody felt so inclined, as the subnames for the models. A telephone call was put through to Henry II, who was vacationing in Nassau. He said that if Edsel was the choice of the executive committee, he would abide by its decision, provided he could get the approval of the rest of his family. Within a few days, he got it.

Eric Larrabee, *Harper's Magazine*, Sept. 1957

## By ERIC LARRABEE

*Drawings by Reese Brandt*

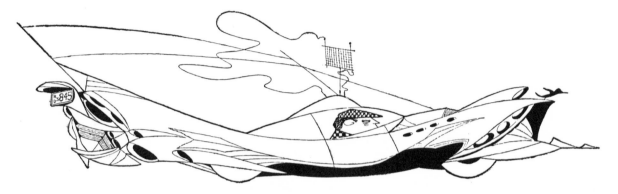

# *the EDSEL*
# *and how it got that way*

**When Ford made its plans to introduce a new car, it did not worry about anything so old-fashioned as engineering or design . . . Instead, it found out what kind of "auto personality" would appeal most to a particular market—and then looked for ways to tap it.**

THE brand-new automobile that Ford will unveil this month, the Edsel, is the first new line of cars in many years to be started by a major manufacturer from absolute scratch. The public has virtually no idea what it will look like, what sort of people it will appeal to, or what will be—in the language of consumer research—its market "personality." The Ford staff, however, has given much thought to these questions, inasmuch as the Edsel is going to be a 250-million-dollar experiment in finding out whether or not they know the answers, and an almost perfect example of how the auto industry—in an era of depth interviews, motivation departments, and "hidden persuaders"—goes about its business.

For such a vehicle the name "Edsel" is poetically and perhaps painfully appropriate. Edsel Ford, named for a childhood friend of his father's, was the son of old Henry and the father of young Henry II. He was president of the Ford Motor Company for twenty-four years, from 1919 until his death in 1943, but for the most part in name only. It was his persistent effort during this period to keep the company in touch with the modern world. He was a new-age man, consumer-minded where his father was production-minded, and he wanted to be more considerate of the public, to have better labor relations and make cars that would be more convenient and attractive. Yet he fought a losing battle with Henry Ford.

Though both were strong-willed, Edsel was also sensitive and considerate, while the old man just didn't give a damn and brutally frustrated his son's desires. Time has shown Edsel right, and for the company under his own son Henry II to say so—by giving his name to such a new-age automobile—is a gesture both sentimental and symbolical.

And ironic. The Edsel is no Lincoln Continental, that design of classic elegance and simplicity on which Edsel Ford lavished his greatest care. Nor is it, for those who look to the automotive industry for images of the American future, any departure from the present pattern—the trend toward the bigger, the gaudier, and the more powerful manifested by what Lewis Mumford has called "those fantastic and insolent chariots with which American motor-car manu-

Eric Larrabee, *Harper's Magazine*, Sept. 1957

facturers now burden our streets and parking lots."

It is, rather, the logical result of trying to give the consumer what he thinks he wants instead of, as the original Henry gave him, the best car at the cheapest price and no nonsense. Now that Edsel's principles are everywhere triumphant, and he has received this well-earned memorial, it is oddly enough to his cantankerous and phenomenally gifted father that we turn with a twinge of rueful nostalgia.

HENRY FORD, like any true hero of tragedy, was betrayed by his own success. More than any other individual, he is responsible for the quality and pattern of modern American life—with its landscape and living habits shaped by the automobile, its economy geared to an expanding mass market, and the majority of its people determined to enjoy the perquisites of middle-class contentment.

Ford liberated the genie of mass production. He saw in the automobile an object of universal desire, susceptible to manufacture in quantity, with which he could unlock the door to trade in enormous volume, constantly lowering prices and raising wages in defiance of the rules of "sound business practice" as then understood. By showing that this could be done with a piece of heavy, complicated, and expensive machinery he led the way for other industries into what has been called the Second Industrial Revolution and what increasingly appears, with the passage of time, to have been a decisive historical event. In doing all this, however, he released precisely those consumer cravings which he himself could not satisfy—and he created a world in which he himself was not at home.

Just as there were kings before Agamemnon, there was (as Allan Nevins has said) mass production before Henry Ford. His role was no more or less than that of the fanatical, unforeseeable, and essential genius who converts what had been obvious into what had been unimaginable. All the constituent elements of mass production (the assembly line, interchangeable parts, repetitive skills, mechanical handling of materials) had been discovered long before Ford applied them to his epoch-making Model T. Even the assembly line, which is so closely identified with him, can be found as far back as medieval Venice; and there is some doubt whether Ford himself was responsible for the first, true, continuously moving line, which was set up in his own Highland Park plant in 1912-13. Certainly there were other men in the com-

pany, notably James Couzens, who were as necessary to its success. But always, and throughout, there was Henry Ford: the one man demoniacally possessed by the simple, incredible fantasy—a cheap car for the masses—that set all else in motion.

## FATHER AND SON

FORD was a farm boy who hated farming, who sought to escape the loneliness and drudgery of the farmer's life by learning to repair machines. With the Model T he did for rural America what he had done for himself, lifting the farmer up out of manual labor and isolation. Model T was the first personal power-plant that everyone could buy. The stream of flivvers seemed endless, more than fifteen million in all, and the price came down and down (in 1924 you could buy a new Model T for $290).

At the same time, to make customers among his urban workers, Ford's wages went up and up —until finally, with a devastating disregard of precedent and public opinion, he announced a five-dollar-a-day minimum wage in 1914. For this he was damned as irresponsible by the best authorities, but that made no impression. To an innovator like Ford, history *is* "mostly bunk." He had done the impossible too often to take anyone else's word for it. Did "they" say that concrete railroad ties would make the engine jump the track? Well, he would find out for himself—and three times the engine jumped the track until Ford was satisfied.

But history caught up with him in the end. By unleashing the productive giant, he had brought into existence an economy far too bounteous to be satisfied with the Model T, with its absence of accessories and decoration, with (in Ford's famous phrase) "any color so long as it's black." As soon as the customers could see that the supply of cars was infinite they began to want the style and variety that Ford, by temperament and principle, had denied them. And, before long, other companies arose to meet these demands.

Other men—with the organizational flair of a promotor like William C. Durant, or the sympathy to design of an engineer like Alfred P. Sloan—challenged Ford's leadership. His pre-eminence gave way to that of General Motors, as the Ford car lost first place to the Chevrolet and later, in the 'thirties, lost second place to Walter Chrysler's Plymouth. (Ford has since regained the lead in the low-price field although GM, with half the market, is otherwise top dog.)

Eric Larrabee, *Harper's Magazine*, Sept. 1957

Henry Ford could never make his peace with these changes in the national temper. He was at heart a populist and a puritan, and in so many respects he remained—in spite of becoming unimaginably rich—a yokel. Lacking the appetites and emulative envy of a Morgan or a Vanderbilt, he could not really visualize these qualities in others; he was totally lacking in talent as a consumer, and he had little regard for those who serviced the consumer or catered to his longings. Ford disliked white-collar workers almost as much as bookkeepers and banks, or any form of methodical management; and it is scarcely possible to imagine the incredulous fury he would have vented on the present generation of industrial designers, market researchers, and other specialists in public whimsy.

He was the last of the old-style industrialists who had both the conviction and the power to restrain their proliferating bureaucracies; the story is told that one day, when he happened on a roomful of people with charts and comptometers, and was informed that this was the Statistical Department, he called over to the plant for his production boss Charlie Sorensen and a crew of men with crowbars—and wiped it out, root and branch, in a single afternoon.

As the world went against him, however, Ford's country-boy canniness turned sour. He came more and more to resemble the crabbed and suspicious crank of his worst caricatures, and increasingly he solaced himself with assembling his museum, that fantastic repository of the slow-moving, handicraft past which he had done more than anyone else to destroy. His hatreds became obsessive—hatred of Wall Street, hatred of the New Deal, hatred of imaginary enemies.

He hired thugs, and relished their company; eventually he carried a gun. Harry Bennett tells how he and Mr. Ford, in a fit of pure spitefulness, went out to Willow Run one evening in World War II and tore up the surveyors' stakes of a federal housing project for workers. He would show them a thing or two—that was what mattered—and the person he wanted most to show, who mattered most, was his own son.

EDSEL FORD grew up with the company. Instead of going to college he went to work in the Highland Park office. His father had great hopes for him, too great: he wanted Edsel to do as he did, be as he was, think as he thought. Edsel was a dutiful son; he became secretary-treasurer, and then president. But he did not become his father's echo. He had a mind of his own, and

the courage to back it up. He fought to put some curves and smoother surfaces into Model T, and for variety in color. He fought to have Ford cars equipped with hydraulic brakes and safety glass.

For thirteen years Edsel tried to get his father to bring out a six-cylinder model to compete with those of Chevrolet and Plymouth. He urged the company into the aircraft business, and the Lincoln and Mercury lines. He long foresaw the coming changes in buying habits; as early as 1924 he was pointing out to the *New York Times* the importance of women in determining the family choice of automobile, and he appreciated the desire of middle-class customers for "something more impressive. . . ." In the effort to make up for his father's aesthetic illiteracy and his own incomplete education, he and his wife had attended classes twice a week at the Detroit Institute of Art and taken a trip to Europe with its director.

All to little avail. Henry Ford wanted his son never to leave home, yet also to be hardened by experience—to be, as Sorenson later put it, "both steeplechaser and harness horse." Any difference that arose he blamed on Edsel's friends, or his diet, or his modest liking for Grosse Point luxuries. Yet the contrast was enormous, an expression through father and son of the oldest of American polarities, that between the Jeffersonian and the Hamiltonian, the rustic tinkerer and the financial sophisticate. It tore and tormented them; only Edsel's dislike of discord and hurt feelings prevented an open break. "But Henry Ford's idea of harmony," Sorenson again, "was constant turmoil."

Orders given by Edsel were countermanded. People fired by Edsel did not stay fired; while people Edsel liked, or who liked him, had a way of mysteriously losing their jobs. When Edsel and Sorensen, with the elder Ford's prior approval, signed a contract in Washington in 1940 to make Spitfire engines for the government, old Henry suddenly and angrily canceled it. Once he told Sorensen to send Edsel to California and not let him come back until asked. Ten years later he gave Edsel the same order for his two grandsons (it was not relayed). He insisted, virtually until the eve of his son's death, that Edsel needed only to "mend his ways" and all would be well again.

Father survived son, but not for long. Henry Ford's memory was lapsing and, though he tried to take over the reins of company control, he could no longer wield them effectively. Toward the end, according to Harry Bennett, he got

Eric Larrabee, *Harper's Magazine*, Sept. 1957

Bennett on the telephone and asked him to shut down the great integrated plant at River Rouge. "Then he began weeping," writes Bennett, "and became incoherent."

The Ford Motor Company was no longer the instrument of a single will; it had become an institution, a living organism, and even its creator could not kill it. It had, almost in spite of him, transformed itself and survived. One final irony: his house, Fair Lane, took its electricity from River Rouge. The night of April 7, 1947, there was a power failure, and Henry Ford died by oil lamp and candlelight.

Reuther and I talked in his office in Solidarity House, UAW headquarters in Detroit. Compared to the meticulous spotlessness of Henry Ford II's offices over the world, the place was a shambles. Reuther was coatless. In his early sixties, he looked twenty years younger with hair still red, eyes sparkling, and bubbling exuberance. As he talked he'd jump up, stick out his chest, strut back and forth, and orate—not with pomp, but with honest enthusiasm.

"Henry Ford," he said, referring to the founder, "was responsible for the great shift in production philosophy on the part of American industry. He was the first to realize the value of the mass market for his products—for everybody's products. I'm convinced that he was sincere in his motivation for the $5 day. It doesn't make any difference how many of the people who were with him then tried to take credit for the idea, the old man had to approve it and he knew what he was doing. It was his most fundamental contribution to our economy, even more valuable than the Model T. Only after Henry Ford showed the rest of them how, did industry begin to build for the large number of consumers. He structured the idea of the mass market which required mass production which made it possible to utilize the advanced technology that science was beginning to furnish at just that time. Some people say Henry Ford was only a good mechanic but he was much more. He combined his personal mechanical genius with a unique understanding of this basic fact—mass consumption makes mass production possible. He was sound mechanically and he was sound economically, and he brought the two together at just the time when scientific advances were becoming available to make the combination work. . . ."

Booton Herndon, *Ford*

FOLLOWING THE golden years of the Twenties, the Ford Motor
Company was coasting down a steep hill toward disaster with
both antiquated brakes and driver. The financial criteria and
operating controls vital to the success of even a crossroads filling
station were nonexistent in the Ford Motor Company, and the
head of the company didn't care. Any decision made with
respect to investment, product, design, and price was made by
Henry Ford on a purely subjective basis, mostly hunch. His
distaste for cost analysis bordered on the psychotic; he had built
the greatest family-owned enterprise with emphasis on mechanical production and to hell with the pencil pushers. As he
neared and then passed the age of three score and ten he reacted with phobic intensity to the new generation of innovators,
the practitioners of the art of cost-finding whom General
Motors was using to become the colossus of the industrial world.

McNamara, in any case, was drawn quickly into the developing political campaign even before Hubert H. Humphrey was nominated to run with Johnson. For months Senator Barry Goldwater of Arizona had made McNamara a particular target as he sought the Republican nomination. Candidate of the Republican right wing, Goldwater was also a major general in the Air Force Reserve. As early as January he charged that American missiles were undependable as a replacement for the manned bomber. McNamara reacted with a private outburst—Goldwater, he said, was a "damned fool"—that startled associates: publicly, he labeled the charges "reckless and irresponsible," and, of course, untrue.

In March Goldwater invaded Detroit, the site of McNamara's industrial triumphs, and zeroed in on the Secretary of Defense personally. McNamara was a loser, he said: "A one-time loser with the Edsel right here in Michigan, a four-time loser in terms of trips to Vietnam, and an all-time loser if his policies and the policies of the Administration that supports and applauds him are not changed in 1964." Even more provocatively, Goldwater claimed that McNamara's policies were reducing U.S. military choices to "withdrawal or nuclear holocaust"—the opposite of the intention of the strategy of flexible response. About the kindest charge he made was that McNamara was pursuing "unilateral disarmament."

*Business Week*, Sept. 26, 1959

# Ford's Peculiar Management Line-Up

**Henry Ford II**

**THE BOSS** — He took over a shattered company in 1945 and rebuilt it. Now only 42, he'll go on being boss as the new management generation moves up under him.

**Ernest R. Breech,** now 62, as executive vice-president, then chairman, was master mind in Ford's growth.

**Lewis D. Crusoe,** 64, now retired. He set up cost controls and planning, built up Ford Div., shepherded Quiz Kids.

**Robert S. McNamara,** group vice-president for cars and trucks.

**Delmar S. Harder,** 67, now retired. He ran basic manufacturing as vice-president, then executive vice-president.

**Theodore O. Yntema,** 59, vice-president, finance. Is a top financial spokesman, helped train some Quiz Kids.

**William T. Gossett,** 55, long a corporation lawyer, handles legal matters as vice-president, general counsel.

**THE OLD HANDS** — These are the men who have run the company under Henry Ford II since the war and have put it back on the track. Mostly they are at or near retirement.

# Ford Hands the Wheel to Youth

As it starts to show its new models next week, the automobile industry enters the 1960s—the decade when the postwar babies become customers for cars. It's a new era for the industry, ushered in by one of the great changes in its history—the compact cars.

At each of the auto companies, the new era has a special significance:

At American Motors Corp. the significance is in the vindication of its small-car concept.

At the Studebaker-Packard Corp. the

new era provides a spur to complete its financial comeback before the full weight of Big Three competition falls upon it.

At General Motors Corp. there is the challenge to continue to win the biggest share of those new customers—most of whom have not yet acquired a loyalty to any brand name.

At Chrysler Corp. the period ahead is the final test of its ability to unravel its multiple marketing system to preserve all its car lines.

At Ford Motor Co., though, the new era offers the most challenging combination of danger and opportunity found at any auto company. Getting and holding the new generation of customers is up to a new generation of management led by 43-year-old Robert S. McNamara (cover), group vice-president for cars and trucks, whose Thunderbird a few years ago signaled that the auto market was ready for sweeping product changes.

• **End of a Period**—Ford Motor Co. has

*Business Week*, Sept. 26, 1959

John S. Bugas          John R. Davis

**HIS CLOSE PERSONAL ADVISERS —** These are the men Henry Ford II turned to after the war to help him take over the company — the men he still turns to for policy advice.

**"THE QUIZ KIDS" —** These men were hired in a package in 1946, when they were rounding 30. The six who are left will have key roles as Ford moves into the 1960s.

**James O. Wright,** *vice-president, general manager, Ford Div.*

**Ben D. Mills,** *vice-president and general manager, M-E-L Div.*

**Arjay R. Miller,** *company comptroller and a vice-president.*

**J. Edward Lundy,** *company treasurer; his specialty is finance.*

**Charles E. Bosworth,** *director of purchasing for Ford Div.*

**W. R. Andreson** *left first, runs California van and storage firm.*

**George Moore** *has string of Ford, Lincoln-Mercury dealerships.*

**Charles B. Thornton,** *original leader, now heads Litton Industries.*

**F. C. Reith** *is president of Crosley Div., Avco Mfg. Corp.*

about reached the end of its swaddling period. At the close of World War II, it underwent a management upheaval, and a new crew took charge. The men brought in by Henry Ford II at that time were experienced business and automobile men. They turned the company around, and turned a fantastic loss into profits that are swelling this year to perhaps the biggest in Ford's 56 years.

The men who, in the late 1940s, started the company up the high road to the 1950s now are turning the wheel over to new drivers. The future of Ford in the 1960s rests with men who were barely starting in business 13 years ago, and most of whom still are relatively unsung in Detroit.

• **Carrying On**—This group, led by McNamara, already has great influence over the policies and direction of a company that is quite unlike any other in the automobile industry today. Not only is much of Ford top management young, it is composed of business

administration and finance specialists who, to a large degree, have enshrined cost control and profitability considerations above extravagant sales volume. In this, they resemble the managers of General Motors 40 years ago.

Since the principal training ground for management at Ford is the finance office, the new leadership is well grounded in this Ford tradition and ready to carry it over into the industry's new era.

At their head, of course, is Pres.

Henry Ford, II, 42 years old this month. Working with him or in major staff posts remain some of the veterans he relied upon for support to rebuild the company.

But operating responsibility for the biggest chunk of business is in the hands of a new generation: McNamara; James O. Wright, 47-year-old vice-president and general manager of the multibillion-dollar-a-year Ford Div.; and Ben D. Mills, 44, vice-president and general manager of the M-E-L Div. (Mercury, Edsel, Lincoln).

All three came to Ford 13½ years ago under circumstances and with results unique in American management. They were part of a "package deal."

## I. Help Wanted

The circumstances of their entry were simple, yet dramatic. Ford Motor Co. needed all kinds of men. For years it was one of the most successful of enterprises, yet it was adrift when Henry Ford II became president on Sept. 21, 1945. His grandfather had been nominal president, but was ailing at his home. Harry Bennett, his long-time confidential aide, ran the company in his name.

Henry II was 28, eager, ambitious—and fully aware that he knew little about the company or the automobile business. What he did know was that everything—plants, management, products, concepts, goals—all had to be modernized. "We needed to improve in every direction," he recently told BUSINESS WEEK.

• **Upheaval**—Henry II fired Bennett and established an informal cabinet of three men. Two of these are still his principal advisers (pictures): John R. Davis, then 51, a family friend and Ford man since 1919, who became vice-president for sales and is now retired and a consultant; and John S. Bugas, 37 in 1945, who became vice-president for industrial relations and is now also vice-president of the international group. The third, Meade L. Bricker, vice-president for manufacturing, retired nine years ago.

To take charge of shaking the rust out of the mammoth Ford machine, Henry II brought in as executive vice-president—now chairman—Ernest R. Breech, who was then president of Bendix Aviation Corp. and had previously been for many years a General Motors executive. Breech set the new organizational pattern, and brought in Lewis D. Crusoe to hack away at

costs and untangle the mess that was putting Ford into the red "at the rate of nearly $9-million a month," as Breech reported later.

Between 1946 and 1950, Breech, Crusoe, and Henry II recruited enough more senior executives to bring Ford's top echelon to a round dozen—not counting Henry II, who, though boss, was still learning.

• **Looking Ahead**—But Ford was building for the future. These dozen men became the teachers of younger men recruited from the lower ranks as Breech made over the company in the General Motors' staff-and-line image to give younger men the chance to learn and grow by exercising authority and responsibility.

Though no one could know it at the time, the most productive of the younger men were already at Ford when Breech moved in. They were there because of a telegram that set in motion an unparalleled chain of events.

## II. The "Quiz Kids"

That story begins during World War II when the Army Air Force established a statistical control office to keep track of its enormous production and flow of materiel. At the head of "stat control" was Col. Charles B. Thornton, before the war a government employee. His principal subordinates were lawyers, economists, accountants, and business administration graduates, many of whom were sent by the Air Force to the Harvard Graduate School of Business Administration.

• **Job Hunt**—As the war drew to a close in 1945, a group of stat control officers began wondering about postwar jobs. From wartime observation they knew that industry did not have the type of statistical controls on production, inventory, and the like that they had developed for the Air Force. From that grew the idea of several of them going into business as a team.

Four of them—Thornton, Ben Mills, George Moore, and F. C. Reith prepared a brochure explaining what statistical control was and how it could be applied in industry, and what kind of men were available to apply it. Mailed to several hundred companies, it drew 10 replies, among them one from Robert R. Young, head of Alleghany Corp.

• **Approach to Ford**—About this time Moore, a native of Detroit, went home on vacation and heard about Henry Ford II's interest in new management.

He returned to the Pentagon and told Thornton; then, as Mills recalls, Thornton, Mills, Moore, and Reith debated how to approach Henry II. They doubted that a letter would get to him —anyway there was need for haste as Thornton and Moore had an appointment in the next few days with Robert Young. They thought a phone call would be a little brash. Finally they decided on a telegram.

Mills remembers that the telegram said something to the effect that "we have a matter of management significance to discuss with you." Moore adds that it also pointed out that the signer (Thornton) had been directing 6,000 people around the world in management activities.

Mills says now they didn't really expect any reply; but the next morning Ford's Washington office telephoned to arrange an appointment in Dearborn. In late November, 1945, Thornton and Moore went first to Cleveland to talk to Young, got an offer and a 10-day period in which to reply, and then went on to Dearborn.

• **Meeting**—Henry Ford II recalls that he got the telegram and turned it over to George Coulton, his office manager. Coulton met with Thornton and Moore and shortly went into Henry II's office saying that he couldn't deal with Thornton and that Ford himself had better talk to him. Ford did, along with Bugas.

They could have struck a deal right there to hire the four—Thornton, Moore, Mills, and Reith; Henry II knew he needed all sorts of management men, and Thornton was impressed with the wide-open opportunity at Ford and the chance of working directly with the company president. Instead they agreed to think about it overnight.

The next morning Thornton telephoned Henry II and found the welcome mat still out. Thornton was to select the number of the men and recommend salary for each.

• **Package**—Back in Washington the four sifted the qualifications of hundreds of stat control officers and finally decided on 10—for no better reason than that it was a nice round number, not too many, not too few. Then each of the 10 prepared a personal evaluation of his capabilities along with a salary recommendation. The lowest salary was $9,000, most were $12,000, and one —likely Thornton's—was higher. The group was presented officially to Henry Ford II and John Bugas early in January, 1946, at a luncheon in the Ford

*Business Week*, Sept. 26, 1959

Rotunda—with Mills, on assignment on the West Coast, and McNamara, recovering from infantile paralysis, absent.

The 10, and their ages at the time, were: Charles B. Thornton, 32; George Moore, 25; F. C. (Jack) Reith, 31; Ben D. Mills, 30; Robert S. McNamara, 29; James O. Wright, 34; Arjay R. Miller, 29; J. Edward Lundy, 31; Charles E. Bosworth, 29; W. R. Anderson, 30. Around the company they always have been known as the "Quiz Kids" for a reason that soon became apparent.

• **Firing Questions**—Henry Ford II knew he needed talent, and here he had one big package of raw talent that he didn't quite know how to use. Obviously, though, the first step was for the 10 to learn the company.

"For three straight months," one of them remembers, "every day we talked to a department supervisor—one a day. Ten of us, all asking questions. We would march in in the morning, sit down, and start firing questions and taking notes. We asked questions no one around Ford was supposed to ask—and we got answers. Henry backed us all the way. At the end of that time we knew more about the company than anyone else—and more than anyone had ever known."

"They were," mildly says a Ford veteran whom the passing years has made tolerant, "pretty obnoxious."

• **Facts of Life**—At the end of the training period the 10 became a "programing department" headed by Thornton, who reported to Henry Ford II. In a few months Crusoe came to Ford and the group went under his direction. Then their real education began.

This is not surprising considering how the episode of the Quiz Kids began and unfolded. When they first started discussing going into business together, none of them had had extensive experience in private industry. They had a hot idea, great self-confidence, ambition—and little notion of how corporate management really works internally. Privately, they probably expected to remold Ford Motor Co.

• **Change of Mind**—Anderson was first to find that Ford wasn't his dish of tea. A native Californian, he prepared to live in that state, so he left before the training period was even over; now he runs a moving and storage company in Los Angeles. Moore was next to realize that working for a big corporation wasn't what he had wanted after all. He wanted his own business, and quit Ford in the spring of 1947. Now he has a string of Ford and Lincoln-Mer-

cury dealerships.

Thornton's departure explains a lot about how Ford was developing. He was the group's leader, both in the service and at Ford. Any dreams the group may have had about really running the company centered on Thornton. Now there was the Breech-Crusoe-Harder hierarchy calling the shots and planning a long, careful development of the Quiz Kids. This wasn't at all the "management environment" that Thornton had envisioned when he made the package deal. So he resigned in the spring of 1948.

After a successful stint as vice-president at Hughes Aircraft, he bought into Litton Industries and has made it a fast-growing electronics firm.

• **From 10, Six Left**—Although it happened nearly 10 years later, Reith left for somewhat the same reason. He rose fast, becoming managing director of Ford of France in 1952. When Ford sold out to Simca he returned to Dearborn, and in 1955 was elected a vice-president and general manager of the Mercury Div.

When the market for medium-priced cars turned sour, Ford collapsed Mercury and Lincoln into a single division under James J. Nance. With his division and his job taken by a relative newcomer to the company, Reith resigned in October, 1957, and became president of the Crosley Div. of Avco Mfg. Corp.

So now the 10 Quiz Kids are only six.

## III. How to Grow Management

The six who stayed got a broad education in the automobile business—and under well-qualified teachers.

Since Sept. 21, 1945 there never has been any doubt about who is top man at Ford Motor Co. It is Henry Ford II. But after July 1, 1946, the major business decisions at Ford were made by Ernest Breech—with Henry II's concurrence. The principal executor of those decisions, in all but purely manufacturing matters, was Lewis D. Crusoe. Delmar S. Harder handled manufacturing. It was his job to get new facilities, and Crusoe's to use them to best advantage. And from 1949 on, Theodore O. Yntema has been the fountainhead of economic efficiency. These four had most to do with molding the Quiz Kids.

For several years the young men worked together as a planning and programing group under Crusoe—although they dealt with requirements for manpower, facilities, and money, and the

hard facts of cost control. When Crusoe set up the Ford Div. in 1949, their novitiate was over, their education in exercising responsibility just beginning.

• **Up the Ladder**—Take Wright as an example of six men in motion. He went to the new division as assistant to Crusoe. Then he got into the production end of the division's business as assistant general manufacturing manager. Next stop was purchasing in the Ford Div., as assistant general purchasing agent. In both of these jobs, the boss was a veteran.

Back to central staff in 1955, he was company director of purchasing. With broad manufacturing and purchasing experience under his belt, he showed up again at Ford Div. in 1956 as assistant general manager—by this time McNamara was general manager of the division. Wright succeeded McNamara when the latter was appointed to his present post.

• **Intelligence, Not Instinct**—Their varied experience in the company hasn't changed their basic character and outlook. Because of their educational backgrounds they never have been business pragmatists; although McNamara and Mills, in particular, have a tendency to be pragmatic regarding socio-economic affairs. They are not auto men in the old-time Detroit context; they are professional management men with an interest in sociology and philosophy unheard of in the hard-nosed auto business.

They are more inclined to apply intelligence than instinct to anything they do—not a bad idea in itself, but car customers notoriously buy by instinct rather than intelligence. While running the Ford Div., McNamara (and Mills, too, at Mercury) was hipped on the idea that by proper detailed analysis of buying habits and economic statistics of an area you could practically pinpoint a dealer's customers and selling would be fairly routine—an idea partly borrowed, it must be admitted, from Crusoe.

Despite this basic concept, however, McNamara has never underrated the importance of dealers.

• **Their Company**—It is the intellectual approach taken by the Quiz Kids that is likely to have the greatest imprint on Ford Motor Co. in the years ahead. The ranks of the teachers have thinned. Crusoe retired in 1957 after a heart attack. Harder retired this year. Breech, now 62, is gently trying to disengage and turn the detailed direction

*Business Week*, Sept. 26, 1959

of the company over to Henry Ford II and the younger men.

The six remaining Quiz Kids all have enormous responsibilities. Bosworth, as general purchasing agent of Ford Div., is involved in buying materials costing billions of dollars a year. McNamara, Wright, and Mills are in charge of the cars and trucks. Miller and Lundy are in over-all charge of cost control. Over the next decade, at least, Ford Motor Co. largely will be the kind of company they make it.

## IV. In the Shadow of the Dollar

What kind of company is it today? It is a company still young enough–using 1946 as the base year–to be cast in the image of its creators. That means it is oriented to cost analysis and finance considerations above all others. The most influential builders of the company, Breech, Crusoe (who claims to have inaugurated cost accounting in the automobile industry), and Yntema–and Gossett should be included as a powerful policy voice–have always worked in a frame of dollar signs rather than machines or sales charts.

• **Fundamental Difference**–Structurally, the company resembles General Motors, but behind the organization chart of Ford Motor Co. today there is a philosophy fundamentally different from what is found in the General Motors of today. Look back 30 to 40 years, however, and you see the outlines of a remarkable parallel.

In the early years of General Motors after 1920, its dominant men were specialists in finance and management–Pierre du Pont, Alfred Sloan, John J. Raskob, Donaldson Brown, John Lee Pratt (BW–Apr.18'59,p142). It was not until years later that the type of executive who has recently been preeminent in GM–the manufacturing man, the engineer, the salesman–came into prominence.

What the present-day GM executive knows by rote–thanks to the drilling of his corporate ancestors–the present day Ford executives are proving by charts and statistics. Oversimplified, at GM the dominant objective is higher sales, grounded on a philosophy that high volume itself maintains a favorable profit-to-sales ratio–for production efficiency was bred in years ago. Again oversimplified at Ford the rule is that low production cost will permit a low enough selling price to get satisfactory volume.

• **Finance Training**–Whether the type of man running Ford will change over the years–as the type of man running GM changed (although with Frederic G. Donner GM once again is in the hands of a finance-oriented executive) –is doubtful.

The principal training ground for management at Ford still is the finance office. For years it has been signing on and fanning out through the company intellectual twins of the Quiz Kids: for example, Tom Lilley, 47, vice-president and general manager of the International Div., who went to Ford in 1948 when he was 36; Robert J. Hampson, 42, general manager of the Transmission and Chassis Div., who was 30 when he joined Ford in 1947.

• **New Leader**–Another reason for doubting that such a change will take place is the character of today's young men, who should be around for a long time. Their leader, both on the organization chart and by common acknowledgement is McNamara. San Francisco-born, he was graduated from the University of California with a degree in economics and philosophy. In 1939 he got a master's degree in business administration from the Harvard B. School. (He also has an honorary doctor of laws from the University of Alabama.) He taught at Harvard before entering the Air Force.

A man of wide-ranging intellectual interests, he has a mental brilliance that impresses even the other Quiz Kids. An innate shyness is often mistaken by lower echelons for sternness. That, combined with an unalterable determination for company (not necessarily personal) success, makes him a bit more feared than adored by underlings.

Actually, he's a man of considerable patience with those who can't follow his rapid mind, and with an understanding of and sympathy for the problems of employees–years ago he served a brief spell as a union organizer on the West Coast.

• **Group, Not Clique**–While Ford is still largely the reflection of Breech and Crusoe, Henry II and the Quiz Kids are making their own indent. McNamara, Mills, Wright, Miller, and Lundy have worked together so long there is unusual rapport–which has a disadvantage as well as an advantage.

The disadvantage quite obviously is the notion that the Quiz Kids are a clique–if you don't belong your path is blocked. That opinion persists in some lower ranks despite the example of Reith's departure, and the objections of the Quiz Kids themselves who are well aware the idea exists.

• **Accent on Youth**–The other major characteristic that makes Ford the kind of company it is plainly is the youth of its management. That worries no one at Ford. "We used to say," Crusoe recently explained, "'don't worry about him being young; we'll take care of that pretty fast.'" It certainly doesn't worry other close observers of the Detroit scene. Says a man who knows intimately all the auto companies and their management: "Just give those fellows at Ford a few years to mature and nothing can stop them." **END**

WHILE THE gnarled old trunk of a company was putting forth new shoots in the form of personnel, organization, plants, and equipment, it still had to produce hardware. All automotive companies, in the immediate postwar years, had brought out updated versions of the 1942 models. Ford planned a smashing new model for 1948. Breech decided that the model on the drawing board would be too big, heavy, and expensive to compete in the low-priced field, and it was brought out instead as a Mercury. But that left Ford with the tired old 1942 model.

On the morning of September 4, 1947, while driving to the office, Breech received the inspiration to start afresh. He recommended to the policy committee that morning that they waste no more time or money phonying up the old Ford, but begin a crash program, immediately, from scratch. Not completely satisfied with the design of Eugene Gregorie, the Ford stylist, he took Henry, Jack Davis, and Harold Youngren of engineering over to visit George W. Walker, a free-lance designer. As the four men discussed their ideas for the new car, Walker started sketching it. His design was accepted, and Gregorie quit in a huff.

With a spirit of teamwork that would have made Edsel Ford glow, the factory brought the new car out in record time. During the period from drawing board to metal reality, young Henry must have been overwhelmed by the high-powered executives Breech had brought in. Even the second and third echelon people who had left GM for a future with Ford were older and more experienced than the young president. But when the car came out, Henry Ford was in his element. Jack Davis, who was entrusted with introducing the car, was delighted with Henry's creative pictorial sense. He was particularly good at suggesting and selecting photographic angles to bring out the best features of the new car.

Though the 1949 Ford was a tribute to the production and organizational genius of Breech and his top-flight associates, the presentation of the automobile demonstrated the direction Henry Ford II was bringing to the product. The car was introduced in the gold-and-white ballroom of the Waldorf-Astoria. Champagne flowed. Orchestras played. Hundreds of thousands of people inspected the first truly postwar beauty.

Davis had to fight off would-be dealers; there were 25 applicants for every opening. Though Davis later said the car had 8000 bugs in it, a hyperbolic comment taken mistakenly as serious criticism, he knew he could sell that car. It was sleek with elegant simplicity and a minimum of gingerbread and chrome. It was long and low for its time, and no running boards marred its lines.

Promotional and advertising photographs showed the new

Ford at a country club or in the driveway of a stately mansion. Henry I had brought out a car for the masses; the 1949 Ford established Henry II as the producer of the classless car. Anybody could drive it; you could even be rich.

In 1949, the company's total sales, including the new Lincoln and Mercury models, passed the million mark. Plymouth was definitely put back into third place, and though Chevrolet felt no hot breath on its rear windows, it heard footsteps. Despite the heavily augmented payrolls and vast capital improvements in the works, Ford Motor Company showed a profit of $177 million.

During the Korean War, for which the factory furnished large amounts of materiel, Ford continued to grow. Organization had brought order; every man on the organization chart knew what he was supposed to do and who would see to it that he did it. Breech was particularly proud of the engineering department, whose personnel quadrupled and whose budget was increased by a factor of nine. Del Harder, who had coined the word automation, automated manufacturing. Defining it as the use of machines to run machines, Peter Drucker compared the automation installed under Henry Ford II to the assembly line developed by his grandfather. The 1952 model Ford, second generation of the '49 with the 8000 bugs removed, gained on Chevrolet, and the 1954 model either outsold it or came mighty close, depending on whose figures you believe.

The Gold Dust Twins, Ernie and Henry, were elated with their progress. But there was still some sludge in their engine. After 15 years, Mercury was selling only about one out of every 150 cars manufactured in the country. As a car owner's income increased to, say, $5000 in the mid Fifties, he began dreaming of trading up to a more expensive car. That car was more often than not a BOP—Buick, Oldsmobile, Pontiac. "We're growing customers for General Motors," Lewis Crusoe, head of the new Ford Division, said.

In January of 1952, Henry Ford II appointed Jack Davis head of a committee composed of several top executives to make a full study on how to get more of the middle-priced market. The directive setting up the committee hinted strongly at a new car with a new name and a new dealer organization. The Davis committee produced a six-volume report, known as the Davis book, which clearly reflected Davis's personal experiences along this line, as with the Zephyr, Edsel Ford's attempt to break into the medium-priced market, and his observation of General Motors flops like the Marquette, Viking, and La Salle.

His recommendation was modest indeed in the light of what was later adopted. He recommended a new car that would be a little bigger than Ford to compete with Pontiac, and another version of the same name which would be a little smaller than Lincoln to compete with Buick.

The company at the time had only two body shells, that for Ford and Mercury which covered more than 97 per cent of all models, and the Lincoln which took care of the rest. Davis would continue using these shells for the new car, with interchangeability of parts,· and would peddle it primarily through existing dealers, though a few would be set up in large communities to handle the new car exclusively. Purely for convenience in referring to it, he called it the E car, in which E stood for experimental.

But the top echelon did not buy the Davis book. Henry and Ernie were big and they wanted to get bigger. One indication was the creation of a more prestigious title for Breech; in 1955 he became chairman of the board. H. F. II remained president and chief executive officer. It took two men to fill Breech's shoes as executive vice president: Harder for manufacturing and Crusoe for cars and trucks. Both rode clouds to work.

Crusoe, as head of the Ford Division, had not only pushed Ford automobiles to their highest penetration point, but had, as a kind of sideline, brought out a surprisingly successful new car. Designed merely as a competitor to the Chevrolet Corvette, the two-seater Thunderbird suddenly became the In car of 1954. It had pizazz with a capital P.

With the stubbornness of a drunk looking for trouble until he finds it, Henry and Ernie set up the Product Planning Committee on top of the Davis committee and named Crusoe chairman. About this time, early in 1955, Jack Reith returned from so excellent a performance in France that Crusoe gave him the ball. Reith ran with it. He drew up a far more ambitious plan and presented it in a masterpiece of exposition.

Reith pointed out that in the price range between Mercury and Lincoln, Ford had nothing. In that Ford vacuum GM offered two cars, the big Oldsmobile and Buick, and Chrysler the De-Soto and small Chrysler. In effect he proposed an increase to three body shells with a total of seven products. From the top down, there would be the Lincoln, a big new Mercury, an almost as big new E car, the standard Mercury, a smaller edition of the E car, the new Ford Fairlane, and the standard Ford.

Incidentally, in fairness to the planners of both committees and in answer to those who criticize Ford for not bringing out a compact car at that time, I should point out that the company had been making exhaustive studies of the potential of a light car all along and had even designed one. But from the pragmatic standpoint at that point in time—that's the way they talk at Ford's—the American people just didn't want an economical small car. Remember the Henry J, the Willys, the Hudson Jet, the small Nash? Only the Nash ever got anywhere, under the name of Rambler American. Dealers couldn't give the economical Ford Mainline away, and it was discontinued. As for the small foreign cars, in the early and mid-Fifties they were curiosities.

Reith's program called for an entire new dealer organization to sell the E car, but the car itself was to be only part of a comprehensive package involving a major reorganization of the company. Reith did not spring his program on the board of directors without warning that April 15, 1955. Nobody with any sense would have thrown a program of this magnitude before a board without softening up its members first, and Reith had plenty of sense. He planned his pitch, discussed it, and organized his forces long before the meeting. He was tireless, enthusiastic, and almost hypnotic and he had Crusoe behind him.

When the proposal was brought before the board, it was adopted unanimously. Henry Ford II was present, and he voted for it. McNamara was also present.

As for Ernie Breech, the chairman, he has since maintained that he was the only person in the room opposed to the car, but that he yielded to the majority. Several executives with whom I've discussed the ensuing fiasco maintained that Breech could have prevented it if he had strongly disapproved it, but they said so off the record. Not Jack Davis, who doesn't know how to speak anonymously.

"You may think that the Edsel is a dead issue," he told me, chuckling, "but it's no dead issue as far as a fellow like Ernie is concerned. He's got to prove to the world that he can't be blamed for the Edsel. The truth is that he was the one man who could have stopped it. The Edsel was Reith's baby. He worked it up and made a presentation for it—for Crusoe, he was working for Crusoe—at the board meeting. I wasn't there, I had just had a coronary. But I'd headed the committee to consider and make a separate recommendation on the Edsel, and the Davis committee recommended against it. Further, I'd shown Breech a copy of my report before the meeting and he had agreed with me. I asked Ernie later, 'Why did you go along, Ernie? You had my report, you said you were against it.' And Ernie just shrugged and said something about not rocking the boat. He was chairman of the board. He could have stopped it. He could have put sand on the track. He may be kidding himself, but he's not kidding me. Further, I believe if Breech had opposed it, Henry would probably have gone along with him. Breech was chairman of the administrative committee and Henry listened to him."

*Harper's Magazine*, Feb. 1971

IS GROWING UP HAD BEEN SIMPLE—and enviable. Good parents. Good values. Good education. Good marks. He was born in San Francisco in 1916 the son of Robert J. McNamara and Claranell Strange (thus the middle name, upon which his critics would so joyously seize in later years). His father, who married late, was fifty when his namesake was born. He was sales manager for a San Francisco wholesale shoe firm. The father was Catholic, the mother Protestant, and young McNamara was brought up a Protestant.\*

When Bob and his sister were young, the family moved across the Bay to Oakland, which boasted a good school. They lived in Annerly, a pleasant middle-class neighborhood. More than forty years later, his teachers would recall him with pleasure. Bob always had his homework done, and was always well-behaved. In high school, Piedmont High, he received excellent marks, joined all the right clubs and honor societies, worked on the yearbook, sang in the glee club, was president of a secret fraternity pledged to service. An early IQ test put him above the norm, very bright but not exceptional. From Piedmont he went on to Berkeley, at a time when Robert Gordon Sproul was making Berkeley into a great university. Here his gift for math was beginning to show, the work coming so easily that he had time to read and work in other courses. His professors assumed that he would become a teacher; he did not seem to have the kind of drive, the hustle, which one felt went with a business career, but seemed rather on the scholarly side. Vacations he spent gold mining (unsuccessfully), climbing mountains, learning to ski. From Berkeley to the Harvard Business School, where for the first time his enormous ability in accounting control began to show and where for the first time he worked at applying this ability to management techniques. He graduated in 1939, moved back to the Bay area to work for Price Waterhouse, started seeing an old friend named Marg Craig, was asked back to Harvard Business to teach, and married Marg Craig (whom everyone would consider a good and humanizing influence on McNamara, much of what was good in Bob, friends thought, coming from Marg's generous instincts). At Harvard he taught accounting and was a particularly good, well-organized teacher, but he was restless. America's involvement in World War II was approaching. The Navy had turned him down because of weak eyes, and he was trying to join the Army when the Harvard Business School went to war.

\*Once, during the height of Lyndon Johnson's love affair with McNamara, the President thought of the Secretary of Defense as a Vice-Presidential possibility and called around to Democratic pols with the idea. "You could even see Lyndon thinking it out—the Protestants will assume he's a Protestant, and the Catholics will think he's a Catholic," a former White House aide would reminisce.

ROBERT LOVETT HAD BEEN A WORLD WAR I aviator ("I have Naval Air Wings number 57"). As a young banker overseas between the wars he had been plagued with a bad stomach, had lived on baby foods, and thus had forsworn most of the social life expected of a successful, well-connected young banker. Instead he had devoted himself to the political and military study of a decaying Europe and of the meaning of the Hitler buildup. He had predicted accurately the fall of France and had sensed that it would be a war no one could contain, a war, moreover, in which air power—a mere embryo in the first world war—would become the decisive factor. He had returned to America, and as a private citizen had made his own study of what America's air needs and resources were. He had made a private tour of all U.S. air plants and airfields, shocked by the inadequacy of what he found. He had already decided that with Europe at war, and given the limit of German transcontinental bombers, American industry could by flexing its muscles build the greatest air force in the world, and that this air force could wreak massive saturation bombing on the enemy's industrial might. James Forrestal he knew through banking connections, and Forrestal, then Secretary of War, had sent him to see Robert Patterson at Air. Lovett quickly became Assistant Secretary, and when the U.S. entered the war, his private planning was to save the country crucial, vital time. But it was a very difficult period; Lovett could not even find out how many airplanes there actually were in the country. Lovett and one of his top deputies, Charles Thornton, had decided to try to harness American industry for the great war effort, and what they needed first and foremost was a giant statistical brain to give them a rundown on the current condition. To train the officers they needed for statistical control, the brain of this giant—which would send the right men and the right parts to the right places, or make sure that when crews arrived at a base there were enough instructors—they went to the most logical place, Harvard Business School. This was the symbolic step in America's becoming a superpower: already the real problem was not so much might as control, the careful and accurate projection of just how powerful we were. (Thus, twenty years later, when we were an acknowledged superpower, Kennedy turned for his Secretary of Defense to someone who was not so much a production man as the supreme accountant, the determination of what we had and what we needed being more essential than the qualities of the old-style professional production man who ramrodded manufacturing schedules through, who went by instinct, and who knew nothing about systems control.) The Business School readily agreed to the project, and McNamara agreed to become a teacher in Lovett's and Thornton's program. He was an

David Halberstam
# THE PROGRAMMING OF ROBERT McNAMARA

*Harper's Magazine*, Feb. 1971

David Halberstam
# THE PROGRAMMING OF ROBERT McNAMARA

assistant professor at the time, and he was so effective that Thornton soon pulled him from Harvard and attached him to the Air Force. Finally Mc-Namara had found something on which to fasten his energy, and his curious cold passion. He had a larger cause, and those traits of mind and personality which would eventually make up his legend began to show themselves. Until then he had been another bright young man, intelligent, hard-working, able. Thornton would remember the young McNamara of those early days as being strikingly similar to the mature McNamara. ("I'm sure that now that he's at the World Bank, only the Bank exists and Defense is behind him, just as when he was at Defense, Ford was behind him," he would say.) Thornton sent him to England to work out problems on the B-17 bomber program, finally got him a commission as a temporary captain in the Army Air Force. Then he went to China with the 20th Air Force, where, it has been said, he was the best and most effective statistical officer of any unit, creating new and more exacting criteria, the creative statistician. And when the problem of organizing the B-29 program arose—to become the major project for the Air Force—McNamara was put onto it. Other men would make their reputations out of the development of the B-29, but Thornton came to believe that the real genius of the operation was McNamara, putting a group of infinitely complicated pieces together, doing program analysis, operation analysis, making sure that the planes and the crews were readied at roughly the same time; all this before the real age of computers so that he had to work it out himself. He worked endlessly and sought no credit. He held the operation together, kept its timing right, kept everything on schedule. It was an awesome performance for a man not yet thirty.

McNamara had planned to return to Harvard after the war. His years there had been happy, and he was not by instinct a businessman; he got, then or later, little pleasure from the mere making of money. Challenges fascinated him, but neither worldly goods nor profit as things in themselves. Thus why not return to Harvard and the teaching of those beloved statistics? It was amazing what statistics had done, it was awesome to imagine what they might do in the future. Cambridge, where one could enjoy the university atmosphere, talk with men who were in other fields, and yet still involve oneself in statistics and their use, was an appealing place. Throughout his life he would tell friends that the years at Harvard had been among his happiest (something no one has ever heard him say about Detroit).

But Thornton, more outgoing and imaginative, more entrepreneurial than McNamara, had other ideas. To Thornton, the Air Force had not been simply a part of a vast and impressive wartime enterprise, but something more, a case study in instant corporate success. It had gone from 295 pilots trained in the year before Pearl Harbor to 96,000 trained the year after, planes built, flight crews trained, all dovetailed. It had been a staggering task and an enormous success. And they had done it, not the old, tired men who had headed prewar companies, but this group of talented young people that Thornton and Lovett had created, young modern minds not tied to the myths, the superstitions, and the business prejudices of the past. Thornton knew there would be a reconversion from military to civilian production, and the business world would be filled with new opportunities. He saw his team, men who had gained twenty-five years of experience in four years and who had delivered. Under normal business conditions they might not have attained comparable positions of power and influence until they were nearly fifty. Thornton himself, the oldest of them, was now thirty. He began to think of the possibility of selling them as a group, all that expertise and managerial talent bound together. It was not just that they could bring a better price as a group, but, more important to Thornton, if they were really to create something new and bold in the business world, then the chances were far greater that they·could really affect that world and its ways. ("If you went in with one or two people you could get lost or chewed up; if you were going to convert a relatively large company quickly, you needed a group," he would recall.) He talked it over with some members of his team, and most of them were enthusiastic. Only Mc-Namara had serious objections: he wanted to return to Harvard, the idea of business did not excite him. But he had come up with a mild case of polio, and Marg with a more serious case, necessitating considerable doctor bills. ("I said, 'Bob, you've got those doctor bills and you can't go back there to Harvard on $2,600 a year,' and he thought and said, 'I guess you're right,' and he was on board," Thornton said.)

For the team, there were two immediate possibilities; one was Robert Young of Canadian-Texas and the other was the Ford Motor Company. Thornton went by to see Young, who offered him a job and said he could bring two or three men with him. Ford seemed a better idea. The company would have to be retooled and reconverted. They knew that financially it had not done well (though they did not know how badly it had done during the preceding twenty years, showing a profit only once since 1927, in the year 1932), and it had been taken over by young Henry Ford, their own age—he was twenty-eight—who now needed desperately to modernize the company that his grandfather had founded and then let slip. They sent Ford a cable, saying, in effect: bright young management team, ran Air Force, ready to work. Thornton made an

*Harper's Magazine*, Feb. 1971

early contact; eight of them went out there and impressed Henry Ford, and the deal was set. Ford told Thornton to set the salaries; they ranged from $10,000 to $16,000, and Thornton gave McNamara the second highest. The group became the famous Whiz Kids: Thornton, McNamara, Arjay Miller, J. E. Lundy, Charles Bosworth, Jack Reith, Jim Wright, Ben Davis Mills, Wilbur Anderson, and George Moore. Ford, at that bleak moment in his company's history, had nowhere to go but up: nonetheless, it was an extraordinary decision for him to have made. He was reaching out beyond the normally closed auto business for non-auto men, and he was hiring a group which had just come out of the most terrible war in modern times, but whose experience was not in the failure and stupidity of war, but rather in the technology of it, indeed the technological success of war, their chief lesson being that you could control an organization by having an abundance of facts and data which were in turn convertible to industrial production. They were, in short, purveyors of what would be a new managerial art in American industry.

So THE FORD MOTOR COMPANY AT THE END of the war was a very sick company. Its practices, both in production and in personnel, had an almost medieval quality to them. Under old Henry and Harry Bennett there was to have been no unionism and virtually no sharing of authority. The public was a problem, the unions were a problem, the bankers were a problem. If Ford built a car, it was the public's responsibility to like it. And the company had no credit. Edsel Ford had tried to fight his father's policies, but Bennett had destroyed him; young Henry had led a family revolt and as a result had inherited the shell of a company, the name and perhaps not that much more, at a time when General Motors seemed to exemplify everything modern in production and managerial techniques. What young Henry needed, above all else, were instant executives; Ford was losing nine million a month. But he needed, as one friend would admit, two levels of management; one now, instantly, and one to come along. So in hiring the Whiz Kids he was hiring for the future, the near future, but the future nonetheless. At the same time he shrewdly covered all bets and hired a senior level of management from General Motors, men in their late forties and early fifties, who could go to work that day and help train his new intellectuals in the auto business. This was to be known in automotive circles as the Breech-Crusoe-Harder group, headed by Ernie Breech, then forty-nine, who had been at General Motors for most of his adult life, and was at the time the president of Bendix. Breech brought with him Lewis Crusoe, another high General Motors executive, now retired, and Delmar

"McNamara was, in business philosophy no less than in personal life, the Puritan."

Harder, former chief of production of GM. The arrival of the GM executive group, which the Whiz Kids had not known was to happen, slowed down the latter's takeover of Ford (Thornton, restless, left after a year and a half for Hughes Aircraft, where he sensed greater possibilities, finally ending up at Litton Industries). But the system worked very well for Henry Ford. The young men were scattered throughout the company (with McNamara and Arjay Miller, who succeeded McNamara as president of Ford, working in finance). There they worked to convert the incredibly archaic, helter-skelter operation of old Henry to the new classic corporate style used at General Motors, with its highly accountable decentralized units, the different company operations turned into separate profit and loss centers where each executive would be held directly responsible, and where slippage and failure would be quickly spotted. The lead of General Motors in that postwar period was enormous: Ford had very little in the way of a factory, its machinery was badly outdated, not easily retooled. In contrast, GM had converted to war production but it had been very careful to establish in its factory and production lines the kind of systems that could be easily converted to peacetime production. Chevy thus had a massive lead; it could bring out a car for much less than it actually did, but if it lowered its prices it would kill Chrysler and bring the wrath of the Congress down for antitrust. ("Don't ever hire anyone from the auto industry," Gene McCarthy, one of McNamara's severest critics, later said of him. "The way they have it rigged it's impossible to fail out there.") So Chevy kept its prices higher and produced a much better car than Ford. The true difference between Ford and Chevy then was reflected in the used-car market: a two-year-old Chevy sold on the used-car market for

*Harper's Magazine*, Feb. 1971

David Halberstam
## THE PROGRAMMING OF ROBERT McNAMARA

about $200 more than a two-year-old Ford, a very considerable gap. The prime aim of the two new management teams at Ford was to close the gap. Here Breech and McNamara combined their talents; they had to figure out how to produce a car that was at least partially competitive with Chevrolet, and at the same time make enough profit that could be ploughed back into the company to build the desperately needed plants. They couldn't do it by borrowing from the banks, Ford's credit rating simply wasn't good enough, so they did it by skinning down the value of the car, mainly on the inside where it wouldn't be seen. Ford had always been known for styling and speed, so they kept that, and worked on having a modern design, with a zippy car, good for the youth market; though eventually, and sometimes not so eventually, the rest of the car would deteriorate (as was also reflected in the used-car price). The Ford buyers seemed to know it, but curiously enough continued to buy Fords. By these means Breech got the money to buy and modernize the plants, while it was McNamara's particular genius to raise the quality without raising the cost, a supreme act of cost effectiveness. This was, of course, McNamara's specialty, and he had a bonus system to reward stylists and engineers who could improve the car without increasing the cost. The McNamara phrase—it came up again and again at meetings, driven home like a Biblical truth—was "add value rather than cost to the car." And slowly he and Breech closed the gap on the used-car differential while at the same time modernizing the company.

It was at Ford during this period that McNamara was being converted from a bright, hard-charging young statistician into a formidable figure, a legend, *McNamara* the entity, someone to respect, someone to fear, a man who rewarded those who met his standards handsomely, and coldly rejected those who did not.

If someone were to be driving with Bob during work hours, he would see it: Bob was driving, but he was thinking of grilles that day, only grilles existed for him, cheap ones, expensive ones, flashy ones, simple ones, other cars rushing by on their way to lunch, on their way home, and Bob running it through his mind, oblivious to oncoming traffic, frightening his companions. Bob, watch the road, one would say, and, if he were in a good mood, he might apologize for his mental absence. McNamara never stopped pushing—in those days he was watching Chevy, how was Chevy doing. The night each year they got hold of the first Chevy, everyone gathered around in a special room, and broke it down piece by piece into hundreds of pieces, each one stapled to a place already laid out for it, and they concentrated on it—no brain surgeon ever concentrated more—everyone muttering,

wondering how Chevy had done this or that for a tenth of a cent less, cursing them slightly, so *that* was how they had done it.

When Thornton left, there was considerable curiosity as to who would emerge as the top Whiz Kid; the answer soon became clear. McNamara was brilliant at telling Ford where it was going before it got there. He set up a corporate accounting system which reduced the element of surprise in the business. His system of rewards for reducing costs provided incentive (though occasionally, in the view of his critics, this system backfired, the rewards going to people and ideas whose efficiency would be only short-range). In addition, he had the advantage of moving in something of a leadership vacuum. Henry Ford was new and unsure of himself, particularly in the field of financial systems. To an uneasy, uncertain Ford, McNamara offered reassurance; when questions arose he always seemed to have the answers, not vague estimates, but certitudes, facts, numbers, and lots of them. Though his critics might doubt that he knew what the public wanted or what it was doing, he could always forecast precisely the Ford part of the equation. He had little respect for much of the human material he found around him, the people who claimed, when he reeled off his overwhelming statistics, that they had always done it the other way in the auto business. Such people, when they challenged him, were often proven wrong. Slowly he surrounded himself with men who met his criteria, men who responded to the same challenges and beliefs, and he would respect their judgments. This was a formative experience in his life, because years later, when the doubters about Vietnam began to express themselves, they at first tended to be people who did not talk his language and who were very different from his kind of people. They did not think in terms of statistics, or rationalizing systems, and they did not support their judgments with facts as he knew them, but rather by saying things like it all smelled wrong, or that it just didn't feel right; he would trust his facts and statistics and instincts against theirs just as he had before at Ford when confronted by the businessmen who had doubted his facts and charts.

IN DETROIT SOCIETY, HE WAS ODD MAN IN. The auto world represents a very special piece of American society, one in which the already exaggerated American normal gets exaggerated even more. It is like a mini-Texas. Detroit feels not so much like the automobile capital as the very core and regulator of the consumer drives of this country. The city believes in building, selling, moving, above all, expansion—always more, always up, a bigger car with more on it, a newer car with more comfort.

*Harper's Magazine*, Feb. 1971

David Halberstam
# THE PROGRAMMING OF ROBERT McNAMARA

The rest of the world might be content to ogle last year's car, or even the year's before that, but Detroit is perpetually on its way to the new one. At its upper levels, the auto world is pleasantly closed in, speaking only to itself. In the rest of the country people might be tearing at one another, feeling the bitterness, say, of racial tension or international crises, but in the Detroit of the auto executive, if more cars have been sold this year than last, all is well; if you sell more cars, Detroit is healthy. Auto men talk to other auto men, auto traditions are passed on from generation to generation. Ford people live among Ford people, General Motors, among GM people; there is a Ford country club, a General Motors country club. Cocktail conversations and dinner conversations are of cars and the company.

McNamara, then, was never of this Detroit, never really, even, of the auto industry. They were back-slappers, and he was never one for the slapped back, either his or theirs. Even his public-relations man was different. Other PR men specialized in expense-account lunches, plush trips, the usual lures to journalists. McNamara paid a handsome salary to a man named Holmes Brown because Brown knew a lot about the auto industry and was very well informed, and his treatment of reporters was considered by Detroit standards unusually Spartan. While his counterparts frolicked, McNamara ploughed through the unabridged Toynbee. He made a point of living in Ann Arbor among the eggheads, many of them liberals and Democrats (at Ford executive meetings, Henry Ford would occasionally mention contributions to the Republican party and then note with a certain distaste that "Bob here" would probably donate to the Democrats), reading books, buying paintings; he socialized with his colleagues as little as he could. When the dealers and their wives showed up each year, by tradition the head of Ford would show the men around for a day while the wife took care of the ladies. Normally the wives were given a fashion show. Under Marg McNamara they went on a tour of the University of Michigan Cyclotron. It was said that the McNamaras deliberately managed to be elsewhere when Henry and Anne Ford gave gala coming-out parties for their daughters.

But all this was more than just a stylistic difference with Detroit. McNamara was, in business philosophy no less than in personal life, the Puritan. The auto business is not necessarily the place for someone with an abiding faith in man as a rational being, for the buying of a car is not necessarily a rational act. Detroit has been happiest when it is selling a potential customer more than he needs, adding space, chrome, hard tops, soft tops, air conditioners, speakers, extra horsepower. McNamara not only thought the customer *should* be rational; what was even worse, in the eyes of some of his colleagues, McNamara thought he *was* rational. It pained him to approve a convertible, the idea that a customer would pay $200 more for a dangerous car that would deteriorate more rapidly being personally offensive to him. (After he left Ford and they made a convertible version out of his beloved Falcon, he wrote a rare message to a friend at Ford—"you must be crazier than hell.") It was as if he felt there were certain things which were good for people and other things which were bad, and that he would be the arbiter. His, said one friend, was a quiet kind of arrogance: he simply knew better, and these facts that he came up with were the proof. He believed deeply in the simple utilitarian car. His opponents in the auto industry argued that this is not the way the world is, that man will opt for comfort and status every time and has done so throughout history. One of his colleagues remarked that McNamara should have been the head of production at the Moskva works in the Soviet Union—no worry about frills there. A friend said of him that he not only believed in rationality, he loved it. It was his only passion. If you offended it at a meeting, you were not just wrong, you had violated something far greater, like offending a man's religion. If you did it, showed a flash of irrationality, supported the wrong position, he would change, speaking faster, the voice like a machine gun, cutting into you. Chop chop chop. You miscalculated here. Chop. You left this out. Chop. You neglected this. Chop. Therefore you're wrong. Chop. Chop. Chop.

He was overpowering; his power was facts, no one had more, and no one used them better, firing them out, one after another, devastating his opponents (though sometimes friends would feel that there was a missing piece, that sometimes this brilliant reasoning was based, yes, on a false assumption). He was, if anything, too strong a personality; he so dominated meetings that other men felt submerged and suppressed. Sometimes his meetings seemed to less friendly eyes to have a sham quality. There would be a meeting, say, to plan a car, its style, content, and prospective price. McNamara would arrive at the meeting with his own homework done, his own decisions made, so that he came with a fixed position. He would seemingly defer to the others, ask what they thought, yet there was an overpowering personality and ego there. He perhaps did not mean it to be that way, but despite the appearance of give and take, the whole thing would become something of a sham, the classic Harvard Business School approach with loaded dice. Those who attended the meetings learned to play the game; the McNamara requests to speak freely were not to be taken too seriously. He would telegraph his own viewpoint, more often

*Harper's Magazine*, Feb. 1971

"His greatest triumph was the Falcon, the vindication of his years at Ford, the definitive car, the direct descendant of the Model T ."

than not unconsciously, in the way he expressed the problem, and in particular he would summarize in an intimidating way, outlining point by point, using the letters of the alphabet, A through J, if necessary, and his position always seemed to win out in the summation. If you dissented or deviated, he listened, but you could almost hear the fingers wanting to drum on the table; if you agreed and gave pro evidence, he would respond warmly, his voice approving in tone. Gradually those who disagreed learned their lesson, and just as gradually he would reach out to men who were like him until he was surrounded by men in his own image. Those who knew him well could tell when he was angry, when he was going to explode. He would become tense, and if you looked under the table you could see him begin to hitch up his pants, a nervous habit, done because he knew he could not control his hands if they were on the table. The more restless he became, the more his antagonist assaulted his senses, the higher the pants would get, showing thick hairy legs. On bad days the pants might reach to the knees, and then suddenly he would talk, bang bang bang. You're wrong for these reasons. Flicking his fingers out. One. Two. Three. He always ran out of fingers.

THOUGH HE WAS OFTEN BLAMED FOR the Edsel (particularly by Barry Goldwater in 1964), he had remarkably little to do with it; the car was essentially antithetical to his position. The old GM people at Ford had long wanted to emulate the GM pattern, a different car in each of several different markets, different stalls in the market place (Ford-Mercury-Lincoln dealers were together, whereas the GM lines were sold separately). Finally they saw their chance: upgrade Mercury and slip the Edsel in between. The decision was made in 1955, a prime year, but the car came to fruition in 1958, which was a bad auto year, post-Sputnik, the worst year, for instance, Buick had. When the Edsel went bad, Lewis Crusoe had a heart attack, and McNamara was put in charge of all the car divisions. He consolidated some of the other divisions and put a stop to the Edsel.

Instead of playing games with consumer tastes, he spent those years fighting the battle to keep the prices down and the cars simple, fighting with the other people at Ford, fighting with the dealers. Always trading and swapping to hold the line. The dealers wanted more frills. The dealers wanted a crank on the front-window vents. And McNamara would say, all right, you can have that, but we'll have to take all the chrome off the car. Some of the men fought about the width of the car, wanting it wider so it could be a hardtop, which entailed a wider frame. McNamara would listen and tell them

(words which would be remembered long after), "If you persist in demanding this, I'll have to take the car away from you." The men around him began to shade things in talking to him, not really lies, just a certain hedging of the truth to please him. He for instance wanted a two-speed automatic transmission. So he promoted a design which would perform as well as a three-speed but cost less. There were considerable doubts that the two-speed would work as well, but he was finally given assurances that it would; the engineers wanted it to work because *he* wanted it to work, because there would be bonuses and smiles of approval, but sadly it never did; it performed durably, but sluggishly, just as his critics had predicted.

Yet he was good at Ford, no mistake of that. He brought his system to that declining empire at just the right time, they held the line, they did not decay and collapse as they might have, and they finally grew back, in part owing to his enormous drive and pressure, his utilitarian view, probably perfectly suited to what Ford needed and could afford at the time. His greatest triumph was the Falcon, the vindication of his years at Ford, the definitive utilitarian car, the direct descendant of the Model T, his ultimate contribution to cost effectiveness, a car low enough in price to compete with foreign imports but large enough to transport an American family around. He did not want a revolutionary car, just a classic, simple car. It was a great success, though not as great as McNamara had hoped; he envisioned a million in the first year, and it went instead to 600,000. Its success was to come just before he left Ford; it enabled him to gain the presidency, and he left on a note of triumph. But after he left, Lee Iacocca, who would eventually succeed him, said that Bob McNamara had damn near ruined Ford by pushing that Falcon, too simple a car, with too small a profit for the company. Iacocca symbolized exactly the opposite of McNamara in the auto world. For instance, he brought racing to Ford, and Henry liked that, Henry pictured with his pretty new wife in Europe after having virtually bought LeMans, an invasion of American power and industry somewhat short of that flashed on D-Day. McNamara hated all that, hated racing, and now here was Henry and the Ford name advertising for it. Lee brought in the Mustang, a car designed for the American consumer in just the way McNamara's cars were not. They had looked at the design and thought, we have a doll of a car and people will buy it, and now let's figure out how to build it. Lee liked bigger, plusher, flashier cars, and to him the Falcon was a reminder that Ford might be growing customers for GM, bringing them into auto consumption and then as they grew wealthier turning them over to GM, which was stronger in the middle range of cars. So Lee was

*Harper's Magazine*, Feb. 1971

critical of McNamara, and so occasionally was Henry Ford, now more confident, now more his own man, and sometimes given to making statements which indicated a measure of disenchantment with McNamara, that perhaps the good old-style auto people were better than the new intellectuals.

In 1954 the Ford Division reported "a definite 'swing toward the Ford,'" and was in a neck and neck race with Chevrolet. From one prestige contest it emerged definitely a victor. Chevrolet in 1953 had introduced a sports car, the Corvette, and expected in the ensuing season to dispose of 10,000 units. Ford countered quickly with the Thunderbird, which Crusoe explained was not merely a sports car but "is more truly a personal or boulevard car for the customer who insists on comfort and yet would like to own a prestige vehicle that incorporates the flair and performance characteristics of a sports car." The Thunderbird proved a winner from the start, surpassing even Ford hopes, for in three years 53,166 cars were sold.

All these improvements steadily edged the Ford toward the middle-class market, but apparently the company's leaders saw nothing doubtful in the trend. Certainly they did not seriously consider finding a new small car rather than placing a middle-priced car between the Mercury and the Lincoln. Perhaps in 1954 to do so would not have been a sound move. Buyers of the Ford approved of its being "upgraded," and plenty of customers could be found in the middle-and-upper-price fields which General Motors and Chrysler were holding altogether too successfully. In early 1954 the Lincoln-Mercury Division was still studying how to invade this area, and on May 18 laid some findings before the Executive Committee.

They tallied closely with those of the Davis Committee. The new car should use a Lincoln shell and the Mercury chassis, and should compete in the price class above the Mercury. The only difference, in fact, between this report and that of the Davis Committee was that the Lincoln-Mercury executives did *not* reject a new name for the car. They referred to it as "the Edsel," using the term for "identification purposes." From that time forward it was to be known as "the E car." At this meeting Robert S. McNamara, who had become Assistant General Manager of the Ford Division in 1953, spoke against "putting a lid" on specifications for the Ford car. He also asked: "What is the new car intended to offer the car-buying public?" This shrewd question was not intended to challenge the E car, for he believed in it; however, a full discussion of the point might have been useful.[13]

13. L-M Div. to Ex. Com., May 18, 1954, and minutes of ensuing discussion; interv. Breech (he termed this the "Davis car" or "Davis Edsel"); Mins. Ex. Com., May 18, 1954.

TODAY transcript, Feb. 17, 1961

[Extract from the transcript of an interview
with Secretary of Defense Robert S. McNamara, on
the National Broadcasting Company's Today program,
February 17, 1961 (italics added.)]

"I think that the role of public manager
is very similar to the role of a private
manager; in each case he has the option of
following one of two major alternative
courses of action. He can either act as a
judge or a leader. In the former case, he
sits and waits until subordinates bring to
him problems for solution, or alternatives
for choice. In the latter case he immerses
himself in the operations of the business
or governmental activity, examines the
problems, the objectives, the alternative
courses of action, chooses among them, and
leads the organization to their accomplish-
ment. In the one case, it's a passive
role; in the other case, an active role. . . .
_I have always believed in and endeavored to_
_follow the active leadership as opposed to_
_the passive judicial role._"

The Department of Defense provides another example of the development of government planning in the 1960s, narrower in range than manpower planning though more spectacular in its effects. The aim here was the familiar one of using a common intellectual framework, in which trends were projected and future needs established by all the service departments and their subordinate offices, in order to compel them to co-ordinate their decisions here and now on what to buy and how much. The combined buying power of the three services is enormous. Particularly in the development of new products and techniques their impact is decisive; they finance over half of all the research and development done in the United States.

The chief objective of the Secretary of Defense, Robert McNamara, who was personally responsible for the thorough-going reforms in the Department from 1961 onwards, was to eliminate the element of duplication in this immensely costly business of the development of new weapons. In order to do this, each of the services had to collaborate in an exercise in systematic prediction covering its armoury of weapons as they would be several years ahead. All the weapons in the pipeline, i.e. those covered by the huge research and development programme—absorbing as much as 15 per cent of the whole defence budget—were thus subjected to review. It was in fact closely analogous to the first step in the preparation of a French Plan, when firms which have been competing with one another come together in order to establish an investment programme with a timetable over a stated period of years for their industry as a whole. The different services and their subordinate branches engaged in the $50 billion defence programme of the United States tended to behave, as we have seen, precisely on the model of rival firms in a keenly competitive market. The technique of confrontation and joint planning imposed on them by the Secretary of Defense, in the face of a powerful resistance movement, has resulted in some remarkable savings. Those which have attracted the greatest attention are the cancellations of some expensive and beloved project of a single service, found on closer examination to add an insufficient amount to the military output of the United States to justify the additional cost.[29]

[29] McNamara's most controversial project in his programme for cutting costs by better co-ordinated planning to meet the needs of the different armed services was the fighter-bomber called TFX, developed in the early 1960s. The special feature of the machine, which was estimated to cost around $1,000m. to develop, was that its basic design was intended to meet both navy and army air force needs. Previously the two services had kept their design work jealously under their own separate control. In the end the contract was awarded, in the face of strong opposition from the army side and noisy protests from Congress, to the General Dynamics Corporation. The special advantage of the winning design over its nearest rival, presented by Boeing, was that 91 per cent of its components consisted of interchangeable parts (common to the machines required to meet the needs of the two services) compared with Boeing's proportion of 44 per cent. It was, it seems, the principle of the thing, the idea that a firm should win a contract on the grounds that it had found the highest common factor of two different service customers, instead of concentrating exclusively on meeting the design specifications of each one of them, which prompted an especially violent attack on McNamara, including an attack on his personal character, on this occasion (see *Sunday Times*, 17 Jan. 1965).

McNamara thus found himself in a rather difficult, if not highly uncomfortable, situation. From the Evaluation Group's conclusions, from his staff's analysis, and from his own rough estimates, he knew that both bids were too low. He also knew that one bid was lower than the other. But from none of the figures before him could he know *how* low the two bids were or how *much* lower one was than the other. Faced with this situation, unable to use any of the figures developed by the Air Force, not trusting those submitted by the contractors, how did McNamara arrive at his final conclusions with respect to costs? The following passage gives a clue:

> The Secretary said that, after finding the Air Force estimates inadequate for judging the cost implications of the two proposals, he had made rough judgments of the kind he had made for many years with the Ford Motor Co.*

* It is certainly fair to ask why McNamara relied *only* on what he called "rough judgment," rather than having his own staff prepare more detailed, rigorous analyses. From the public record and from the interviews I held, there seems to be no conclusive answer to this question. There are, however, several *possible* answers. First, McNamara may have felt he had all the information he needed to make a sound decision. In this case more detailed staff analysis would have been superfluous. Second, he may have felt that the information he would have gained by having his staff do such analysis would have been outweighed by the delay required for them to do so. In this case more detailed staff analysis would have been unjustifiable.

Neither of these answers seems to be the correct one. About the first, McNamara stated that neither the contractors' own estimates nor the Air Force's estimating standards were useful to him in projecting either the likely costs of the TFX development program or the difference in costs between the two competitors' programs. (The fact that the development program has run well over $1 billion suggests that he was correct.) It is hard to imagine that McNamara would therefore not have wanted something that could have provided him with more information than he had. With his predisposition for knowing the alternatives and with his known bent for rigorous analysis, it is hard to imagine McNamara relying upon "rough judgment" unless he felt he had been forced to do so. With regard to the second answer, McNamara had already delayed the awarding of the development contract ten months — from January to November — in order to get better estimates and designs. It is hard to imagine that McNamara would not have found justifiable those few extra weeks or even months that would have been required for a staff analysis if such an analysis might have produced some valuable information.

Thus the unlikelihood of either of these possibilities points to the same conclusion: McNamara probably felt that he was not going to receive any *more* useful cost data (useful in the sense that the data would help him make a choice between the two competitors) because he felt that he had not received *any* useful cost data as a result of the four rounds. He did not obtain it from the Air Force nor would he obtain it from his staff. For McNamara believed that neither he nor his staff nor the Air Force possessed at that time either the historical backlog of cost information or the statistical equations based on such a backlog to make more than "rough judgments" about the actual costs of major aircraft development programs.

In addition to the evidence from interviews I received for this hypothesis, there are two other shreds of information. The first is a short statement on the TFX case by a man who worked in the Defense Department while the key decisions were being made on the TFX, and who was very close to McNamara while there. In an article on McNamara's methods of running the Defense Department, Adam Yarmolinsky said: "It is an essential element of his management philosophy to reach out for decisions. But he could not find the factual background for decision making if the system did not dredge it up for him. A case in point was the decision to choose General Dynamics over Boeing as the contractor for the TFX. In order to evaluate properly the cost estimates submitted by the two final bidders, both of which were unreasonably optimistic, the Secretary would have needed a compilation of experience statistics based largely on so-called learning curves, which was simply not available at that early stage in his administration. Instead he had to base his decision on his own business experience." See "How the Pentagon Works," *The Atlantic Monthly,* CCXIX (March, 1967), 60–61.

A second bit of evidence lies in two of the steps that McNamara took to remedy the situation that Yarmolinsky describes above. Early in 1963, probably as a direct result of his experience with the TFX, McNamara instructed his office of Systems Analysis to produce some techniques that would enable him to estimate development costs for aircraft with greater accuracy than he could have in the TFX case. One result has been a series of estimating equations developed through multiple regression analysis that have proved remarkably accurate in estimating the costs of tactical fighter aircraft programs. These equations may be found in *Methods of Estimating Fixed-Wing Airframe Costs,* Vol. 1 (Revised), PRC R-547A, Prepared for the Office of the Secretary of Defense under contract by the Planning Research Corporation (Los Angeles, 1961). ("Fixed wing" includes aircraft but excludes helicopters. It does include variable-sweep wing aircraft.)

Another of these steps was to involve Systems Analysis (SA) more in the actual making of development decisions than they appear to have been in the early stages of the TFX program. If DDR & E has asked whether it is technically and technologically *feasible* to build a new weapon system, then SA has asked, first, is it *necessary* to do so and, second, what operational features *should* the system have to meet the mission requirements it was designed for. McNamara thus involved people at the beginning of a new program who would ask the kind of questions he considered vital. (Such a thing was done in the C-5A military aircraft transport program.) It was through steps like these that McNamara tried to build into the development decision-making process methods and pressures that would produce the analyses and results that he wanted.

*The Wall Street Journal*, June 7, 1973

# General Dynamics F-111 Output to Be Ended By Pentagon; Rockwell B1 Seen Benefiting

By Richard J. Levine
*Staff Reporter of* The Wall Street Journal

WASHINGTON — The Defense Department decided to end production of the controversial General Dynamics Corp. F-111 fighter-bomber. It appears to be a major victory for Air Force proponents of the new B1 strategic bomber.

Deputy Defense Secretary William Clements announced late yesterday that he had advised Congress of Pentagon plans to halt production of the F-111 in December 1974, when the 543rd aircraft is due to roll off the line.

"We have again reviewed the F-111 program and have concluded that the need for additional F-111s is . . . less demanding than a number of other critical Defense Department requirements," Mr. Clements said.

One of the arguments used by those who favored keeping the F-111 line open was that it would give the Air Force an alternative to the B1 bomber, should that Rockwell International Corp. development program encounter technical and cost problems. With the F-111 production line closed down, the Air Force will be in a stronger position to argue for B1 production, regardless of any problems.

### General Dynamics "Flabbergasted"

"The Air Force probably thinks if we keep this F-111 line open someone might argue we should reconsider about the B1," says a Capitol Hill staffer who specializes in defense issues.

A General Dynamics spokesman said the company was disappointed and "flabbergasted" to learn of the decision. Terming the past controversy misleading, he added, "From every standpoint—cost, safety, and effectiveness—it makes sense to keep the production line going even if at a minimum level." He added that he is confident a reexamination of the decision will result in additional orders for the plane.

The decision on whether to put the B1 into production is scheduled to be made about six months after the closedown of the F-111 line in Fort Worth. While the F-111F models currently coming off that line aren't comparable to the B1, General Dynamics believes it could produce a "stretched" version of the present FB-111 bomber that would be adequate for a strategic nuclear role. The F-111 bomber is much smaller and less sophisticated that the B1 and has less range and capability.

### Hard Lobbying

Some Congressional aides believe that Congress could yet reverse the Clements decision on the F-111, which is a major blow to General Dynamics. The company has lobbied hard in recent months on Capitol Hill and at the Pentagon to continue the program which started as the TFX in the early 1960s, when Robert McNamara was Defense Secretary.

The company's immediate objective had been to get the Air Force to spend the $30 million that Congress included in this year's budget for long-lead items for the F-111. This would have preserved the Air Force's option to keep the production line open beyond 1974.

It appeared that the company was making progress when Elliot Richardson, the recently departed Pentagon boss, mentioned the pending production-line decision at a news conference. But top Air Force officials have vigorously opposed continuation of the F-111, saying they like the plane but that budgets are tight and other projects more imperative. Still, the suspicion has lingered among defense analysts that an unspoken reason for Air Force reluctance was the possible threat the F-111 posed to the B1.

The B1 is clearly the Air Force's highest-priority, highest-priced new weapons program. And it's rapidly getting more expensive.

Last month, the Air Force disclosed that the cost of the B1, including research and development, is currently projected at $54.6 million each, up from $45.6 million only two years ago. Most of the increase, the Air Force stresses, is the result of a bigger inflation factor in its cost estimates. But added weight has also contributed to the rising price tag.

This huge increase in projected cost seems certain to make the Air Force job of selling the B1 to Congress even more difficult at production time. For many years, a sizable group of lawmakers has argued that it's folly to build a new bomber in a missile age.

The F-111 has hardly been without its critics over the years, either. Originally, Mr. McNamara envisioned the plane as serving the needs of both the Air Force and the Navy. But the Navy was never happy with that decision and eventually the Navy version was canceled when it grew too heavy to operate off aircraft carriers.

The swing-wing F-111 has also been plagued with a wide range of technical problems and mounting costs. But Air Force pilots have argued that its performance in Vietnam last year was outstanding, despite losses. And in today's aircraft market, its price tag doesn't look so big anymore. A tactical F-111 goes for $15.5 million, a strategic bomber model for $16.5 million.

Eugene J. McCarthy, *The New Republic*, July 10, 1971

The papers show also a strong and almost frighten-ing callousness and detachment on the part of those who were managing the war, manifest in the use of terms such as these: when it had gone badly, for example, the situation was described in one memo as our having been brought to *square one* – a figure of speech, I assume, drawn from parlor games in which a bad spin might bring you into a square which required you to move your pawn back to square one and then to start over; manifest also in the recurrence of the phrase *on balance* as though without it being defined, it described a kind of minimal justification for what-ever happened, since the matters being weighed were always of a different order and that the person reading the scales could conclude that "on balance" the policy had worked out satisfactorily.

The same attitude is manifest in the tendency to quantify what had to be personal, subjective, military, political or moral judgments. The most striking example of this was in the much quoted report of Assistant Secretary of Defense John McNaughton which, according to the Pentagon Papers, met with the approval of Secretary McNamara. McNaughton de-fined and measured US aims in Vietnam as follows: 70 percent to avoid United States defeat; 20 percent to keep South Vietnam territory from Chinese hands; 10 percent to permit the people of South Vietnam to enjoy a better life.

This use of percentages is essentially the same as that which is used today in making weather forecasts – a technique which I have always thought to be if not dishonest at least misleading: a 20 percent chance does not tell you very much about when the rain will come, if it is to come, or how much rain will fall, whether to expect a light shower or a cloud burst or a flood. Certainly the forecasters in Vietnam gave no indication of what was to follow.

Barnet, in Stavins, Barnet, and Raskin, *Washington Plans an Aggressive War*

The pervasive ignorance of the National Security Managers concerning the politics of Vietnam led them into the trap of collecting isolated facts and figures. Robert McNamara was the leading specimen in the national security bureaucracy of *homo mathematicus*, the man who believes other men behave primarily in response to "hard data," usually numbers (infiltration rates, "kill ratios," bomb tonnage). Like the classic private eye on television, *homo mathematicus* always looks for "the facts." In the process, he misses reality, for he never gets close enough or related enough to another society to do more than count things in it.

If you relate to a country as a military target you do not need to know anything about it except such details as are easily supplied by reconnaissance satellites, spy ships, secret agents, etc. You need never know who the victims of your attack were. Your job is merely to count. Things that stay still long enough to be counted are either inanimate or dead. Living human beings, complex and changing political relationships, such intangibles as national pride, elude the best analysis. All foreigners who do not know a society are at an enormous disadvantage, but *homo mathematicus* is intellectually crippled in special ways. When Desmond Fitzgerald, top CIA specialist in covert intelligence operations, briefed McNamara and told him that he had a "feeling" for the events in Vietnam that contradicted the optimistic "hard data" which lower echelons were feeding Washington, the Secretary of Defense glared icily at him and never invited him to give another briefing.

Charles Yablon

# T H E   R I S E   O F   T H E   T E C H N O C R A T

A Venture into Intellectual History

Charles Yablon

The concept of the technocrat may be traced to Thorstein Veblen. Although the idea that the technician was the "man of the future," the individual able to assert human control over the industrial corporation, appears in some earlier writers, notably Henry Adams,(1) it is Veblen who used the concept to distinguish the growth of corporations from the growth of technological progress. By doing so, he separated the industrial corporation into two processes. One, the business enterprise, is pictured as outmoded and dangerous. The other, the machine process, is seen as inevitable and beneficial. The technician acquires a crucial role because he is the means whereby control of the machine process will be taken from the corporations and returned to humans.

Veblen recognized the corporation as the dominant economic entity of his time, commenting, "Through the latter half of the 19th century corporations multiplied and increasingly displaced other forms of business concerns, and took over more and more of the control of the industrial system."(2) Basically a Darwinian, Veblen saw this development as a natural and inevitable adaptation to historical developments.

> The rise of the corporation toward the middle of the century, and its subsequent growth, was not due to any access of iniquity: nor on the other hand does it appear to have resulted in increased hardship. It came on by force of circumstances, because the conditions and methods of business were maturing into such shape as to head up in this outcome. The incentives which drove on to this outcome were the sound and laudable incentives of greater expedition and larger net gains to be got by a more exhaustive use of credit.(3)

While Veblen clearly perceived the rise of the corporation as an evolutionary development, his disclaimer of any ethical reservations is more problematic. Veblen often made his moral points while denying that he was making them. For example, when discussing the complaint that monopolistic corporations destroy competition, he asserts, "It is not that competition ceased when this "Competitive system" fell into decay, but only that the incidence of it has shifted. The competition which then used to run mutually between the producing-sellers has since then increasingly come to run between the business community on one side and the consumers on the other.(4) Veblen's tongue is even more firmly in cheek when he discusses the "principle" of "what the traffic will bear," "which underlies all sound business, and more particularly, all corporation business." "This principle," he notes,

> "has come to be formally recognized and accepted as good and final ever since the corporation came into general use as the standard form of business concern. Doubtless, and obviously, the spirit of it has always been present and decisive wherever men have done business, from time immemorial, but in concession to ancient prejudice it used to be decently covered over with professions of something else. . . . And the corporation incorporates this underlying principle of business enterprise more singly and adequately than any form of organisation that had gone before."(5)

The happy solution to the problem adumbrated in this passage is achieved by denying that technology and corporate structure are inextricably linked. The idea that the corporate form itself was a kind of technological innovation is rejected by Veblen as erroneous. The idea that corporations are necessary fully to develop new technology had been true at one time, but had ceased to be so. All that is needed, according to Veblen, is the full and open cooperation of the technicians.

The technician, to Veblen, has an attitude toward work first evidenced by the medieval craftsman.

> Wherever manual dexterity, the rule of thumb, and the fortuitous conjunctures of the seasons have been supplanted by a reasoned procedure on the basis of a systematic knowledge of the forces employed, there the mechanical industry is to be found, even in the absence of intricate mechanical contrivances. It is a question of the character of the process rather than a question of the complexity of the contrivances employed.(6)

The knowledge of the technician is knowledge of

law student paper

"forces" which produce goods, not profits: "Production" is a matter of workmanship, whereas earnings are a matter of "business." The productive process remains a matter of human control and human value, the instinct of "workmanship--" even if business is solely concerned with pecuniary gain.

The human values inherent in the idea of the technician take a number of forms. First, there is the "instinct for workmanship." To Veblen this is the elemental need of man, to manipulate his environment, to impose his own mark on the workings of nature. This "humanness" of the technician was also manifested in his autonomy. He is described as the "masterless man."(7) On one level this is a reference to his feudal situation, but it is also a name indicating freedom from corporate manipulation. In short, the technician as envisaged by Veblen is the exact opposite of the alienated, dehumanized worker who exists as the slave of the corporation.

Veblen's discussion of the feudal craftsman makes these ideas clear.

> But the craftsmen were, after all, masterless men working for a living; men on whose productive industry no absentee claimant had any claim which they felt bound to respect. Out of this workday experience appears to have arisen the common-sense notion that ownership is a "natural right"; in the sense that what a man has made, whatsoever "he hath mixed his labor with," that has thereby become his own, to do with as he will. He has extended over and infused into the material of his work something of that discretionary force and control which, in the nature of things, the masterless man of right exercises in the movements of his own person.(8)

The differences between the medieval craftsman and the modern engineer are presented primarily as ones of degree. The skills of the engineer are infinitely more complex--and much more central to the functioning of the economy-- than those of the medieval craftsman. But the process is the same: he is the one who shapes inanimate forces into useful goods, solely through his own skill.

> This mechanical system of work, "has the peculiar quality that it can be managed at will, that it is not subject to seasonal and fortuitous circumstances over which men have no control. . . . The system is complex, intricate and extensive; but it is a creature of human information and initiative, and all its complex and interwoven motions have been formulated out of experience and run wholly within the lines of known objective fact."(9)

In contrast, the businessman, "the Captain of Industry," exerts no control over the productive process. His talent lies not in manipulating nature, but in manipulating men. "Salesmanship"

is the instinct of the businessman, as workmanship is that of the technician. Advertising and packaging are means by which goods are sold, not produced. "[T]he containers account for one-half the shop-cost of what are properly called "package goods," and for something approaching one-half of the price paid by the consumer. In certain lines, doubtless, as, e.g., in cosmetics and household remedies, this proportion is exceeded by a very substantial margin."(10) In a typically Veblenian footnote, he demonstrates the absurdity of these methods by treating them seriously:

> This is not said by way of aspersion. In these intimate matters of health and fabricated beauty the beneficent workings of faith are manifest; if it should not rather be said that the manifest benefit derived from these many remedies....is in the main a work of faith which acts tropismatically on the consumer's bodily frame, with little reference to the pharmaceutical composition of the contents of the purchased container.... The case may, not without profit, be assimilated to certain of the more amiable prodigies wrought in the name of Holy Church, where it is well known that the curative efficacy of any given sainted object is something quite apart from its chemical constitution. Indeed, here as at many other points salesmanship touches the frontiers of the magical art; and no man will question that, as a business proposition, a magical efficacy is a good thing to sell.(11)

Veblen denies that larger concentrations of capital lead to more efficient production, calling that assertion part of the "folklore of Political Economy."(12) All that the addition of capital does, on his theory, is to raise the price of producing the goods, and thereby raise the price of the goods themselves. Capital adds nothing tangible to the machine process, which is totally involved in tangible forces.

> Measured by physical units or physical usefulness the total effect is nil, at the best; but measured in money-values there has been an appreciable addition to the total wealth, represented immediately by the corporate capital in which the funds in question have been invested and indirectly by an enhanced level of prices.(13)

Veblen's idea of the technician was an enormously appealing one. In part, this may have been due precisely to the vagueness which permitted various groups to find in it what they wanted. Nevertheless, the separation of technology from the corporate form solved the problem of the corporation. The benefits of technological progress could be preserved and even advanced by curtailing the power of corporations. The Veblenites could argue that laws which preserved corporate power were futile and harmful, much in

Charles Yablon

the way the previous generation had argued that the antitrust laws seeking to curtail corporate power were futile and harmful.

The 1930s gave these theoretical positions an added immediacy. As in the 1890s, the economy seemed to be breaking down. As in the 1890s, there was a dispute about the type of governmental action necessary to deal with the problem. But, as Ellis Hawley(14) notes, there were now three competing views of the problem. Two of them, the idea that concentrations of wealth should be broken up and free competition restored, and the idea that business cooperation was beneficial and should be allowed, were both familiar. A third position was new:

> The spectacle of poverty in the midst of plenty, of millions of workers idle while the community lacked goods, had led many intellectuals to question the very assumptions of the private enterprise system. And in their quest for a solution, they turned to the old dream of a planned economy. . . . [T]he great majority elaborated a planning ideology that was indigenous to America. One line of inspiration here came from the discipline of scientific management, from the system of ideas developed by such men as Frederick W. Taylor and Henry L. Gantt and applied to the economy as a whole by writers influenced by Thorstein Veblen. From Veblen these men drew such concepts as the technological imperative, the work-a-day, matter-of-fact discipline of the machine process, and the distinction between the business interest and the industrial interest."(15)

These Veblenian ideas were manifested in two political movements, Technocracy, and the League for Independent Political Action: both were attempts to reform society along the lines suggested by Veblen; both were failures.

Technocracy was a curious and shortlived phenomenon, which sought to put into effect the "soviet of engineers" which Veblen had envisioned. Howard Scott, an economist at Columbia, announed in 1932 that he and a small group of engineers were working on a system to rationalize the economy. The system was to be based on the energy produced by economic enterprise, rather than on money. It would be possible, according to Scott, to provide everyone in the country with an abundance of material goods. All that would be necessary was to turn the economic production of the country over to Scott and his engineers for rationalization.

For a short time in 1932, the concept had become, according to one historian, "a national sensation."(16) Although he ascribed this to the sheer audacity of the scheme, the fact is that the Technocrats knew how to exploit some of the most appealing aspects of Veblen. Foremost <u>certainty</u>: Scott believed that he was dealing with objective forces which could be quantified

and controlled: a belief supported by the mystique of science, which Veblen had equated with technology, "governed by the same logic as the scientific laboratories."(17)

More ominous than the use of science to provide assurance of objectivity was the elitist nature of Technocracy. The Technocrats saw themselves as saviors and expected to be treated as such. The small number of people involved in the "planning," and the use of abstruse scientific jargon, fostered the view of the engineer as a member of the aristocratic elite. Their demand for dictatorial power over the economy was a logical outcome of their certainty that they had possessed incontrovertible knowledge.

The League for Independent Political Action was organized in 1929 as a political party, patterned after the Minnesota Farm-Labor Party, one of the few third parties which had achieved any real political success in the United States. The League sought to put together a coalition of farmers, wage earners, and intellectuals. Veblen was one of the few social theorist whom agrarian, urban, and intellectual radicals could all find congenial. The Veblen of the League for Independent Political Action, however, was not the elitist Veblen of the Technocrats. This was the Veblen who saw almost everybody as a craftsman, and saw almost everybody as exploited by absentee ownership.

The ambiguity in Veblen's thought, however, was manifest in the problems of the League. Veblen as a symbol could unite urban intellectuals and agrarian reformers; Veblen as a social theorist could not. To urban intellectuals, his ideas were a justification for social planning. Their platform in 1932 was the product of "over one hundred economists and experts."(18) Their concept of planning, although not as elitist as that of the Technocrats, nevertheless involved an ascertaining of the various interests involved, and then a process where those interests would be "perfected, coordinated and enforced by a central board of technicians, economists, engineers and other 'qualified experts'."(19) Inherent in this concept, of course, is Veblen's idea of the objective and impersonal nature of science and technology. Once a process of negotiation among societal groups had determined what the societal goals should be, the central planners would scientifically determine the best way to achieve them. The concept of a negotiating process to develop policy goals, however, was an attempt to curb the elitist notion inherent in "scientific planning." As Hawley points out

> Repeatedly, the planners expressed concern about the preservation of democracy. They did hope, on the one hand, to create a planned system of abundance, one that would make the most efficient use of technological advances, distribute the proceeds equitably

law student paper

among all claimants, and provide adequate security for everyone. Yet they also hoped, on the other, to maintain a democratic system of procedure, a system based on compromise, conciliation, persuasion and popular consent. The two objectives, perhaps, were not necessarily incompatible, but the achievement of both required great faith in the efficacy of the conference table, the sweet reasonableness of mankind, and the ability of disinterested experts to resolve interest conflicts through scientific research and the amassing of factual material.(20)

Galbraith's discussion of the power and inevitability of greater and greater economic concentrations is reminiscent of turn-of-the-century economists who argued that the corporations' large size gave them a tremendous advantage in the competitive struggle. Size is once again equated with technological achievement, although Galbraith's emphasis is not economies of scale, but of planning:

> with the rise of the modern corporation, the emergence of the organization required by modern technology and planning, ...the entrepreneur no longer exists as an individual person... The most obvious requirement of effective planning is large size. This, we have seen, allows the firm to accept market uncertainty where it cannot be eliminated; to eliminate markets on which otherwise it would be excessively dependent; to control other markets in which it buys and sells; and it is very nearly indispensable for participation in that part of the economy, characterized by exacting technology and comprehensive planning, where the only buyer is the federal government.(21)

Galbraith rejects the idea that technology and corporate interests are incompatible. On the contrary, he finds them to be identical, thus completing the process that Veblen identified. His technostructure does not simply gain power in the corporation; it controls the corporation.

> The requirements of technology and planning have greatly increased the need of the industrial enterprise for specialized talent and for its organization.... Unlike capital it is not something that the firm can supply to itself.... [O]ne should expect, from past experience, to find a new shift of power in the industrial enterprise, this one from capital to organized intelligence. . . . This has, indeed, occurred.(22)

Galbraith does admit that "there must be consistency in the goals of the society, the organization and the individual. And there must be consistency in the motives which induce organizations and individuals to pursue these goals."(23)  If all the members of the techno-

structure could agree on the goals of a humane society, such a society could be achieved. But underlying Galbraith's description of the technostructure is a pessimism about the capacity of individuals to favor such social concerns. As members of the technostructure, the group in power, their primary interest is simply to preserve that power. "For any organization, as for any organism, the goal or objective that has a natural assumption of pre-eminence is the organization's own survival. This, plausibly, is true of the technostructure."(24)  In effect, Galbraith creates a new monster to run the old monster.

Nevertheless, Galbraith seeks a way out of the dilemma of how to control and humanize the corporation:

> For this emancipation, education--higher education in particular--is obviously strategic. It is, among other things, an apparatus for affecting belief and hopefully, inducing more critical belief. The industrial system, by making trained and educated manpower the decisive factor of production, requires a highly developed educational system. If the educational system serves generally the beliefs of the industrial system, the influence and monolithic character of the latter will be enhanced. By the same token, should it be superior to and independent of the industrial system, it can be the necessary force for skepticism, emancipation and pluralism."(25)

Like Veblen's technicians, the university professors do not recognize their importance to the system, but they do in fact have the power to control it: "The educational and scientific estate has the power to exercise its option. It holds the critical cards. For in committing itself to technology, planning and organization, the industrial system has made itself deeply dependent on the manpower which these require.(26)

Moreover, just as Veblen's technician, by the nature of his profession, was possessed of autonomy and human values, Galbraith's scientific and educational estate appears to be equally blessed:

> The needed changes, including those in the images by which military and foreign policy are shaped, all involve the sensibilities and concerns of the mind. Their natural, although by no means exclusive, interest therefore is to those who are called intellectuals. The largest number of intellectuals with an occupational identification are those in the educational scientific estate. It is to the educational and scientific estate, accordingly, that we must turn for the requisite political initiative.(27)

Veblen skirted the problem of elitism by

Charles Yablon

asserting that the technician was defined by his
matter-of-fact attitude to the world and its
inanimate forces.  Such a definition potentially
included almost everyone.  Galbraith does not
skirt the problem; he rams right into it.  The
leadership potential of the educational estate is
derived not from any special insight they can
impart to the public at large, but because they
regularly deal with "concerns of the mind."  They
are, in other words, the experts, and are therefore under an obligation to lead others.

Basically, because he trusts academicians as
a class more than business managers, Galbraith,
in effect, proclaims an aristocracy newer than
Veblen's and drawing its members from a different
vocational status.

1. "All New York was demanding new men, and all the new forces, condensed into corporations, were demanding a new type of man" Henry Adams, The Education at 499
2. T. Veblen, Absentee Ownership and Business Enterprise in Recent Times (1923) at 82
3. Absentee Ownership at 83-84
4. Ibid., p.99
5. Id. at 85-86
6. T. Veblen, The Theory of the Business Enterprise, (1904) at 6
7. Absentee Ownership at 44
8. Id. at 47-48
9. Id. at 267-268
10. Id. at 301
11. Id. at 301 n.7
12. Id. at 86
13. Id. at 88
14. E. Hawley, The New Deal and the Problem of Monopoly (1966)
15. Id. at 43-44
16. R. Alan Lawson, The Failure of Independent Liberalism, (1971) at 47
17. Absentee Ownership at 261
18. R. Lawson, op cit at 43
19. Hawley, op cit at 45
20. Id. at 176
21. J. Galbraith, The New Industrial State, (2d ed. 1971) at 70, 74
22. Id. at 56 (emphasis in original)
23. Id. at 159
24. Id. at 167
25. Id. at 372
26. Id. at 378
27. Id. at 382

Faithfully executing the prescribed routine, the Special Products Division called upon its director of planning for market research, David Wallace, to see what he could do about imparting a personality to the E-Car and giving it a name. Wallace, a lean, craggy-jawed pipe puffer with a soft, slow, thoughtful way of speaking, gives the impression of being the Platonic idea of the college professor—the very steel die from which the breed is cut—although, in point of fact, his background is not strongly academic. Before going to Ford, in 1955, he had worked his way through Westminster College, in Pennsylvania, ridden out the depression as a construction laborer in New York City, and then spent ten years in market research at *Time*. Still, impressions are what count, and Wallace admits that during his tenure with Ford he consciously stressed his professorial air for the sake of the advantage it gave him in dealing with the bluff, practical men of Dearborn. "Our department came to be regarded as a semi-Brain Trust," he says. He insisted, typically, on living in Ann Arbor, where he could bask in the scholarly aura of the University of Michigan, rather than in Dearborn or Detroit, both of which he declared were intolerable after business hours. Whatever the degree of his success in projecting the image of the E-Car, he seems, by his small eccentricities, to have done splendidly at projecting the image of Wallace. "I don't think Dave's motivation for being at Ford was basically economic," his old boss, Krafve, says. "Dave is the scholarly type, and I think he considered the job an interesting challenge."

Among the former executives of the Edsel Division, opinions differ as to the exact moment when the portents of doom became unmistakable. Krafve feels that the moment did not arrive until sometime late in October. David Wallace, Edsel's pipe-smoking, professorial director of planning for market research, who concentrated his attention on the vagaries of sociology and mass psychology, conducted the Edsel's motivational-research program, and

frequently referred to his department as a "semi-Brain Trust," goes a step further by pinning the start of the disaster to a specific date—October 4th, the day the first Soviet sputnik went into orbit, shattering the myth of American technical preëminence and precipitating a public revulsion against Detroit's fancier baubles.

Wallace's sputnik theory provides an answer to Doyle's question about why people weren't in the mood, and, furthermore, it is sufficiently cosmic to befit a semi-Brain Truster. It also leaves Wallace free to defend the validity of his motivational-research studies as of the time when they were conducted. "I don't think we yet know the depths of the psychological effect that that first orbiting had on us all," he says. "Somebody had beaten us to an important gain in technology, and immediately people started writing articles about how crummy Detroit products were, particularly the heavily ornamented and status-symbolic medium-priced cars. In 1958, when none of the small cars were out except the Rambler, Chevy almost ran away with the market, because it had the simplest car. The American people had put themselves on a self-imposed austerity program. Not buying Edsels was their hair shirt."

* * *

Wallace, the semi-Brain Truster, was asked to continue semi-Brain Trusting for Ford, and, since he didn't like living in Detroit, or even near it, was permitted to move to New York and to spend only two days a week at headquarters. ("They didn't seem to care any more where I operated from," he says modestly.) At the end of 1958, he left Ford, and he has since finally achieved his heart's desire—to become a full-time academic. He is now working for a doctorate in sociology at Columbia, and his thesis is to be on social change in Westport, Connecticut, which he is investigating by busily quizzing its inhabitants; meanwhile, he is teaching a course on "The Dynamics of Social Behavior" at the New School for Social

Research. "I'm through with industry," he declared the other day with evident satisfaction, as he boarded a train for Westport, a bundle of questionnaires under his arm.

Joseph Kraft, *The Washington Post*, Feb. 7, 1974

*Joseph Kraft*

# Government by Professor

As the Nixon administration presents its 1974 face to the world, it turns out to be a government by—of all things — professors: Dr. George Shultz, the Secretary of the Treasury, Dr. Henry Kissinger, the Secretary of State, and Dr. James Schlesinger, as Secretary of Defense, command among them more influence than intellectuals ever have had in Washington.

Secretary Schultz is the unquestioned master of national economic policy. He dominated the recent briefings on the 1975 budget and the essential budgetary decision is a decison close to his heart.

That is the decision not to seek a tax reduction as the way to avoid a recession in the coming year. Moreover, energy policy and the fight against inflation have been delegated to two of Dr. Shultz' closest associates — John Dunlop, who is head of the Cost of Living Council, and William Simon, the Under Secretary of the Treasury who heads the Federal Energy Office.

Secretary Kissinger has unmatched sway over foreign policy. As a presidential adviser on national security, he handled negotiations with Russia, China, Europe, Japan and the two Vietnams.

As Secretary of State he has added the rest of the world to his portfolio. The international energy conference, which he has convoked for Washington next week, will probably play a central role in the future economic welfare of all countries. Peace itself seems to hang on his travels through the Mideast.

Secretary Schlesinger, who has only been at the Pentagon for a few months. is a lesser known quantity. Still he has obviously made a big dent on the budget. If the $2.2 billion supplementary spending for replenishing supplies is included in the 1975 budget, as it should be, then total obligatory authority will be $95.4 billion, an increase of over 13 per cent from last year.

Moreover, Dr. Schlesinger has already made a dent on defense doctrine with a plea, voiced in a press conference on Jan. 10, for more emphasis on a nuclear force capable of hitting Soviet missile sites rather than Soviet cities. He seemed to take a step backward in a news conference two weeks later, perhaps because Dr. Kissinger has misgivings about the impact of a counterforce strategy on his arms control negotiations with the Russians. Still the new budget includes $250 million for research and procurement of counterforce weapons—a clear sign of Secretary Schlesinger's weight.

No one would ascribe the rise of these professors to a personal bias in favor of intellectuals on the part of President Nixon. So how did the schoolmen rise?

Watergate, of course, played a part. The professors had no direct involvement in the scandal at any time. So as the President needed to cleanse his regime, it made sense to push them forward.

But there is a deeper factor at work. Between advanced intellectual labor and the presidential perspective there is a hidden harmony — a harmony that does not work for businessmen.

In general, businessmen get ahead by doing one thing — sales or production or finance or public relations — very, very well. They overwhelm the competition. And what applies to them applies to the lawyers who represent them as clients.

But all advanced academic disciplines these days go beyond doing one thing well. They typically involve balances and trade-offs among competing objectives. High ability in abstraction almost always involves creative skill in developing schemes for the analysis and ordering of highly complex functions, many with interrelations and feedbacks that are only poorly understood. That is what economics and political science are all about these days.

It is also what presidential leadership is about. A central aspect of the presidency is to establish a hierarchy of interest among competing bureaucratic entities, each of them remarkably complex. Most recent Presidents, accordingly, have used intellectuals as special assistants to get a grip on the management of the bureaucracy. Indeed, Messrs. Schlesinger, Kissinger and Shultz all served as presidential assistants before moving on to their present posts.

So my sense is that their present emergence expresses a longterm trend. The presidency has been weakened by Watergate among many other things. As the personal leadership of the President recedes, men with the presidential perspective are going to be called on to take over the major departments of government. Now, and for some time to come, I think, that means a role of special importance for the intellectuals.

Anthony Burgess, *The New York Times Magazine*, Nov. 7, 1971

No wonder the guilt of the thoughtful Americans I met in Princeton and New York and, indeed, all over the Union tended to express itself as an extravagant masochism, a desire for flagellation. Americans want to take on all the blame they can find, gluttons for punishment. "What do Europeans really think of us?" is a common question at parties. The expected answer is: "They think you're a load of decadent, gross-lipped, potbellied, callous, over-bearing neoimperialists." Then the head can be bowed and the chest smitten: "*Nostra culpa, nostra maxima culpa....*" But the fact is that such an answer, however much desired, would not be an honest one. Europeans think more highly of Americans now than they ever did. Let me try to explain why.

# Facts and Values

Given the title of the succeeding section, I think it important to note that I personally value John Kenneth Galbraith's insights into economic reality, and that I believe that the concept of the technostructure embodies a truth important to the development of our society, which is that organizations do assume lives of their own, in the sense that organizational goals and ideals motivate individual behavior. The truth of this insight is, however, something that has long been evident in the work done by historians, whose trade is the study of institutions. In this sense, I think the purpose of *this* section has been to indicate, on the basis of a description of the Edsel event, Galbraith's inadequacy as an historian.

It should be noted, however, that the absence of this historical dimension is a peculiarly American phenomenon. A sense of political history—of social living and human interaction—is one way of phrasing what I think is lacking in the Galbraithian theory of the New Industrial State.

Indeed, even in the language of John Kenneth Galbraith's own vocation—an academic economist—it seems to me significant that Robert M. Solow can laugh at himself, while John Kenneth Galbraith cannot. One of the things that makes United States innocence so striking is that it so easily turns to arrogance.

# Values

If the issue raised by the *New Industrial State* is how the technostructure is to be controlled, the answer must be phrased in terms of political as well as economic reality. Whether or not his scholarly peers approve of the techniques he has employed, in short, the argument being made is that Galbraith has given an inadequate answer to the questions he has posed. The answer argued for in this section is phrased in terms of law.

J. G. D., *Stanford Law Review*, Jan. 1968

# Neutrality, Legitimacy, and the Supreme Court: Some Intersections Between Law and Political Science

## I.

The work of Professor Martin Shapiro is distinguished by lucidity, an analytical turn of mind, formidable sophistication, and a thoroughly readable style. A political scientist by training, Shapiro is very much at home with the tools and techniques of the lawyer. His flair for case analysis is much in evidence in *Law and Politics in the Supreme Court*.[1] In the chapters on tax and labor policy, for example, his view of the Court as a political agency furthering its interests through interaction with other agencies such as the Internal Revenue Service and the National Labor Relations Board is developed through close readings of decisions[2] and comparisons among groups of cases.[3] Indeed, Shapiro's analysis of the reapportionment controversy demonstrates a regard for lawyers' sensibilities seemingly above and beyond the call of duty—considerably more than half the chapter is devoted to a closely reasoned parsing of the "political question" cases.[4]

Shapiro's regard for "lawyer's law," however, is only apparently excessive. His focus on the interaction among governmental agencies inevitably involves consideration of cases in which the Court paces the boundaries of its own jurisdiction. And as Professor Bickel's work in *The Least Dangerous Branch*[5] testifies, this judicial mapping of spheres of competence is preeminently "lawyer's law," with compass directions provided in the arcane terminology of "case and controversy," "standing," and "ripeness." Yet it is precisely here that Shapiro breaks decisively with conventional legal approaches.

Shapiro denominates his view "political jurisprudence."[6] Postulating

---

Anything of value in this Article owes much to three men associated with the Stanford Law School: Jared G. Carter, formerly assistant professor of law, who first suggested many of these ideas to me; Professor William F. Baxter, who helped me to refine them in the course of long and, at least on his side, gracious conversations; and Dean Bayless A. Manning, who first afforded me the opportunity of offering the seminar in which they were developed.

1. M. Shapiro, Law and Politics in the Supreme Court: New Approaches to Political Jurisprudence (1964).
2. *See, e.g., id.* at 107–09.
3. *See, e.g., id.* at 113–24.
4. *Id.* at 175–216.
5. A. Bickel, The Least Dangerous Branch: The Supreme Court at the Bar of Politics (1962).
6. M. Shapiro, *supra* note 1, at 15.

170

that Court opinions represent political decisions embodying the policy preferences of the Justices, he perceives the doctrines surveyed by Bickel as political accommodations between the judiciary and rival centers of political power. Devotees of polemical literature concerning the Court will recognize this delineation.

The starting point for the recent debate has been Judge Hand's eloquent Holmes Lectures. In those lectures, Hand confessed his inability satisfactorily to justify a doctrine of judicial review that enables a Court not responsible to the electorate to nullify acts of political agencies deriving their powers directly from that electorate.[7] Professor Wechsler's essay on neutral principles, by rooting the power of judicial review in the text of the Constitution itself,[8] attempts to lay the ghost of judicial usurpation raised by Hand.

Shapiro, so to speak, stands Hand on his head. He accepts as given—as the normal state of affairs—the very attempt by the Court to substitute its policy preferences for those of the political agencies that Hand found so difficult to justify even in exceptional circumstances.[9] Shapiro's characteristically trenchant assessment of the Court's need for neutral principles defines the gulf that separates his starting point from those of Hand and Wechsler.

> To put it bluntly, the real problem is how the Supreme Court can pursue its policy goals without violating those popular and professional expectations of "neutrality," which are an important factor in our legal tradition and a principal source of the Supreme Court's prestige. It is in these terms, not in terms of the philosophic, jurisprudential, or historical correctness of the concept of neutral principles, that the debate should now proceed.[10]

Demonstration of the superiority of one or another theory about the role of the Court hinges upon the understanding such a theory affords of the results embodied in particular decisions. Shapiro's most recent book[11] advocates more vigorous implementation of first amendment guarantees than would be deemed proper by Hand, Wechsler, or Justice Frankfurter— a group whose reiterated concern that the Court might be overstepping the legitimate boundaries of its authority leads Shapiro to designate them the "modest."[12] That Shapiro regards this difference in attitude toward the first amendment as dependent upon differences between his theory of judicial review and that espoused by the "modest" is clear. The introduc-

---

7. *See* L. HAND, THE BILL OF RIGHTS 1–30 (1958).
8. *See* H. WECHSLER, *Toward Neutral Principles of Constitutional Law*, in PRINCIPLES, POLITICS, AND FUNDAMENTAL LAW 3, 4–15 (1961).
9. *See* L. HAND, *supra* note 7, at 1–30, 56–77.
10. M. SHAPIRO, *supra* note 1, at 31.
11. M. SHAPIRO, FREEDOM OF SPEECH: THE SUPREME COURT AND JUDICIAL REVIEW (1966).
12. *See id.* at 108–11.

J. G. D., *Stanford Law Review*, Jan. 1968

tory section of his book concludes: "Having cleared away the hesitancies of judicial modesty, it is possible to proceed to the problem of what level of protection the Supreme Court ought to give freedom of speech."[13]

The first amendment, however, does not provide a satisfactory area in which to demonstrate Shapiro's thesis more successful than the "modest" view. True, much of the opposition to the Hand and Wechsler positions came from those who approved results reached by the Court in decisions that both Hand and Wechsler found illegitimate. And Shapiro does arrive at first amendment conclusions considerably divergent from those reached by the judge and the professor. But we are not justified in regarding one view of the judicial role as more valuable than another simply because it, more frequently than the other, produces substantive results with which we agree. We might well prefer such a theory, but we could regard it as demonstrably better than alternative views only on the basis of the criterion by which all theories are judged: the ability satisfactorily to account for a range of phenomena. Thus, when we say that the value of a theory concerning the Court rests on its application to particular decisions, what we mean is that successful theories satisfactorily account for results that alternative hypotheses fail to explicate.

Given this criterion, what does Shapiro's view of the Court's function explicate—in first amendment cases—that is not also accounted for by the views of the "modest"? Shapiro argues that the Court's clientele consists of those groups and potential groups in our society that are not represented by other political agencies;[14] that the Court, like other political agencies, ought to act so as to create and support that clientele;[15] that groups seeking to protect speech are normally not represented by agencies other than the Court; and, hence, that the Court ought to grant protection of their interests a high priority.[16] Shapiro's view thus accounts for the phenomenon of the Court's affording a special status to first amendment guarantees.

But the fact is that both Hand and Wechsler also account for this phenomenon. Wechsler accepts the "preferred position" conception of first amendment rights "insofar as it recognizes that some ordering of social values is essential; that all cannot be given equal weight, if the Bill of Rights is to be maintained."[17]And Hand concludes his Holmes Lectures by "considering [in connection with the first amendment] whether, even assuming that I am right in thinking that the Constitution does not warrant the courts in annulling any legislation because they disapprove it on the

13. *Id.* at 44.
14. *See id.* at 34–38.
15. *See id.* at 2, 38–39.
16. *See id.* at 111–15.
17. H. WECHSLER, *supra* note 8, at 35.

172

merits, nevertheless it is desirable that they should exercise such an author-ity on extreme occasions."[18]

Wechsler's and Hand's acceptance of a special status for first amend-ment guarantees does not, however, imply that their decision in any given case would accord with that arrived at by Shapiro. A great many value judgments other than that concerning the propriety of judicial review are involved in any given case. Consequently, even a regularly divergent pat-tern of results might be accounted for—to choose only the most obvious of a spectrum of possibilities—by different weights being assigned to one or more of the other values involved in the decisions. Once the "modest" and Shapiro reach agreement on the existence of a special status for first amend-ment guarantees, therefore, the verdict on the superiority of Shapiro's view of the proper role of the Court must be "not proven."

Phenomena for which the "modest" cannot account, however, are not difficult to come by. Both Wechsler[19] and Hand[20] made clear their inability to construct doctrinal substantiation for the *Segregation Cases*,[21] and similar claims of illegitimacy have recently been made[22] concerning the *Reap-portionment Cases*.[23] These two sets of cases, moreover, represent the most controversial recent examples of the Court's implementation of policy pref-erences—of, in the language of the "modest," "political" action. This fact alone, putting aside problems of demonstrating the superiority of Shapiro's theory, would seem a sufficient basis for expecting explication of the re-apportionment and segregation decisions to be central to his thesis.

Here, then, are the conclusions arrived at by Shapiro on the basis of his analysis of the *Reapportionment Cases*:

> The Court's failure to grapple with the complex philosophical and theoretical issues that lie behind the notion of constitutional democracy led it away from the delicate and tentative adjustments that our peculiar form of democracy requires and into the formulation of appealing slogans. The "one man, one vote" slogan, in equating the whole of democracy with majority-rule elections represents naive political philosophy, bad political theory, and no political science. It remains that the *Reapportionment Cases* are, in one important sense, imprudent political action. One of the first rules of politics at any level is that a politician must keep his word. Great tactical advantage may occasionally be gained from breaking promises, but a politician who earns a reputation for breaking promises cannot survive very long. Courts are not immune to this rule. One of the principal tactics of the Supreme

---

18. L. HAND, *supra* note 7, at 56.
19. *See* H. WECHSLER, *supra* note 8, at 36–48.
20. *See* L. HAND, *supra* note 7, at 54–55.
21. Brown v. Board of Educ., 347 U.S. 483 (1954); Barrows v. Jackson, 346 U.S. 249 (1953); Shelley v. Kraemer, 334 U.S. 1 (1948); Smith v. Allwright, 321 U.S. 649 (1944).
22. *See, e.g.*, Neal, *Baker v. Carr: Politics in Search of Law*, 1962 S. CT. REV. 252.
23. Reynolds v. Sims, 377 U.S. 533 (1964); WMCA, Inc. v. Lomenzo, 377 U.S. 633 (1964); Maryland Comm. for Fair Representation v. Tawes, 377 U.S. 656 (1964); Davis v. Mann, 377 U.S. 678 (1964); Roman v. Sincock, 377 U.S. 695 (1964); Lucas v. Forty-Fourth Gen. Assembly, 377 U.S. 713 (1964).

173

Court's opponents has always been to seize upon a narrowly circumscribed opinion, to inflate it to its logical extreme, and then to attack the extreme rather than the actual opinion. Defenders of the Court have traditionally replied by pointing to the limited nature of the opinions and by insisting that the Court really means only what it says and nothing more. The Court, in its two most important postwar decisions, has obviously meant more than it said, and its subsequent actions have justified those who attacked the most extreme interpretation of its decisions. The Court has, in a sense, not kept its word to those of its defenders who have relied on the initially limited arguments.

The opinion in the school segregation cases was strictly limited to education and rested upon a rationale narrowly drawn to cover only public education. Yet we learned from the subsequent *per curiam* opinions that, at the time the school cases were decided, the Court had already made up its mind that segregation, not only in schools but also in all public facilities, was unconstitutional.

In *Baker v. Carr*, the Court said, as far as the jurisdictional niceties would allow, that patently unreasonable districting was unconstitutional, but it carefully avoided the "one man, one vote" rule and hinted strongly in other directions. . . . [T]he *Reapportionment Cases* made it perfectly clear that what the Court had really meant, although it had not said so, in *Baker* was that "one man, one vote" is the universal rule applicable to both upper and lower houses of the state legislatures.

The advantage to the Court of such an approach in both the segregation and apportionment cases is obvious. The first and greatest battle rages around the relatively narrow and therefore most easily defended opinion. Then, when the shouting has died down somewhat and the position is solidified by widespread public acceptance, the Court goes on to what it really intended all along, the broadest and most extreme application of its initial decision. Such tactics are politically clever, but they may be too clever. It will hardly be possible in the immediate future to defend any Supreme Court position by pointing to its limited scope. Attackers of the Court will be perfectly safe in painting the most wildly exaggerated pictures of the Court's intentions in any field it enters. It remains to be seen whether or not the tactical advantage gained by its "delayed action" approach will compensate for the Court's loss of that precious political asset, a reputation for candor.[24]

The verdict on the comparative utility of Shapiro's approach to judicial review must once again be "not proven." Here too Shapiro and the "modest" are in agreement. Of course, convergence of Shapiro's and the "modest" assessment of these particular results, no less than divergences, might well be accounted for by policy preferences having nothing to do with judicial review. In fact, Shapiro seems to share with many of those he denominates "modest" a policy preference for the result reached in the *Segregation Cases* and against that arrived at in the *Reapportionment Cases*.

The real importance of the quoted passage is the tone and sweep of the condemnation of the Court's works. Indeed, if neither the segregation nor the reapportionment decisions can satisfactorily be accounted for in terms of Shapiro's theory, what have the "modest" to fear from it? True, Shapiro substitutes the charge of imprudent political action for Wechsler's accusa-

---

24. M. SHAPIRO, *supra* note 1, at 250–52.

174

tion of unprincipled—and therefore illegitimate—behavior. But that exchange can represent progress only for those who, on aesthetic grounds,
prefer the dull click of value-free social science to the sonorous moralism
of the law. The crucial fact remains that Shapiro characterizes as dangerously improper both the reapportionment and segregation decisions. If
this be the music of political jurisprudence, the "modest" ought to urge
Shapiro to play on.

What makes this coalescence of Shapiro and the "modest" startling is,
of course, the wide divergence in their starting points. Shapiro postulates
the Court as a political agency competing with other political agencies.
The "modest" postulate a need for the Court to avoid opposing political
agencies on political matters. Yet Shapiro converges with the "modest"
in disavowing two sets of "political" decisions. Unraveling the paradox
exemplified by that coalescence constitutes the task of the remainder of this
Article.

## II.

Our inquiry begins with Justice Black, whose "activist" first amendment
philosophy, approved by Shapiro,[25] constitutes the unnamed target of many
of the "modest" strictures.[26] Our goal, the assessment of theories concerning
the proper role of the Court, requires a focus upon cases in which the issue
of the Court's relationship with other governmental agencies is squarely
faced—in short, "lawyer's law."

During the 1962 term Black joined in two decisions that significantly
altered the relationship between federal and state courts in criminal cases:
*Townsend v. Sain*[27] delineated a series of standards substantially expanding the circumstances in which federal review of state convictions could
take place in habeas corpus proceedings; *Fay v. Noia*[28] held inapplicable to
habeas corpus the doctrine that an adequate and independent state ground
of decision would bar federal review.

Two terms later the Court rendered its decision in *Henry v. Mississippi*,[29] in which Mississippi argued that the proceedings under attack were
insulated from Supreme Court review by the existence of an adequate and
independent state ground. Since Henry was seeking direct review of his
conviction in the Supreme Court, rather than attempting a collateral attack
in a federal district court by means of habeas corpus, Mississippi could—and
did—rely directly on *Murdock v. Memphis*,[30] which had derived the ade-

---

25. *See* M. SHAPIRO, *supra* note 11, at 108–11.
26. *See, e.g.,* L. HAND, *supra* note 7, at 77 (penultimate sentence); *cf.* A. BICKEL, *supra* note 5,
at 85–86.
27. 372 U.S. 293 (1963).
28. 372 U.S. 391 (1963).
29. 379 U.S. 443 (1965).
30. 87 U.S. (20 Wall.) 590 (1875).

quate-state-ground doctrine from a construction of the statute governing direct review of state cases by the Supreme Court,[31] and which *Fay v. Noia* had carefully confined to cases involving direct review.[32]

The Court in *Henry* noted that, given *Noia,* the existence of an adequate state ground would not suffice to bar federal review in collateral proceedings,[33] and it also indicated some doubts as to the adequacy of the state ground.[34] But the Court did not dismiss the case outright, which would have "remanded" Henry to whatever remedies he could obtain in a subsequent federal habeas proceeding. Nor did it find the state ground inadequate and proceed to review the state conviction on the merits. What the Court did was to remand the case to the state courts for a hearing on evidence not included in the record—evidence that the Court regarded as essential to a determination of the adequacy of the state ground.[35] In support of this remand procedure, the Court relied on its earlier decision in *Jackson v. Denno.*[36] There, after finding New York's procedure for determining the voluntariness of challenged confessions constitutionally defective, it had remanded the case to the state courts for a hearing restricted to the issue of voluntariness.

Perhaps the most surprising aspect of the *Henry* decision (besides the fact that neither of the two dissenting opinions raised the issue[37]) was its undercutting of the rationale of *Townsend v. Sain. Townsend* rested on a recognition of the overriding importance of providing a federal forum for determination of the facts underlying a claim of unconstitutional state detention. And a federal forum was precisely what Henry was deprived of by the Court's remand to the state, rather than the federal, judicial system.

The departure, moreover, was far from unintentional. It represented, rather, a conscious attempt to harmonize relations between state and federal courts so as to promote the efficient administration of criminal justice:

> By permitting the Mississippi courts to make an initial determination of waiver, we serve the causes of efficient administration of criminal justice, and of harmonious federal-state judicial relations. Such a disposition may make unnecessary the processing of the case through federal courts already laboring under congested dockets, or it may make unnecessary the relitigation in a federal forum of certain issues. . . . The Court is not blind to the fact that the federal habeas corpus juris-

---

31. Act of Feb. 5, 1867, ch. 28, § 2, 14 Stat. 385, *as amended*, 28 U.S.C. § 1257 (1964).
32. *See* 372 U.S. at 426–35.
33. *See* 379 U.S. at 452.
34. *See id.* at 448–49.
35. *Id.* at 452.
36. 378 U.S. 368 (1964).
37. Justice Harlan, joined by Justices Clark and Stewart, dissented, 379 U.S. at 457, in an opinion stressing the adequacy of the state ground, *id.* at 458–63, and warning that the decision in *Henry* presaged substantial erosion of the adequate-state-ground doctrine even in direct-review proceedings, *id.* at 463–65. The other dissenting opinion was by Justice Black. *Id.* at 453.

176

diction has been a source of irritation between the federal and state judiciaries. It has been suggested that this friction might be ameliorated if the States would look upon our decisions in [*Fay v. Noia* and *Townsend v. Sain*] . . . as affording them an opportunity to provide state procedures, direct or collateral, for a full airing of federal claims. That prospect is better served by a remand than by relegating petitioner to his federal habeas remedy.[38]

Although Shapiro does not canvass these decisions, they provide considerable support for his view of the Court as a political agency, whose decisions reflect the need to accommodate rival govermental agencies—in this case, the state courts. *Henry*, on this view, is explained by the fact that federal judicial resources are too exiguous to implement the comprehensive supervision of state criminal proceedings portended by *Fay v. Noia* and *Townsend v. Sain*. Having recognized this fact, the Court would thus be led by considerations of efficiency as well as harmony to attempt to enlist the aid of state judicial resources.[39]

Justice Black dissented from the remand procedure in *Henry* as he had in *Jackson v. Denno*. In both cases, the objection was to "piecemeal prosecution," which was characterized as "unjust" and in violation of "the spirit of the constitutional protection against double jeopardy."[40] As indicated in *Jackson v. Denno*, where he bitterly dissented from the Court's invalidation of a procedure in which the jury alone could resolve evidentiary disputes concerning the voluntariness of a confession, Black's reluctance to sanction remand procedures involving hearings before judges draws heavily upon his conviction that juries are to be preferred as factfinding bodies: "[T]he Constitution itself long ago made the decision that juries *are* to be trusted."[41]

Yet Black joined the decision in *Townsend v. Sain*, which considerably expanded the number of cases in which federal judges sitting without juries in habeas corpus proceedings will be obliged to review findings of fact embodied in the verdicts of state juries. And in *Jackson v. Denno* itself Black indicated:

It is our duty when a conviction for crime comes to us based in part on a confession to review the record to decide for ourselves whether that confession was freely and

---

38. *Id*. at 452–53 (footnotes omitted).

39. Shapiro's view of the Court's role also contributes to an analysis of the decision in *Fay v. Noia*. The obvious alternative to the decision arrived at in that case would have been a holding that reliance by the state upon the procedural default there at issue to bar reexamination of a conviction based on an admittedly coerced confession ran afoul of federal due process standards. Such a holding, however, would have resulted in a substantial increase in the Court's workload. Any reliance by the state upon a procedural default would have been open to a due process attack on direct review, and the Court would have been forced to develop viable standards on a case-by-case basis. In effect, the decision in *Fay v. Noia* can be seen as a shifting of this potential workload—as well as the substantive issues that have to be considered once reliance on the procedural default is held to be unavailing—to the lower federal courts. The decision in *Henry* can be viewed as an attempt to shift the burden yet further—to the state courts. Considerations of workload were explicitly canvassed in *Murdock v. Memphis. See* 87 U.S. (20 Wall.) at 628–29.

40. 378 U.S. at 410; *accord*, 379 U.S. at 454–55.

41. 378 U.S. at 405.

voluntarily given. In so doing we must reexamine the facts to be certain that there has been no constitutional violation, and our inquiry to determine the facts on which constitutional rights depend cannot be cut off by factfindings at the trial, whether by judge or by jury.[42]

Are these positions of Black's reconcilable? By what warrant does the Court, implementing constitutional guarantees, override the factual determination arrived at by a jury, if that very Constitution grants to the jury a preferred status as a factfinder?

The answer, phrased in terms of a contrast between judges rendering constitutional decisions and those making nonconstitutional law, rather than between judges and juries, is to be found in *Linkletter v. Walker*.[43] There the Court refused to make retroactive the holding in *Mapp v. Ohio*,[44] which had held that illegally seized evidence was inadmissible in state criminal proceedings. The reasoning of *Linkletter* was that (1) retroactivity would have no deterrent effect on police conduct (since the evidence in question had already been seized) and (2) a holding of retroactivity (due to the need for new hearings on the admissibility of evidence long since forgotten, destroyed, or deteriorated) "would tax the administration of justice to the utmost."[45] Dissenting, Black noted:

> In making this ruling the Court assumes for itself the virtue of acting in harmony with a comment of Justice Holmes that "[t]he life of the law has not been logic: it has been experience." Justice Holmes was not there talking about the Constitution; he was talking about the evolving judge-made law of England and of some of our States whose judges are allowed to follow in the common law tradition.[46]

This discounting of the factor of experience in constitutional adjudication accounts for Black's willingness to override jury determinations where constitutional rights are at stake. It need only be recalled that it is precisely the factor of experience—of greater familiarity with contemporary community views and standards—that juries bring to the adjudicatory process. Black's association of the process of constitutional adjudication with the rigor of logic rather than the flexibility of experience is, moreover, wholly consonant with the fact of his dissent from the "political" decision in *Henry*. Thus, while the *Henry* dissent is based, substantively, on the inadequacy of the state ground there at issue,[47] the *Linkletter* dissent strongly suggests that even in the absence of such substantive factors Black would in many instances find political jurisprudence, with its emphasis on flexible accom-

---

42. *Id.* at 408.
43. 381 U.S. 618 (1965).
44. 367 U.S. 643 (1961).
45. 381 U.S. at 637.
46. *Id.* at 642. For an analogous attempt by Justice Black to set limits on the discretion of the Court to give less than full retroactive effect to its decisions, in this instance in the interpretation of statutes defining criminal conduct, see James v. United States, 366 U.S. 213, 222 (1961).
47. *See* 379 U.S. at 455–57.

178

modations among rival agencies, incompatible with the rigorous demands of constitutional "logic."

We must defer further exploration of the issues raised by Black's contrast between common-law development and the processes of constitutional adjudication until part VI of this Article. What is important for present purposes is that Black's logic-experience dichotomy can be derived directly from his insistence on constitutional "absolutes." As demonstrated by Professor Reich's concise delineation of the connection between "absolutes" and Black's opposition to the "balancing" approach long utilized by the Court in first amendment and due process cases, Black sees an emphasis on "experience" as underlying the constitutional "balances" he so strongly disapproves:

> [T]he Court's ad hoc balances are on a "slippery slope." Each is likely to reflect present-day needs and views. Each has for a standard its predecessor, and by degrees what is thought shocking to the conscience or necessary to the maintenance of democratic society may become far different from what was first conceived. The urgencies of the day, like gravity, pull the Court along; there is no counterweight in its formula to maintain a constant level.
>
> . . . .
>
> The notion of "absolutes" can best be seen, then, as an answer to a process of judging which Black believes to be out of keeping with the Constitution. It developed as a dissenting position. It represents a plea for constitutional adjudication with definite standards.[48]

Black's insistence on "absolutes" served as the focal point for the "modest" attack on his views.[49] Yet that insistence eventuates in a call for definite standards in constitutional adjudication that strangely echoes Wechsler's demand for neutral principles. Delineation of the differences between the views of Black and those of the "modest" thus hinges on an analysis of the neutrality of neutral principles, an issue to which we must now turn.[50]

## III.

The problem to which Wechsler's essay is devoted is posed by him in the following terms: The *Segregation Cases* (Wechsler analyzes in detail those involving white primaries, restrictive covenants, and segregated schools) "have the best chance of making an enduring contribution to the quality of our society of any that I know in recent years."[51] Yet Wechsler cannot approve those decisions because they do not "rest on neutral prin-

---

48. Reich, *Mr. Justice Black and the Living Constitution*, 76 HARV. L. REV. 673, 743–44 (1963).
49. *See* authorities cited note 26 *supra.*
50. A bibliography of the considerable literature spawned by the neutral-principles controversy can be found in M. SHAPIRO, *supra* note 1, at 17 n.37.
51. H. WECHSLER, *supra* note 8, at 37.

J. G. D., *Stanford Law Review*, Jan. 1968

179

ciples" and hence are not "entitled to approval in the only terms that I acknowledge to be relevant to a decision of the courts."[52]

## A.

Wechsler derives the postulate that judicial decisions are legitimate only when they rest on neutral principles from the duty of constitutional adjudication that he finds article III to impose on the courts:

> The courts have both the title and the duty when a case is properly before them to review the actions of the other branches in the light of constitutional provisions, even though the action involves value choices, as invariably action does. In doing so, however, they are bound to function otherwise than as a naked power organ; they participate as courts of law. This calls for facing how determinations of this kind can be asserted to have any legal quality. The answer, I suggest, inheres primarily in that they are—or are obliged to be—entirely principled. A principled decision, in the sense I have in mind, is one that rests on reasons with respect to all the issues in the case, reasons that in their generality and their neutrality transcend any immediate result that is involved. When no sufficient reasons of this kind can be assigned for overturning value choices of the other branches of the Government or of a state, those choices must, of course, survive. Otherwise, as Holmes said in his first opinion for the Court, "a constitution, instead of embodying only relatively fundamental rules of right, as generally understood by all English-speaking communities, would become the partisan of a particular set of ethical or economical opinions . . . ."[53]

The central difficulty with this passage is that its core is assertion rather than explanation. It tells us that courts are "bound to function otherwise than as a naked power organ," but it does not tell us why. Wechsler's only approach to explanation of his assertion begins with a catalog of recent Court decisions which, in his view, represent ad hoc rather than principled evaluations: first amendment attacks upon congressional investigations of suspected Communists, which their authors would not feel obliged to press home against investigations of labor racketeers; first amendment objections to the Smith Act, which would not be raised to legislation directed against agitators preaching racial prejudice; attempts to interpret first amendment guarantees so as to void convictions based on advocacy of the abstract doctrine of communism, which would not be forthcoming on behalf of those advocating resistance to court decrees; and enthusiasm for jury trial, which seemingly abates before the prospect of making trial by jury available to white southerners accused of civil rights violations.[54]

The constitutional positions described by Wechsler are, of course, those espoused by Justice Black. Wechsler may or may not believe that Black

---

52. *Id.*
53. *Id.* at 27–28.
54. *See id.* at 20–21.

180

personally would balk at extending first amendment protections to the fact situations delineated above. What is clear is that Wechsler's conclusion—that the positions taken by Black represent ad hoc responses to particular situations—rests on his belief that application of such guarantees to labor racketeers and racial agitators, for example, represent extensions that are impermissible yet necessarily entailed by Black's positions. Implicit in Wechsler's catalog, in short, is the nub of the "modest" case against the "absolutes" of Black's constitutional philosophy.

Wechsler continues:

> All I have said, you may reply, is something no one will deny, that principles are largely instrumental as they are employed in politics, instrumental in relation to results that a controlling sentiment demands at any given time. Politicians recognize this fact of life and are obliged to trim and shape their speech and votes accordingly, unless perchance they are prepared to step aside; and the example that John Quincy Adams set somehow is rarely followed.
>
> That is, indeed, all I have said but I now add that whether you are tolerant, perhaps more tolerant than I, of the *ad hoc* in politics, with principle reduced to a manipulative tool, are you not also ready to agree that something else is called for from the courts? I put it to you that the main constituent of the judicial process is precisely that it must be genuinely principled, resting with respect to every step that is involved in reaching judgment on analysis and reasons quite transcending the immediate result that is achieved. To be sure, the courts decide, or should decide, only the case they have before them. But must they not decide on grounds of adequate neutrality and generality, tested not only by the instant application but by others that the principles imply? Is it not the very essence of judicial method to insist upon attending to such other cases, preferably those involving an opposing interest, in evaluating any principle avowed?[55]

The need for neutral principles is thus derived by Wechsler from the contrast between the ad hoc ways of politics and the principled processes of the courts. This derivation, however, is crucially flawed, at least in part because of Wechsler's use of rhetorical questions to explicate a concept central to his scheme. The most striking difficulty involves Wechsler's assuming the conclusion that he purports to derive. Wechsler begins by asserting that the branches of government whose actions the Court reviews act as "naked power organs" in arriving at ad hoc decisions. The question he puts is why the Court may not legitimately utilize similar processes in constitutional adjudication. His response is that principled adjudication is the "main constituent of the judicial process." But this response is relevant only on the assumption that the process of constitutional adjudication is in fact a judicial process: only, in other words, if Wechsler assumes that the Supreme Court—in the exercise of its constitutional functions—is acting as a court rather than as a "naked power organ."

55. *Id.* at 21.

By deriving the judicial need for neutral principles entirely from a contrast with the ad hoc decisionmaking processes of the "political" branches, Wechsler also seriously undercuts his attack on Black's "absolutes." The extensions of Black's positions drawn by Wechsler are regarded by him as impermissible wholly on prudential grounds. There is nothing in the nature of labor racketeers or racial agitators, for example, that leads Wechsler to desire to protect them as such. Quite the contrary, Wechsler must hold that the situations he sketches are ones in which courts ought to deny any protection allegedly afforded by constitutional guarantees. Otherwise, if Wechsler believed that courts ought to protect civil rights violators and persons who advocate resistance to court decrees—if, in other words, Wechsler held that the first amendment covered such situations—his charge that Black's positions are ad hoc could not be maintained.

Wechsler's point, then, is that the constitutional protection afforded by Black to Negroes and Communists, whom we do wish to protect, makes it impossible to deny those protections to such as labor racketeers and racial agitators, whom we ought not to protect. Given his contrast between wholly ad hoc political branches and a wholly principled judiciary, however, that objection—based, as it is, wholly on prudential grounds—seems one more properly addressed to a legislature than a court.

There is, of course, the alternative of not enforcing the relevant constitutional guarantee in either situation, and it seems significant that the only example of an adequately neutral principle given by Wechsler is the Court's abandonment of any attempt to place limitations upon congressional exercise of the commerce and taxing powers—a retreat so complete that Wechsler is led to speculate on the possibility of principles entailing less comprehensive abdications.[56] This speculation, like the opening section of the essay in which Wechsler derives a justification for judicial review from a reading of the constitutional text, reassures us that there must indeed exist constitutional checks that the Court was intended to impose upon the acts of the political branches.

Once the existence of such limits is admitted, however, the question arises how they are to be enforced. And it is precisely Wechsler's contrast with the prudential, ad hoc nature of political decisions that suggests that judicial enforcement ought to be across the board, to the utmost logical limits of the principle enunciated, untroubled by those prudential con-

---

56. *See id.* at 32–33.

Another possible interpretation of Wechsler's catalog is that it is intended to assert only that the first amendment principles enunciated by Black are ad hoc without asserting that *no* neutral principle could be developed capable of distinguishing between, for example, Negroes and racial agitators. But the views embodied in Wechsler's catalog are not specifically attributed to Black; what Wechsler implies about the necessity of according to racial agitators the same measure of first amendment protections granted to Negroes must therefore be read as referring to the entire spectrum of possible first amendment interpretations, not just those espoused by Black.

182

siderations that the contrast relegates to the sphere of politics. Thus if Wechsler's universe contains constitutional guarantees judicially enforceable otherwise than by abdication, the very contrast on the basis of which neutral principles were found necessary mandates that those guarantees take the form of Justice Black's "absolutes."

The final difficulty with deriving the need for neutral principles from a contrast between ad hoc political decisions and principled judicial processes goes to the heart of the contrast itself. Far from describing reality, that contrast, like the use of rhetorical questions, is ultimately no more than a literary device. Wechsler himself believes that a society governed by political institutions whose decisions were always and entirely unprincipled could not long survive; his catalog of contemporary ad hoc judicial decisions is preceded by an historical survey of constitutional positions taken by a President[57] and in Congress[58]—positions he deems unprincipled. And the implied judgment is not an approving one.

Unfortunately, this commendable recognition of an obligation to principle on the part of the political branches dissolves the very contrast from which Wechsler derives the judicial need for neutral principles. Once it is admitted that political decisions are only sometimes or partially ad hoc, the literary device of a contrast can no longer serve to justify the demand that constitutional adjudications be always and absolutely principled. Yet that is precisely the demand that Wechsler makes.

## B.

The contrast from which Wechsler derives a need for neutral principles thus does not aid in answering the very question with which Wechsler began: Why is it illegitimate for the Court, in the exercise of its constitutional functions, to act (at least partially or sometimes) as a "naked power organ"? Wechsler adverts to the contrast between power organs and courts of law almost immediately after setting out his justification for judicial review, at a juncture in his argument preceding the introduction of the concept of neutral principles:[59]

---

57. See id. at 18: "Was not Jefferson in the Louisiana Purchase forced to rest on an expansive reading of the clauses granting national authority of the very kind that he had steadfastly opposed in his attacks upon the Bank?"

58. See id. at 17–18: "Did not New England challenge the embargo that the South supported on the very ground on which the South was to resist New England's demand for a protective tariff?"

59. The problem to which Wechsler is responding at this point is that "[t]hose who perceive in law only the element of fiat, in whose conception of the legal cosmos reason has no meaning or no place, will not join gladly in the search for [criteria that can be framed and tested as an exercise of reason and not merely as an act of willfulness or will] . . . ." Id. at 16. Once again, Wechsler has structured an issue encompassing an entire spectrum of possible interactions, this time of reason and will, so as to create a single antithesis. But we need not explore the similarities between this formulation and the contrast between ad hoc politics and principled adjudication, since Wechsler immediately disclaims any intention to "try to overcome the philosophic doubt" raised by the possibility of perceiving law as fiat, since "[t]hat battle must be fought on wider fronts than that of constitutional interpretation." Id. at 17.

J. G. D., *Stanford Law Review*, Jan. 1968

The man who simply lets his judgment turn on the immediate result may not, however, realize that his position implies that the courts are free to function as a naked power organ, that it is an empty affirmation to regard them, as ambivalently he so often does, as courts of law. If he may know he disapproves of a decision when all he knows is that it has sustained a claim put forward by a labor union or a taxpayer, a Negro or a segregationist, a corporation or a Communist—he acquiesces in the proposition that a man of different sympathy but equal information may no less properly conclude that he approves.[60]

The Court may not act as a power organ, then, because to do so entails the possibility that persons who disagree with its results might on that basis legitimately object to its decisions. The legitimacy of opposition to executive and legislative decisions based on disagreement with the results reached is, for Wechsler, a necessary concomitant of their status as power organs. If the political branches can survive this state of affairs, however, why does Wechsler assume that the courts could not?

One possible answer is to be found in the reasoning that underlay Hand's position on judicial review. If constitutional adjudication is viewed as an anomaly in a democratic society, as a process in which a politically irresponsible institution reviews the acts of duly elected legislative and executive officials, then of course the Court's constitutional decisions require a species of justification wholly different from that demanded of elected institutions. That this reasoning both provides the basis for the contrast between courts of law and power organs and defines the need for neutral principles emerges from a reading of the passages immediately following the contrast between ad hoc political institutions and principled courts.

Wechsler begins by granting, as "commonplace," "that courts in constitutional determinations face issues that are inescapably 'political' . . . in that they involve a choice among competing values or desires, a choice reflected in the legislative or executive action in question, which the court must either condemn or condone."[61] The argument continues:

But what is crucial, I submit, is not the nature of the question but the nature of the answer that may validly be given by the courts. No legislature or executive is obligated by the nature of its function to support its choice of values by the type of reasoned explanation that I have suggested is intrinsic to judicial action—however much we may admire such a reasoned explanation when we find it in those other realms.

Does not the special duty of the courts to judge by neutral principles addressed to all the issues make it inapposite to contend, as Judge Hand does, that no court can review the legislative choice—by any standard other than a fixed, "historical meaning" of constitutional provisions—without becoming "a third legislative chamber"? Is there not, in short, a vital difference between legislative freedom to

---

60. *Id.* at 17.
61. *Id.* at 22.

184

appraise the gains and losses in projected measures and the kind of principled ap-
praisal, in respect of values that can reasonably be asserted to have constitutional
dimension, that alone is in the province of the courts? Does not the difference yield
a middle ground between a judicial House of Lords and the abandonment of any
limitation on the other branches—a middle ground consisting of judicial action
that embodies what are surely the main qualities of law, its generality and its
neutrality?[62]

Two factors, in addition to the textual evidence, further suggest that,
in Wechsler's scheme, the function of neutral principles is to meet the
difficulties posed by Hand. First, this interpretation provides the basis for
a meaningful statement concerning constitutional adjudication: Because
the Court, as an undemocratic institution, represents an anomaly in our
democratic society, its decisions require a higher degree of justification than
that demanded of the legislature or executive, a degree of justification embodied in the demand for total neutrality. The alternative, as we have seen,
is to reduce neutral principles to a formulation that assumes the answer
it seeks to demonstrate.

Second, to view neutral principles as a response to Hand's dilemma
concerning the undemocratic nature of judicial review serves to explain
Wechsler's objection to Black's "absolutes." If judicial review represents
an exception to democratic norms that otherwise govern our polity, then,
in Wechsler's words, "the courts ought to be cautious to impose a choice of
values on the other branches or a state, based upon the Constitution, only
when they are persuaded, on an adequate and principled analysis, that the
choice is clear."[63] Given Hand's assumption, it is manifest that the Court
cannot justifiably push a constitutional principle to logical extremes; an
undemocratic Court must be a cautious Court, and a cautious Court eschews
"absolutes."

There is a difficulty, however, with the interpretation of neutral principles delineated above. It postulates that the need for neutral principles
is rooted not—as Wechsler has it—in the nature of the judicial process, but
rather in the undemocratic nature of the Court. On this interpretation, the
contrast from which neutral principles are derived is between democratic
political branches and an undemocratic Court, not between ad hoc politics
and principled adjudication. To be sure, it is presumably the democratic
nature of the political branches that, in Wechsler's view, legitimizes their
resort to ad hoc decisions. If, however, the crucial fact in the analysis is not
that the legislature is ad hoc, but rather that it is democratic, the corresponding directive to the Court must prescribe not principle, but caution.

If this interpretation of neutral principles is to be acceptable, therefore,

62. *Id.* at 22–23.
63. *Id.* at 34.

185

it must account for the fact that Wechsler focused on the ad hoc rather than the democratic aspect of the political process. Except in his series of rhetorical questions, Wechsler never adverts to Hand's argument. If the concept of neutral principles was intended to respond to Hand's dilemma, why did that dilemma go unacknowledged?

The answer is that Wechsler had already established the legitimacy of judicial review by means of his gloss on article III. Having thus duly exorcised the spectre of judicial usurpation, no warrant existed for the invocation of yet another remedy. Participation in duly prescribed rites for the warding off of harm does not, however, prevent resort to amulets; it only makes the wearer reluctant to reveal the identity of the evil against which the charm offers protection.

## C.

Even amulets have their uses, of course, if the danger be sufficiently serious. Putting aside Wechsler's reading of the constitutional text, we must, therefore, confront the question of whether the status of judicial review in our society is so anomalous as to justify a demand for total adherence to neutral principles.

The attempt to derive a need for such adherence from the contrast between an undemocratic Court and democratic political branches ultimately suffers from precisely the same defect that marred the earlier contrast between ad hoc politics and principled adjudication. Even superficial analysis reveals, as in the earlier instance, that the contrast between a Court wholly insulated from the desires of the electorate and a legislature and executive devotedly registering the will of their constituents functions rather as a literary device than as a description of reality.

To begin with the political branches, is it at all accurate to describe Senator Fulbright as having represented, over the years, the views of his constituency on international affairs? It might be argued that he has carefully reflected those views on other issues deemed more important by that constituency, but then what of his control over the Senate Committee on Foreign Relations? Insofar as control over that committee's affairs carries with it the power to influence governmental decisions, Fulbright has been exercising irresponsible power. Similarly, Congressman Mills' very considerable power as chairman of the House Committee on Ways and Means is derived not from the importance of his constituency, but rather from the central role accorded to committees in the legislative process. And power exercised by administrative agencies is, of course, even further removed from any direct accountability to the electorate. Shapiro's conclusion, after a survey of the actual workings of the political system,[64] is as follows:

---

64. M. SHAPIRO, *supra* note 11, at 17–34.

186

> [T]he lawmaker, whom the modest so reverently endow with democracy's banner, is none other than precisely this combination of bureaucracy, President, and Congress, for, quite obviously, all three are major participants in the shaping of our laws. In short, the lawmaker to whom the nasty old undemocratic Supreme Court is supposed to yield so reverently because of his greater democratic virtues is the entire mass of majoritarian-anti-majoritarian, elected-appointed, special interest-general interest, responsible-irresponsible elements that make up American national politics. If we are off on a democratic quest, the dragon begins to look better and better and St. George worse and worse.[65]

The other side of the coin—the political irresponsibility of the Court—is similarly far more complicated than the antithetical nature of the contrast might suggest. The ultimate weapons that Congress and the President can bring to bear on the Court are analogous to those they use to influence the decisions of the "independent" administrative agencies: control over appropriations and a refusal to execute decisions. And the Court is certainly not unique among nonelected governmental agencies in having developed sufficient resources of its own to make either a cut in appropriations or an executive refusal to enforce its decisions highly unlikely. Similarly, Professor Dahl has demonstrated the considerable power available to the President to shape the policies of the Court through the appointment process,[66] a degree of "electoral" control analogous to that which is exercised over the "independent" administrative agencies. Indeed, given the relatively fast turnover of Justices revealed by Dahl's statistics, and the development, in connection with several agencies, of a tradition of reappointment, the statistical correspondence may be a quite precise one.

There is, moreover, a fundamental contradiction inherent in the position that the Court, because it is irresponsible, ought not to make political decisions, ought not, in the words of Holmes quoted by Wechsler, to "become the partisan of a particular set of ethical or economical opinions."[67] This difficulty is apparent in a passage from a recent article describing the process by which power in the United States has tended to centralize in federal institutions:

> Sharing in the general euphoria of power, the nine justices of the Supreme Court make major political decisions, unresponsive to the democratic process, in secret meetings on Friday afternoons. Both the number and the scope of such decisions steadily mount. Liberal critics have generally approved this development because they approve the content of the decisions, while the fundamental reshaping of an important institution seems not to trouble them. But it is a transformation which almost certainly will come back to plague us as judicial personnel and social attitudes change, and as an institution which has become more and more political develops an even greater sensitivity to transitory shifts in the political temper.[68]

65. *Id.* at 32.
66. *See* Dahl, *Decision-Making in a Democracy: The Supreme Court as a National Policy-Maker,* 6 J. Pub. L. 279, 284–86 (1957).
67. Text accompanying note 53 *supra.*
68. Goodwin, *The Shape of American Politics,* Commentary, June 1967, at 26–27.

The quoted argument, it should be noted, follows Wechsler in intimating no disapproval of the content of the decisions "approved by liberal critics." The point is, rather, that the Court should not have made such decisions at all, and two arguments are offered in support. First, these decisions are political in nature and hence should not be entrusted to an institution "unresponsive to the democratic process." Second, the making of such political decisions involves a fundamental transformation of the institution that "will come back to plague us as . . . [the] institution . . . develops an [ever] greater sensitivity to transitory shifts in the political temper."

If the difficulty with entrusting political decisions to the Court is its political unresponsiveness, ought we not welcome a "greater sensitivity to . . . shifts in the political temper?" If, on the other hand, we distrust decisions based on transitory shifts in the electorate's mood, is not the solution precisely an institution "unresponsive to the democratic process?" What we cannot do—once we agree that judicial review involves a duty to render decisions that necessarily entail political consequences—is to have it both ways, simultaneously denying legitimacy to decisions of a politically unresponsive institution and to decisions of one that responds to shifts in political sentiment.

The above analysis does not deny, of course, that in many areas of governmental concern the political branches are more responsive than the judiciary to the wishes of the electorate. Nor does it deny that, even on issues as to which the Court might possess a special responsiveness, the quality of that responsiveness ought to differ from the deference accorded electoral opinion by the legislature or executive. Nor, finally, does it deny that Court decisions will typically have far more serious consequences than those reached by administrative agencies and that this fact ought to have a considerable bearing on the scope and frequency of the Court's interventions. The point is simply that the antithesis between democratic political branches and an undemocratic Court is not a complete one, and hence that a demand for *total* neutrality cannot be derived from that contrast.

## D.

On the level of assertion rather than justification, however, Wechsler's demand for neutrality and generality rings true. If the arguments he presents fail to establish the need for total adherence to a concept of neutral principles, his insistence that reasoned opinions have historically been integral to the judicial process nevertheless raises the issue of the role and content of reasoned explanation in constitutional adjudication. Any final assessment of Wechsler's argument hinges upon the resolution of that issue.

The process of reasoned explanation embodies, according to Wechsler, two components, neutrality and generality; but he defines neither the con-

188

tent of these component parts nor the interrelationship between them. Much of the criticism directed against Wechsler's argument presupposes that the concept of neutral principles entails a demand for neutral criteria on the basis of which a choice among competing values can be made.[69] Such a demand ultimately involves a contradiction, since the existence of a neutral criterion, precisely because of its neutrality, eliminates the necessity for choice that Wechsler agrees is "inescapable."[70] On that ground alone the proposed interpretation seems an unlikely one. Moreover, Wechsler's contrast between principled adjudication and ad hoc political decision-making strongly suggests, although the distinction is never explicitly drawn, that he was focusing on the process of applying rather than deriving constitutional principles. Presumably on the basis of arguments such as these, Professor Ernest Brown, in a review of Wechsler's work, suggests that the formulation " 'the neutral application of general principles' . . . would be more explicit of his idea, if less arresting."[71]

Such a formulation exposes the fallacious assumption underlying much of the criticism of Wechsler, but its own foundations are none too secure, since it presupposes the existence of constitutional principles whose generality remains unaffected by the process of application. Constitutional adjudication, however, is a process in which the general content of a constitutional principle is only gradually defined by means of its application in a concrete series of cases. Given this process, the neutrality of application of a constitutional principle depends precisely on the degree to which its formulation takes into account those competing principles that, under some circumstances, require a different result; a principle is neutrally applied, in other words, where its nonapplication in circumstances to which it is arguably applicable can be justified by reference to competing principles.[72]

What this formulation makes clear is that the test of "neutral application" is simply another way of stating a test for adequate generality. Thus, a principle is neutrally applied when it is applied to a sufficiently large number of diverse fact situations; but its application to those situations is a function of the degree of generality in its formulation—of the degree to which competing values were taken into account in the derivation of the principle. We may, therefore, reformulate the concept of neutral principles as requiring the general application of general constitutional principles, and define neutrality as the concept in terms of which Wechsler tests the adequacy of generality.

---

69. *See, e.g.,* Miller & Howell, *The Myth of Neutrality in Constitutional Adjudication,* 27 U. CHI. L. REV. 661 (1960); *cf.* Mueller & Schwartz, *The Principle of Neutral Principles,* 7 U.C.L.A.L. REV. 571 (1960).

70. *See* text accompanying note 61 *supra.*

71. Brown, Book Review, 62 COLUM. L. REV. 386, 387 (1962).

72. A similar analysis is developed at greater length in Golding, *Principled Decision-Making and the Supreme Court,* 63 COLUM. L. REV. 35 (1963).

That Professor Brown sees neutrality as no more than a test for the adequacy of the generality with which a constitutional principle is expressed is clear from the defense he offers for the Court's decision in *Smith v. Allwright*.[73] In that case, involving primary elections conducted by the Texas Democratic Party, which was treated by state law as a private voluntary association, the Court held attempts to exclude persons from the primaries on the basis of race violative of constitutional guarantees. Wechsler condemns the decision as unprincipled because the principle involved seems to him necessarily to entail the impermissible proposition that political parties could not be organized exclusively on the basis of religious, economic, or social classifications or ideologies.[74] Brown responds:

> Cause and effect are difficult to establish in political institutions, but it is at least a tenable thesis that the system of legally significant primary elections is an outgrowth of a party system in which the major parties, to which primaries significantly relate, have historically been amorphous, heterogeneous, and heterodox. In dealing with an institution in what is, I should think, its predominant historical and functional context, it seems questionable that *Smith v. Allwright* can be considered unprincipled because it did not anticipate possibilities lying in a hypothetical, and different, future.[75]

Significantly, Brown denies neither that the extension postulated by Wechsler is necessarily entailed by the *Allwright* principle nor that the extension would be impermissible. His point, rather, is that, given the historical context in which the case arose, it was unnecessary for the Court to consider Wechsler's extension in formulating the constitutional principle involved. According to Brown, in short, the *Allwright* principle was adequately general because the factual situation stressed by Wechsler, in which the principle could not neutrally be applied, was one unlikely to arise in the foreseeable future.

One response to this analysis would deny the legitimacy of relying upon an historical context to set limits on the degree of generality that can be accepted as adequate. Generality is adequate, such a response would run, only when the principle involved can be demonstrated to be applicable neutrally in any conceivable factual situation. Although the phrasing is different, such a response represents simply a reformulation of the demand for totally principled adjudication, a demand that, as we have seen, could not be justified in terms of Wechsler's argument.

The demand for adequately general principles, moreover, is not advanced as part of a theoretical model, but rather as a standard for judging the legitimacy of constitutional decisions. The position that adequacy requires neutral application in any conceivable set of circumstances in fact

---

73. 321 U.S. 649 (1944).
74. H. WECHSLER, *supra* note 8, at 39–40.
75. Brown, *supra* note 71, at 391.

190

demands that judges decide cases on the basis of a constitutional principle only when that principle forms part of a completely coherent system applicable across the board. Such a total system may in theory be possible, although everything in our experience of constitutional adjudication counsels the contrary. But the crucial point in this context is an empirical one: the practical impossibility of constructing a completely coherent system of constitutional law at any given time. The demand for total generality, like the demand for totally principled adjudication,[76] thus renders superfluous any defense of judicial review; a Court that could review only after it had constructed a totally coherent system would in practice not review at all.

We need not, in this connection, assess the validity of the particular justification offered by Brown for the *Allwright* decision. It may be, for example, that only factors other than historical ones may legitimately be used to delimit the generality required of constitutional principles. Similarly, the historical context in which *Allwright* arose may not be capable of supporting the interpretation Brown seeks to place upon the case. Neither of these possibilities, however, detracts from the insight crucial to Brown's analysis: that adequate generality cannot be synonymous with total generality.

## E.

The care with which Wechsler establishes a constitutional justification for judicial review—travail that a demand for total generality would render superfluous—strongly suggests that he would not himself regard the concept of neutral principles as entailing such a demand. Textual arguments aside, however, the issue is one that can best be analyzed in the setting of a concrete case. I choose *Brown v. Board of Education*[77] because that case posed most sharply for Wechsler the dilemma that precisely those cases with "the best chance of making an enduring contribution to the quality of our society" had to be disapproved because they did not rest on neutral principles.

The problem that *Brown* poses for Wechsler is the absence of a neutral principle upon which a choice in favor of integration can be based, "[g]iven a situation where the state must practically choose between denying the association to those individuals who wish it or imposing it on those who would avoid it."[78] Since Wechsler agrees that legitimate Court decisions

76. *See* text accompanying note 56 *supra.*
77. 347 U.S. 483 (1954).
78. H. WECHSLER, *supra* note 8, at 47. Attempts have been made to deny the propriety of this formulation of the issue posed by *Brown*. Dean Pollak, for example, argues that the right not to associate is not involved because the forced association results, not from the decision in *Brown*, but as a consequence of the existence of compulsory school laws, and that children who wished to exercise the right not to associate could in any event do so by attending private schools. Pollak, *Racial Discrimination and Judicial Integrity: A Reply to Professor Wechsler*, 108 U. PA. L. REV. 1, 29–30 (1959).

The difficulty with this argument is, of course, the financial burden involved in attending private

J. G. D., *Stanford Law Review*, Jan. 1968

"inescapably . . . involve a choice among competing values or desires,"[79] why is not a satisfactory justification for *Brown* simply that, in the concrete situation presented, the right to associate weighed more heavily than that not to associate? There exist, of course, situations more or less analogous in which, as Wechsler indicates, the conclusion would most likely be the opposite,[80] but that fact does no more than define the problem. Granted the existence of analogous situations in which the values of association and non-association would be weighted differently, the question remains why a weighting in favor of association in *Brown* does not itself constitute a constitutional principle of adequate generality.

Wechsler's answer is that such a decision does not rest on a neutral principle because the "judgment turn[s] on the immediate result."[81] The examples he cites, described as uses of impermissible bases for assessing, rather than arriving at, decisions, consist of cases in which claims are approved because they have been "put forward by a labor union or a taxpayer, a Negro or a segregationist, a corporation or a Communist."[82] Using these examples, we can more precisely define the question at issue: In what sense is a constitutional principle inadequately general if it states that all claims put forward by Negroes or Communists will be approved, or that all claims advanced by segregationists or corporations will be rejected?

One response is that the principle is inadequate because it is incapable of being applied to all cases involving, for example, claims advanced by Negroes. But what does such an assertion mean? If it means simply that the Court, irrespective of other values embodied in different situations, does not intend to approve all claims advanced by Negroes, then the assertion denies, not the adequacy of the principle's generality, but simply the good faith of the Court in enunciating a principle it has no intention of follow-

schools. The Supreme Court has informed us that first amendment freedoms "are available to all, not merely to those who can pay their own way." Murdock v. Pennsylvania, 319 U.S. 105, 111 (1943). If a right not to associate exists, therefore, by what warrant are those who wish to exercise it required to shoulder an additional financial burden? Why does the fact of that burden not suffice as a basis on which those who wish not to associate can attack a decision that forces them to choose between free schooling and the exercise of the right not to associate?

An analogous argument, based on the financial burden involved in attendance at a private school in which prayers were permitted, was made by Mr. Justice Stewart in dissenting from the Court's decision in School Dist. v. Schempp, 374 U.S. 203, 308, 312–13 (1963). In the context of the prayer decision, Pollak meets this argument by noting that "[i]f as to a particular schoolchild a particular prayerless public school really operates to restrain his religious faith, this surely suggests not that such a religious establishment should be tolerated, but that the child would be constitutionally exempt from compliance with the compulsory school laws." L. Pollak, *Foreword: Public Prayers in Public Schools*, 77 HARV. L. REV. 62, 77 (1963).

Would a similar exemption be available for children desiring to exercise the right not to associate? A decision to the contrary would have to rest on the proposition that the free-exercise claim in the prayer case was more compelling than the claim of a right not to associate in *Brown*. Such a judgment, however, has nothing to do with the compulsory school laws, and represents precisely the sort of weighing of constitutional values that Wechsler finds at the core of *Brown*.

79. H. WECHSLER, *supra* note 8, at 22.
80. *See id.* at 46.
81. *Id.* at 17.
82. *Id.*

192

ing. A Court that refused to apply an enunciated principle to a fact situation involving no values on the basis of which nonapplication could be justified would be deciding solely on the basis of whim and caprice. Quite possibly, then, it is the good faith of the Court, rather than the adequate generality of the principle, that is being challenged.

The assertion that the principle could not be applied to all cases involving claims raised by Negroes could, however, have a different meaning—a meaning that has the virtue of going to the question at issue, that of adequate generality. Thus, the assertion could represent a prediction that the principle will in a concrete case conflict with another principle—for example, the principle that all claims put forward by Communists will be approved in a case in which Negroes and Communists assert conflicting claims. If this is what the assertion means, however, we have come full circle, since the short answer to the dilemma presented by conflicting principles is that the Court's role involves the making of a "choice among competing values or desires." It was precisely Wechsler's assent to the legitimacy of performing that task that gave rise to the inquiry into the legitimacy of the Court's choice of association in *Brown*.

The circle would be broken, of course, if the assertion meant that the possibility of conflict sufficed to render a principle inadequate. But this is simply to restate the demand for total generality, to postulate that no principle can legitimately be applied unless the Court can demonstrate that it would not in any conceivable situation conflict with any other principle. We have already noted the considerable difficulties presented by such a position,[83] further exploration of which must be deferred until part VI of this Article. The important point for present purposes is that analysis of the principle that all Negro claims will be approved eventuates only in a reiteration of the flat assertion that adequate generality is equivalent to total generality. If this were indeed Wechsler's position, then, it would be a consistent one, but one based on assertion rather than explanation.

### F.

Consistency alone, moreover, is not sufficient to make an argument validly persuasive. An argument is validly persuasive only when its persuasive elements stem from the argument itself, and are not extraneous to it. Wechsler's example, the principle that all Negro claims are to be upheld, is persuasive; there exists general agreement that decisions based on such a principle would be illegitimate. But this illegitimacy has nothing whatsoever to do with Wechsler's concept of adequate generality.

As we have seen, Wechsler's test for adequacy is general applicability; his objection to the principle that all Negro claims should be approved

---

83. *See* text accompanying notes 56, 76 *supra*.

is that it represents "ad hoc evaluation"[84] of the case before the Court. This objection would be met, however, if the Court did in fact approve all Negro claims coming before it—a course of action that would neither change the general agreement as to the principle's illegitimacy nor be approved by Wechsler.

Any principle, moreover, can in theory be applied with complete generality, provided only that the Court is willing to disregard the claims of all competing values. The general agreement as to the illegitimacy of the principle that Negro claims should always be favored does not, however, rest on the prediction that that principle might often be held inapplicable; indeed, the more often it was held applicable, the more illegitimate the Court's course of action would be. That agreement rests, rather, directly on disapproval of the content of the principle: disapproval based on the belief that other values are equally or more important than those embodied in Negro claims.

Failure to take these competing claims into account can, of course, be described as a situation in which the content of the principle is inadequately general. Used in this sense, however, the accusation of lack of generality is no longer the "neutral" one of lack of general applicability, but rather expresses disagreement with the weighting of the values from which the principle was derived. Morover, given Wechsler's view that the principle embodied in *Brown* has "the best chance of making an enduring contribution to the quality of our society of any that I know in recent years,"[85] it is difficult to perceive the basis on which he would disagree with the weighting of values it embodies.

Nor can a standard of total generality be applied to the content of principles, any more than to their applicability, since the proposition that a principle is adequately general *only* if it does not involve a conflict among values denies the possibility of the "choice among competing values" that Wechsler agrees is a legitimate part of the Court's task. The short of this matter, then, is that the persuasiveness of Wechsler's examples must stem from factors extraneous to his argument. Analysis of those factors may provide a definition of "neutrality" on the basis of which decisions such as *Brown*—the results of which Wechsler values so highly—can be justified.

What must be investigated is the basis for the general agreement that the principle that all Negro claims should be approved is illegitimate. One of the defects in the principle, embodied in the word "all," has already been noted: the failure to take any competing value into account. Simply delimiting the principle, however, would not suffice to meet the charge of illegitimacy. Thus, in a suitably limited case, we might well find legiti-

84. H. WECHSLER, *supra* note 8, at 17.
85. *Id.* at 37.

194

mate the principle that, all other things being equal, the claims of those exercising the right of free speech should be favored. Yet it is precisely Wechsler's point that we would not find legitimate even in a single case the proposition that, all other things being equal, the Court should favor the claims of those who are Negroes.

Nor can the difficulty be met by the analysis that the Constitution protects rights such as free speech but not groups of people such as Negroes; one need not search long for authority to the effect that the Reconstruction amendments were intended to protect the newly freed slaves. Perhaps the best illustration of the inadequacy of such an analysis is provided by Professor Brown's justification for the *Allwright* result. Wechsler, it will be recalled, asserts that the interpretation of equal protection embodied in *Allwright* could seriously curtail the exercise of first amendment religious and ideological freedoms. Brown dismisses the relevance of this assertion by stressing that the historical context in which *Allwright* arose rendered highly unlikely attempts to form ideological and religious political parties. Brown's view of history, in short, leads him to the proposition that only racial categories need be considered in assessing the legitimacy of the *Allwright* result. But is this different from saying that the *Allwright* principle was legitimate, despite the fact that it threatened the exercise of hypothetical religious and ideological first amendment rights, because it did protect Negroes from actual discrimination?

The difference, of course, is one of phrasing, and the importance of that difference is underlined by the decision in *United States v. Brown*,[86] which struck down as violative of the constitutional prohibition against bills of attainder a statutory provision barring Communist Party members from the executive boards of labor organizations. The heart of the holding was that Congress, in passing the statute, had "exceeded the authority granted it by the Constitution" because

> [t]he statute does not set forth a generally applicable rule decreeing that any person who commits certain acts or possesses certain characteristics (acts and characteristics which, in Congress' view, make them likely to initiate political strikes) shall not hold union office, and leave to courts and juries the job of deciding what persons have committed the specified acts or possess the specified characteristics. Instead, it designates in no uncertain terms the persons who possess the feared characteristics and therefore cannot hold union office without incurring criminal liability—members of the Communist Party.[87]

*United States v. Brown* rests on our society's deep-seated aversion to attaching legal consequences to the fact of group membership vel non, an aversion that is essential in a society as heterogeneous as ours if we are to

86. 381 U.S. 437 (1965).
87. *Id.* at 450.

J. G. D., *Stanford Law Review*, Jan. 1968

avoid the divisive consequences of distrust of that society on the part of minorities. The difficulties involved in attempting to distinguish *United States v. Brown*[88] from the Court's earlier decision in *American Communications Association, CIO v. Douds*[89] make clear, however, that stressing the existence of this aversion is a way of stating, rather than resolving, the issue. The fact is that all lawmaking—judicial as well as statutory—must perforce proceed in terms of groupings larger than the single individual. Thus, a legislative act directed against a specific person would clearly constitute a bill of attainder,[90] and judicial decisions whose principles applied only to the situation then before the Court would represent the acme of ad hoc rather than principled evaluation. Even the category of persons exercising first amendment rights, to return to an earlier example, defines an ascertainable group.

The central difficulty raised by the holding in *United States v. Brown* that Congress' grouping for legal purposes constituted a bill of attainder may, therefore, be generalized. To paraphrase the quotation from Holmes that for Wechsler sets forth the dangers to be avoided by adherence to neutral principles,[91] one man's "relatively fundamental rules of right" may well be another man's "particular set of ethical or economical opinions." What Brown's *Allwright* justification contributes to the resolution of that difficulty is the insight that the historical context may well determine the proper classification of a given principle as either a "fundamental right" or a "particular opinion."[92]

Redefining neutrality in terms of that insight, a neutral principle becomes one that is perceived as adequately general in terms of the historical context in which it is applied. The question that such a reformulation raises, however, is this: perceived as adequately general by whom? The answer can be derived from the fact that the illegitimacy of the principle approving all Negro claims was ultimately traced to a deeply held social aversion to the attaching of legal consequences to membership in groups, an aversion that is expressed in the demand that constitutional principles be generally applicable. Adequate generality in a judicial decision—neutrality, if you will—is, therefore, that degree of generality perceived as adequate by the very society that imposes the requirement of adequate generality to begin with—that same public whose agreement that the principle approving all Negro claims is illegitimate serves to make Wechsler's illustrations persuasive.

---

88. *Cf.* Dennis v. United States, 384 U.S. 855 (1966).
89. 339 U.S. 382 (1950).
90. United States v. Lovett, 328 U.S. 303 (1946).
91. *See* text accompanying note 53 *supra*.
92. Another illustration is provided by the doubt recently cast upon the historically impeccable proposition that legal consequences can legitimately be attached to the status of citizenship by naturalization rather than birth. *See* Afroyim v. Rusk, 387 U.S. 253 (1967).

196

## G.

Shapiro accepts Wechsler's demand for adequately general constitutional principles, which he calls "standards," as a political necessity. He agrees that "[i]f the Court is to be successful as a political actor, it must have the authority and public acceptance which the principled, reasoned opinion brings."[93] He goes on to note, however, that satisfying popular expectations about the legal process

> is not a political body's end but its means. It seeks to satisfy expectations in order to build the prestige necessary to pursue policy goals successfully. A court devoted only to creating the judicial myth and enhancing its own prestige would be simply strutting like a peacock. A court must use its prestige to further whatever long-range goals it has chosen. . . .
>
> . . . .
>
> The question then becomes one of political strategy. The availability of standards becomes one of the factors in the political equation. In those areas where standards are most readily available and reasonably defensible, the Court enjoys the greatest freedom to act. . . . Where the creation or selection of standards would bring the Court into open collision with a politically powerful opponent or force it to do a patent injustice, then standards may not be the order of the day.[94]

What Shapiro's formulation makes clear is the danger that adherence to neutral principles is intended to avoid: loss of the Court's ability to gain public acceptance for its decisions. But if Shapiro agrees that "[p]olitical institutions survive and prosper to the extent that they satisfy widely held expectations about them,"[95] he is also careful to emphasize that the satisfaction of those expectations represents no more than one of the complex of values that the Court must weigh in arriving at a decision. Moreover, if the concern underlying the demand for neutrality is the satisfaction of public expectations, the weight to be accorded to that demand must be determined not only by how strongly some members of the public believe a given principle to be inadequately general, but also by the number and influence of those who share that view—and of those who oppose it.

This last proposition affords a basis for explicating the consequences of Wechsler's disapproval of *Brown v. Board of Education*. Given the high regard in which he holds the *Brown* result, it would be anomalous in the extreme for Wechsler to deny legitimacy to that decision if he alone perceived the principle it embodies as inadequately general. But Wechsler's disapproval entails more than the empirical judgment that the *Brown* principle is widely perceived as inadequately general. Whatever the degree of generality deemed by him to be adequate, and whatever the relationship of that degree to the desirability of the result in a given case—whether, that is,

93. M. SHAPIRO, *supra* note 1, at 29.
94. *Id.* at 30–31.
95. *Id.* at 29.

Wechsler believes that a higher or lower standard of adequacy should be imposed as the desirability of the result increases—his disapproval of *Brown* embodies the judgment that the damage done to public expectations about the Court by *Brown*'s inadequate generality outweighs the desirability of a result which has "the best chance of making an enduring contribution to the quality of our society of any that I know in recent years."

---

It follows, from a definition of neutrality as that degree of generality that the public perceives as adequate, that the Court ought always to decide on the basis of the most general principle that can fairly be derived—the principle that will maximize satisfaction of public expectations of neutrality. Given that proposition, the most troublesome Court decisions are those per curiam opinions in which no explanation at all is offered, and hence no generality at all achieved.

It is thus no surprise that Wechsler begins his review of decisions that cannot be justified in terms of neutrality with per curiam decisions in the areas of film censorship and segregation.[96] Strikingly, however, Shapiro's objection to the segregation decisions also rests upon the Court's per curiam opinions, his objection being that resort to such opinions will result in "the Court's loss of that precious political asset, a reputation for candor."[97] Loss of "a reputation for candor," however, is precisely the consequence entailed by judicial failure to respond to the demand for neutral principles. Is the demand for "candor," then, simply an insistence upon neutral principles under another name? If so, the differences between the prudential maxims of political jurisprudence and the strictures of the "modest" seem once again to be those of style rather than substance.

## IV.

At the heart of Wechsler's concept of neutral principles, as we have seen, is the demand for generality of principle. Yet early in his argument Wechsler warns that courts may ask "what the Constitution may require or forbid . . . only . . . when it is necessary for decision of the case that is at hand"[98]—a requirement that severely limits the permissible generality of constitutional principles. Wechsler never attempts to resolve the contradiction between a demand for maximum generality and the requirement that a court decide only the case at hand, but the tension between them

---

96. *See* H. WECHSLER, *supra* note 8, at 28–31.
97. *See* text accompanying note 24 *supra*.
98. H. WECHSLER, *supra* note 8, at 10; *see id.* at 21: "To be sure, the courts decide, or should decide, only the case they have before them."

198

forms the core of Professor Alexander Bickel's analysis of the work of the
Court in *The Least Dangerous Branch*.[99]

### A.

Bickel, like Wechsler, treats justification of the *Brown* decision as the
ultimate test of his approach. He begins with a basic objection to *Brown*:
that the principle of decision in that case entails the constitutional invalidity
of measures such as benevolent quotas, which, like statutes requiring school
segregation, involve the state's attaching legal consequences to the fact of
race. Like Wechsler,[100] Bickel believes both that benevolent quotas should
not be invalidated by the Court and that the *Brown* principle, fairly read,
is inconsistent with a finding of their validity.[101] What Bickel does not
accept is that these two propositions suffice to render the *Brown* decision
unjustifiable; he rejects Wechsler's view that the Court may invoke only
those principles that can also justifiably be applied to all relevantly analogous situations.

"Our democratic system of government," argues Bickel,

> exists in [the] tension between principle and expediency, and within it judicial
> review must play its role. Mr. Wechsler's dilemma is a false one. The constitu-
> tional function of the Court is to define values and proclaim principles. But this is
> not a function to be exercised with respect to some exceedingly few matters, while
> society is left wholly to its devices of expediency in dealing with the great number
> of its other concerns. Often, as with the segregation problem and slavery before it,
> we require principle and expediency at once. The rule of the neutral principles
> would excise the Court's function of declaring principled goals. More, it would
> require the Court to validate with overtones of principle most of what the political
> institutions do merely on grounds of expediency. . . .
>
> . . . .
>
> The essentially important fact, so often missed, is that the Court wields a three-
> fold power. It may strike down legislation as inconsistent with principle. It may
> validate, or, in Charles L. Black's better word, "legitimate" legislation as consistent
> with principle. *Or it may do neither.* It may do neither, and therein lies the secret
> of its ability to maintain itself in the tension between principle and expediency.[102]

Bickel's argument as to the importance of the Court's leeway to "do
neither" in any given case rests, therefore, on the insight developed at length
by Professor Charles L. Black, Jr.: In any assessment of the work of the
Court, the function performed by that body in legitimating the actions of
other agencies of government has central importance.[103] Bickel states:

99. A. BICKEL, THE LEAST DANGEROUS BRANCH: THE SUPREME COURT AT THE BAR OF POLITICS
(1962).
100. The same objection is cited in H. WECHSLER, PRINCIPLES, POLITICS, AND FUNDAMENTAL LAW
xiv (1961).
101. A. BICKEL, *supra* note 99, at 57–65.
102. *Id.* at 68–69 (italics in original).
103. *See* C. BLACK, THE PEOPLE AND THE COURT—JUDICIAL REVIEW IN A DEMOCRACY 56–86
(1960).

199

[I]t is no small matter, in Professor Black's term, to "legitimate" a legislative measure. The Court's prestige, the spell it casts as a symbol, enable it to entrench and solidify measures that may have been tentative in the conception or that are on the verge of abandonment in the execution. Regardless of what it intends, and granted that it often intends no such thing, the Court can generate consent and may impart permanence.[104]

Bickel's differences with Wechsler are thus defined:

The rule that the Court must legitimate whatever it is not justified in striking down fails to attain its intended purpose of removing the Court from the political arena; rather, it works an uncertain and uncontrolled change in the degree of the Court's intervention, and it shifts the direction. In the course of achieving this result, it excises a great deal of what the institution is capable of doing without undue offense to democratic theory and practice. At the root is the question—in the large—of the role of principle in democratic government. No attempt to lift the Court out of the [tension between principle and expediency] can be successful. The rule of the neutral principles merely distorts the tension, by placing the weight of the Court most often on the side of expediency; for that weight is felt whenever the Court legitimates legislative choices on the constitutional merits. The Court is able to play its full role, as it did in [*Brown*], maintaining itself in the tension on which our society thrives, because it has available the many techniques and devices of the mediating way between the ultimates of legitimation and invalidation.[105]

Thus, Bickel's response to the concrete problem presented by benevolent quotas is to refer to *Naim v. Naim*,[106] in which "the Court found no insuperable difficulty in leaving open the question of the constitutionality of anti-miscegenation statutes [by dismissing an appeal from a state-court decision upholding their constitutionality], though it would surely seem to be governed by the principle of [*Brown*]," and to suggest "that the Court should similarly leave open such an issue as is offered by benevolent housing quotas."[107]

The variety of "mediating devices" that Bickel's theory makes available to the Court, however, includes more than dismissals of appeals and denials of certiorari. The bulk of *The Least Dangerous Branch* is devoted to a comprehensive survey of the work of the Court ranging from cases arising under the commerce clause[108] to such decisions as *Kent v. Dulles*[109] and *Garner v. Louisiana*,[110] which, although they raised constitutional issues, were decided on nonconstitutional grounds. Bickel presents *Kent v. Dulles* as an instance of the Court's using the "delegation" doctrine to "remand" to Congress for a "second look" a statute raising serious constitutional

---

104. A. BICKEL, *supra* note 99, at 129.
105. *Id.* at 131–32.
106. 350 U.S. 985, *dismissing appeal from* 197 Va. 734, 90 S.E.2d 849 (1956).
107. A. BICKEL, *supra* note 99, at 71.
108. *See id.* at 228–32.
109. 357 U.S. 116 (1958).
110. 368 U.S. 157 (1961).

200

doubts[111]—a type of analysis that Bickel, together with Professor Harry Wellington, had earlier adumbrated in an article suggesting application of the "remand" technique to Section 301 of the Taft-Hartley Act.[112]

In *Garner*, the Court reversed the Louisiana convictions of a group of "sit-ins" who had been prosecuted under a statute that prohibited the commission of certain acts "in such a manner as would foreseeably disturb or alarm the public."[113] The ultimate constitutional issue raised by the case was the validity, under the fourteenth amendment, of the use of state power to enforce the discriminatory policies of lunch-counter owners. The Court, however, did not reach the constitutional merits: The ground for reversal was that the state had introduced no evidence at trial to show that the public was being unreasonably disturbed or alarmed.

Analyzing the case, Bickel first notes that "[i]t is not credible that a conviction of disturbing the peace would be reversed for lack of evidence that the public might be alarmed"[114] in analogous circumstances—a peaceful demonstration involving nudity, for example, or a peaceable refusal either to produce a ticket for, or to leave, a seat at a Carnegie Hall concert. But "[t]he defendants were Negroes sitting at a white lunch counter; and as Justice Douglas, who differed from the majority and spoke to the merits, pointed out, this was Louisiana."[115]

"[E]verything else being equal," Bickel argues,

> the Court would normally have left to the local trier of facts the choice of which inference [as to whether or not the public was unreasonably disturbed or alarmed] to draw. Surely the decisive factor in *Garner* was that everything else was jarred into being unequal by the looming presence, in the background, of a momentous constitutional issue. All this is not to say that the holding in the *Garner* case is intellectually untenable. It is to say only that by its own intrinsic significance such a holding was not necessarily to be expected or even likely. It is explained and justified as probably the most suitable and certainly the narrowest method of avoidance consistent with the equities that favored the defendants, the method with the fewest surrounding implications. For the upshot is merely that this prosecution failed for reasons that are easily curable . . . .[116]

Whether the Court's disposition is phrased in terms of lack of ripeness, excessive delegation, or vagueness, whether what is involved is a denial of certiorari, dismissal of an appeal, or a decision so narrowly confined as to be applicable only to the facts then before the Court, whether the "remand" for a second look is to the legislature, as in *Kent v. Dulles*, or to the prose-

---

111. *See* A. BICKEL, *supra* note 99, at 164–66.
112. *See* Bickel & Wellington, *Legislative Purpose and the Judicial Process: The Lincoln Mills Case*, 71 HARV. L. REV. 1, 28–35 (1957).
113. 368 U.S. at 165.
114. A. BICKEL, *supra* note 99, at 178.
115. *Id.*
116. *Id.* at 179.

cutor, as in *Garner*, the distinguishing characteristic of the "mediating devices and techniques"—the Court's "passive virtues"—is the avoidance of a decision on the constitutional merits. What makes the passive virtues so important, in Bickel's view, is:

> When the Court . . . stays its hand, and makes clear that it is staying its hand and not legitimating, then the political processes are given relatively free play. Such a decision needs relatively little justification in terms of consistency with democratic theory. . . . [I]n withholding constitutional judgment, the Court does not . . . abandon principle. It seeks merely to elicit the correct answers to certain prudential questions that . . . lie in the path of ultimate issues of principle. To this end, the Court has, over the years, developed an almost inexhaustible arsenal of techniques and devices. Most of them are quite properly called techniques for eliciting answers, since so often they engage the Court in a Socratic colloquy with the other institutions of government and with society as a whole concerning the necessity for this or that measure, for this or that compromise. All the while, the issue of principle remains in abeyance and ripens. "The most important thing we do," said Brandeis, "is not doing." He had in mind all the techniques, of which he was a past master, for staying the Court's hand. They are the most important thing, because they make possible performance of the Court's grand function as proclaimer and protector of the goals. These are the techniques that allow leeway to expediency without abandoning principle. Therefore they make possible a principled government.[117]

What needs to be noted, finally, is the intimate connection between Bickel's "mediating devices" and the techniques of adjudication long since embodied in the common-law tradition as canons of judicial craftsmanship. Law made by judges—common law—is not law until it is applied by a court, and it is crucial to Bickel's theory that constitutional law is judge-made law.[118] At the level of craftsmanship, a common-law judge might well appraise the passive virtues as no more than applications of the venerable injunction that decisions be based on the narrowest possible ground, a connection Bickel himself draws at one point.[119] Given Bickel's presuppositions, however, the techniques for applying constitutional law in con-

---

117. *Id*. at 70–71.
118. *See id*. at 69–70: "When it strikes down legislative policy, the Court must act rigorously on principle, else it undermines the justification for its power. It must enunciate a goal, it must demonstrate that what the legislature did will not measure up, and it must proclaim its readiness to defend the goal—absolutely, if it is an absolute one. But it is not obligated to foresee all foreseeable relevant cases and to foreclose all compromise. Indeed, it cannot. It can only decide the case before it, giving reasons which rise to the dignity of principle and hence, of course, have a forward momentum and broad radiations. But the compelling force of the judgment goes only to the actual case before the Court. If it were otherwise, another part of the justification for the existence of the power [of judicial review] would be destroyed. For, as we have seen, the Court's peculiar capacity to enunciate basic principles inheres in large part in its opportunity to derive and test whatever generalization it proclaims in the concrete circumstances of a case. This is an opportunity that a legislature, constrained to generalize prospectively and hence in a sense abstractly, cannot have. I have remarked that the function of judicial review arises in the limiting context of cases, and yet, while the Court should not surmount the limitation, it must rise above the case. And while the Court should rise above the case, it must not surmount the limitation."
119. *See id*. at 112.

202

crete cases have implications far beyond those of judicial craftsmanship. At the center of Bickel's analysis of the work of the Court is the importance of "not doing"—the insight that the timing and vehicle of constitutional decisions are deserving of the same attention as their content. The resolution of questions of timing and circumstance, moreover, simultaneously defines the terms of the "colloquy" between the Court and other agencies of government. Thus, the passive virtues are far more than craft techniques governing the application of judge-made constitutional principles. They are also, in Shapiro's terms, maxims of political jurisprudence.

**B.**

Bickel's entry into the lists as a defender of the Court was met with cries of outrage from the "modest."[120] The objections to Bickel's thesis were basically three: First, use of the mediating devices eventuated in unprincipled, albeit nonconstitutional, grounds of decision in cases raising constitutional issues; second, some of the mediating devices, notably dismissals of appeals based on considerations of ripeness, constituted an unprincipled flouting of jurisdictional directives imposed on the Court by Congress; and third, once the Court accepted Bickel's counsels of expedience as to nonconstitutional decisions, it would inevitably apply the techniques for accommodating political pressures to decisions on the constitutional merits, which would themselves thus become unprincipled.[121]

The content of the first two objections can be illustrated briefly in terms of cases that have already been discussed. The objection to *Garner*, for example, would be that the Court there avoided the constitutional merits only by deciding that southern prosecutors, in "disturbing the peace" cases, would have to proffer more evidence than their northern counterparts—in short, that in the service of avoiding the "momentous constitutional issue" looming in the background, the *Garner* convictions were ultimately voided on the wholly unprincipled ground that "[t]he defendants were Negroes sitting at a white lunch counter; and . . . this was Louisiana." Similarly, the *Naim* dismissal, which Bickel explains "in terms of the discretionary considerations that go to determine the lack of ripeness,"[122] was branded by Wechsler as being "wholly without basis in the law."[123]

The basic "modest" objection to Bickel's view that dismissals of appeals rest largely in the discretion of the Court is that, in contrast to the discretion embodied in the certiorari jurisdiction, the relevant congressional

---

120. *See, e.g.,* Gunther, *The Subtle Vices of the "Passive Virtues"—A Comment on Principle and Expediency in Judicial Review,* 64 COLUM. L. REV. 1 (1964).

121. *See id.*

122. A. BICKEL, *supra* note 99, at 126.

123. H. WECHSLER, *Toward Neutral Principles of Constitutional Law,* in PRINCIPLES, POLITICS, AND FUNDAMENTAL LAW 3, 46–47 (1961). *See also* Gunther, *supra* note 120, at 16–20; Wechsler, Book Review, 75 YALE L.J. 672, 675–76 (1966).

statutes appear to make the appellate jurisdiction mandatory. It is pre-eminently these dispositions, therefore, that provide the basis for the charge that Bickel would transform a principled institution into a political one. Bickel himself admits:

> It follows that the techniques and allied devices for staying the Court's hand, as is avowedly true at least of certiorari, cannot themselves be principled in the sense in which we have a right to expect adjudications on the merits to be principled. They mark the point at which the Court gives the electoral institutions their head and itself stays out of politics, and there is nothing paradoxical in finding that here is where the Court is most a political animal.[124]

But why do the "modest" refuse to accept the justifications offered by Bickel for the political accommodations that he prescribes? As we have seen, the "modest" insistence on adhering to the terms of the congressional mandate is derived from the premise that the Court, because it is an institution incapable of being held to account by the public, ought not, except in extraordinary circumstances, to impose its own views where those views contradict decisions reached by the electorally responsible agencies of government. As his many references to "democratic theory and practice" suggest, however, and as his discussion of "The Counter-Majoritorian Difficulty" makes explicit,[125] the limitations on the Court's power derived by the "modest" from the fact of political irresponsibility are central to Bickel's approach. Indeed, the thrust of his effort is precisely to afford the Court the maximum possible opportunity to avoid taking stands on constitutional issues.

The differences between Bickel and, for example, Wechsler thus have nothing whatsoever to do with the opposition of those who counsel judicial activism to those who advocate judicial restraint. There is simply nothing in Bickel's system that would lead a Court following his prescriptions to be any more active than one embracing Wechslerian edicts. The source of their differences is, rather, that Bickel's view of the Court's "legitimation" function requires him to postulate that the Court acts politically even when it validates another agency's actions and that the consequences of such a decision must therefore be weighed as carefully as the consequences of an invalidation on constitutional grounds.

In Bickel's view, therefore, the Court's lack of electoral accountability requires not acts of legitimation that necessarily involve political consequences, but rather the "doing nothing" that "gives the electoral institutions their head." Consequently, what separates the two approaches to dismissals of appeals is that it is Bickel, not Wechsler, who is "modestly"

---

124. A. BICKEL, *supra* note 99, at 132.
125. *See id.* at 16–23.

204

willing to let the Court protect itself and the society from exercise of the power of decision that the statute governing appeals seeks to thrust upon it.

The structure of the judicial "politics" delineated by Bickel, moreover, is composed of elements developed in the schools of his most vociferous critics. Thus, the functional and institutional significance of concepts such as ripeness, standing, and case and controversy have been elucidated in a succession of both scholarly works and judicial opinions attributable to such men as Wechsler, Frankfurter, Louis Jaffe, Henry Hart, Albert Sachs, Philip Kurland, and Gerald Gunther. These are the men who so ably delineated for the profession the precise senses in which courts and legislatures interact to "make" law. It was, indeed, Hart and Wechsler's monumental *The Federal Courts and the Federal System*[126] that expounded the myriad ways in which doctrines such as ripeness not only define jurisdiction but, by deciding jurisdiction, simultaneously determine the timing and impact of judicial decisions.

Bickel's analysis of the Court's "legitimation" function is thus thoroughly grounded in the approach to the work of the Court that informs *The Federal Courts and the Federal System*. Similarly, his focus, in analyzing *Garner*, on the actual impact of that decision in terms of the interplay among state and federal trial and appellate courts, prosecutors, state legislatures, and Congress is wholly consistent with the perspectives developed by Hart and Wechsler in that work. The fact is, moreover, that the system developed in *The Federal Courts and the Federal System* was proving itself too rigid to be capable of accounting satisfactorily for much of the recent work of the Court. Over time, the tone of commentators' analyses had gradually shifted from one that marks the explications of the critic to one more characteristic of the strictures of the opponent.[127] Bickel's modification of that system, therefore, as contrasted, for example, to the approach of Wechsler's article on neutral principles, has at least the compelling virtue of providing a structure in terms of which much of that work can satisfactorily be explained.

Against this formidable array of merits, Bickel's critics bring to bear the insistence that dismissals of appeals on the grounds of ripeness are unjustified, not only because they involve the flouting of a congressional mandate, but also because they represent denials of a judicial obligation to decide properly tendered constitutional issues—abdications of that duty to

---

126. H.M. HART & H. WECHSLER, THE FEDERAL COURTS AND THE FEDERAL SYSTEM (1953).

127. *See, e.g.,* the following forewords to the *Harvard Law Review* annual survey of the work of the Supreme Court: Jaffe, *Foreword*, 65 HARV. L. REV. 107 (1951); Freund, *Foreword: The Year of the Steel Case*, 66 HARV. L. REV. 89 (1952); Sacks, *Foreword*, 68 HARV. L. REV. 96 (1954); Brown, *Foreword: Process of Law*, 72 HARV. L. REV. 77 (1958); Hart, *Foreword: The Time Chart of the Justices*, 73 HARV. L. REV. 84 (1959); Griswold, *Foreword: Of Time and Attitudes—Professor Hart and Judge Arnold*, 74 HARV. L. REV. 81 (1960); Kurland, *Foreword: "Equal in Origin and Equal in Title to the Legislative and Executive Branches of the Government,"* 78 HARV. L. REV. 143 (1964).

J. G. D., *Stanford Law Review*, Jan. 1968

decide from which Wechsler drew his justification for the institution of judicial review.[128] As in the instances we have already examined, Bickel's response to this argument is wholly faithful to the tradition of *The Federal Courts and the Federal System*, focusing sensitively on the functional differences in the roles our system of government assigns to the lower state and federal courts and to the Supreme Court:

> The pressure for individual justice is, of course, all the stronger when one may fairly surmise that the tendency of the Court, if pushed to the wall of principled judgment, would likely be to vindicate the moving party's constitutional claim. How should a man feel who has lost on what he must regard as a technicality, having asserted a principle that two years later, in a similar case, carries the field?[129]

In considering this problem, Bickel notes first that the fact that "the equities on the side of the moving party will vary in intensity . . . is not an argument relevant to the issue of principle itself. It can only make more palatable [if those equities are weak] the use of a device of avoidance that works against the moving party."[130] His argument continues:

> In any event, the policy of avoidance, if otherwise applicable, must prevail, despite hardship to the litigant and despite what is in other circumstances a strong policy in favor of authoritative and speedy pronouncement of governing rules. There are crucial differences—which, of course, the opinions in *Marbury v. Madison* and *Cohens v. Virginia* seek to obscure—between the role of the Supreme Court in constitutional cases and the function of courts of general jurisdiction. The latter sit as primary agencies for the peaceful settlement of disputes and, in a more restricted sphere, as primary agencies for the vindication and evolution of the legal order. They must, indeed, resolve all controversies within their jurisdiction, because the alternative is chaos. The Supreme Court in constitutional cases sits to render an additional, principled judgment on what has already been authoritatively ordered. Its interventions are by hypothesis exceptional and limited, and they occur, not to forestall chaos, but to revise a pre-existing order that is otherwise viable and was itself arrived at by more normal processes. Fixation on an individual right to judgment by the Supreme Court is, therefore, largely question-begging.[131]

The vociferousness of the opposition to Bickel's counseling dismissals of appeals cannot, therefore, be explained simply as an expected reaction to a radical departure, for it is clear that Bickel built entirely on the foundations previously laid out by his critics. The basis for that opposition can perhaps best be illuminated by reference to another tradition that, like the law, attempted the necessary but impossible feat of defining relevance and thus ordering existence—that of Gothic cathedrals.

Sainte Chapelle, the chapel of the French kings in Paris, consists of one tall room whose walls, with the exception of one area near the base, are

---

128. *See* H. WECHSLER, *Toward Neutral Principles of Constitutional Law*, in PRINCIPLES, POLITICS, AND FUNDAMENTAL LAW 3, 4–15 (1961).

129. A. BICKEL, *supra* note 99, at 172.

130. *Id.* at 173.

131. *Id.*

206

composed entirely of glass. Clearly Sainte Chapelle is Gothic; the elements of design indicate immersion in that tradition, and the search for light, which marked the transition from Romanesque to Gothic, is consummated in the luminosity its construction made possible. Sainte Chapelle in this sense represents the culmination of the Gothic tradition.

Yet, in another way, the chapel must have been a thoroughly disturbing presence for those habituated to the Gothic pattern. For the illusion created by the building is that there is nothing but luminosity, that the structural members, the elements that the chapel was to order, have completely disappeared. The child, then, if child it was, was an offspring difficult to recognize, and therefore to legitimate—not because it was not within the tradition, but because, like *The Least Dangerous Branch*, it was more than the culmination of an old style. It was also the beginning of a new perspective.

## C.

In one sense, therefore, the objections to *The Least Dangerous Branch* are understandable, for the new elements introduced by Bickel must eventually prove irresistible. The old tradition is exploded and the new begins.

The instability of the equilibrium between the traditional and the novel embodied in Bickel's approach is demonstrated by at least three factors that that approach fails to explain satisfactorily. First, there is the problem presented by the number and variety of the considerations that Bickel assumes the Court brings to bear upon its utilization of the mediating devices. Thus, if Bickel's Justices need be no more activist than those of Wechsler, it is nevertheless true that they have a great deal more discretionary power with which to be nonactivist. And for Bickel, who shares Hand's premises as to the limitations imposed upon the Court by the fact of its political irresponsibility,[132] the existence of such discretion necessarily presents a dilemma.

Bickel's response to this dilemma, like that of his predecessors to the more limited discretion entailed by their more limited conception of the Court's permissible leeway, is to insist upon rationality, upon "intellectually tenable" dispositions, in those areas of accommodation where wholly principled decisions are untenable. Wechsler had tried to confine the Court's discretion within boundaries sufficiently narrow to obviate the possibility of the Justices becoming the Platonic Guardians feared by Hand; Bickel's modification of that theory postulates Guardians who are Platonic not only in their exercise of power, but also in their wisdom: possessed of a degree of rationality exceeding that vouchsafed to Wechsler's Justices by precisely the extent to which the discretion Bickel bestows on the Court exceeds that conceded by Wechsler.

132. *See* text accompanying note 124 *supra.*

207

We need not be cynics to conclude from what we know of the Justices, and especially of the processes that lead to their appointment,[133] that a Court meeting those specifications could be produced only by the sheerest accident. Yet, under Bickel's theory, only such Justices would be capable of legitimately exercising the discretion granted the Court. Bickel has not, then, in fact, satisfactorily accounted for the recent work of the Court we know. What he has done is to explain how a hypothetical Court might justifiably have arrived at many of those same decisions.

Secondly, Bickel's analysis of the Court's "legitimation" function—the fulcrum that enabled him to move the Wechslerian world—itself rests on the dubious assumption that the society will always perceive the difference between "doing nothing" and "legitimation." If, however, the Court "does nothing" long enough, if it leaves undisturbed—because the issue is unripe, because further experimentation is needed, or because it wants to "give the electoral institutions their head"—a sufficient number of lower-court dispositions at variance with those the Court would reach "if pushed to the wall of principled judgment," those decisions may well be perceived as legitimated. Indeed, given a sufficiently notorious case, even denial of certiorari might have such an impact. Conversely, a sufficiently prolonged series of invalidations on nonconstitutional grounds might well be perceived as an attempt to implement an unspoken constitutional judgment.

Bickel's counter to this objection is to stress the Court's "resources of rhetoric," its educational role, in Eugene Rostow's phrase, as "teacher in a vital national seminar."[134] But that rejoinder is convincing only if we assume that the public responds rather to what the Court says than to what it does, and that "legitimation" is effective only when the deed is accompanied by words of approval. The more likely hypothesis is that the public responds to the results the Court reaches as well as to the rhetoric it employs.

Given these limits on the usefulness of rhetoric, the objection that Bickel raises to Wechsler's "rule that the Court must legitimate whatever it is not justified in striking down" can be applied to his own counsel to "do nothing": It "fails to attain its intended purpose of removing the Court from the political arena."[135] What it does do is to change, and to some extent limit, the degree of the Court's intervention in that arena. But this consequence, which is also entailed by Wechsler's rule, must ultimately be as unsatisfactory for Bickel as Bickel assumed it would be for Wechsler. Both Bickel and Wechsler, for the same reason—the desire to render exercise of the Court's power compatible with the fact of its political irresponsibility

133. *See, e.g.*, D. DANELSKI, A SUPREME COURT JUSTICE IS APPOINTED (1964).

134. Rostow, *The Democratic Character of Judicial Review*, 66 HARV. L. REV. 193, 208 (1952); *see* A. BICKEL, *supra* note 99, at 26.

135. *See* text accompanying note 105 *supra*.

208

—attempt to formulate courses of action that will take the Court out of politics. Both, though for different reasons, fail.

There remains, finally, the problem raised by Bickel's barring of anything analogous to the mediating devices from the formulation of decisions on the merits of constitutionality—what Professor Gunther refers to as "the novelty and vulnerability of the Bickel thesis: the emphasis on principle as the highest Court duty, but only in a limited sphere of Court actions; the 100% insistence on principle, 20% of the time."[136] Gunther, of course, is concerned with the other 80 percent of the cases. What he regards as unjustifiable is, for example, the stress on prudential factors contained in the following explanation offered by Bickel for the dismissal of the appeal in *Naim*:

> But would it have been wise, at a time when the Court had just pronounced its new integration principle, when it was subject to scurrilous attack by men who predicted that integration of the schools would lead directly to "mongrelization of the race" and that this was the result the Court had really willed, would it have been wise, just then, in the first case of its sort, on an issue that the Negro community as a whole can hardly be said to be pressing hard at the moment, to declare that the states may not prohibit racial intermarriage?[137]

But if, contrary to Gunther, we accept Bickel's view as to the propriety of the mediating devices, the query implicit in Gunther's characterization of that view nevertheless remains unanswered. If, that is, Bickel is correct in asserting that prudential factors properly influence dispositions based on the unprincipled mediating devices, on what basis does he deny that such factors ought properly to influence decisions on the constitutional merits: decisions that, because they attract greater public attention, are most likely to entail the type of consequences that, for Bickel, justified the dismissal of *Naim*?

Similarly, the structure of Bickel's analysis of *Garner* makes it likely that he would meet the objection that that analysis involves southern prosecutors having to produce more evidence than northern prosecutors in "disturbing the peace" cases by asserting that the relationship between the dangers involved in "legitimating" a given statute or conviction and the demand for "intellectual tenability" is an inverse one: that the greater the dangers involved in "legitimation," the more readily the Court may properly resort to a mediating device.[138] Thus, Bickel would argue that in *Garner* the constitutional issue "looming in the background" was sufficiently momentous to justify resort to an extremely narrow ground of decision, one open to the objection canvassed above. Again, if, contrary to Gunther,

---

136. Gunther, *supra* note 120, at 3.
137. A. BICKEL, *supra* note 99, at 174.
138. *See* text accompanying note 116 *supra*.

we accept this analysis, the question implicitly posed by Gunther nevertheless remains: Why, in Bickel's view, is an analogous equation not applicable
to constitutional decisions? If, in short, the sorts of factors that for Bickel
justify the dismissal of *Naim* and the disposition in *Garner* properly enter
into the Court's decision as to *when* to decide constitutional issues, why
does Bickel deny the propriety of those factors playing any part in the
Court's decision as to *how* to decide such issues—as to the terms of the
constitutional decision itself?

The answer, in simplest terms, is that, as we have seen, Bickel is with
Hand and Wechsler in drawing the need for principled constitutional decisions from the fact of the Court's political irresponsibility. Like Wechsler,
moreover, Bickel defines principle in terms of generality; "By 'principle,' "
according to Bickel, "is meant general propositions . . . organizing ideas
of universal validity in the given universe of a culture and a place . . . ."[139]
Given this agreement, it is perhaps to be expected that two of the three
major constitutional decisions whose lack of neutrality Wechsler analyzed
at length,[140] *Shelley v. Kraemer*[141] and *Smith v. Allwright*,[142] are not discussed by Bickel at all. They are mentioned, indeed, only once each, and
then in footnotes.[143] As for *Brown v. Board of Education*,[144] the third of
Wechsler's examples, Bickel's proposed dismissal of cases raising the constitutionality of benign quotas obviously presupposes that the Court ought
not strike down such quotas on the merits—that the principle underlying
*Brown*, the impermissibility of racial classifications, does not, at least in
this place and this culture, possess "universal validity."

Bickel accepts, then, Wechsler's proposition that constitutional decisions are justified only when they are based on neutral principles, and, on
the level of concrete cases, he fails to traverse Wechsler's averment that
certain of the Court's most important recent decisions are to be found
lacking in neutrality. *The Least Dangerous Branch* can thus truly be characterized as an exercise in the usefulness of mediating devices, for Bickel's
response to Wechsler, in terms of the cases on which the latter relies, is
ultimately explicable only as an instance of confession and avoidance.

## D.

That Bickel's analysis of the Court's work eventuates in assessments that
are congruent with those of Wechsler is clearly apparent in his recent ap-

---

139. A. BICKEL, *supra* note 99, at 199; *cf. id.* at 69: "When it strikes down legislative policy, the
Court must act rigorously on principle, else it undermines the justification for its power. It must
enunciate a goal, it must demonstrate that what the legislature did will not measure up, and it must
proclaim its readiness to defend the goal—absolutely, if it is an absolute one."
140. *See* H. WECHSLER, *supra* note 128, at 36–42.
141. 334 U.S. 1 (1948).
142. 321 U.S. 649 (1944).
143. *See* A. BICKEL, *supra* note 99, at 191 n.124, 241 n.55.
144. 347 U.S. 483 (1954).

210

praisal of the obscenity decisions.[145] Bickel there condemns the per curiam decision in the three cases jointly decided in *Redrup v. New York*[146] as having "made an utter shambles of the law of obscenity."[147] His objection is that the publications held in *Redrup* not to be obscene cannot meaningfully be distinguished from the material on the basis of which the conviction of Ralph Ginzburg had been upheld one year earlier:[148]

> All there is of an effort to differentiate Mr. Ginzburg's case in the short order— it is hardly an opinion—that the Court wrote in the three cases . . . is the remark that in these cases there was no "evidence of the sort of 'pandering' which the Court found significant in *Ginzburg v. United States*." The pandering notion was based on Ginzburg's advertising, and embodies the bizarre proposition that Ginzburg's publications, even if not otherwise obscene, were made so by his sales pitch, which emphasized that they were sexually interesting. That, as Mr. Justice Douglas very sensibly said in dissent in the *Ginzburg* case, would make the constitutional protection of the Song of Solomon depend on the way it was sold, and might turn into unlawful obscenity a lot of "lotions, tires, food, liquor, clothing, autos, and even insurance policies," sold with the aid of displays "of thighs, calves, bosoms" *etc.* But be that as it may, and assuming that the pandering test does have some validity, it is impossible to see how publications . . . held not obscene [in *Redrup*] pander any less than Ginzburg's product.[149]

The deficiencies Bickel finds in the *Redrup* opinion are aggravated, moreover, by the fact that "there was hardly any explanation this time. Most of that, such as it was, came [in *Ginzburg* and its accompanying cases]. Now the Court said virtually nothing; it simply acted."[150] In deciding *Redrup* in a per curiam order that briefly adumbrated the bases on which various Justices, by differing routes, reached the conclusion that the material at issue was not obscene, the Court was seemingly returning to a "practice that it had previously followed for nine years, from 1957 to 1966."[151]

1957 was the year of *Roth v. United States*,[152] in which the Court first attempted to develop guidelines for the obscenity area.[153] What followed, as a recent commentary has put it, is that

> [f]or nearly a decade afterwards, the Court could muster a majority only for cryptic *per curiams*; in the two cases where the Justices wrote full-dress opinions . . . no more than three of them could agree on a common rationalization. Initial efforts to clarify *Roth* broke down in a dispute whether the "community" re-

145. *See* Bickel, *Obscenity Cases*, NEW REPUBLIC, May 27, 1967, at 15.
146. 386 U.S. 767 (1967).
147. Bickel, *supra* note 145, at 17.
148. Ginzburg v. United States, 383 U.S. 463, *rehearing denied*, 384 U.S. 934 (1966).
149. Bickel, *supra* note 145, at 16.
150. *Id.* at 15.
151. *Id.*
152. 354 U.S. 476 (1957).
153. For a concise and perceptive analysis of the difficulties inherent in those guidelines see Comment, *More Ado About Dirty Books*, 75 YALE L.J. 1364, 1365–77 (1966).

J. G. D., *Stanford Law Review*, Jan. 1968

ferred to in the *Roth* definition was a national or local one; attempts to establish the relevance of "social importance" were similarly unsuccessful. One Justice suggested that the prurient interest rule be supplemented by elements such as "patent offensiveness"; another, that *Roth* be applied in conjunction with a "sufficient evidence" rule in reviewing lower-court decisions; still another, that *Roth* be limited to federal cases. Mr. Justice Stewart urged the Court to replace *Roth* entirely with a "hard core pornography" rule, promising that although he was unable to define the hard core, he would know it when he saw it. From the start Mr. Chief Justice Warren offered a "purveying" test as an alternative, claiming that the conduct of the distributor rather than the content of his wares should be the central issue. Few of the proposals won the support of anybody but their authors.[154]

That Bickel finds these dispositions objectionable is clear, since it was this course of decision that he believes led lower courts, and Mr. Ginzburg, to the conclusion that "just about anything is printable in the US today"[155] —a conclusion emphatically, and, according to Bickel, unjustifiably, rejected in *Ginzburg v. United States*.

"The problem [of obscenity]," Bickel concludes,

is exceedingly difficult—quite likely insoluble at the hands of the Supreme Court. On principle it would seem clear that, while government may take a hand in helping parents and schools to control what juveniles read and see, and while government should also have the power to control displays that thrust themselves unavailingly at people who may feel offended by them—with these two exceptions, anyone should have the right to print and publish and show anything that anyone else may wish to read and see. But . . . it seems equally clear that a majority of our people are not prepared to accept such a broadly permissive rule, and that their unwillingness to accept it is based in some part on surmises about the possible connection between pornography and crime. That there is no such connection may be likely. But no one is able to prove it.

In such circumstances, it is neither wise nor is it possible, as a practical matter, for the Court to impose and enforce a broadly permissive constitutional rule. And short of a broadly permissive rule, as the Justices have amply demonstrated, there is no coherent and consistent constitutional principle on which to rest judicial judgment. There is merely—but that is a great deal—an opportunity, through procedural, interpretive and other decisions falling short of the attempt to impose ultimate constitutional prohibitions, to discourage, circumscribe, reduce and contain the application of obscenity statutes. This is the business the Supreme Court ought to get on with.[156]

The principled disposition of the obscenity problem being ruled out, for prudential reasons analogous to those that for Bickel governed the disposition in *Naim*, we are thus left with the counsel of the passive virtues. Unlike the areas with which Bickel dealt in *The Least Dangerous Branch*, however, his analysis of the obscenity issue in fact involves a wholesale

---

154. *Id.* at 1373–77 (footnotes omitted).
155. Bickel, *supra* note 145, at 15.
156. *Id.* at 17.

212

condemnation of the Court's recent work in the area. The per curiam dispositions in *Redrup* and the post-*Roth* cases are only explicable as holdings on the merits of the constitutional issue of obscenity, and such holdings, on Bickel's analysis, are unjustifiable. In other words, Bickel can avoid Wechsler's characterization of *Naim* as "wholly without basis in the law" by arguing, as he does, that dismissals of appeals, even dismissals "for the want of a substantial federal question," need not be principled because they do not in fact represent dispositions on the merits.[157] But this avenue is closed to Bickel in the obscenity area since, whatever else may be said of the per curiam dispositions we have been canvassing, it is apparent that they disposed of the issue presented on its constitutional merits.

Shapiro's fears for the Court's loss of a "reputation for candor," it will be recalled, are in part based on the per curiam dispositions in the segregation cases.[158] And Wechsler, while agreeing that those dispositions are rightly to be condemned, begins his survey of illegitimate recent decisions with a number of pre-*Roth* per curiam dispositions in the area of film censorship.[159] On the basis of Bickel's analysis of the obscenity issue, therefore, we may conclude that he is with Shapiro and Wechsler in being unable to offer a satisfactory account of the Court's recent per curiam practice. Bickel's strictures may be couched in more sophisticated language, but that fact in no way mitigates the severity of the indictment of the Court's recent work that his analysis of the obscenity cases entails.[160]

157. "It can be said, and indeed it is commonly assumed, that dismissals 'for the want of a substantial federal question' are decisions on the merits, though without opinion. But when the Court decides the merits without opinion, it is in the habit of telling us so by issuing a summary order that reverses or affirms the judgment below. There is and has been for many years a great deal that is pure fiction in this explanation. Many are the dismissals for the want of a convenient, or timely, or suitably presented question." A. BICKEL, *supra* note 99, at 126 (footnote omitted).

A striking confirmation of Bickel's view is to be found in Mr. Justice Harlan's dissenting opinion, which Mr. Justice Clark joined, in *Redrup*: "The three cases were argued together at the beginning of this Term. Today, the Court rules that the materials could not constitutionally be adjudged obscene by the States, thus rendering adjudication of the other issues unnecessary. In short, the Court disposes of the cases on the issue that was deliberately excluded from review, and refuses to pass on the questions that brought the cases here [the issues of *scienter*, "vagueness," and "prior restraint"].

"In my opinion these dispositions do not reflect well on the processes of the Court, and I think the issues for which the cases were taken should be decided. Failing that, I prefer to cast my vote to dismiss the writs in *Redrup* and *Austin* as improvidently granted and, *in the circumstances, to dismiss the appeal in Gent for lack of a substantial federal question*. I deem it more appropriate to defer an expression of my own views on the questions brought here until an occasion when the Court is prepared to come to grips with such issues." 386 U.S. at 772 (emphasis added).

The description given by Mr. Justice Harlan of the Court's handling of certain summary dismissals in early reapportionment cases is also instructive: "Each of these recent cases is distinguished on some ground or other in *Baker v. Carr*. . . . Their summary dispositions prevent consideration whether these after-the-fact distinctions are real or imaginary. The fact remains, however, that between 1947 and 1957, four cases raising issues precisely the same as those decided today were presented to the Court. Three were dismissed because the issues presented were thought insubstantial and in the fourth the lower court's dismissal was affirmed." Reynolds v. Sims, 377 U.S. 533, 614 (1964) (dissenting opinion) (footnote omitted).

158. *See* text accompanying note 97 *supra*.

159. *See* text accompanying note 96 *supra*.

160. *Cf.* Bickel & Wellington, *supra* note 112, at 3: "The Court's product has shown an increasing incidence of the sweeping dogmatic statement, of the formulation of results accompanied by little or no effort to support them in reason, in sum, of opinions that do not opine and of per curiam orders that quite frankly fail to build the bridge between the authorities they cite and the results they decree."

## V.

The ultimate source of the difficulties in Bickel's analysis is, as we have seen, the postulate that he shares with Hand and Wechsler: that the Court's political irresponsibility requires—though, for Bickel, only in a delimited category of cases—an absolute adherence to principle. That what we know of the legislative and executive branches renders meaningless a comparative characterization of the Court as politically irresponsible has already been indicated.[161] Nor can it realistically be asserted that the absolute form of limitation that Bickel and Wechsler would impose is required to prevent the Court from becoming excessively powerful. Unlike Congress or the President, the Court has access to neither sword nor purse, and in many areas, including such crucial contemporary concerns as foreign affairs, its recognition of its own limitations has amounted to almost total abdication.[162]

The issue central to both Bickel's and Wechsler's analyses is, therefore, not power but propriety. The charge is not that the Court is in some abstract sense exercising more power than our system of government allocates to it. What Bickel and Wechsler conclude, rather, is that recent dispositions, because they are not based on neutral principles, betray an abuse of the Court's admitted power to render constitutional decisions. The issue, then, is one of defining criteria for justifiable decisions.

## A.

The starting point for any such formulation must be the insight that underlies Bickel's development of the passive virtues: that the Court, as an institution, has certain institutional needs—for example, the needs to ensure survival and to operate efficiently—and that those needs are necessarily reflected in the form and content of its work. The active role played by the Court in securing passage of the Judiciary Act of 1925,[163] the "Judges' Bill" whose introduction of certiorari made possible control of the docket at a time when the number of cases awaiting decision threatened to cripple the Court as an effective institution, constitutes a response to the need for efficient operation. And Bickel's rationale for dispositions such as *Naim*— the necessity for maintaining the "tension between principle and expediency"—ultimately rests on the Court's need to ensure its own survival as a viable institution.

"The Court's authority to employ [mediating devices]," notes Bickel, "derives from its ultimate function of rendering principled adjudications;

---

161. *See* part III–C *supra*.

162. *See, e.g.*, Banco Nacional de Cuba v. Sabbatino, 376 U.S. 398 (1964); text accompanying note 56 *supra*.

163. Act of Feb. 13, 1925, ch. 229, 43 Stat. 936 (codified in scattered sections of 10, 11, 15, 28, 48 U.S.C.).

214

for this is a function that can be wisely and fruitfully exercised only if the Court is empowered also to decide whether and when to exercise it."[164] The Court's duty to render constitutional decisions thus entails, for Bickel, the power to determine the timing and scope of such decisions—entails, in other words, the Court's power to determine its own institutional capacity. It is precisely this reasoning that forms the basis for Bickel's approval of dismissals of appeals on grounds of ripeness.

In an earlier article, Bickel and Wellington, quoting Mr. Justice Frankfurter, advanced the view that the Court's power to determine its own institutional capacity derives directly from the principles of article III of the Constitution:

> The earliest declaration of unconstitutionality of an act of Congress—by the Justices on circuit—involved a refusal by the Justices to perform a function imposed upon them by Congress because of the non-judicial nature of that function. . . . Since then, the Court has many times declared legislation unconstitutional because it imposed on the Court powers or functions that were regarded as outside the scope of the "judicial power" lodged in the Court by the Constitution. . . .
>
> One may fairly generalize from these instances that the Court has deemed itself peculiarly qualified, with due regard to the contrary judgment of Congress, to determine what is meet and fit for the exercise of "judicial power" as authorized by the Constitution.[165]

Whatever the merits of this attempted derivation from the constitutional text, however, there exist a variety of devices for avoiding "controversy" and thereby ensuring survival, many of which have become so integral a part of adjudicatory techniques that the Court is often criticized for failure to observe them. One instance is provided by the maxim that a decision ought always to be based on the narrowest possible ground, as a means both of preserving flexibility for the future and of avoiding the conflict of judicial and public opinion that would likely result from more sweeping dispositions. Bickel commends this course to the Court,[166] and Gunther takes pains to argue that nothing Wechsler proposes is inconsistent with that maxim.[167] Cognate propositions, such as the importance of submerging individual doctrinal differences in compromise opinions that can speak for a majority of the Court and the importance of refraining from dissent in order to make unanimous decisions possible,[168] rest, like that mandating the choice of the narrow ground, both on the desirability

---

164. A. BICKEL, *supra* note 99, at 205.

165. Textile Workers Union v. Lincoln Mills, 353 U.S. 448, 464–65 (1957) (dissenting opinion), *quoted in* Bickel & Wellington, *supra* note 112, at 28.

166. *See* A. BICKEL, *supra* note 99, at 112.

167. *See* Gunther, *supra* note 120, at 20 (discussing Cohens v. Virginia, 19 U.S. (6 Wheat.) 264 (1821), on which Wechsler heavily relies).

168. *See* A. BICKEL, THE UNPUBLISHED OPINIONS OF MR. JUSTICE BRANDEIS: THE SUPREME COURT AT WORK 18–19, 28–32, 58, 65, 99, 161–62, 199–200, 203, 209–10 (1957); Murphy, *Marshaling the Court: Leadership, Bargaining, and the Judicial Process*, 29 U. CHI. L. REV. 640, 656–72 (1962).

J. G. D., *Stanford Law Review*, Jan. 1968

of the Court's maintaining a united front and on the importance of obviating the possibility of conflicting decisions.

It was these considerations that underlay the assertion by Justices Frankfurter, Clark, Harlan, and Whittaker that the noting of probable jurisdiction in *Ohio ex rel. Eaton v. Price*[169] "manifest[ed] disrespect by the Court for its own process."[170] Regarding *Eaton* as "completely controll[ed]" by a case decided within two weeks of the time the *Eaton* papers came before the Court,[171] the four Justices objected to the Court's "willingness to create an opportunity to overrule a case decided only a fortnight ago after thorough discussion at the bar and in the briefs and after the weightiest deliberation within the Court."[172]

The issue involved in *Eaton*, however, was admittedly a weighty one—the propriety of warrantless searches in a noncriminal setting. Might it not be argued, therefore, that the four Justices who voted to note probable jurisdiction, far from manifesting disrespect for the Court's processes, were actually following Wechsler's injunction that they act on principle? Since they regarded the earlier decision as a serious infringement of constitutional rights, might not their insistence that the Court give plenary consideration to every extension of that case, no matter how small the variation in the facts presented, be characterized, again borrowing Wechsler's terms, as a praiseworthy refusal to bow to "controlling sentiment" and "to trim and shape their speech and votes accordingly"?[173] A year later, when *Eaton* was affirmed by an equally divided Court, the four Justices who had voted to note probable jurisdiction took care to point out, referring to the earlier, controlling decision: "We would not be candid to say that on its own facts we have become reconciled to that judgment."[174] Does this avowal of refusal to be bound by decided cases help to provide a basis for that "reputation for candor" whose loss Shapiro fears?

The proper answer to these questions, a negative one, entails the assertion that a Court that often indulged in controversies like *Eaton* would suffer greatly—not only from the inability to utilize its time and resources efficiently that must result from the insistence that certain issues never be regarded as even temporarily settled, but also from the loss of public esteem that must eventually be caused by spectacles as unseemly as that provided by *Eaton*. Such an answer indicates much about the extent to which the institutional values of efficient operation and survival form the necessary

---

169. 360 U.S. 246 (1959).

170. *Id.* at 248–49.

171. Frank v. Maryland, 359 U.S. 360 (1959).

172. 360 U.S. at 249.

173. H. Wechsler, *supra* note 128, at 21.

174. Ohio *ex rel.* Eaton v. Price, 364 U.S. 263, 269 (1960). The four Justices who voted to note probable jurisdiction joined in an opinion urging that *Frank* be either reversed or distinguished. The *Frank* case has since been overruled in Camara v. Municipal Court, 387 U.S. 523 (1967).

216

underpinning for any analysis of the work of the Court. But it indicates more than that as well, for the emphasis on loss of public esteem as providing a justifiable basis for criticism of *Eaton* recalls the earlier analysis of the degree of generality—of neutrality, in Wechsler's terms—that suffices to render a decision justifiable. A decision is to be regarded as justifiable, it was there concluded, when its generality is perceived as adequate by the public.[175]

## B.

As the *Eaton* analysis makes clear, the necessary limitation on judicial "candor," like the Wechslerian insistence on neutrality as necessary to the enforceability of the Court's decisions, ultimately represents a requirement of public acceptance. Nor is this a limitation peculiar to the judicial branch, for in the last analysis, obedience over the long term even to congressional statutes can be enforced neither by the sword nor by the purse. The continued existence of all branches of our government, not just the judiciary, is at bottom dependent upon public acceptance. That acceptance is not at issue, however, in the normal course of events. Inertia is a guiding principle in politics as well as physics, and the very existence of our institutions —the persuasive testimony of history—itself serves to produce a significant degree of acceptance.

It is the reservoir of acceptance produced by this inertia that is drawn upon by the Court whenever it renders a decision less than adequately general, and the reservoir is far from inexhaustible. Why, then, render such decisions at all? Why not follow Wechsler's advice and validate acts of other governmental agencies or, following Bickel, resort to the "passive virtues"? The answer is that public acceptance of the Court does not rest solely on perceptions of adequately general decisions. That acceptance rests also, to a very considerable degree, on a view of the Court as the guardian of our constitutional rights. Given this view, each approval of a statute perceived as involving an infringement of constitutional rights—even, in some instances, refusals to rule on the merits of such a statute—results in a loss of credibility, and therefore public acceptance, of the Court.[176]

The loss of acceptance resulting from a loss of credibility, like that produced by a decision perceived as inadequately general, depends, of course, on the seriousness with which the public views a given constitutional infringement or a given instance of inadequate generality. The requirements of credibility and generality will, moreover, be inconsistent wherever a statute perceived as constituting an infringement of constitutional rights

---

175. *See* part III–F *supra*.
176. *See* Scharpf, *Judicial Review and the Political Question: A Functional Analysis*, 75 YALE L.J. 517, 562–66 (1966).

J. G. D., *Stanford Law Review*, Jan. 1968

can be struck down only on a basis perceived as inadequately general. The crucial point, however—the point that Bickel refuses to accept—is that resort to the "passive virtues" does not resolve this dilemma. It simply ignores one factor in the equation, for the fact is that every decision not to decide, just like decisions on the constitutional merits, may result either in adding to the reservoir of public acceptance (if only by remaining unnoticed, and thus adding to the inertial acceptability produced by the Court's continued functioning) or in depleting that accumulation. And depletion may as easily be the consequence of a lack of credibility as a lack of generality.

Bickel's significant contribution to analysis of the Court's work is the description of the multitude of factors that may necessitate a compromise with doctrinal purity—with the adequate generality on which Wechsler insists. There is the Court's need to ensure itself the flexibility that will be required in future cases, where the issue presented is manifested in such a diverse variety of circumstances that no principle is yet at hand, or where available principles are seen to entail ramifications in other areas that have not yet fully been explored. There is the Court's need, wherever possible, to maintain a united front, both to retain public acceptance and to preserve uniformity and therefore stability within the law. There is the need to accommodate the pressures and needs of other governmental institutions, including lower federal and state courts and federal and state administrative agencies, whose attitudes towards a given decision may have a significant impact on the way in which it is enforced, as well as federal and state executive and legislative institutions, which may be considering taking action in a field with which the Court is presently concerned, or whose later actions may have drastic implications for any decision reached by the Court. There is, finally, as in Bickel's analysis of *Naim*, the limitation imposed by the public acceptability of the result reached in the given case.

What Bickel failed to see, the flaw upon which Gunther correctly insists, is that this analysis is workable only if it is applied to decisions on the constitutional merits as well as to the mediating devices. Thus, that same public whose refusal to accept the *Naim* result justified the disposition of that case may, in another case, regard a given result as so urgently required that refusal to reach it would entail a loss of credibility far outweighing the consequences of inadequate generality. The point is that the weighing of the factors delineated by Bickel is a task that the Court must undertake in each and every case, whether what is involved is a mediating device or a decision on the constitutional merits. If these factors represent "political" considerations, in other words, then the Court is in politics, and the counsel of passive virtues ultimately avails as little as the injunction of neutral principles to extricate the Court from that status.

218

It is precisely this failure that makes it impossible for Bickel convinc-ingly to distinguish dismissals for want of a substantial federal question from per curiam dispositions without opinion. Thus, as his analysis of the obscenity issue indicates, Bickel subjects per curiam dispositions involv-ing constitutional questions to the same rigorous requirements of prin-ciple applicable to cases decided with full opinion. Appeals dismissed for want of a substantial federal question, however, often involve, as *Naim* did, a constitutional question, and the existence of a congressional statute making the hearing of appeals mandatory seems to entail the proposition that such a dismissal involves a decision on the merits about the substan-tiality of the constitutional question presented. Denial of this proposition, which Bickel characterizes as "pure fiction,"[177] is mandated, as we have seen, by the necessity for the Court to be able to determine its own insti-tutional capacity.[178] Yet the only distinction Bickel offers between such dismissals and decisions on the merits without opinion is the fact that the latter "habitually" involve "issuing a summary order that reverses or affirms the judgment below."[179] The point seems somehow too formal, too con-cerned with the mechanics of the Clerk's office, to account satisfactorily for the distinction between dispositions subject to a requirement of rigorous adherence to principle and dismissals for which that requirement may justifiably be treated as a "fiction."

The question Bickel never satisfactorily answers, the query insistently put by Gunther, may thus be reformulated in more precise terms: If the Court's need to preserve its institutional capacity by avoiding needless pub-lic controversy justified the dismissal of *Naim*, notwithstanding the exis-tence of a mandatory appeals jurisdiction, why would not a similar need to avoid loss of the Court's credibility in a situation where enunciation of the principle involved would cause needless public controversy justify a per curiam disposition, reaching the required result without opinion? One response given in connection with criticisms of the Court's per curiam practice[180] is that reasoned opinions constitute the source of the Court's power, and that a refusal to make clear the grounds of decision in each case must ultimately result in the Court's decrees becoming unenforceable. Such a response ignores the reservoir of public acceptability provided for the Court by the inertial effects we have already analyzed. But the more serious difficulty in terms of Bickel's theory is that acceptance of this argu-ment would go far towards rendering unjustifiable many of the mediat-ing devices, including, of course, dismissals for want of a substantial fed-eral question.

177. *See* A. BICKEL, *supra* note 99, at 126.
178. *See* text accompanying note 164 *supra*.
179. A. BICKEL, *supra* note 99, at 126.
180. *Cf.* Brown, *supra* note 127; Sacks, *supra* note 127.

Thus, Bickel agrees that reasoned, principled opinions constitute the source of the Court's power, but his description of the importance of the mediating devices rests on the insight that not every case provides the proper occasion for such an opinion—that often, as in *Naim*, what is called for is not the reasoned opinion, but rather the passive virtue. Bickel's more likely response, therefore, is that a disposition without opinion in the per curiam situation is unjustifiable because such a disposition represents a decision on the merits that must be principled; because it, unlike the dismissal of an appeal, is not truly a mediating device. Such an argument, however, serves only to restate the question why dismissals of appeals do not represent decisions on the merits. Bickel cannot, after all, simply wish out of existence the congressional statute making appeals mandatory; and the argument that dismissals can be differentiated from per curiams because the Court does not in fact treat the former as binding precedents[181] can be met by reference to Bickel's own analysis of *Ginzburg*, which convincingly demonstrates that the Court there did not regard earlier per curiams as entitled to precedential weight.[182]

The search, therefore, must be for the factor that makes dismissal of an appeal a justifiable mediating device—the significance, in Bickel's terms, of the absence of an order affirming or reversing the judgment below. Viewed in terms of a focus upon public acceptability, the significance of that absence seems clear, for it results in a decision that in form, in appearance, represents not a decision on the merits, but simply a refusal to decide. The justifiability of treating dismissals as a mediating device thus lies precisely in the disparity between the public and the lawyer's view of the significance of such a decision. We can therefore say, with Bickel, that it is a fiction that dismissals of appeals involve decisions on the merits, not because that proposition is a fiction in the universe of the legal scholar, but because the scholar's world does not in itself contain all the relevant materials from which a satisfactory account of the work of the Court can be drawn.

If, however, we focus with Bickel on the impact of a given decision on the public that is ultimately the source of the Court's power, it is clear that decisions without opinion do often serve as mediating devices. The limitations on the use of this device are, of course, considerably more severe than in the case of dismissals; but what is involved are differences, not antitheses. Thus, there is a significant probability that certain cases will be sufficiently notorious that a decision without opinion would be perceived as enunciating an inadequately general principle, just as there is a lesser probability that certain dismissals would be perceived as refusals to enforce constitu-

---

181. *See* note 157 *supra.*
182. *See* text accompanying notes 154–56 *supra.*

220

tional rights sufficiently significant to lead to a loss of credibility. Similarly, it is probable that a whole series of dispositions without opinion in a given area would lead to a significant loss of public acceptance resulting from a perception of inadequate generality, and this eventuality is more likely than a series of dismissals resulting in a loss of credibility. But the question ultimately is one of a difference in probabilities, not of antitheses. To further complicate matters, moreover, any complete description would require modification of Bickel's unlikely assumption that legal scholarship is so completely isolated from the world on which Court decisions impinge that scholarly criticism of an opinion's refusal to give precedential weight to a series of "fictional" dismissals cannot become sufficiently vociferous and well known as to result in a loss of public acceptance.

The crucial point, once again, is that the same factors that provide justification for the passive virtues come into play in connection with decisions avowedly on the constitutional merits. If it is the *form* of dismissals of appeals—the appearance of not deciding—that accounts for their designation as mediating devices, then the stringently limited form of dispositions without opinion—the appearance of deciding without any radiating effects—must also suffice to qualify the per curiam practice as a passive virtue. The relevant characteristic of the per curiam is thus precisely the absence of any full-dress opinion, ensuring, in the absence of other circumstances leading to public notoriety, that the public impact of the Court's action, as in the case of dismissals, is held to a minimum.

Such an analysis does not, of course, purport to demonstrate that dispositions without opinions invariably represent a mediating device as desirable as dismissals. As indicated above, the limitations on the use of this device are more severe than is true of dismissals, and the likelihood that factors outside the Court's control, such as the actions of the press or the scholarly community, will result in the public's perceiving the disposition as inadequately general is greater than in the case of dismissals. With those qualifications, however, the same reasoning that leads to the designation of dismissals as legitimate passive virtues must also be applicable to the per curiam practice. We may, therefore, criticize the Court's per curiam practice, as we might criticize its dismissal actions, for discounting too drastically the likely reactions of the press and the scholarly community, for example, or for resorting to dispositions without opinion for too extended a period in any given area, since any long series of such decisions tends to increase the likelihood of a public perception of inadequate generality. What we cannot do, and this is precisely what Bickel attempts, is simultaneously accept dismissals as legitimate mediating devices and yet criticize the per curiam practice on the basis that dispositions without opinion are not entitled to the same status.

221

Assimilation of per curiams to the status of passive virtues, moreover, involves a good deal more than simply expanding the scope of application of the latter. For, as we have seen, Bickel's justification for drawing the line between per curiams and dismissals of appeals is that the former truly embody what the latter only "fictionally" represent—decisions on the constitutional merits. And decisions on the constitutional merits, unlike the mediating devices, are subject to the rigorous requirements of principle. Recognition of per curiams as one of the passive virtues entails, therefore, the proposition that the pressures that compel resort to the mediating devices, which for Bickel justify the decision in *Naim*, also have their part to play in the disposition of cases on the constitutional merits. To some extent, of course, this view is implicit in Bickel's treatment of *Garner*, which, as we have seen, ultimately rests on the proposition that justifiable demands for "intellectual tenability" are inversely related to the dangers involved in legitimating the situation before the Court.[183] *Garner*, however, although a decision on the merits, was not a decision on the constitutional merits; and the crucial point about many of the per curiams, once again, is precisely that they *are* decisions on the constitutional merits. In this sense, therefore, classification of per curiams as a mediating device ultimately does far more than simply shift the line that Bickel draws between dismissals of appeals and the per curiam practice. What it entails, rather, is destruction of the barrier Bickel seeks to erect between principled decisions and the mediating devices.

## C.

A satisfactory theory of the work of the Court cannot stop, however, with the assimilation of the per curiam practice into the world of passive virtues. It must also account for the phenomenon against which much of the recent criticism has been directed, for what Bickel and Wellington referred to as the

> increasing incidence of the sweeping dogmatic statement, of the formulation of results accompanied by little or no effort to support them in reason, in sum, of opinions that do not opine and of per curiam orders that quite frankly fail to build the bridge between the authorities they cite and the results they decree.[184]

That description has since been echoed in numerous critical appraisals,[185] and the phenomenon it reports is presumably also what Shapiro depicts as the Court's lack of "candor" and Wechsler as a lack of "principle."

Criticism has, of course, always accompanied the work of the Court, and the accusation of a lack of "candor" or "principle" may to some extent

---

183. *See* text accompanying note 138 *supra*.
184. Bickel & Wellington, *supra* note 112, at 3.
185. *See, e.g.*, L. HAND, THE BILL OF RIGHTS (1958); Brown, *supra* note 127; Griswold, *supra* note 127; Hart, *supra* note 127; Kurland, *supra* note 127.

222

rest simply on a refusal to accept the legitimacy of the mediating devices. As Bickel demonstrates, however, the Court has resorted to such devices throughout its history. Even if one views them as unprincipled, or as lacking in candor, their use means only that the Court's product has continued to be as deficient as it always has been. What Bickel reports, however, and what the recent critics object to, is something more—not the same old level of imperfection, but an "increasing incidence" of failure.

One could, of course, simply brand these failures as illegitimate decisions and leave it at that. Imprecation, however, is a poor substitute for understanding. And even a work that purports not to describe the ongoing work of the Court, but only to delineate the role that such an institution may legitimately fulfill, is more likely to persuade if it is based on an accurate diagnosis of the institution's ills. Any satisfactory theory, therefore, must account not only for the necessary level of lack of principle that has always characterized the work of the Court, a requirement Bickel ably satisfies, but also for the fact of an "increasing incidence" of failure, a task Bickel wholly ignores.

Assuming that the quality of personnel staffing an institution remains reasonably stable and that no significant changes occur in the internal institutional processes (and there is nothing in the recent history of the Supreme Court to vitiate either of these assumptions), striking variations in work product are likely to represent responses to change in the environment in which the institution operates. The environment in which the Supreme Court operates has recently been subject to two significant changes—neither of them unknown in prior eras, neither of them without considerable roots in history, but both having assumed significant proportions only in the years following 1945.

The first of these changes has to do with increased public awareness of the possibilities for social change inherent in constitutional litigation. In part this is a diffuse, general consciousness resulting simply from more widespread education and from developments in communications that ensure that an increasing proportion of the public learns of Court decisions, and has access to speculation concerning the consequences of those decisions, almost as soon as they are handed down. More significantly, it is this awareness that has increasingly guided the behavior of organized groups, a phenomenon symbolized by the carefully conceived campaign of litigation that eventuated in the *Brown* decision.[186] A decisive effect of such group activity is the extent to which it predetermines the sequence of issues brought before the Court in any given area. One of the most important of the passive virtues has historically been the property of randomness in the

---

186. *See generally* Vose, *Litigation as a Form of Pressure Group Activity*, 319 ANNALS 20 (1958).

flow of litigation, which made it unlikely that the Court, after deciding any given case, would immediately be faced with the situation that most stringently tested the principle enunciated. It is precisely this saving element of accident, this opportunity to avoid the testing of the outermost limits of a principle, that has been eliminated by the activity of groups whose aim it is to utilize litigation as a means of pursuing social goals.

One response by the Court to this activity has been to utilize an organization possessing considerable legal resources that, in addition to furthering its own interests through litigation, has also demonstrated a regard for the institutional needs of the Court. The Office of the Solicitor General has increasingly been cast in this role, as is demonstrated by its recent participation in cases in which the interests of the United States were not directly involved—the *Reapportionment Cases* and the *Brown* decision provide two striking examples. In instances such as the second *Brown* decision,[187] the Court's request for participation by the Solicitor General has eventuated in arguments displaying a sensitive regard for the importance of mediating devices and the Court's institutional capacity.[188]

A second response, rooted in the considerations so thoroughly canvassed in *The Least Dangerous Branch*, has been an increasing incidence of resort to the passive virtues, including the mediating device represented by the per curiam practice. The series of cases denying retroactive effect to various decisions in the field of criminal procedure[189] represents one such instance, analogous to the second *Brown* decision. To understand a second instance, the handling of the obscenity issue, requires consideration of the second significant change in the Court's environment—the breakdown of accepted limitations on the meaning of constitutional concepts.

Dean Bayless Manning, in an incisive analysis demonstrating the inapplicability of constitutional limitations to the exercise of power by private business corporations, stresses the narrowly delimited nature of the freedoms embodied in our constitutional guarantees. His conclusion that those guarantees cannot meaningfully be applied to the corporate area is based on the fact that the freedoms they ensure are freedoms from arbitrary interference only by governmental agencies and only in a restricted number of areas, largely political rather than economic. The economic freedoms, including freedom from hunger and deprivation; the cultural and intellectual freedoms, including freedom to develop talents to the utmost limits of capacity and to express those talents; "positive" rather than "negative" freedoms; and freedoms whose attainment would implicate the actions of non-

---

187. Brown v. Board of Educ., 349 U.S. 294 (1955) (implementation decision).
188. *See* A. BICKEL, *supra* note 99, at 252–53.
189. *See, e.g.,* Johnson v. New Jersey, 384 U.S. 719 (1966); Tehan v. United States *ex rel.* Shott, 382 U.S. 406 (1966); Linkletter v. Walker, 381 U.S. 618 (1965).

224

governmental agencies, all were largely ignored when our Constitution was written.[190]

Strict observation of such limitations vastly simplified the task of the Court in defining the applicability of constitutional guarantees. Thus, the Court has not historically been in danger of losing its "reputation for candor" when it failed to consider the applicability of a given constitutional principle to deprivations of economic or cultural freedoms. And a constitutional principle was perceived as adequately general even when it was applied only to attempts by governmental agencies to interfere with political freedoms. As the scope of the freedoms regarded as relevant expands, however, both candor and adequate generality must become increasingly difficult to achieve.

The limitations that have thus helped to make the Court's work manageable are not to be found explicitly set out in the constitutional texts. They exist, rather, as cultural understandings, as implicit assumptions, and it is precisely these agreements that have increasingly been breaking down. A primary example is the traditional understanding of the scope of the equal protection guarantee. The Court's recent expansion of the applicability of this guarantee has been designated "the egalitarian revolution" by Professor Kurland, one of the Court's most vociferous scholarly critics, who considers this expansion the most "novel" of the themes that have characterized the work of the Court over the past decade.[191]

When he wrote those words, Kurland had in mind the reapportionment and segregation decisions;[192] but he might with equal justification have included the recent decisions in the area of criminal law, which he considers primarily as examples of "the effective subordination, if not destruction, of the federal system."[193] True, decisions such as *Gideon v. Wainwright*[194] and *Escobedo v. Illinois*[195] are phrased in terms of sixth amendment guarantees, and *Miranda v. Arizona*[196] is couched in fifth amendment language. But *Gideon* emphasizes the fact that "there are few defendants charged with crime, few indeed, who fail to hire the best lawyers they can get to prepare and present their defenses,"[197] and *Escobedo* relies on the "lesson of history that no system of criminal justice can, or should, survive if it comes to depend for its continued effectiveness on the citizens' abdication through unawareness of their constitutional rights."[198] Clearly, then,

190. *See* Manning, *Corporate Power and Individual Freedom: Some General Analysis and Particular Reservations*, 55 Nw. U.L. Rev. 38, 46–53 (1960).
191. *See* Kurland, *supra* note 127, at 144.
192. *See id.* at 145–62.
193. *Id.* at 144; *see id.* at 163–65.
194. 372 U.S. 335 (1963).
195. 378 U.S. 478 (1964).
196. 384 U.S. 436 (1966).
197. 372 U.S. at 344.
198. 378 U.S. at 490.

the theme that underlies these cases is one of equality: in *Gideon*, the imposition of a duty on the State to provide the same access to counsel for those who cannot afford to hire an attorney as for those who can; in *Escobedo* and *Miranda*, the duty to equalize, between those who are aware of their constitutional rights and those who are not, the opportunity for access to counsel prior to interrogation that may result in invocation of fifth amendment rights.

The equal protection basis for decision is most nearly explicit in cases such as *Douglas v. California*,[199] which invalidated the practice of denying appointment of counsel for an indigent upon the independent determination of an appellate court that no purpose would be served by the appointment. The opinion in *Douglas* relied on *Griffin v. Illinois*,[200] which had held that indigents must be given equal access to the procedures established by the States for reviewing criminal convictions. But as Mr. Justice Harlan pointed out in dissent, *Douglas*, unlike *Griffin*, did not deal with a problem of access to appellate review, for the procedures struck down in *Douglas* required the appellate court to make a complete review of the trial proceedings in determining that no purpose would be served by the appointment of counsel.[201] What *Douglas* involved, rather, was the imposition of a duty on the State to equalize the *quality* of the indigent's participation in appellate procedures.

Mr. Justice Harlan clearly saw the implications of such a decision for the other criminal-procedure cases canvassed above:

> [I]f the present problem may be viewed as one of equal protection, so may the question of the right to appointed counsel at trial, and the Court's analysis of that right in *Gideon v. Wainwright* . . . is wholly unnecessary. The short way to dispose of [that case] . . . would be simply to say that the State deprives the indigent of equal protection whenever it fails to furnish him with legal services, and perhaps with other services as well, equivalent to those that the affluent defendant can obtain.[202]

Justice Harlan's basic objection to the decision was precisely the "novelty" of its interpretation of the constitutional guarantee of equal protection:

> [T]he Equal Protection Clause does not impose on the States "an affirmative duty to lift the handicaps flowing from differences in economic circumstances." To so construe it would be to read into the Constitution a philosophy of leveling that would be foreign to many of our basic concepts of the proper relations between government and society. The State may have a moral obligation to eliminate the evils of poverty, but it is not required by the Equal Protection Clause to give to some whatever others can afford.[203]

---

199. 372 U.S. 353 (1963).
200. 351 U.S. 12 (1956).
201. *See* 372 U.S. at 363–64.
202. *Id.* at 363.
203. *Id.* at 362 (footnote omitted).

226

The extent to which the accepted limitations on the concept of equal protection have been eroded—whether the Court's "novel" interpretation will eventually be extended to such areas as payment for expert witnesses, and beyond—is not yet clear. As *Douglas* demonstrates, however, the process is under way. Ultimately, therefore, Kurland's failure to point to the criminal cases as exemplifications of "the egalitarian revolution" seems to stem from a failure to appreciate the real source of the "novel" constitutional doctrine he finds in the segregation decisions: the Court's partial recognition, reflecting a new awareness on the part of the public, that the freedom embodied in constitutional guarantees as they have historically been limited is, for the economically and socially disadvantaged, no freedom at all. Once that fact had been recognized in *Brown*, in connection with the impact on Negroes of segregated educational facilities, the drawing of its obvious implications for criminal law required only a further recognition of the empirical connection between poverty and crime.

The "novel" element in recent segregation and criminal decisions can thus largely be accounted for in terms of the relatively recent public (and judicial) awareness of the extent to which the world of the poor and of the Negro differs from that in which the bulk of the public lives, and of the consequences entailed by that disparity for the content of a meaningful constitutional guarantee of "equal protection." Moreover, the discovery of previously unknown universes existing within our boundaries is not the only example of an area of increased public and judicial consciousness in the United States in the post–World War II period. Due in part to the enforced world tours required of so many citizens by that conflict, and perhaps more to ongoing developments in communication and transportation, there developed a growing awareness of the divergent sexual standards characteristic of even closely related Western cultures.

The predictable result was confusion. Both a public that continued to hold to the accepted truth that society ought not to permit the dissemination of obscenity, and a Court that had translated that premise into the *Roth* formula that obscenity was not speech and was therefore not protected by first amendment guarantees,[204] found themselves increasingly unable to agree on just what it was that had—of course—to be banned. Reflecting the public confusion, the absence of even a potential consensus on the nature and content of permissible areas of candor in sexual matters, a badly fragmented Court increasingly resorted to the passive virtues. Wherever possible, for nearly a decade after the *Roth* decision, "cryptic per curiams" were the order of the day.

---

204. *See* Roth v. United States, 354 U.S. 476, 482–84 (1957).

## D.

Bickel, of course, is fully aware of this lack of consensus, and it forms the basis for his counsel that the Court restrict the scope of obscenity statutes without ever ruling on the constitutional merits.[205] But the circumstances in which several of the cases arose foreclosed, in the Court's view, avenues other than that of constitutional adjudication;[206] and decisions on the merits, given the relatively acceptable content of the material that was usually at issue and the need of the Court to preserve credibility, had, in the main, to uphold the freedom to print and to read. Bickel correctly suggests that a "principled" exception to this pattern should be made for cases involving "displays that thrust themselves unavailingly at people who may feel offended by them."[207]

Would application of this "principled" exception, however, entail the inconsistency noted by Mr. Justice Douglas, dissenting in *Ginzburg*, of making the obscene content of material depend on the advertising that preceded or accompanied it? That inconsistency could be avoided only if what the Court in fact condemned was the method and content of the advertising rather than the material being advertised. But that, of course, is precisely the purport of the "pandering" test advanced in *Ginzburg*. The content of the material involved in *Redrup*, as Bickel notes,[208] cannot meaningfully be distinguished from that condemned in *Ginzburg*. But the Court in *Ginzburg* did not focus on the content of the material being disseminated; the pivotal inquiry was, rather, into the nature and content of the advertising campaign that accompanied it.[209]

The *Ginzburg* test is, admittedly, not stated in these terms, just as the per curiams that both preceded and followed that decision are impenetrably "cryptic" concerning the bases of decision. But that, as Bickel himself acknowledges in terms reminiscent of his justification for *Naim*, is surely attributable to the fact that "a majority of our people are not prepared to accept such a broadly permissive rule, and . . . their unwillingness to accept it is based in some part on surmises about the possible connection between pornography and crime. That there is no such connection may be likely. But no one is able to prove it."[210] The obscenity cases, therefore, no

---

205. *See* text accompanying note 156 *supra*.
206. *See, e.g.,* A. BICKEL, THE LEAST DANGEROUS BRANCH: THE SUPREME COURT AT THE BAR OF POLITICS 133–43 (1962), outlining an alternative to the Court's having reached the merits in Times Film Corp. v. City of Chicago, 365 U.S. 43 (1961), a film-censorship case.
207. *See* text accompanying note 156 *supra*.
208. "[The materials involved in *Redrup*] . . . are no more distinguishable from Mr. Ginzburg's publications than were all those items that went before, from 1957 to 1966." Bickel, *Obscenity Cases*, NEW REPUBLIC, May 27, 1967, at 15, 16. *See also* text accompanying note 149 *supra*.
209. *See* Comment, *More Ado About Dirty Books*, 75 YALE L.J. 1364, 1386–88 (1966).
210. Bickel, *supra* note 208, at 17.

228

less than the other examples surveyed by Bickel of the use of mediating devices, represent dispositions "seek[ing] merely to elicit the correct answers to certain prudential questions that . . . lie in the path of ultimate issues of principle."[211] They are attempts by the Court "to maintain itself in the tension between principle and expediency"[212]—the tension "on which our society thrives."[213]

Bickel's objection to the obscenity decisions is not, however, an objection in the large. It focuses, rather, on "the rank injustice of punishing [Ginzburg] under a rule applicable to no one else, past *or* future."[214] Because the per curiams preceding *Ginzburg* had seemed to indicate that "just about anything is printable in the US today," and because *Ginzburg* itself refused to make explicit the "principled" exception on which it was based, Bickel can only conclude:

> The Court, we now know, made of Mr. Ginzburg an example which exemplifies nothing. Had any other institution been responsible for this performance—say some hapless administrative agency—the Court would have been well-justified in holding that it violated the Due Process and Equal Protection Clauses.[215]

In another context, as we have seen, Bickel himself exposed the flaw in this contention. In response to the argument that devices of avoidance could not legitimately be employed where they resulted in refusals to uphold individual claims that "the Court, if pushed to the wall of principled judgment, would likely . . . vindicate,"[216] Bickel countered:

> The Supreme Court in constitutional cases sits to render an additional, principled judgment on what has already been authoritatively ordered. Its interventions are by hypothesis exceptional and limited, and they occur, not to forestall chaos, but to revise a pre-existing order that is otherwise viable and was itself arrived at by more normal processes. Fixation on an individual right to judgment by the Supreme Court is, therefore, largely question-begging.[217]

We are all creatures of the injustices to which we have become accustomed. Ginzburg's conviction had already been upheld by one appellate court when the Supreme Court granted certiorari in his case. Had the Court simply denied certiorari at that point, would there then have been a rank injustice? The conclusion to be drawn from a negative answer, one that Bickel's prescription of mediating devices strongly suggests, must be that the *Ginzburg* decision and the obscenity per curiams, no less than the other passive virtues described by Bickel, represent the price society must

---

211. A. Bickel, *supra* note 206, at 70.
212. *Id.* at 69.
213. *Id.* at 132.
214. Bickel, *supra* note 208, at 16.
215. *Id.*
216. A. Bickel, *supra* note 206, at 172.
217. *Id.* at 173.

pay for maintaining the Court as a viable institution capable of fulfilling its assigned constitutional task.[218]

That price may be expected to increase as the factors of change sketched above continue to accelerate. It is not only the growth of self-conscious group litigation—although that is important and likely to become vastly more so as the legal agencies associated with the War on Poverty come into full operation—and the gradual breakdown of accepted limitations on constitutional concepts that dictate an increasing resort to the full panoply of mediating devices. In the last analysis, this trend toward "expediency" can be accounted for as a reaction to the continuing increase in both the tempo and content of constitutional litigation—an intensification and expansion that at bottom are produced not by a Court imperiously attempting to impose its will upon the nation, but rather by a nation with a population growing both in numbers and in education, a population ever more aware both of decisions of the Court and of the potentiality for social change inherent in those decisions.

In terms of any given decision, therefore, the Court may be open to criticism for espousing a wrong, or an inadequate, principle; for failing to resort to a passive virtue where such resort is both possible and proper;[219] or for resorting to per curiam dispositions where a more limited and less controversial mediating device is available.[220] In general, however, it is clear that the direction of change is such that the Court's task of constitutional adjudication must necessarily become an increasingly difficult one. The prognosis, then, is precisely one of an "increasing incidence" of failure.

## VI.

Professor Bickel, moreover, is not alone in disapproving of the Court's handling of cases in the areas of obscenity and film censorship. Almost a decade ago, Mr. Justice Black made clear his objection to the Court's procedure of dealing with such cases at retail:

---

218. A similar price involving subordination of individual goals is exacted by the process of group litigation delineated in the text accompanying notes 186–88 *supra*. In the NAACP campaign that led to the *Brown* decision, for example, may there not have been individual plaintiffs who were condemned to an experience of exclusively segregated schooling, to a practical denial of the right being contended for, by the grade-a-year desegregation programs on which agreement was often reached?

Acceptance of the fact that in every viable society individual desires must at some point be sacrificed to institutional needs presumably also represents the solution to the equal protection problems raised by the practice, described in the text at notes 187–88 *supra*, of having the Office of the Solicitor General intervene in cases in which the United States has no direct pecuniary or governmental interest. Assuming that this practice has become an established one, suppose that after a Supreme Court decision has established a certain constitutional right, the Solicitor General receives a letter from someone being denied that right, reporting that no lawyer whom the writer can afford to hire is willing to take the case, and requesting assistance. Must the Solicitor General—an agency of government—respond affirmatively if the facts contained in the letter are true, or can he—and the Supreme Court—restrict at will the occasions when, and the parties on whose behalf, intervention will take place?

219. *See* note 206 *supra* and accompanying text.

220. *Cf.* text accompanying note 156 *supra*.

230

We are told that the only way we can decide whether a State or municipality can constitutionally bar movies is for this Court to view and appraise each movie on a case-by-case basis. Under these circumstances, every member of the Court must exercise his own judgment as to how bad a picture is . . . . The end result of such decisions seems to me to be a purely personal determination by individual Justices as to whether a particular picture viewed is too bad to allow it to be seen by the public. Such an individualized determination cannot be guided by reasonably fixed and certain standards. . . . [The resulting] uncertainty cannot easily be reconciled with the rule of law which our Constitution envisages.[221]

Black's emphasis on "fixed and certain standards," like his objection to a case-by-case process of adjudication, recalls the differentiation between constitutional and common-law adjudication that he expressed in his *Linkletter* dissent[222] in terms of the logic-experience dichotomy.[223] But what is the danger posed for the development of constitutional law by resort to common-law methods of adjudication? A persuasive argument can be made that, far from eschewing such methods, a Court desiring to achieve that precision of analysis essential to the formulation of enduring constitutional principles could do no better than to adhere to the process of case-by-case adjudication:

> [T]he framing of concepts and the integration of a conceptual system for the purpose of finding out where we are at, as a preliminary to seeing where we are to go next—that will remain eternally necessary to scientific advance. And at this point, the process of argument in court, or the judicial process, affords in the rival claims of the opposing lawyers a clarity of appreciation, forced upon few other men, as to the weasel ways of verbal symbols, as to the need for rigorous definition, the need for hunting postulates to their foul holes and yanking them out into brutal, healthy sun, the need for step-by-step reasoning which stays at every step within the premises as defined, whenever one sets about any such integration.[224]

What Black fears sufficiently to justify his sacrifice of the intellectual precision made possible by common-law processes is the exercise by the Court of that measure of discretion that a system of case-by-case adjudi-

---

221. Kingsley Int'l Pictures Corp. v. Regents, 360 U.S. 684, 690–91 (1959) (concurring opinion).
222. *See* note 46 *supra* and accompanying text.
223. Mr. Justice Black has recently reiterated this distinction in support of his dissenting position in Griswold v. Connecticut, 381 U.S. 479, 507 (1965): "Observing that 'the right to privacy . . . presses for recognition here,' today this Court, *which I did not understand to have power to sit as a court of common law*, now appears to be exalting a phrase which Warren and Brandeis used in discussing grounds for tort relief, to the level of a constitutional rule which prevents state legislatures from passing any law deemed by this Court to interfere with 'privacy.'" *Id.* at 510 n.1 (emphasis added).
224. Llewellyn, *Legal Tradition and Social Science Method—A Realist's Critique*, in Brookings Institution, Essays on Research in the Social Sciences 89, 111 (1931); *cf.* Corbin, *Hard Cases Make Good Law*, 33 Yale L.J. 78 (1923).
Bickel shares this appreciation of the virtues of common-law methods of adjudication: "Another advantage that courts have is that questions of principle never carry the same aspect for them as they did for the legislature or the executive. Statutes, after all, deal typically with abstract or dimly foreseen problems. The courts are concerned with the flesh and blood of an actual case. This tends to modify, perhaps to lengthen, everyone's view. It also provides an extremely salutary proving ground for all abstractions; it is conducive, in a phrase of Holmes, to thinking things, not words, and thus to the

cation inevitably entails. The connection between discretion and common-law adjudication is explicitly drawn by the prevailing opinion in *Linkletter*, which begins by establishing the Court's agreement with Austin, who "maintained that judges do in fact do something more than discover law; they make it interstitially by filling in with judicial interpretation the vague, indefinite, or generic statutory or common-law terms that alone are but the empty crevices of the law."[225]

Black's *Linkletter* opinion also makes explicit the basis for his opposition to the exercise of such discretion by the Court. The sentence immediately following the passage that objects to the reading of Holmes as identifying constitutional law with "experience" is as follows: "It should be remembered in this connection that no member of this Court has ever more seriously criticized it than did Justice Holmes for reading its own predilections into the 'vague contours' of the Due Process Clause."[226] In other words, the Court may not in constitutional cases rely on "experience," may not exercise the discretion that case-by-case adjudication would entrust to it, because to do so would run the risk of repeating the occurrences of the 1930's. That period, as the then Senator Black was well aware, was one in which the Court's attempts to block economic measures deemed necessary by the legislature and executive came near to destroying it as a viable institution.

It might be argued that, if the function of the Court is truly to afford our society an opportunity for "sober second thought" concerning measures that challenge, in some significant way, either cherished ideals or deep-rooted social beliefs, then the actions of the thirties were thoroughly in accord with that function. The fact is that the impropriety of government intervention in the economy did represent such a belief; and the effect of the Court's decisions was precisely to impress upon the society the magnitude of the departure from received tradition entailed by acceptance of the view that there exist no principled checks on governmental economic actions. The full implications of that acceptance are only now becoming apparent, as property rights once again begin to be perceived as necessary bulwarks of individual freedom.[227] Even on a less long-range view, it is apparent that the Court's 1930's decisions performed the task of legitimation that the cumbersomeness of the machinery for amending the Constitution has historically imposed upon the Court. Thus, the public

evolution of principle by a process that tests as it creates." A. BICKEL, *supra* note 206, at 26. Indeed, as we have previously seen, it is essential to Bickel's theory that constitutional cases are decided by means of common-law processes. *See* note 118 *supra* and accompanying text.

225. 381 U.S. at 623–24. *See also* K. LLEWELLYN, THE COMMON LAW TRADITION 62–120 (1960).
226. 381 U.S. at 642.
227. *See, e.g.*, McCloskey, *Economic Due Process and the Supreme Court: An Exhumation and Reburial*, 1962 S. CT. REV. 34; Reich, *The New Property*, 73 YALE L.J. 733 (1964); *cf.* Struve, *The Less-Restrictive-Alternative Principle and Economic Due Process*, 80 HARV. L. REV. 1463 (1967).

232

consensus on the propriety of the economic legislation of the 1930's was ultimately strengthened, not weakened, as a result of the Court's intervention.

Whether or not that intervention was proper, the *Linkletter* dissent makes clear that Black's objection to case-by-case adjudication is rooted in his fear that the Court will abuse the discretion such a process necessarily involves. That fear is confirmed by what Black sees as the record of the Court's use of common-law "experience" as a guide to constitutional decisions. In Black's view, reliance on "experience" led, in the 1950's, to a supplanting of the excesses of the 1930's by the constitutional "balances" he so bitterly opposed. Black's solution to this dilemma is an insistence on "logic" —the logic of textual "absolutes" and of historical meanings.

The efficacy of relying on these two sources of logic for satisfactory guidelines in constitutional adjudication has been searchingly questioned by Bickel.[228] What is crucial for present purposes, however, is that Black's system of constitutional "logic" can successfully eliminate the element of discretion in constitutional adjudication only if it provides a totally coherent and comprehensive system, whose principles never conflict with each other in any conceivable set of circumstances. Such a system, of course, satisfies Wechsler's criterion of neutrality interpreted as total generality. Under such a system, moreover, there would be no need for mediating devices and the avoidance of constitutional issues. Consequently, the Court, in each and every case, would be able to fulfill completely the requirement of "candor" with regard to the basis for decision that Shapiro seeks to impose upon it.

But to return momentarily to the Gothic mode, the fact is that the structure of the law embodies the diversity and incongruity of Chartres, not the rational order of Amiens or even of Notre Dame. It is no less true for constitutional law than for tort law that precedents serve, not as logical axioms from which conclusions can mechanically be derived, but as an accumulated store of wisdom against which the validity of new conclusions can be assessed. Nor are constitutional cases exempt from the transformations of meaning produced by history. Is the proposition for which *Marbury v. Madison*[229] stands today the holding of that case? Is not *Pierce v. Society of Sisters*[230] cited as establishing a first amendment right of which no trace can be found in the opinion? Is not *Buchanan v. Warley*[231] cited as establishing an equal protection rather than a due process right?

As then Dean Rostow put it :

228. *See* A. BICKEL, *supra* note 206, at 84–110.
229. 5 U.S. (1 Cranch) 137 (1803).
230. 268 U.S. 510 (1925).
231. 245 U.S. 60 (1917).

Any lawyer who has worked through a line of cases about easements or trusts or bills and notes or any other legal subject, knows that no court has ever achieved perfection in its reasoning in its first, or indeed in its twentieth opinion on the same subject. . . . [Even our greatest and most insightful judges] grapple with a new problem, deal with it over and over again, as its dimensions change. They settle one case, and find themselves tormented by its unanticipated progeny. They back and fill, zig and zag, groping through the mist for a line of thought which will in the end satisfy their standards of craft and their vision of the policy of the community they must try to interpret. The opinions written at the end of such a cycle rarely resemble those composed at the beginning. Exceptions emerge, and new formulations of what once looked like clear principle. If we take advantage of hindsight, we can see in any line of cases and statutes a pattern of growth, and of response to changing conditions and changing ideas. There are cases that lead nowhere, stunted branches and healthy ones. Often the judges who participated in the process could not have described the tree that was growing. Yet the felt necessities of society have their impact, and the law emerges, gnarled, asymmetrical, but very much alive—the product of a forest, not of a nursery garden, nor of the gardener's art.[232]

To substitute "logic" for "experience" in constitutional adjudication, therefore, would be to dispense altogether with the judicial process, at least the judicial process as known in the United States and in England.

The connection between the judicial process and the discretion that Black fears is perhaps best illustrated by the following example: Assume a logical chain of propositions (a) through (e), with the Court already having decided (a) and (b) in such a way as to indicate a particular result in (c), which result has not, however, yet been promulgated. Assume further, that case (e) then arises and that some combination of factors—with the Supreme Court, perhaps a need to maintain credibility that outweighs any loss of public acceptance foreseeable from a perception of inadequate generality—presses strongly for a resolution that conflicts with the indicated outcome, the "logical" decision, in (c). It is precisely here that the process of case-by-case adjudication maximizes the attention given to the "flesh and blood" of the case before the court, "to things," in the phrase of Holmes quoted by Bickel, "not words." Outweighing the need to maintain doctrinal consistency, in short, is the fearsome pressure of decision, the knowledge that even a refusal to decide involves not only a continuation, but also in part a legitimation, of the (by hypothesis) undesirable status quo contained in the case presently at issue. In such a situation the measure of discretion inevitably entailed by common-law methods of adjudication is embodied in the pressure toward simply deciding the single case, toward reaching a decision in (e) that conflicts with the result indicated in (c),

---

232. Rostow, *American Legal Realism and the Sense of the Profession*, 34 Rocky Mt. L. Rev. 123, 141–42 (1962).

234

and leaving to a later case, or to a later bench, the possibility of formulating an acceptable distinction in (d).

The description given above is not, of course, intended to suggest either that sloppiness in opinion writing ought to be condoned in common-law adjudication or that the dilemma being delineated will often be encountered. Nor can decisions such as that suggested in (e) long survive in the law if the issue on which they bear continues to be actively litigated. Unless within a reasonable period of time they become incorporated into an articulated, rationalizable exception to the general rule, they must inevitably become, in Rostow's phrase, "stunted branches," "cases that lead nowhere."

There is, however, another possibility, one canvassed by Bickel in connection with his justification for the Court's avoidance of the "momentous constitutional issue" lurking in the background of the *Garner* case:[233] "But then, nothing may have to be faced, or what must be faced may arise in a different social and political context. As many a southern and border city has demonstrated, the sit-in problem is soluble—and beyond a doubt best solved—by processes other than judicial."[234] Case (d), in other words, may never arise or, if it does, the factors that represented the potentiality for conflict with (c) and (e) may have been transformed beyond recognition by the passage of time. Is it too early to suggest that the Communist cases of the 1950's are rapidly being assimilated to that status, that the recent transformations in the monolithic quality of the world Communist movement are rapidly rendering irrelevant the justification offered in those cases for the inapplicability of first amendment guarantees?

Whatever the applicability of this analysis to those particular decisions, it is clear that the alternative suggested by Bickel, the possibility that any particular formulation of a social or political problem may be only transitory, is what ultimately makes possible the art of government. That today's problems, even if not completely or rationally or logically soluble, will eventually be replaced by tomorrow's, is an insight that lies at the core of all political wisdom. It is also, of course, what Brandeis had in mind when he said of the Court: "The most important thing we do is not doing."[235] And it is, finally, the ultimate justification for the common law's reliance on "experience," for the case-by-case methods of adjudication in terms of which common-law judges make the law.

In the last analysis, the wisdom of "experience" is a humbling one. "Often," Rostow tells us, "the judges who participated in the process could not have described the tree that was growing." Thus when a judge decides simply the case before him, when he focuses on things rather than words,

233. *See* text accompanying notes 115–17 *supra*.
234. A. Bickel, *supra* note 206, at 177.
235. *Id.* at 71.

J. G. D., *Stanford Law Review*, Jan. 1968

235

the ultimate justification for his actions is not the certainty that he will reach the correct result in the particular instance. The certainty, rather, is that the words are inadequate, that even if a totally coherent and comprehensive system of law is theoretically possible, there is no warrant for believing that our judges are capable of finding and administering it.

Reliance upon common-law methods of adjudication, however, has consequences for society as well as for the judge. Thus, as we have seen, the rising incidence both of awareness concerning the Court and of group litigation tends to create a situation in which case (d) will rapidly be brought before the courts. Similarly, the breakdown of accepted limitations on the meaning of legal concepts, most evident in constitutional law but by no means confined to that area, makes it increasingly difficult to formulate even partially complete and coherent systems. This problem, the reverse side of the coin of "candor," arises because a widening of the meaning of fundamental legal concepts increases the number of situations to which a given principle is arguably applicable, and in which it may arguably conflict with some other principle.[236]

The heart of the difficulty is that stability represents one of the paramount demands that we make on the law. And stability is the child of "logic," of "clear and definite standards," and of the absence of conflict. The common law can meet this demand, it can achieve the status of "logic," but it can do so only over time, as the slow accretion of individual decisions works itself into a recognizable pattern. The key to the stability of the common law is, therefore, time: time in which to develop a pattern of decision whose meaning will be accessible to hindsight, and time in which to accommodate, in terms of shifting doctrine, the changes required of the law by changing social conditions. As the pace of social change accelerates, however, it is precisely the element of time that is increasingly denied to the common law. As a result, the prognosis for the continuing acceptability of case-by-case adjudication as the method by which constitutional litigation is conducted must eventually be the same as that for the Court's efforts to maintain satisfactory levels of principle and candor in the resolution of constitutional issues—one of an increasing incidence of failure.

## VII.

Even apart from the effects of accelerating social change, it has always been true that the common law has existed in an uneasy tension between the "logic" of doctrine and the "experience," the "flesh and blood," of the individual case. As is true of all common-law courts, much of the Supreme Court's prestige stems from the public's identification of the law with

---

236. *Cf.* Gilmore, *Legal Realism: Its Cause and Cure*, 70 YALE L.J. 1037 (1961).

236

"logic," with the pattern of decision rather than with the individual case. And, as is again true of all common-law courts, it is this identification that ultimately accounts for the reservoir of public acceptance upon which courts draw, not only when adherence to doctrine results in an unpopular decision, but also when the need to preserve institutional capacity leads to a decision inexplicable in terms of received doctrine or when an error is committed in the exercise of discretion.

It is thus only partially correct to assert, as Bickel does in demonstrating the "question-begging" nature of a demand for "an individual right to judgment by the Supreme Court," that "[t]here are crucial differences— which, of course, the opinions in *Marbury v. Madison* and *Cohens v. Virginia* seek to obscure—between the role of the Supreme Court in constitutional cases and the function of courts of general jurisdiction."[237] It would be more accurate to say that what the opinions in *Marbury* and *Cohens* are seeking to obscure is the fact that "logic" is not the whole of the law. The pressures requiring resort to "experience" are, of course, greater for the Supreme Court than for lower federal courts and the state judiciary. But the fact is that the Supreme Court is not alone, that it shares with all common-law courts the status of existing in the tension between the principled universe of "logic" and the expedient requirements of "experience."

## A.

As Bickel stresses, however, this tension assumes a significantly greater dimension with the Supreme Court. In large part, the source of this additional dimension is to be found in what Bickel refers to as "The Mystic Function" of the Court;[238] the sense in which the Court, because it "is seen as a continuum," because "[i]t is never, like other institutions, renewed at a single stroke," serves "to concretize the symbol of the Constitution," which, for our society, serves as "the symbol of nationhood, of continuity, of unity and common purpose."[239] One of the consequences of being cast in a symbolic role—the need to assume a stance that can be apprehended by the public in terms of moral norms—has been evocatively portrayed by Dean Manning:

> To the extent that our politics partake of the nature of a Morality Play, they have inevitably required, and generated, a set of theatrical conventions as arbitrary, and as acceptable, as those of any dramatic form. The vocabulary of our politics conforms to its role as a national Morality drama. That vocabulary is formal, dogmatic, simplified, symbolic, repetitive, and goal-setting; it is not descriptive and must not be thought of as being descriptive. And the actors in the political drama must, as in epic drama, appear as more than life-size, establishing, declaring, and

237. A. BICKEL, *supra* note 206, at 173.
238. *Id.* at 29–33.
239. *Id.* at 31.

237

appearing to live in accordance with, standards that are not of this world. We therefore demand ultimate moral pronouncements from our parties and our officials. We beatify or apotheosize our former Presidents, feeling the need for unifying national moral norms and having no national established church to do the job or to produce national saints.[240]

Manning, in the passage quoted, was considering the rhetoric of United States political campaigns and offering an explanation for the imposition upon our government officials of requirements for the divestment of holdings in commercial enterprises that go far beyond the purported necessity to avoid conflicts of interest, and that serve in fact to deprive government of so large a proportion of the society's administrative and technological talent that the effective formulation and implementation of national policy may seriously be threatened. Insofar as the Court also has a symbolic role to play in our society, however, it too is subject to the mandate of "establishing, declaring, and appearing to live in accordance with, standards that are not of this world." In the case of the Court, those standards require the maintenance of an appearance not only of incorruptibility—which the society largely, and correctly, takes for granted—but also of adherence to principle, to "logic," and to neutrality.

The impact of such requirements is most clearly apparent in the rhetoric of decision, in what was referred to in part III–F as matters of "phrasing." When a dissent characterizes the majority's disposition as an impermissible "amending of the Constitution," for example, the rhetoric serves precisely the same function as an accusation by the minority in the House that the majority are "employing steamroller tactics" or "playing partisan politics." The dissenting judge is fully aware, of course, that any judicial interpretation of a constitutional principle involves a pro tanto "amendment" of the Constitution, just as the House minority knows full well that "partisan politics" are an integral part of the legislative process and that the majority's electoral mandate involves, in part, a commitment to enact certain policies and, if necessary, to use "steamroller tactics."

Neither the dissenting judge nor the House minority, then, is suffering from any illusions concerning the nature of the judicial or legislative process. What they are doing is adverting to the existence of certain overriding goals that those processes are expected to fulfill: stability and continuity, in the case of judicial interpretation of the Constitution, and the need for compromising competing interests and for giving some recognition to the legitimate demands of the minority party, in the case of the legislative process. In both instances, therefore, the appeal is to the symbols in terms of which those overriding goals are expressed: an unchanging Constitution,

---

240. Manning, *The Purity Potlatch: An Essay on Conflicts of Interest, American Government, and Moral Escalation*, 24 Fed. B.J. 239, 243 (1964).

238

whose meaning is clear and accessible to all, and which is simply applied by the judiciary to the cases that are brought before it; and a legislative process that represents the work, not of members of political parties or agents of interest groups, but of statesmen whose sole concern is the attainment of the national good.

Another example of the impact of the requirement that symbolic appearances be maintained is to be found in the Court's refusal to assign significance to changes in the policymaking personnel of an administrative agency, the refusal to treat such changes as a reason for either more or less stringent scrutiny of that agency's decisions. The suggestion offered is not, of course, that the Court ought to scrutinize an agency's decisions more closely because individual Justices personally dislike or distrust the policymaking members of the agency. No court could long survive public awareness of such flouting of the ideal of dispassionate inquiry to which our judiciary is held. But assume that the legislative history of a given statute indicates that it was to be interpreted in a certain fashion, and that both the administrative agency charged with its implementation and the Court had agreed on the propriety of that mode of interpretation over a period of years. And assume further a change in agency personnel resulting from the entry into office of an administration out of sympathy with the aims of the statute (does the NLRB under Eisenhower's administration at least partially fit this description?). Why, under such circumstances, does not the change in personnel provide a proper occasion for a judicial announcement that that agency's decisions will henceforth be subject to more stringent scrutiny?

The answer, it is suggested, is not that the Court is under any illusion as to the unimportance of the political persuasion of agency personnel in determining the spirit in which congressional statutes are implemented; a Court that suffered from such an illusion would have to regard as meaningless the many statutory provisions that specify the political composition of the policymaking arms of administrative agencies. The crucial point is, rather, that the Court is charged with the function of upholding the symbol of an evenhanded Government, characterized by continuity of policy and devoted to the interests of the nation as a whole rather than to the attainment of parochial, partisan goals. And that ideal, symbolized by the belief that we are ruled by a "government of laws, not men," would be seriously compromised by overt recognition of the fact that a change in party, even without an accompanying change in legislative mandates, can nevertheless result in a change in law.

Recognition of this consequence of the Court's symbolic role severely limits the applicability of any requirement of "candor" in measuring that institution's achievements. Shapiro's fears concerning the possibility of "the

J. G. D., *Stanford Law Review*, Jan. 1968

239

Court's loss of that precious political asset, a reputation for candor," are based on the premises that the public looks at opinions, not results, and that it demands of those opinions the utmost candor concerning the bases of decision. The short answer is that matters are far more complex than that. To begin with, it is a far more likely hypothesis, as we have seen, that the public responds as much to results, to the outcome of a given decision, as to the rhetoric contained in the opinion.[241] Even more important, however, are the complicating factors introduced by the Court's symbolic function.

It is true, of course, that there exist severe limits on the extent to which the content of symbols such as those considered above are taken literally by the public. The public is aware, and to some extent accepts as inevitable, that, for example, the staffing of many governmental offices is dictated by narrowly political considerations; that our government is, in a sense—as the statutory provisions specifying the political composition of administrative agencies attest—a government of men as much as of laws. But that fact alone does not entail the proposition that an increase in public sophistication will, or ought to, lead to a public willingness to accept a rhetoric that substitutes greater candor concerning the processes by which the polity is governed for continued adherence to the symbols cherished by the society.

In some cases, where the conflict between symbol and reality is particularly acute, and where continued adherence to symbolic rhetoric would seriously interfere with the efficient performance of the workaday governmental task, such a result may well follow. But the point remains that continued adherence to the symbolic content of government is not just a matter of "keeping up appearances," that the overriding social goals embodied in those symbols have both meaning and importance. It is thus of the highest importance that our legislators be reminded constantly of their obligation to be more than members of a political party or agents of an interest group, and that our judges display a proper regard for the traditional wisdom contained in precedents and the social utility of continuing adherence to established patterns of social organization.

But these requirements are only half of the story of government, for the work of this world, the world in which the symbols are only partially and sometimes operative, also urgently requires doing. If society is to continue to function efficiently, in other words, parochial interests must continue to be represented effectively in the legislative process; and political parties, despite the fact that they are unsanctioned by any mention in the constitutional text, represent the means developed by our polity for fulfilling this task. Similarly, a Court concerned exclusively with adherence to the "logic" of precedent could not long succeed in the task of keeping relevant to

---

241. *See, e.g.*, text accompanying notes 134–35 *supra*.

240

present-day social needs a constitutional text phrased in the language of 18th-century concerns and concepts.

That task, it might be argued, is properly performed, not by the Court, but by the people of the society through the democratic process of amending the Constitution. Two factors, however, militate against such a conclusion. First, the cumbersome and complicated machinery provided for amendment casts serious doubt on both the efficacy and the democratic nature of reliance on this process, if by democratic we mean responsive to the majority will. More importantly, a Constitution that had been amended, rather than judicially interpreted, in the majority of instances in which such interpretation was required to maintain it as a continuingly relevant document, would by that very fact cease effectively to serve as the symbol of continuity that represents its greatest contribution to the continuing stability of our society.[242] The short of the matter, then, is that the Court's symbolic function is best fulfilled in terms of what Dean Manning designates a "dramatic form" and that our society requires, from that dramatic form, a far more complicated mixture of appearance and reality than Shapiro's insistence on candor would allow for.

It is precisely because we entrust them with so important and complex a function that being a Supreme Court Justice, rather than a law professor, regularly appears in public opinion polls as the most desirable occupation in our society. Law professors tend to be more skilled than many Justices in the "logic" of the law and would no doubt be more capable, in many instances, of meeting Shapiro's criterion of candor in opinion writing. But the task that we entrust to our Justices requires the political sensitivity of the statesman as well as the doctrinal skills of the lawyer. It is for this reason that Justices are selected by means of a political appointment process rather than by a nationwide system of examinations, and that the high degree of rationality required of Justices by Bickel,[243] even if it were possible of attainment, would in the end prove to be an insufficient criterion.

The objection might be taken that the description given above represents an apotheosis of the role of a Supreme Court Justice that no actual incumbent could hope to achieve. But such an objection confuses a job description with an assessment of the degree of skill required to perform a given task satisfactorily. No marriage is perfect, and precious few are great, but the fact that any marriage would disintegrate under the stress of an insistent demand for complete candor is nevertheless sufficient to convince us that intellectual honesty is inadequate as the sole criterion for selection of a marital partner.

---

242. *See, e.g.,* A. BICKEL, POLITICS AND THE WARREN COURT 155 (1965).
243. *See* text following note 132 *supra.*

J. G. D., *Stanford Law Review*, Jan. 1968

Similarly, in the case of the Court, we cannot legitimately withhold our consent from its activities until we become convinced that the nine men who staff it are capable of performing perfectly. We need only agree that there exists a role that must be performed, and that our selection process for filling that role is as satisfactory as possible. After that, as in all human endeavors, we can only ask that the nine men we have chosen do the very best they can. In government as in marriage, there comes a point where consent is based on trust. It is precisely at such a point that the possibility of abuse of power is greatest. But that, of course, is the meaning of trust, the meaning that ultimately gives content to the "Morality Play."

## B.

Even if one accepts these consequences of the Court's symbolic function, however, the question remains how the Court's power is to be confined within its legitimate boundaries. As we have seen, it was this concern, based on his view that the Court during the 1930's was making decisions properly entrusted to Congress, that underlay Mr. Justice Black's insistence that the Court rely on the "logic" of constitutional principles rather than the "experience" of the common law.

To a considerable extent, Shapiro simply ignores the question thus posed by Black. "[I]n the free speech area," for example, Shapiro argues that "the Supreme Court represents some interest groups while other government agencies represent others."[244] Consequently, "[t]he Supreme Court can actually contribute to greater democracy by vigorously furthering the interests of its groups, which are not being protected by other parts of the government, so that all interests in our society may have a voice in making policy decisions."[245] Such an analysis assumes, however, that the impact of a decision by the Court and one by Congress are the same; whereas the problems posed by judicial review, not only for Black but also for Hand and Wechsler, inhere precisely in the finality embodied in a finding of unconstitutionality, in the fact that such a holding, unlike legislative action, largely forecloses further action by other agencies of government representing other interest groups.

Both Congress in passing a statute and the Court in upholding its validity are, after all, passing judgment on the same statute. If all that is involved is the same type of policy decision made by bodies whose difference is simply that they represent different interest groups, on what basis is Congress compelled to respect the decisions of the Court? Shapiro himself betrays awareness of this point when he argues that Congress cannot itself make final determinations of the constitutionality of measures that argu-

244. M. Shapiro, Freedom of Speech: The Supreme Court and Judicial Review 2 (1966).
245. *Id. See also* text accompanying notes 14–16 *supra.*

242

ably infringe first amendment rights because its deliberations focus too much on the "marginal adjustments and compromises" of the legislative process.[246] Yet his analysis of the work of the Court would make it simply one more participant in that process.

If the Court's decisions are entitled to a special sort of deference denied to acts of Congress, there must be some set of differences between the two institutions that can account for this phenomenon—a set of differences ignored in Shapiro's analysis. The best starting point for delineation of those differences is Shapiro's description of Congress as a social system in which participants can efficiently attain their legislative goals only by minimizing conflict within the system, by helping to preserve that system through cooperation with the floor leadership and heads of committees.[247] Contrast with this the degree of independence from such institutional pressures enjoyed by Supreme Court Justices: the absence of any committee system; the freedom from party discipline; and the very considerable freedom, afforded by life tenure, even from any analogue to constituent pressure, all of which ensure that decisions of the Court represent neither attempts to preserve a given social system nor the result of "marginal adjustments and compromises" among competing power centers, but rather the expression of what the individual Justices collectively interpret the constitutional mandate to be.

Equally important in defining the institutional differences between Congress and the Court is the greater importance of craft pressures in connection with the latter's work—the need to present an adequate justification for the result reached. This factor is based in considerable part on the tradition of scholarly criticism of the Court's work, which enforces demands of intellectual coherence on the rationale offered for decision.[248] But it rests also on the procedures that the Court has adopted from the common law: the setting forth of the rationale for decision in an opinion open to public scrutiny, and the acceptance of the limitation that, with the narrowly confined exception of judicial notice, a decision is to be arrived at, and support for its rationale obtained, exclusively from the evidence in the record before the Court. It is ultimately these differences that justify the conclusion that the majority of constitutional issues are better resolved through the processes of the Court than through the processes of Congress, and that the Court's resolution of those issues is properly entitled to a degree of deference and finality not normally accorded to acts of Congress.

It is therefore not sufficient to determine, when deciding whether or not the Court has acted properly in taking cognizance of a given issue, that the

246. *Id.* at 29–30.
247. *See id.* at 20–21.
248. *Cf.* A. BICKEL, *supra* note 206, at 51–55.

J. G. D., *Stanford Law Review*, Jan. 1968

other branches of the government have long disregarded, and are likely to continue to disregard, the problems involved. It is necessary further to determine whether the issue is one with which the Court can deal while continuing to satisfy both craft pressures and the needs of its symbolic role—the complex and often conflicting demands for adherence to logic, to neutrality, and to experience that our society makes upon it. It is this second step that Shapiro, in his analysis of the *Reapportionment Cases*,[249] fails to take.

Shapiro approves of the decision in *Baker v. Carr*[250] precisely on the basis that a serious problem existed that no other agency of government was capable of dealing with.[251] What Shapiro disapproves are the decisions following *Baker*, the *Reapportionment Cases*, which established the "one man, one vote" principle. Shapiro's objection is not, of course, that the "one man, one vote" principle lacks neutrality. Quite the contrary, Shapiro sees that principle as embodying all of the worst faults that result from an insistence on a relentlessly generalizable rule of decision,[252] and his penetrating survey of the complex and unresolved issues in political philosophy raised by a democratic form of government[253] makes clear his conviction that "one man, one vote" constitutes an oversimplified political slogan rather than a desirable solution to the problems of malapportionment:

> Majoritarian elections and representative government are not ends or values in themselves but are at best instrumental values, "good" only to the extent that they contribute to the goals of liberal democracy. Democratic theorists cannot simply say—and American democratic theory has never consistently held—that "one man, one vote" majority rule is "good." They can say only that "one man, one vote" majority rule is good so far and only so far as it contributes to maximum individual political equality and freedom. No democratic theorist can state flatly and finally just how much of the "one man, one vote" principle should be introduced into American politics. He can only make rough adjustments based on estimates of the political consequences.
>
> It is exactly this approach that the Court took in *Baker* when it, in effect, said that Americans have reached a consensus that a proportion of eighteen to one is a hindrance to democracy. Neither they nor we, however, can say that a one-to-one proportion always maximizes democracy. In *Baker*, the Court stated the American balance between "Madisonian" and "populistic" democracy and avoided binding itself to precise standards of representation, any one of which would be theoretically incorrect because democratic theory does not contain any such precise standards.
>
> It is at this point that the Court as political theorist might have become Court

---

249. Reynolds v. Sims, 377 U.S. 533 (1964); WMCA, Inc. v. Lomenzo, 377 U.S. 633 (1964); Maryland Comm. for Fair Representation v. Tawes, 377 U.S. 656 (1964); Davis v. Mann, 377 U.S. 678 (1964); Roman v. Sincock, 377 U.S. 695 (1964); Lucas v. Forty-Fourth Gen. Assembly, 377 U.S. 713 (1964).

250. 369 U.S. 186 (1962).

251. M. SHAPIRO, LAW AND POLITICS IN THE SUPREME COURT: NEW APPROACHES TO POLITICAL JURISPRUDENCE 233–34, 236 (1964).

252. *See id.* at 232–33, 236.

253. *See id.* at 216–32.

244

as political scientist, analyzing the actual operation of the political forces around it. For once the democratic theorist recognizes that electoral equality is not equivalent to political equality or freedom but is simply a means that sometimes contributes to and sometimes conflicts with these ends, he must decide when, where, and how much electoral equality should be added to or subtracted from the political system in which he operates, in order to make it more democratic. Given the complexity of contemporary American politics, such assessments are always difficult, but one thing is fairly certain. Whatever the assessments, they are likely to suggest delicate adjustments rather than sledge-hammer blows. It seems highly unlikely that either a continuation of the present crazy quilt of malapportionment or introduction of total and immediate equalization of votes will yield a democratically ideal result. The *Baker* decision allowed the Supreme Court to make its own case-by-case assessment of the political balance in any given state and to fit its remedies to the situations it found. When it is recalled that the processes of group politics may give to members of certain groups far greater political influence than to others and that the relative strength of various groups is markedly affected by the geographic distributions of population, resources, industries, and so forth—distributions that vary markedly from state to state—whoever attempts to achieve greater equality must be prepared to make differing adjustments in differing areas.[254]

Shapiro then shifts his focus to those decisions following *Baker—Gray v. Sanders*,[255] *Wesberry v. Sanders*,[256] and the *Reapportionment Cases*—the decisions that resulted in the "one man, one vote" formulation:

The new decisions fundamentally ignore all that we have learned about the group nature of politics. By adopting the most simplistic view of the political process, and particularly of the process of representation, the Court equates the electoral and the political processes and thinks to assure each citizen "equal protection of the laws" in the political sphere by giving each citizen a vote equal to every other's. I have tried to show earlier that such a position glosses over or ignores the basic paradox hidden behind the notion of government by the people and mistakes an imperfect expedient, majority voting, for the essence of democracy. . . . A vision of the political process as no more than the electoral process and of each citizen as exercising his whole political power in the individual act of voting cannot properly serve even the most populistic philosophy. For in the complex politics of group bargaining and shifting temporary majorities that we actually have in the United States, inequalities in voting strength may contribute in the over-all equality of all participants in the political process as a whole. Blanket and blind enforcement of electoral equality will only decrease the political inequalities in some states at the cost of increasing them in others. The result of the Court's new rulings in terms of real political equality will be largely random. In the end they may achieve somewhat greater over-all equality but only because the sum of new equalities will exceed the sum of new inequalities. Viewed as an attempt actually to contribute to greater political equality in the United States, rather than simply as a philosophical editorial, the Court's new position is little more than a random stab.[257]

254. *Id.* at 244–45.
255. 372 U.S. 368 (1963).
256. 376 U.S. 1 (1964).
257. M. SHAPIRO, *supra* note 251, at 249.

J. G. D., *Stanford Law Review*, Jan. 1968

245

Shapiro's view of the proper role of the Court in the *Reapportionment Cases* is echoed in Mr. Justice Stewart's dissent from those decisions:[258]

Representative government is a process of accommodating group interests through democratic institutional arrangements. Its function is to channel the numerous opinions, interests, and abilities of the people of a State into the making of the State's public policy. Appropriate legislative apportionment, therefore, should ideally be designed to insure effective representation in the State's legislature, in cooperation with other organs of political power, of the various groups and interests making up the electorate. In practice, of course, this ideal is approximated in the particular apportionment system of any State by a realistic accommodation of the diverse and often conflicting political forces operating within the State.

I do not pretend to any specialized knowledge of the myriad of individual characteristics of the several States, beyond the records in the cases before us today. But I do know enough to be aware that a system of legislative apportionment which might be best for South Dakota, might be unwise for Hawaii with its many islands, or Michigan with its Northern Peninsula. I do know enough to realize that Montana with its vast distances is not Rhode Island with its heavy concentrations of people. I do know enough to be aware of the great variations among the several States in their historic manner of distributing legislative power—of the Governors' Councils in New England, of the broad powers of initiative and referendum retained in some States by the people, of the legislative power which some States give to their Governors, by the right of veto or otherwise, of the widely autonomous home rule which many States give to their cities. The Court today declines to give any recognition to these considerations and countless others, tangible and intangible, in holding unconstitutional the particular systems of legislative apportionment which these States have chosen. Instead, the Court says that the requirements of the Equal Protection Clause can be met in any State only by the uncritical, simplistic, and heavy-handed application of sixth-grade arithmetic.

. . . .

The fact is, of course, that population factors must often to some degree be subordinated in devising a legislative apportionment plan which is to achieve the important goal of ensuring a fair, effective, and balanced representation of the regional, social, and economic interests within a State. And the further fact is that throughout our history the apportionments of State Legislatures have reflected the strongly felt American tradition that the public interest is composed of many diverse interests, and that in the long run it can better be expressed by a medley of component voices than by the majority's monolithic command. What constitutes a rational plan reasonably designed to achieve this objective will vary from State to State, since each State is unique, in terms of topography, geography, demography, history, heterogeneity and concentration of population, variety of social and economic interests, and in the operation and interrelation of its political institutions. But so long as a State's apportionment plan reasonably achieves, in the light

---

258. Justice Stewart's dissenting opinion in the *Reapportionment Cases* appears in 377 U.S. at 744. The dissent applied to Lucas v. Forty-Fourth Gen. Assembly, 377 U.S. 713 (1964), and WMCA, Inc. v. Lomenzo, 377 U.S. 633 (1964). In the other cases he did not dissent, but issued separate opinions stating either that the legislative apportionment in issue was irrational or (in *Maryland Comm. for Fair Representation v. Tawes*) that the case should be remanded for a determination of whether the "Maryland apportionment 'could be shown systematically to prevent ultimate effective majority rule.'" 377 U.S. at 677.

246

of the State's own characteristics, effective and balanced representation of all substantial interests, without sacrificing the principle of effective majority rule, that plan cannot be considered irrational.[259]

As the above quotations indicate, Stewart's interpretation of the requirements of the equal protection clause in apportionment cases is that the clause bars arbitrariness and systematic frustration of the will of the majority,[260] not that it mandates absolute equality. Such an interpretation is supportable by reference to both what the Court had said in *Baker*[261] and the equal protection doctrine contained in decisions applicable to other than apportionment situations.[262] If, in addition to these virtues, Stewart's position also embodies a superior grasp of the principles of political science and political philosophy, why did the Court refuse to adopt it?

The answer to that question is surely not that the factors involved are inherently too complex for judicial analysis. That apportionment cases involve a formidable degree of complexity is undeniable, but the Court has long dealt with the complexities inherent in fields such as antitrust, and there is no reason to believe that the Court would be less successful at analyzing a given reapportionment problem than will the Governors' commissions and legislative committees presently undertaking this task. The answer is to be found, rather, in Shapiro's insistence that the Court examine "more than the electoral process," in Stewart's view that what must be considered is whether "a realistic accommodation of the diverse and often conflicting political forces operating within the State" has been achieved.

What both Stewart and Shapiro would require the Court to do in apportionment cases is to examine the realities of the distribution of political power within the State—the existence of voting blocs, the degree of party control over voters and officials, the position of the mass media, and the extent of financial backing available to the various factions, to mention only a few of the crucial inquiries. In dissenting from the invalidation of New York's apportionment,[263] for example, Stewart quotes Elihu Root's remarks to the New York constitutional convention of 1894, justifying the giving of fewer seats to New York City than a "one man, one vote" rule would require:

The question is whether thirty separate centers of 38,606 each scattered over the country are to be compared upon the basis of absolute numerical equality with one center of thirty times 38,606 in one city, with all the multiplications of power that comes [*sic*] from representing a single interest, standing together on all measures

259. Lucas v. Forty-Fourth Gen. Assembly, 377 U.S. 713, 749–51 (1964) (dissenting opinion) (footnote omitted).
260. *See id.* at 753–54.
261. *See* M. SHAPIRO, *supra* note 251, at 242–43.
262. *See* Lucas v. Forty-Fourth Gen. Assembly, 377 U.S. 713, 751–53 (1964) (dissenting opinion).
263. WMCA, Inc. v. Lomenzo, 377 U.S. 633 (1964); *see* note 258 *supra*.

247

against a scattered and disunited representation from the thirty widely separated single centers of 38,606. Thirty men from one place owing their allegiance to one political organization, representing the interest of one community, voting together, acting together solidly; why, they are worth double the scattered elements of power coming from hundreds of miles apart.[264]

Whether or not it is correct to assume that the representatives of a large city are under pressure to represent only a single, homogenous interest, the quotation makes crystal clear that the formula espoused by Stewart and Shapiro would indeed require the Court to canvass the actual workings of the floor leadership in the legislative branches, the mechanisms of party control not only over voters and the city government but also over elected representatives—in short, the details of the petty corruption and networks of personal influence that all too often constitute crucial sources of power in municipal politics. Given the Court's institutional arrangements, however, it could investigate these matters only by requiring lower courts to build records on these issues. Is this a demand we can reasonably make of our courts? Even assuming that the evidence was available and would be forthcoming, is it likely that our society could accept, as a steady diet, the spectacle of the judiciary solemnly ruling on the accuracy of a political boss's testimony concerning the sources of his power over voters and the degree of control that he exercised over elected officials?

If the analysis, adumbrated earlier, of the function performed by political rhetoric has any validity whatsoever, the answer must be in the negative. The issue is not that the almost imperceptible gradations such investigations would reveal might go far toward undermining the neutrality of the principle being applied. The decisive point is, rather, that the content of the records that would necessarily have to be made, the image of our politics that the Court would be projecting, would be so totally incompatible with the content of the "Morality Play" as seriously to compromise the symbolic role not only of the judiciary[265] but primarily of the political system that was being surveyed.

---

264. 3 REVISED RECORD OF THE CONSTITUTIONAL CONVENTION OF THE STATE OF NEW YORK 1215 (1900), *quoted in* 377 U.S. at 764.

265. *Cf.* Mr. Justice Frankfurter, dissenting, in *Baker v. Carr*: "Manifestly, the Equal Protection Clause supplies no clearer guide for judicial examination of apportionment methods than would the Guarantee Clause itself. Apportionment, by its character, is a subject of extraordinary complexity, involving—even after the fundamental theoretical issues concerning what is to be represented in a representative legislature have been fought out or compromised—considerations of geography, demography, electoral convenience, economic and social cohesions or divergencies among particular local groups, communications, the practical effects of political institutions like the lobby and the city machine, ancient traditions and ties of settled usage, respect for proven incumbents of long experience and senior status, mathematical mechanics, censuses compiling relevant data, and a host of others. Legislative responses throughout the country to the reapportionment demands of the 1960 Census have glaringly confirmed that these are not factors that lend themselves to evaluations of a nature that are the staple of judicial determinations or for which judges are equipped to adjudicate by legal training or experience or native wit. And this is the more so true because in every strand of this complicated, intricate web of values meet the contending forces of partisan politics. The practical significance of apportionment is that the next election results may differ because of it. Apportionment battles are

248

The Court cannot, in Bickel's terms, legitimate the politics of, for example, one-party rule by basing a constitutional decision on firsthand testimony concerning its operations. Nor could evidence consisting solely of charts, graphs, electoral statistics, and the testimony of expert witnesses meet the requirements of the Stewart and Shapiro formulas, which insist that apportionment involves "more than the electoral process" and that the proper inquiry must consist of a comprehensive analysis of the distribution of political power throughout the state. Given that quest, resort to the testimony of political-power holders concerning the existence of informal channels of power seems well-nigh unavoidable.

It will not do, therefore, to approve the decision in *Baker v. Carr* and then to disavow the principle arrived at in the *Reapportionment Cases*, for the institutional needs of the Court and the interplay between the demands made upon it by its symbolic function and the requirement that decisions be based on evidence contained in the record inevitably resulted in the adoption of a standard that does not require involvement of the judiciary in the spectacle portrayed above—in short, "one man, one vote." The significant question in the apportionment controversy is the one that both Stewart and Shapiro ignore, the analogue to the question Wechsler must be taken to have answered in the negative in assessing the *Brown* decision:[266] Whether, *given the fact that a "one man, one vote" standard*

overwhelmingly party or intra-party contests. It will add a virulent source of friction and tension in federal-state relations to embroil the federal judiciary in them." 369 U.S. at 323–24 (footnotes omitted).

266. *See* text accompanying note 96 *supra*.

The question as posed here is, however, subject to several qualifications. First, adoption of a "one man, one vote" standard by no means answers the question of the number of situations to which the Court will apply such a standard. Thus, as both Bickel and Wechsler implicitly predicted, the "colorblind" standard that underlay *Brown* has not been applied to "benign quota" situations. And similar limitations have already been imposed by the Court on the applicability of the "one man, one vote" standard. *See, e.g.,* Sailors v. Board of Educ., 387 U.S. 105 (1967) ("one man, one vote" standard irrelevant to local nonlegislative school officials chosen by essentially appointive process); Fortson v. Morris, 385 U.S. 231 (1966) (state legislature not disqualified, by reason of malapportionment, from voting in runoff election for governor where previously held that legislature had until 1968 to reapportion). Nor does adoption of such a standard, even apart from the possibility of permissible degrees of variation from an ideal apportionment, bar the utilization of devices such as gerrymanders for accommodating many of the same political pressures that had previously resulted in malapportionment. *See In re* Apportionment of Mich. Legislature, 376 Mich. 410, 137 N.W.2d 495 (1965), 376 Mich. 410, 138 N.W.2d 16 (1965), 377 Mich. 396, 140 N.W.2d 436, *appeal dismissed sub nom.* Badgley v. Hare, 385 U.S. 114 (1966) (per curiam) (want of substantial federal question); Neal, *Baker v. Carr: Politics in Search of Law,* 1962 S. CT. REV. 252, 277–78.

There is, finally, the question whether, given the inevitability of a "one man, one vote" standard, the *Baker* opinion should have "candidly" canvassed the jurisdictional issue in these terms. To do so would have required the Court to discount several possibilities that appeared at least feasible, if not likely, at the time the decision was rendered: the possibility that the analysis given in the text above was erroneous, and that some standard short of "one man, one vote" could have been developed; the possibility that litigation would proceed in such a fashion as to make it unnecessary for the Court at any early date to reach the issue of the ultimate standard to be applied, either because cases could be disposed of upon the basis of more limited issues, or because the state and lower federal courts would apply standards approximating "one man, one vote" without further guidance; and finally, the possibility that an aroused electorate would force state legislatures to undertake their own reapportionments, the possibility, in short, that further judicial intervention would not be required at all. History, of course, has seen none of these possibilities realized, and in this limited sense Shapiro's call for greater "candor" in *Baker v. Carr* seems on balance to be justified. The issue, however, was a good

*would have to be applied*, the consequences of malapportionments were sufficiently serious that greater injury would have been done to the Court's prestige by a refusal to deal with them than by the public controversy that application of that standard aroused.

Shapiro's condemnation of the reapportionment and segregation decisions, like the insistence on candor that results in the coalescence of his assessments of the Court's work with those of the "modest," thus arises from his disregard of the institutional needs of the Court, a failure that seems all the more startling in the context of his insistence that the Court be viewed as a political institution. Our final inquiry must be, therefore, a search for the sources of that failure.

## VIII.

The considerable interest demonstrated by legal scholars in the institutional structure of courts has been part of the search for limitations on judicial discretion. Much of the significant literature in this area is premised on the hypothesis that analysis of the institutional role and capacity of the judiciary will make possible the formulation of guidelines in terms of which courts can be confined within their legitimate sphere of authority.[267] It is this quest, as we have seen, that underlies Justice Black's prescription of logic rather than experience in constitutional adjudication and that makes so important the question insistently raised by Black and ignored by Shapiro of the existence of standards by which the decisions that are properly Congress' can be distinguished from those properly the Court's.[268] Bickel's mediating devices represent one response to this dilemma, and their derivation from the doctrines of "lawyer's law" on which Shapiro also focuses[269] underlines the extent to which the lawyer, in this instance, has displayed a far more sensitive regard for institutional considerations than has the political scientist.

The most important clue to the origins of this anomaly is provided by the fact that Shapiro's focus, unlike Bickel's, is not on the activity of the Court as such, but rather exclusively on the interaction of the Court with other agencies of government. This difference is clearly apparent, for example, in the argument offered by Shapiro to justify his central postulate, the propriety of treating courts as political institutions:

> That courts are political agencies is self-evident. They are part of government, they make public policy, and they are an integral part of the law-making and enforce-

---

deal more complicated than Shapiro suggests, precisely because of the existence of those institutional demands that an insistence on "candor" necessarily overlooks.

267. *See, e.g.*, H.M. HART & A. SACKS, THE LEGAL PROCESS (tent. ed. 1958); H.M. HART & H. WECHSLER, THE FEDERAL COURTS AND THE FEDERAL SYSTEM (1953); K. LLEWELLYN, *supra* note 225, at 19–51; H. WELLINGTON, LABOR AND THE LEGAL SYSTEM (tent. typescript ed. 1967).

268. *See* text accompanying note 244 *supra*.

269. *See* text accompanying notes 4–5 *supra*.

250

ment process which is the central focus of political activity. If legislatures are political and executives are political, then courts must be political since all three are inextricably bound together in the process of making law, and each sometimes performs the functions that each of the others performs at other times.[270]

Such a view, as we have seen, offers many valuable insights, but it utterly fails to provide a framework in terms of which boundaries among the various political institutions can be delineated; and precisely that, as the opinions of Black and the scholarly work of Wechsler and Bickel testify, is the important task.

Shapiro's focus on the process rather than the actor, on interactions within a given system rather than on the component parts of that system, is not, however, peculiar to his analysis of the work of the Court. It is evident in many recent studies by political scientists, including, for example, Professor Robert Dahl's pathbreaking exploration of the distribution of political power in the New Haven municipal setting, *Who Governs?*[271] As is stressed in the companion volume, Professor Nelson Polsby's *Community Power and Political Theory*,[272] the New Haven study had a theoretical as well as a descriptive function: that of demonstrating the extent to which power in our cities is decentralized and, consequently, of correcting the conclusions of those Polsby refers to as "social stratification" theorists to the effect that communities are ruled by a single "power elite."[273]

The method used in *Who Governs?* is to identify a number of important political decisions and the participants in them, to study the behavior of those participants in the course of decisionmaking, and to analyze the benefits and disadvantages accruing to various participants as a result of the outcomes that ensued. What Dahl found was that no single social or economic group either controlled the decisionmaking process or regularly benefited from the results reached. Further, there was remarkably little overlap among the participants in the various New Haven decisions studied by Dahl.[274] In connection with the urban renewal program, for example, although the mayor created a citizens' action commission composed of representatives of the economic elite, Dahl's study revealed that the commission almost never initiated any proposal, nor vetoed or altered one put before it by the mayor.[275] Dahl concluded, therefore, that power in New Haven is held by constantly shifting, issue-oriented coalitions, with consid-

270. M. Shapiro, *Stability and Change in Judicial Decision-Making: Incrementalism or Stare Decisis?*, 2 Law in Transition Q. 134 (1965). For a similar view see Dahl, *Decision-Making in a Democracy: The Supreme Court as a National Policy-Maker*, 6 J. Pub. L. 279 (1957).
271. R. Dahl, Who Governs? Democracy and Power in an American City (1961).
272. N. Polsby, Community Power and Political Theory (1963).
273. *See id.* at 69–97.
274. R. Dahl, *supra* note 271, at 175.
275. *Id.* at 131.

J. G. D., *Stanford Law Review*, Jan. 1968

erable scope being given to a vigorous mayor determined to exploit his political resources to the utmost.

The primary difficulty with *Who Governs?* as an analysis of the existing distribution of power is its assumption that the decisions canvassed represented conflicts sufficiently serious to force all potentially affected powerholders to mobilize their resources in the hopes of obtaining a favorable outcome. As Dahl himself recognizes, however, in connection with two of the three areas he studied—public schools and political nominations— it can convincingly be argued that the economic and social elite, which lives primarily in the suburbs, is largely indifferent to possible outcomes.[276] Moreover, in connection with the third area studied, that of urban renewal, it is far from clear that New Haven's economic elite saw its interests as being significantly threatened rather than advanced. And even if members of the elite were aware that the urban renewal program had certain implications that ran counter to their interests, it nevertheless remains possible that those implications were perceived as being outweighed by the advantages accruing to them.

The important question, then, the question that Dahl never asks in connection with, for example, the power of the citizens' action commission, is whether that commission failed to assert itself because it was powerless or because, given the program as proposed by the mayor, it was indifferent to further modifications. The inquiry is whether the commission's failure to oppose the mayor's proposals represents an index of powerlessness or can be explained, rather, by the hypothesis that the mayor never proposed to the commission anything that he thought that body might reject. If the latter hypothesis is true, and the mayor would in fact have formulated different proposals had he thought the commission would accept them, who then holds power in New Haven?

Such a question ultimately raises the issue of the possible priorities of an elite. Dahl's method of investigation could reveal the true distribution of power in New Haven only if every possible elite assigned the highest priority to never suffering any disadvantage whatsoever from the outcome of any decision reached in any area of New Haven life. Given that postulate, the fact that Dahl's studies reveal the absence of elite participation in certain decisions and the existence of outcomes that to some extent disadvantage the elite would indeed indicate a lack of power on their part. The more likely hypothesis, however, one that Dahl himself apparently accepts,[277] is that members of the elite will not feel compelled even to enter the arena studied by Dahl unless they perceive what they regard as important interests to be threatened. The difficulty is that Dahl resolutely refuses

---

276. *See id.* at 70–71.
277. *See id.* at 224–25, 237–38, 270–301.

252

to address the difference between those conflicts that an elite would perceive as both significant and threatening and those to which it would remain relatively indifferent.[278]

None of the above, of course, purports to deny the significant contribution made by *Who Governs?* to the study of the functioning of political power in local communities. As Dahl convincingly demonstrates, the ways in which such power is exercised are far more complicated than the social-stratification theorists would have us believe. But that demonstration, as we have seen, falls far short of embodying a convincing delineation of the actual distribution of power. The absence of a covert and all-encompassing network of influence that ensures elite participation in, and dictation of the outcome of, all New Haven decisions is not, after all, very startling news. Only the most ruthless and heavyhanded elite, or an elite fearing imminent loss of its power, would feel compelled to act in so assertive and undiscriminating a manner. In the end, therefore, rather than offering an analysis of the distribution of political power, what *Who Governs?* largely accomplishes is to supply a correct answer to an often irrelevant question.

In part, the objections advanced above to Dahl's methods can be epitomized as exemplifications of his failure to take into account what Professor Carl Friedrich first described as the rule of anticipated reactions: the hypothesis that much political behavior is governed by the actor's perceptions of, and adjustments for, the reactions he expects to be provoked by possible actions on his part.[279] Thus, if the citizens' action commission did exercise any power in New Haven's urban renewal program, it did so exclusively by forcing the mayor to propose only those measures that would not conflict with the reactions he anticipated from the commission. The total absence of overt conflict between the mayor and the commission, however, means that such a hypothesis would be viable only on the assumption that the mayor's assessment of the commission's probable reaction was unfailingly accurate.

Given the mayor's political skill, such an assumption is not untenable,[280] but the necessity for invoking it points up the major methodological problem inherent in the anticipated-reaction hypothesis: the extreme difficulty involved in obtaining data on the basis of which it can be either confirmed or disproved in any given situation. Dahl himself noted this difficulty in connection with a study of influence ranking in the United States Senate; there he encountered a problem he called

278. For a similar and more detailed discussion of these objections to Dahl's method see Bachrach & Baratz, *Two Faces of Power*, 56 AM. POL. SCI. REV. 947, 950–52 (1962).

279. *See* C. FRIEDRICH, CONSTITUTIONAL GOVERNMENT AND POLITICS: NATURE AND DEVELOPMENT 16–18 (1937); Simon, *Notes on the Observation and Measurement of Political Power*, 15 J. POL. 500, 505–06 (1953).

280. *See* Bachrach & Baratz, *supra* note 278, at 952 n.29.

J. G. D., *Stanford Law Review*, Jan. 1968

253

the problem of the chameleon. Suppose a Senator takes no prior position on any bill and always decides how to vote by guessing how the Senate majority will vote; then, if he is a perfect guesser, according to the ranking method used he will be placed in the highest rank. Our common sense tells us, however, that in this case it is the Senate that has power over the Senator, whereas the Senator has no influence on the votes of other Senators.

. . . .

. . . In order to identify chameleon behavior and separate it from actual attempts at influence, one cannot rely on roll-calls. One needs observations of the behavior of Senators prior to the roll-calls. But if it is true, as I have been arguing, that observations of this kind are available only with great difficulty, rarely for past sessions, and probably never in large numbers, then in fact the data needed are not likely to exist. But if they do not exist for the Senate, for what institutions are they likely to exist?[281]

We need not examine here the extent to which the absence of such data makes it impossible to reach judgments about who wields power in a given situation, although the existence of historians, whose trade consists of making such judgments, is persuasive evidence that the task is a possible one. Our primary concern is with a phenomenon that, although analogous to anticipated reactions, operates both more widely and less consciously—the phenomenon of the shared community expectation.

In connection with New Haven, Polsby makes explicit the impact of this phenomenon on the distribution of political power within the community:

Some, perhaps most, *possible* courses of action are never considered in community decision-making simply because they are inconceivable to the actors involved. No one seems ever to have seriously considered turning the privately owned New Haven Water Company over to the city, for example, although there seems to be no reason why this could not be done. The array of alternatives presented for community decision-making seems likely, then, to be determined by consideration [*sic*] very different from a rational canvassing of all technically feasible possibilities. What determines the agenda of alternatives within which community decision-making takes place?

There are several plausible answers to this question, but the current state of affairs seems to be centrally important in determining the future course of action. . . .

Dahl has suggested as a general principle that: "If A's goal requires a slight change or weak response from B, and C's goals require a great change or a strong response, then with equal resources, rate [*sic*] and efficiencies [of resource employment], A is more likely to succeed than C. Or, to put it another way, A can attain his political goals with *less influence* than C can. Thus, if A's goals fall well within 'political consensus' he may have to do little beyond maintaining the consensus; whereas if C's goals fall well outside the 'political consensus,' then for him to achieve his goals may require access to enormous resources."

. . . It is not enough . . . for an alternative to be technically feasible. It also

281. Dahl, *The Concept of Power*, 2 BEHAV. SCI. 201, 212–14 (1957).

254

must be politically palatable and relatively easy to accomplish; otherwise great amounts of influence have to be brought to bear with great skill and efficiency in order to secure its adoption. Conclusions that might be drawn from this are that the community agenda of alternatives is relatively insensitive to any but very great differences in the power of actors and that only influence differences of the greatest magnitude as between actors are likely to be reflected in changes in the alternatives presented to decision-makers.[282]

As exemplified by the quotation just given, investigators such as Dahl and Polsby typically devote little attention to ascertaining the origins of the "current state of affairs" or the content of the "community agenda of alternatives." This lack of attention is in part due precisely to the fact that the community agenda represents a shared set of expectations. In other words, because the agenda is the community's, because its content is not a source of conflict among groups within the community, the methods utilized by Dahl in *Who Governs?* are wholly inappropriate to the task of analyzing those origins or that content.

The contents of the agenda may of course—indeed, probably will—significantly favor one set of groups within the community. But as long as the disadvantaged groups do not disassociate themselves from that agenda, analysis of the conflict of interests thus created would require the postulate that the disadvantaged groups have a "real" interest that they are prevented from perceiving by their acceptance of the agenda. Such a postulate, however, because it involves making value judgments that cannot be correlated with the actual behavior of participants in the decisionmaking process, is extremely difficult to integrate into the conceptual structure underlying *Who Governs?*

Dahl's failure to explore the consequences of the existence of a community agenda is also at least partially due to a methodological problem analogous to that posed by the "chameleon." Thus, rejecting the suggestion that the power of a ruling elite might inhere precisely in the control that it exercises over the community consensus embodied in an agenda of alternatives and therefore that such control is inaccessible to an analysis of conflicts between the ruling elite and other groups, Dahl has argued that

either the consensus is perpetual and unbreakable, in which case there is no conceivable way of determining who is ruler and who is ruled. Or it is not. But if it is not, then there is some point in the process of forming opinions at which the one group will be seen to initiate and veto, while the rest merely respond. And we can only discover these points *by an examination of a series of concrete cases where key decisions are made*: decisions on taxation and expenditures, subsidies, welfare programs, military policy, and so on.[283]

---

282. N. POLSBY, *supra* note 272, at 133–35 (italics in original) (footnotes omitted).
283. Dahl, *A Critique of the Ruling Elite Model*, 52 AM. POL. SCI. REV. 463, 469 (1958) (italics in original).

J. G. D., *Stanford Law Review*, Jan. 1968

Two points need to be made concerning this theoretically unassailable proposition. First, the fact that the existence of the consensus benefits the elite does not provide a sufficient basis for assuming that the elite in some conscious sense controls or manipulates that consensus. The elite would presumably mobilize its resources in opposition to any attempt to change the consensus to its disadvantage, but as long as no such attempt occurs, as long as the consensus truly represents a shared set of *community* values, there is no reason to suppose that the elite's acceptance of those values is more self-conscious than their acceptance by any other group. Dahl's insistence on attacking only a model of an elite that actively manipulates the community consensus, rather than considering the possibility of an elite that is the passive beneficiary of the consensus, once again runs the risk of supplying a correct answer to an irrelevant question.

Second, and more important, there is the problem of the time scale. Dahl's assertion that unless there is a conflict concerning the community agenda there is no way to distinguish the rulers from the ruled is true. But such a conflict is most likely to arise over failures of the community consensus to shift in accordance with changes in economic and social conditions. Given a comfortably affluent society, such changes become apparent only over fairly long periods of time, and the resulting conflicts may therefore occur only near the end of such periods, when the disparity between the old consensus and the new social and economic reality is particularly great. The absence of conflict concerning the community agenda during any reasonably limited period of time does not, therefore, imply that such a conflict is not likely in the future. The question, to repeat, is always whether the time scale chosen was a sufficiently long one. In the case of *Who Governs?* no attempt is made to demonstrate that it was.[284]

Moreover, as Polsby explicitly notes, the existence of a community agenda of alternatives imposes stringent limitations upon the changes that can be introduced through the processes of community decisionmaking. As long as that agenda continues to benefit the elite, therefore—and if an elite exists at all it is presumably because the agenda *does* favor it—it seems reasonable to expect that the elite will remain largely indifferent to the outcomes of community decisions. The changes to which we would not expect it to remain indifferent, changes in the community agenda itself, are precisely those that Polsby and Dahl convincingly demonstrate to be the most difficult to bring about.

Polsby also accounts for the mechanism by means of which the community agenda limits the possible outcomes of community decisions—the fact that "some, perhaps most" outcomes "are inconceivable to the actors

---

284. For an analysis of the cognate problem that arises in connection with the anticipated-reaction hypothesis see Simon, *supra* note 279, at 505–06.

256

involved." This internalization of the community agenda by the actors involved in community decisionmaking is not, of course, a phenomenon limited to municipalities. Dahl, for example, makes this argument:

> If the military leaders of this country and their subordinates agreed that it was desirable, they could most assuredly establish a military dictatorship of the most overt sort; nor would they need the aid of leaders of business corporations or the executive branch of our government. But they have not set up such a dictatorship. For what is lacking are the premises I mentioned earlier, namely agreement on a key political alternative and some set of specific implementing actions. That is to say, a group may have a high potential for control and a *low potential for unity*. The actual *political effectiveness* of a group is a function of its potential for control *and* its potential for unity. Thus a group with a relatively low potential for control but a high potential for unity may be more politically effective than a group with a high potential for control but a low potential for unity.[285]

We have been spared a military dictatorship, then, because the military, in Dahl's terms, have "a low potential for unity," which is to say that they have not agreed "on a key political alternative and some set of specific implementing actions." The "key political alternative," however, must surely be the decision to set up a military dictatorship, and if this decision were made, our military organization would presumably be capable of producing plans outlining a "set of specific implementing actions." In the end, therefore, to say that we have not had a military dictatorship because the military have "a low potential for unity" seems to amount to saying that we have not had a military dictatorship because the military have not (yet) agreed among themselves that one ought to be imposed.

The important question must surely be why the military do not so agree, and the phenomenon of the internalized community agenda goes far toward answering that question. Under most circumstances, our national agenda of alternatives does not include the possibility of a military dictatorship; it embodies, rather, the shared value—the symbol, if you will —of civilian rule. And the military, who have historically perceived themselves as part of our society, also share in the consensus on that agenda. They do not agree, in other words, on courses of action that are "inconceivable" to them because not within the agenda they have internalized.

On the basis of the above analysis we may conclude that any study of the distribution of political power that does not include a detailed analysis of the origins and content of the community agenda must be adjudged incomplete.[286] What is crucial, as one incisive analysis of Dahl's study of New Haven has put it, is an exploration of the ways in which "the dominant values and the political myths, rituals and institutions ... tend to

---

285. Dahl, *supra* note 283, at 465 (italics in original).
286. *Cf.* Simon, *supra* note 279, at 510–12.

J. G. D., *Stanford Law Review*, Jan. 1968

favor the vested interests of one or more groups, relative to others."[287] It is precisely such an analysis that is lacking in *Who Governs?*

The ultimate source of the failure of *Who Governs?* fully to describe the distribution of power in New Haven is thus to be found in the focus, which Shapiro shares with Dahl, on the process rather than the actor, on interactions within a given system rather than on the component parts of that system. Such a focus permits a highly accurate description of the system as it actually operates at any given time. But it does not permit an assessment of whether the system is operating within proper limits, whether the community agenda is an equitable one, for any such assessment, as we have seen, would require the postulation of "real" as opposed to perceived interests.

Nor does such a focus, as our examination of Dahl's military-dictatorship example indicates, even permit satisfactory analysis of the question how the existing limits of the system are maintained. The continuing operation of the system, the internal checks and balances, of course limit the changes that can be introduced by any given component part. But if we inquire into the source of the particular set of existing checks and balances or ask why the actors accept the constraints represented by those checks and balances, we are led directly to the community agenda of alternatives: the consensus that defines the existing set of checks and balances and whose internalization by the actors results in the acceptance of the constraints that it imposes.[288]

---

287. Bachrach & Baratz, *supra* note 278, at 950.

288. *Cf.* D. TRUMAN, THE GOVERNMENTAL PROCESS 348–49 (1951).

In one of the footnotes omitted from the text accompanying note 282 *supra*, Polsby notes that the "current state of affairs" is not the only possible determinant of the "community agenda of alternatives": "Other plausible answers might be that the agenda of alternatives is determined by the ideologies of choosers; by the 'real' interests of choosers; by accident; by certain underlying 'structural' characteristics of the community (*e.g.*, company town vs. dormitory suburb vs. metropolis). In presenting my own candidate for the best answer, I do not mean to exclude these possibilities. A theory that claimed some measure of comprehensiveness would probably have to consider the extent to which each of these factors determined the course of community decision-making." N. POLSBY, *supra* note 272, at 134 n.34.

But Polsby has previously found unacceptable at least one of these "plausible answers"—the "real" interests of choosers. Polsby's comment on an attempt by C. Wright Mills to delineate the possibility of a "false consciousness" on the part of a given social stratum is as follows: "Note the presumption that 'objective interests' exist; that there is a set of allegiances and actions which is appropriate for *all* members of a class. This presupposes a homogeneous set of 'accepted values' for all class members. Secondly, Mills presumes that these particular allegiances and actions 'have to be followed.' This means in effect that a 'best' strategy also exists. But are not these 'objective' circumstances actually constructs of the analyst?" *Id.* at 23 n.55 (italics in original).

The salient issue raised by Polsby's comment on Mills is the possibility that Polsby's agenda of alternatives is itself a "construct of the analyst." The short answer is that it clearly is. Certainly there exist no empirical data in direct support of the proposition that all members of any existing community share a single, coherent, and comprehensive body of values. Indeed, one of the most fascinating aspects of *Who Governs?*—Dahl's speculations in book VI on the sources of stability in pluralistic democracies —takes as its point of departure recent empirical findings indicating that "although Americans almost unanimously agree on a number of general propositions about democracy, they disagree about specific applications to crucial cases" and that "a majority of voters frequently hold views contrary to the rules of the game actually followed in the political system." R. DAHL, *supra* note 271, at 312.

Dahl's hypothesis concerning the stability of those rules suggests that, although the majority of voters prefer different rules, their preference is not a strong one, in the sense that they are unwilling

258

An analogous set of problems arises in connection with the "group" theory of politics, which explicitly underlies Shapiro's analysis of the Court's role in first amendment cases.[289] The group theory simply assumes, on the part of groups within the society, the existence of a consensus about the legitimacy of the system that defines the conditions of their interaction.[290] It assumes, in other words, that groups accept the constraints the system imposes on their possible goals and the methods to be followed in achieving those goals.

The difficulties involved in this assumption are most clearly apparent when group theorists attempt to account for a change in the consensus—for society's acceptance of, for example, a set of social, economic, or political demands that had formerly been unacceptable. Because group theory

to expend many resources to realize it; that no agreement exists regarding the desirability of any single set of alternatives; and that the politically active stratum of society, marked by a high degree of consensus concerning the desirability of the existing rules, is often capable of blocking changes because of its superior political skills and resources. Such a hypothesis, suggesting that "public" acceptance of democratic norms is really a matter of their acceptance by a strategically placed subpublic, could obviously be applied to Polsby's "community agenda of alternatives." But this is only to suggest that the agenda of alternatives is indeed an analytical construct, one that may or may not be verified by empirical data. It does not answer the question whether this particular construct is a valuable one.

The "community agenda of alternatives" does account for an empirically observable phenomenon, the fact that "[s]ome, perhaps most, *possible* courses of action are never considered in community decision-making . . . ." N. POLSBY, *supra* note 272, at 133 (italics in original). Dahl's hypothesis suggests that Polsby's explanation (that most possible courses of action are inconceivable to the actors involved because those actors share a community agenda) represents a considerable simplification of a complex reality involving the agendas held by various subpublics, the intensity of the preference of each subpublic for its own agenda (in terms of willingness to expend resources to realize it), and the ability of each subpublic (in terms of access to sufficient resources) to enforce that preference. The methodological difficulties involved in giving empirical content to any of these categories are, to say the least, considerable. Given the absence of data—and the comprehensiveness of Dahl's categories suggests that the vacuum will not soon be filled—a first approximation, a simplification such as that represented by the "community agenda of alternatives," may therefore be good enough. Dahl's hypothesis, after all, in the absence of empirical data, must remain just that—a hypothesis.

Whether a given construct is good enough depends on what questions that construct is being used to answer. Thus, the "public" whose acceptance of Court decisions has often been referred to in this Article is as much an analytic construct as the "public" whose acceptance of democratic norms Dahl has further analyzed in terms of subpublics. Because this Article is concerned with the empirical phenomenon of public reaction to Court opinions only insofar as the existence of that phenomenon requires certain conclusions about the proper role of the Court, detailed analysis of the components of that "public" seems unnecessary. Conversely, there are inquiries for which Dahl's categories of "political professionals, the political stratum, and the great bulk of the population," R. DAHL, *supra* note 271, at 316, will lack adequate precision.

The point, then, is that labeling a category a "construct of the analyst" poses the question rather than answers it. Any general category that purports to encompass a larger group of events than those actually studied represents, in Polsby's sense, a "construct of the analyst" as to those events that have not actually been observed. Further, in a sense that may or may not be different, even categories that refer only to actually observed events represent constructs of the observer. The question in each case can only be whether the construct adequately accounts for the phenomenon it is being used to describe.

The construct of the "community agenda of alternatives" adequately accounts for the phenomenon that most possible courses of action are never considered in community decisionmaking, *if* the focus of inquiry is on the process of decisionmaking, on "how" those decisions get made. That the analysis offered by Dahl and Polsby is inadequate to answer the question "why" decisions get made, to account for the fact that certain decisions *are* inconceivable, is the argument made in part VIII of this Article. As an answer to that question, the construct of a "community agenda of alternatives" is of course unsatisfactory, since the question at issue is precisely what factors determine the content of that agenda. What is striking is that Polsby should regard as a "plausible answer" to that question the very hypothesis of "real" interests that underlies so much of social-stratification theory.

289. *See* text accompanying notes 14–16, 244 *supra*.

290. *See* Rothman, *Systematic Political Theory: Observations on the Group Approach*, 54 AM. POL. SCI. REV. 15, 28–29 (1960).

J. G. D., *Stanford Law Review*, Jan. 1968

postulates that all social attitudes are the product of group membership, the shift in attitudes implied by the acceptance of such demands is accounted for in terms of the crystallization of what had previously been only a "potential" group. Shapiro, for example, explicitly resorts to the concept of potential groups in defining the Court's group "clientele."[291]

The difficulty with this construct, however, is that it fundamentally contradicts the postulate that attitudes are derived solely from group membership, for a potential group is in essence nothing more than a shared attitude that at some point may lead to membership in, and activity as, a group. For potential groups, therefore, attitudes precede group formation, rather than follow from group membership.[292] The root of the difficulty, once again, is the refusal of group theorists to examine the origins and content of the community agenda that defines the conditions for group interaction, and the degree to which that agenda has been internalized by participants in such interaction. Potential groups simply represent potential changes in the community agenda, and an adequate account of their crystallization therefore crucially involves a description of the psychological mechanisms in terms of which changes are introduced into individuals' perceptions of the norms and goals of the society in which they live, the roles they are to play within that society, and the constraints society has imposed upon those roles.

It is such mechanisms of internalization that provide the ultimate answer to the fears of judicial discretion that underlie Black's insistence on "logic" rather than experience. Of course both the existence of other agencies pursuing their own interests—the checks Shapiro postulates as limiting judicial overstepping of legitimate boundaries—and the threat of a massively unfavorable public response do place some constraints on the abuse of that discretion. But those constraints, as the experience of the 1930's demonstrated, operate only belatedly and in the most extreme circumstances. Therefore, if we are concerned about the day-by-day operation of the Court, about the routine decision rather than the isolated, spectacular exception, the question whether the Court will confine itself to those decisions the society regards as legitimately within its authority can ultimately be answered only by examining the extent to which individual Justices have internalized the community consensus that defines the Court's sphere of competence.

It is striking, for example, that immediately upon assuming his seat on the Court, Senator Black was certain that he had assumed a wholly different governmental role. To some extent, awareness of the content and limits of the judicial role can be ascribed either to prior judicial experience

---

291. M. SHAPIRO, *supra* note 244, at 34–36.
292. For a more detailed exposition of this analysis see Rothman, *supra* note 290, at 23–25.

260

or to what might be designated "on-the-job learning." However, in Black's case at least, it is unlikely that much significance can be ascribed to his service, in 1910 and 1911, as a police-court judge in Birmingham, Alabama.

Similarly, there are serious difficulties involved in attempts to derive this awareness from the institutional experiences that Justices undergo during their service on the Court. It is true that much can be learned from an examination of the pressures exerted on a Justice by the institution of the Court, and we already possess studies that considerably advance our knowledge in this area.[293] We could presumably learn even more from an accurate and detailed study of the changes in life style that result from appointment to the Court—changes in luncheon partners, dinner guests, and recipients and initiators of telephone conversations, for example. Ultimately, however, the value of such studies must be considerably less than in the case of a Congressman, for example, or the head of an administrative agency, primarily because the Court as an institution imposes far less pressure on a member than does the social system that is Congress or the interlocking web of bureaucratic and client pressures that constitutes an administrative agency.

The utility of studies such as those suggested above is severely limited, then, by facts already noted: The Court, unlike Congress, is not a social system; the task of a Justice is far more an individual than a group endeavor; and the influence of other Justices and of the institution on a new member of the Court is correspondingly limited.[294] To a far greater extent than is true in the case of a Congressman, therefore, the search for factors that effectively impose restraints on the discretion of the individual Justice must be carried beyond the realm of his work experience to that of his schooling, both formal and informal. Such an investigation, a branch of the study of political "socialization," might profitably begin with an examination of the impact of their professional training on given Justices. For example, to what extent can a particular Justice's perception of the range of discretion he can legitimately exercise be ascribed to a professional training that was primarily "policy-oriented"?

Given the growing awareness on the part of the profession as a whole of the discretion that necessarily inheres in common-law methods of adjudication, it seems unlikely that the study proposed above would produce any startling results. But such a study would at least represent a start toward explorations of far earlier and less formal learning experiences from which more relevant information might be obtained. To propose studies of child-

293. See, e.g., Danelski, The Influence of the Chief Justice in the Decisional Process, in COURTS, JUDGES, AND POLITICS (W. Murphy & C. Pritchett eds. 1961); Murphy, Marshaling the Court: Leadership, Bargaining, and the Judicial Process, 29 U. CHI. L. REV. 640 (1962); Snyder, The Supreme Court as a Small Group, 36 SOCIAL FORCES 232 (1958).
294. See text accompanying notes 247–48 supra.

hood learning experiences is not, of course, to suggest that there do not exist formidable methodological problems that would first have to be overcome. It is to suggest only that such studies will ultimately prove necessary if we insist on definitive answers to the dilemma posed by the possibility of judicial discretion.

As the decisions of the Court increasingly lose the appearance of "logic" that has historically constituted the basis for their public acceptability, studies of the institutional differences between Congress and the Court[295] and of the extent to which the Justices have internalized the constraints on their power implicit in those institutional differences could thus gradually serve to replace appearance with reality, could in time make possible the discarding of those symbols in terms of which the Court's authority has historically been accepted by the public. Even if studies both of childhood learning experiences and of the functioning of the Court as an institution could in principle provide us with complete and coherent descriptions, however, would there not remain significant limitations on the efficacy of those studies?

Thus, as we have seen, the symbols such studies would regard as meaningless abstractions—the need to achieve "logic" in judicial decisions that they would be explaining away—in fact perform a function that is vitally necessary: the function of continually reminding participants in government of the overriding social values our society seeks to impose upon the governmental process, of the ideals in terms of which we desire to be ruled.[296] The Supreme Court's conferences are conducted in secret, and the Latin in which the Roman Catholic Mass was formerly invariably conducted presumably veiled from many of the participants in that rite the meaning of the words being spoken. But is the saying of the Mass in the vernacular now the beginning, or the end, of the relevance of that sacrament to the lives of believers?

That the limits on the utility of such studies continue to be observed, that the processes of the Court not be completely open to public view, is, moreover, no less important for the Justices than for the public they serve. For the short of the matter is that trust has a meaning for both partners to a relationship. If a government based on consent is to survive, the "Morality Play" must have content for the actors as well as for the audience. And that content, as we have seen,[297] is based precisely on the possibility of abuse of discretion.

295. *See, e.g., id.*
296. *See* text accompanying notes 241–43 *supra.*
297. *See* the concluding paragraphs of part VII–A, following note 243 *supra.*

Nelson W. Polsby, *Stanford Law Review*, Nov. 1968

I

# On Intersections Between Law and Political Science

And as they went, Tigger told
Roo (who wanted to know) all about
the things that Tiggers could do.
"Can they fly?" asked Roo.
"Yes," said Tigger, "they're
very good flyers, Tiggers are.
Strornry good flyers."
"Oo!" said Roo. "Can they
fly as well as Owl?"
"Yes," said Tigger. "Only
they don't want to."[1]

The "intersections" between law and political science mapped out by
Professor Jan G. Deutsch appear, on Deutsch's own showing, to be lightly
traveled indeed.[2] In the first 80 pages of an article ostensibly upon this subject, only one political scientist is mentioned except in passing. This scholar,
Professor Martin Shapiro, is commended for his "regard for lawyers' law,"
and his views on the political role of the Supreme Court are considered at
length, along with those of law professors Bickel and Wechsler, and other
lawyers and jurists. The 270 footnotes accompanying these 80 pages advert
but momentarily to the work of five other political scientists.[3] On the 81st
page of text, and thereafter almost to the end of the article, some dozen
pages later, Deutsch abruptly blossoms forth with criticisms of work mainly
by two political scientists, of whom I am one and Professor Robert A.
Dahl is the other.[4] The work under consideration in these few pages is
not about the Supreme Court, as is the rest of Deutsch's article, but about
the study of community power as illustrated by a study of politics in New
Haven, Connecticut, which Dahl directed and in which I played a part.
How does Deutsch arrive at a discussion of community power from a dis-

For much of this chapter, I wish to thank Nelson W. Polsby, Professor of Political
Science at the University of California at Berkeley. Chapter I was published by him
in 21 *Stanford Law Review* 142 (1968), and much of the remainder of this chapter
consists of correspondence between Professor Polsby and myself.

1. A. A. MILNE, THE HOUSE AT POOH CORNER 60 (1928).
2. Deutsch, *Neutrality, Legitimacy, and the Supreme Court: Some Intersections Between Law
and Political Science*, 20 STAN. L. REV. 169 (1968).
3. They are Professors Robert A. Dahl, *id*. at 186 n.66, 250 n.270; David Danelski, *id*. at 207
n.133; Walter Murphy, *id*. at 214 n.168; Clement E. Vose, *id*. at 222 n.186; and Robert McCloskey,
*id*. at 231 n.227.
4. *Id*. at 250–61.

Nelson W. Polsby, *Stanford Law Review*, Nov. 1968

cussion of the Supreme Court? If I have the argument right, it happens this way:

(1) Shapiro, a political scientist, in his discussion of the Court "utterly fails," says Deutsch, in "the important task," which is "to provide a framework in terms of which boundaries among the various political institutions can be delineated." Instead, he focuses "on the process rather than the actor, on interactions within a given system rather than on the component parts of that system."[5]

(2) Dahl, a political scientist, does the same thing in *Who Governs?*,[6] his study of New Haven.

(3) The "utter failure" is, thus, characteristic of political science.

This argument is self-evidently so far from a serious comment upon the contemporary writing of political science in general that it scarcely merits rebuttal. It also seems to me quite wrong. That is, Deutsch makes no persuasive case for the notion that there is a single, sovereign "important task"; he fails to differentiate the important task he seems to care about from adjacent, supplementary, and similar important tasks; he fails to show that Dahl, in fact, commits the errors he fastens upon Shapiro; and, finally, he does not show that what Dahl and Shapiro allegedly share in any way typifies or constrains political science as a whole.[7]

In short, it appears that the connection between 80 pages of Deutsch on the Supreme Court and 10 pages or so of digression on community power is tenuous. It may be, however, that a reasonable case for a useful dialogue between the two disciplines can be made to emerge from a brief consideration of the "political science" part of Deutsch's article, on community power.

The central question addressed by *Who Governs?* is contained in its title; the answer is spread over 350 pages, and it proves to be a rather complex answer. New Haven in the late 1950's, when the book was written, was a political system in which a great deal was going on—some of it visible to the casual observer, some of it not. For several years Dahl and his assistants studied New Haven in a variety of ways: by reading about the history of the community, holding interviews with community leaders, conducting two sample surveys of the local population, arranging for extensive participant observations of key actors and events, reading and clipping

---

5. *Id.* at 250.

6. R. DAHL, WHO GOVERNS? DEMOCRACY AND POWER IN AN AMERICAN CITY (1961).

7. Even readers who do not share Deutsch's view that "the important task" is the discussion of the proper roles of various component parts of political systems in terms of some general theory, argument, or "framework" (if that is what he is advocating) should be aware that there is an extensive political science literature more or less meeting this description. *See, e.g.,* R. DAHL, A PREFACE TO DEMOCRATIC THEORY (1956) (especially 105–18); E. HERRING, THE POLITICS OF DEMOCRACY (1940); V. KEY, JR., PUBLIC OPINION AND AMERICAN DEMOCRACY (1961); E. SCHATTSCHNEIDER, PARTY GOVERNMENT (1942).

the local newspapers, and analyzing census and election material.[8] Dahl's conclusions about the political order of the community are embodied in a lengthy discussion that differentiates between various issue-areas, direct and indirect influence, routine and nonroutine decisions, innovation and the maintenance of status quo, various resource factors in the exercise of influence, and so on. The book is empirical in that evidence is carefully marshaled in support of assertions about the community. It is analytical in that a major attempt is made to show how the various events the book discusses can be knitted together into a description of a political order. It is theoretical in that it advances lawlike general propositions attempting to account for what it describes.[9] And, finally, it is speculative in that it attempts to say how these propositions may illuminate settings other than the one for which evidence is presented. *Who Governs?* is an ambitious, artful, intelligent, persuasive, and on the whole impressively successful book. Because Professor Deutsch engages a small part of it, my discussion will be correspondingly limited; I hope nothing either of us says dissuades some possible reader from undertaking the rather more spacious and refreshing experience of tackling the book itself.

Let me begin, in any event, with Deutsch's listing in consecutive sentences of some findings from *Who Governs?*:

> What Dahl found was that no single social or economic group either controlled the decisionmaking process or regularly benefited from the results reached. Further, there was remarkably little overlap among the participants in the various New Haven decisions studied by Dahl. In connection with the urban renewal program, for example, although the mayor created a citizens' action commission composed of representatives of the economic elite, Dahl's study revealed that the commission almost never initiated any proposal, nor vetoed or altered one put before it by the mayor. Dahl concluded, therefore, that power in New Haven is held by constantly shifting, issue-oriented coalitions, with considerable scope being given to a vigorous mayor determined to exploit his political resources to the utmost.[10]

Each sentence, considered separately, more or less accurately reflects a finding in *Who Governs?* Strung together, with Deutsch-supplied connectives ("further," "for example," "therefore"), they are non sequiturs, and I am afraid they do less than justice to the book. To sort things out a bit: The finding that few participants overlapped issue-areas contributed to the conclusion that no one social or economic elite controlled decisionmaking, not vice versa. So did the finding that there was not much overlap between New Haven's social and economic elites. So did a large number

8. Professor Dahl explains his methods at length in R. DAHL, *supra* note 6, at 330–40.
9. Professor Deutsch in his article, *supra* note 2, at 250, mistakenly attributes to Dahl's book the more limited theoretical purposes of my own companion volume, N. POLSBY, COMMUNITY POWER AND POLITICAL THEORY (1963), which are to describe and test a special theory of community power I call the "stratification theory."
10. Deutsch, *supra* note 2, at 250–51.

Nelson W. Polsby, *Stanford Law Review*, Nov. 1968

of other findings, in which decisionmaking in several issue-areas was reconstructed from the testimony of participants, from newspaper reports, and from direct observations. Deutsch, not Dahl, offers the citizens' action commission as an example of lack of overlap among issue-areas. Dahl demonstrates this point quite differently—by showing lack of overlap among several issue-areas. What this example does show is that in urban renewal the mayor successfully co-opted New Haven's business elite. The final conclusion, heralded by Deutsch's "therefore," was based on much evidence given in the book rather than the sentences Deutsch gives us as Dahl's reasoning.

These small matters reflect unfavorably upon the accuracy of Deutsch's reading (or at least of his rendering) of *Who Governs?*, but they do not touch the heart of his critique of the book, to which he then turns.

> The primary difficulty with *Who Governs?* as an analysis of the existing distribution of power is its assumption that the decisions canvassed represented conflicts sufficiently serious to force all potentially affected powerholders to mobilize their resources in hopes of obtaining a favorable outcome.[11]

Deutsch goes on to make a prima facie case: Many of the economic and social elite lived in New Haven's suburbs; therefore, why should they have cared about public education or political nominations? And perhaps they did not feel threatened by urban renewal.

> The important question, then, the question that Dahl never asks in connection with, for example, the power of the citizens' action commission, is whether that commission failed to assert itself because it was powerless or because, given the program as proposed by the mayor, it was indifferent to further modifications. The inquiry is whether the commission's failure to oppose the mayor's proposals represents an index of powerlessness or can be explained, rather, by the hypothesis that the mayor never proposed to the commission anything that he thought that body might reject. If the latter hypothesis is true, and the mayor would in fact have formulated different proposals had he thought the commission would accept them, who then holds power in New Haven?[12]

---

11. *Id*. at 251.

12. *Id*. It is possible to dispute whether Dahl "never" asks the question Deutsch insists he never asks. *See* DAHL, *supra* note 6, at 136–37: "Thus, properly used, the CAC was a mechanism not for settling disputes but for *avoiding* them altogether. The Mayor and the Development Administrator believed that whatever received the full assent of the CAC would not be strongly opposed by other elements in the community. Their estimate proved to be correct. And the reason was probably not so much the direct influence over public opinion of the CAC collectively or its members individually, as it was that the CAC *was* public opinion; that is, its members represented and reflected the main sources of articulate opinion in the political stratum of New Haven. The Mayor and the Development Administrator used the CAC to test the acceptability of their proposals to the political stratum; in fact, the very existence of the CAC and the seemingly ritualistic process of justifying all proposals to its members meant that members of the administration shaped their proposals according to what they expected would receive the full support of the CAC and therefore of the political stratum. The Mayor, who once described himself as an 'expert in group dynamics,' was particularly skillful in estimating what the CAC could be expected to support or reject. If none of the administration's proposals on redevelopment and renewal were ever opposed by the CAC, the explanation probably lies less in the Mayor's skill in the arts of persuasion than in his capacity for judging with considerable precision what the existing beliefs and commitments of the men on the CAC would compel them to agree to if a proposal were

law and political science

Deutsch then argues this position at length, making essentially two points. First, invoking the "rule of anticipated reactions,"[13] Deutsch asserts that Dahl never really demonstrates that an economic or social elite is relatively powerless in New Haven. This can only be done, Deutsch says, by studying issues which are important to such an elite. Second, Deutsch asserts that there is some reason to believe that in fact such an elite exists because of the existence of a political status quo in the community, of which the elite is the "passive beneficiary."

> As long as that agenda [the status quo] continues to benefit the elite, therefore— and if an elite exists at all it is presumably because the agenda *does* favor it—it seems reasonable to expect that the elite will remain largely indifferent to the outcomes of community decisions.[14]

Dahl "resolutely refuses to address the difference between those conflicts that an elite would perceive as both significant and threatening and those to which it would remain relatively indifferent,"[15] Deutsch says, concluding that "any study of the distribution of political power that does not include a detailed analysis of the origins and content of the community agenda must be adjudged incomplete."[16]

In advancing this argument, Deutsch is making the following asymmetrical inferences: Inactivity by the mayor—that is, his presumed failure to do some unspecified things that he might otherwise do—shows his lack of power, since he is controlled by anticipated reactions. Inactivity by social and economic leaders—that is, their actual failure significantly to influence decisionmaking—shows that they are powerful because the existence of any community agenda "presumably" benefits them. This reasoning is not appealing. On what grounds are we to infer that anticipated reactions apply only to the mayor? And why must we "presume" that the receipt by one group of some unspecified benefit from the status quo thereby invests them uniquely with political power?

It is doubtful that any presently known method of research can produce a "complete" description of community power such as Professor Deutsch advocates. To start with, "all potentially affected powerholders" and "a detailed analysis of the origins and content of the community agenda" are so vaguely specified as to admit of no reasonable limits. Who is not a "po-

---

presented in the proper way, time, and place." Dahl's conclusion is nevertheless that the Mayor's direct influence upon urban renewal was of overwhelming importance. I think this passage indicates, however, that he gives due and generous consideration to the indirect influence of the CAC and the other constituencies of the Mayor and his redevelopment team. *See id.* at 137 and following.

13. The coinage is, of course, Carl Friedrich's. *See* C. Friedrich, Constitutional Government and Democracy 589–91 (1946).

14. Deutsch, *supra* note 2, at 255.

15. *Id.* at 251–52.

16. *Id.* at 256.

Nelson W. Polsby, *Stanford Law Review*, Nov. 1968

tentially" affected powerholder? What constitutes a sufficiently "detailed analysis" of the community agenda?

In fact, far from ignoring these problems, Dahl has addressed them, or problems much like them, on a number of occasions, and reached reasonable compromises that advanced the goals he set himself in studying who governs in New Haven.[17] While it is true that many of those who made up the economic and status elites of New Haven lived outside the city limits, many did not; those that did nevertheless had a sizeable stake in public education because of its heavy demand upon the finances of the city. Likewise, political nominations were crucial in determining the management of the central city in which these people made their livelihoods. As New Haven became ever more firmly committed to the nation's most ambitious urban renewal program, the managerial capacity of elected public officials became a matter of life-and-death concern to the community. It was, after all, the mayor and his redevelopment team that went out and got the federal grants to subsidize knocking down a sizeable part of the central city, that identified the areas to be redeveloped, that mobilized support in the community in behalf of the program, and that would have to find investors to finance the reconstruction. How could local bankers, utility executives, department store owners, holders of downtown real estate, and manufacturing executives wherever they lived fail to see the connection between these matters and their own well-being? As a matter of fact, many did fail to get the point until Mayor Lee explained it to them. *Who Governs?* is filled with evidence that leaders of the business community became concerned, especially with urban renewal, as the direct result of the mayor's prodding and persuasion.[18] Some economic leaders opposed aspects of the program; others were not actively involved. But there can be no serious doubt that the urban renewal program, and therefore who sat in City Hall, was important to the community, and especially so, in varying ways, to those with heavy economic investments there. So I do

---

17. Here is a sample statement from *Who Governs?*, on the origins of a part of the community agenda: "What Lee did as a mayor was to push redevelopment and renewal to the center of focus and to hold it there year after year. He determined that a large share of energy, time, skills, and money would go into redevelopment. He devoted most of his own time and attention to it. He saw the need for a Citizens Action Commission and an extensive system of subcommittees, knew what kind of men he wanted for the CAC, persuaded them to accept membership, brought in Logue, induced him to abandon his attempt to start a law practice in order to work full-time on redevelopment, identified himself fully with redevelopment, and made it into a major issue of his unceasing campaign for reelection." R. Dahl, *supra* note 6, at 126. For the origins of Lee's commitment to urban redevelopment see *id.* at 117 and following. Other analyses of the origins and content of the community agenda and of problems associated with "potential" power holders and anticipated reactions may be found in *Who Governs?* *Id.* at 89–103, 271–75, 330–40. *See also* Dahl, *The Analysis of Influence in Local Communities,* in Social Science and Community Action 25–42 (C. Adrian ed. 1960); Dahl, *A Critique of the Ruling Elite Model,* 52 Am. Pol. Sci. Rev. 463–69 (1958); Dahl, *The Concept of Power,* 2 Behav. Sci. 201–15 (1957). Finally, for discussions of "potential" for power, of groups that exert "just enough control" to get what they want, but not enough to be observed in the act, and related problems in the community power literature see N. Polsby, *supra* note 9, at 14–68.

18. *See, e.g.,* R. Dahl, *supra* note 6, at 130–39 *passim.*

not think that Deutsch's claim that the issues Dahl studied were too trivial to matter should be taken seriously.

Dahl studied the mayor's relations with the citizens' action commission carefully and in a variety of ways and could find no direct evidence of the limitations upon the mayor's power that Deutsch suggested. But were there in fact such limitations, unnoticed by Dahl? Dahl took every reasonable step to investigate this possibility. Did Deutsch, for his part, take reasonable steps in his bid to discredit Dahl's explanation?

Here, I think, we may observe a bit of pile up at an intersection between law and political science. To a political scientist, at least an empirical political scientist with the impressive evidence of New Haven residence to which Professor Deutsch's string of Yale degrees and current Yale employment attest,[19] it might have been worth a few minutes on the telephone, or a few days downtown, to find out how accurately Dahl had described the political roles of the economic leaders of New Haven. The innuendoes Deutsch substitutes for such an investigation, having to do with anticipated reactions, would, of course, vex a nonexperimental empirical study of any kind; they lie with equal force against all methods presently known for studying nonmanipulable phenomena.[20] The essential form of Deutsch's methodological objection is the charge that Dahl fails to exclude hidden causes of the effects he observes in community policymaking. That Dahl is aware of the problem is plain from much of his writing, some of which Deutsch cites.[21] The problem is, by strict standards, intractable. Reasonable ground rules, explicitly stated, have to be established—a responsibility Dahl discharged. That is, Dahl went to great lengths to determine whether,

19. A.B. 1955, LL.B. 1962, Ph.D. (in political science) 1962, all from Yale University. Associate Professor of Law, Yale University, at the time his article was published, and now Professor of Law at Yale.

20. The same is true of what Deutsch refers to as his "more important" objection to Dahl's conclusions: the problem of the time scale. "The absence of conflict concerning the community agenda during any reasonably limited period of time does not . . . imply that such a conflict is not likely in the future. The question . . . is always whether the time scale chosen was a sufficiently long one." Deutsch, *supra* note 2, at 255. One may inquire: Sufficient to explain what? Clearly not to explain everything about "the future." The time scale of Dahl's inquiry did reach as far back as the incorporation of New Haven in 1784; it included an interpretation—with evidence—of changes in patterns of local leadership over the late 18th, 19th, and early 20th centuries; and it included an intensive discussion of the evolution of local politics in the fifties. Even so, I know of no claim by Dahl or his associates that they could thereby predict the future. In this connection, I wrote in 1963: "[A]ssuming the findings from New Haven presented here are correct, what can we infer from them about . . . New Haven ten years from now? Strictly speaking, the answer is little or nothing. New Haven bears certain similarities to other cities, but our theory has not yet progressed to the point where we know with any degree of confidence *which* other similarities predict political similarities. Similarly, aside from some primitive notions of 'habit' or 'inertia,' we have little to go on which helps us predict the effects on future decision-making processes of present ones." N. POLSBY, *supra* note 9, at 97.

In short, one would have to say Deutsch's diagnosis is faulty. It is not the time scale of the New Haven study, which for some purposes stretched from 1784 to 1958, that renders prediction difficult; it is the lack of relevant theory. Readers may decide for themselves whether Deutsch's own attempts to fashion such a theory in the second paragraph of page 255 seem worthwhile. To me they seem jejune.

21. *See* Deutsch, *supra* note 2, at 253 n.281, 254 n.283.

Nelson W. Polsby, *Stanford Law Review*, Nov. 1968

on empirical grounds, a case could be made for the proposition that New Haven was governed by means or by persons other than those he describes as governing New Haven.[22] To my knowledge this description has never been seriously challenged except in minor ways by anyone who bothered to find out about New Haven politics. That Deutsch did not so trouble himself is painfully apparent: He offers not a shred of evidence of any kind in support of his critique of Dahl's interpretation. Further, he ignores much relevant material that Dahl presents on relations between New Haven economic and political leaders. These I believe to be serious shortcomings. It is true, to be sure, that in making his criticisms of Dahl, Deutsch is merely repeating more or less verbatim points that have long since surfaced in the literature of political science;[23] but Deutsch was in an ideal position to ascertain that these criticisms were for the most part weak, frivolous, and incompetent.

Ultimately, Deutsch concedes that *Who Governs?* supplies "a correct answer to an irrelevant question."[24] I take him to mean by this that, on the whole, he has no quarrel with Dahl's account of how New Haven is actually governed. Deutsch says:

> Dahl's insistence on attacking only a model of an elite that actively manipulates the community consensus, rather than considering the possibility of an elite that is the passive beneficiary of consensus, once again runs the risk of supplying a correct answer to an irrelevant question.[25]

The "relevant" question, it appears, is not "who governs?" (to which Dahl has apparently supplied a correct answer), but "who benefits?" It is not clear how Deutsch wishes to regard the relationship of these two questions. I think his position is that "who governs?" is in some sense dependent upon, subsidiary to, or epiphenomenal to, the answer to "who benefits?" And, no doubt, in some sense, it is (as is also true of the reverse). But I think it is a mistake to insist too hard on this mutual dependency; there is something to be gained also from distinguishing the two questions rather sharply, as the following example should suggest:

> Suppose . . . we notice that it rains in Seattle. We speculate that taxi drivers make more money on rainy days. Therefore . . . taxi drivers cause it to rain in Seattle. This conclusion will still be defective even if we are energetic in buttressing some empirical points: we can test the theory that taxi drivers do indeed benefit from rain; we can learn if they know they benefit from rain; we can find out if they

---

22. *See, e.g.,* R. Dahl, *supra* note 6, at 63–84.

23. *See* W. Connolly, Political Science and Ideology 13–54 (1967); W. Mackenzie, Politics and Social Science 230–35 (1967); Bachrach & Baratz, *Two Faces of Power*, 56 Am. Pol. Sci. Rev. 947–52 (1962). *See generally* A Political Politics: A Critique of Behavioralism (C. McCoy & J. Playford eds. 1967).

24. Deutsch, *supra* note 2, at 252, 255.

25. *Id.* at 255.

actually favor rain. But it is still impossible to conclude that they cause rain since we do not show *what they did* to bring about rain and how these actions fit into existing knowledge about the phenomenon.[26]

The central empirical problem is this: Even if we can show that a given status quo benefits some people disproportionately (as I think we can for any real-world status quo), such a demonstration falls short of showing that these beneficiaries created the status quo, act in any meaningful way to maintain it, or could, in the future, act effectively to deter changes in it.[27] On all of these matters, we must, I think, look to the political powers and activities of variously advantaged groups. This, of course, is what Dahl does. "Who benefits?" may, after all, be an interesting question—though to me it is less interesting than "who governs?" In any event, it is susceptible to empirical investigation by those genuinely interested in studying it.

To say this, therefore, is to admit that not all conceivable questions or important questions about community politics, in New Haven or elsewhere, have been answered satisfactorily in *Who Governs?* Thus I think we would have no difficulty in agreeing with Deutsch's observation that Dahl's book and my own must be "adjudged incomplete." In a recent article, Dahl takes this position quite explicitly:

> Some of the links that a power analyst may take as "effects" to be explained by searching for causes are the outcomes of specific decisions; the current values, attitudes, and expectations of decisionmakers; their earlier or more fundamental attitudes and values; the attitudes and values of other participants—or nonpar-

---

26. Payne, *The Oligarchy Muddle*, 20 WORLD POL. 52 (1968) (emphasis in original).

27. This was what I argued in *Community Power and Political Theory*. N. POLSBY, *supra* note 9, at 132–36. Deutsch discusses these pages in a long footnote, Deutsch, *supra* note 2, at 257–58 n.288, but the point seems to have slipped past him. What I tried to show there (in part) was that it was possible to describe many community political systems as conservative without assuming anything about the pattern of leadership—that, in short, there was a probable gap between the distributions of benefits by any system and the exercise of power within it. Hence, the answer to the question "who governs?" could not be assumed to be the same as the answer to the question "who benefits?"

*See also* R. DAHL, MODERN POLITICAL ANALYSIS 39–54 (1963). Under the heading "Some common errors in the analysis of power," Dahl lists "[f]ailing to distinguish clearly between participating in a decision, influencing a decision, and being affected by the consequences of a decision." *Id.* at 53.

As for the rest of footnote 288, perhaps a few words are in order. Deutsch's discussion turns on a few phrases from my work, which I can, perhaps, clarify. As one "plausible answer" to the question "what determines the community agenda?" I listed the "real interests" of decisionmakers. I should have made clearer that I did not intend by this to withdraw the strictures against this sort of explanation, which, as Deutsch notes, I had earlier advanced. Rather, I meant only to indicate that "real interests" were one among a number of alternatives that scholars would quite likely find plausible and hence discussable. The phrase "construct of the analyst" also seems to have given Deutsch difficulty. He quotes me as accusing C. Wright Mills of using a particular "construct" and quite rightly observes that I, too, use "constructs of the analyst" rather liberally in my own work. What I should have said, since it apparently was not, as I had supposed, crystal clear from context, was that the construct in question was offered by Mills as a representation of a set of real world conditions that palpably did not exist in the real world. I can assure everyone that I have no general objection to the use of "constructs of the analyst." Finally, the phrase "community agenda" seems to have caused difficulty. I meant by it simply the population of decisions in some sense under consideration by a community. The extent to which this population is controlled by internalized norms of decisionmakers (as Deutsch seems to think) rather than other factors (such as Dahl enumerates in the text to which footnote 28 *infra* refers) is, of course, an empirical question. In the meantime, Deutsch's guess is not only as good as mine, but apparently more or less the same as mine.

Nelson W. Polsby, *Stanford Law Review*, Nov. 1968

ticipants—whose participation is in some way significant; the processes of selection, self-selection, recruitment, or entry by which decision-makers arrive at their locations in the political system; the rules of decision-making, the structures, the constitutions. No doubt a "complete" explanation of power relations in a political system would try to account for all these effects, and others. Yet this is an enormously ambitious task. Meanwhile, it is important to specify which effects are at the focus of an explanatory theory and which are not. A good deal of confusion, and no little controversy, are produced when different analysts focus on different links in the chain of power and causation without specifying clearly what effects they wish to explain; and a good deal of criticism of dubious relevance is produced by critics who hold that an investigator has focused on the "wrong" links or did not provide a "complete" explanation.[28]

In short, the agenda of research that Professor Deutsch prescribes is well known, and may be a fruitful one; his testimony on this point would, of course, carry greater conviction if he had taken the trouble to pursue the matter a short way himself. In that case, he might have come to the view that to counsel perfection is often easier than to achieve it. He might even concede that "correct" answers to the question "who governs?" may be as valuable for some purposes as insistent nonanswers to the question "who benefits?"

From all this I believe we can salvage a modest lesson: Perhaps political science as it is presently being written can help those who study the law by offering as a supplement to the naked exercise of their forensic skills a sense of the possible that is imposed upon scholars committed to empirical research. Thus in a small way we may be able to help our brethren in the law recall that, as James Thurber once said, "Skepticism is a useful tool of the inquisitive mind, but it is scarcely a method of investigation."[29]

28. Dahl, *Power*, 12 INTERNATIONAL ENCYCLOPEDIA OF THE SOCIAL SCIENCES 412 (1968).
29. J. THURBER, *Look Homeward, Jeannie*, in THE BEAST IN ME AND OTHER ANIMALS 114 (1928).

II

My objections to Who Governs? are not disputes concerning the validity of the conclusions
arrived at, but fundamental methodological ones.
Thus, I have talked to one person fairly highly
placed in the administrative hierarchy charged
with the making of urban renewal decisions who
indicated his agreement with my belief that, to
some extent, the anticipated reactions of the
business community played a role in the decisions
reached by that hierarchy. I failed to cite
this fact in my article because the conversation
failed to focus on any specific decision, and
because a variety of issues--involving such matters as the reliability of one person's memory,
the significance of the beliefs concerning
determinants of decisions held by one member of
a fairly large administrative hierarchy charged
with making those decisions, the accuracy of his
hypotheses concerning his (and others') unre-
vealed motivations, the importance to be attributed to any specific decision, and the extent
to which any given decision should be accepted
as other than the product of an exceptional set
of circumstances--could all validly be raised
concerning the significance of that conversation.
In this sense I agree with you that perhaps the
best way of stating the dilemma I tried to make
clear is to examine the sense in which the answer
to the question "Who Governs?" is distinguishable from the answer to the question "Who Benefits?" Put briefly, my point is that so long
as the community agenda of alternatives favors
a group other than that which is governing,
there seems no reason why the favored group
should attempt to interfere in decisions which
do not threaten that agenda. Thus, my answer to
comments on my underestimation of the interest of
the economic and social elite in school-board and
political-nomination affairs can only be that I
am postulating precisely what you accuse me of
ignoring: a very considerable level of indifference on the part of the elite to community
decisions.

Indeed, it seems to me that it was precisely
the burden of the argument advanced by the social
stratificationists--and today by the New Left--
that one important index of power is measured
by the answer to the question "Who Benefits?",
and that the results of that index of power are
wholly compatible with permitting other actors
to control decisions which do not affect such
benefits. The people who govern, in other
words, may either be exercising power or serving
as "fronts"; and identification of those people
does not answer the question which role they are
playing.

To recapitulate, then, my argument is not
that the method utilized in Who Governs? does not
represent a wholly workable means of studying
particular decisions. What I do argue is that,
given that method, one is unable--on the basis of

any particular set of decisions--to make valid
statements about the distribution of power in any
arena larger than the one bounded by the set of
decisions being studied.

The basic answer I find you making to my
criticism is that it is a counsel of perfection-
ism and that, since I fail to demonstrate that
it could be implemented, I ought to regard
myself as estopped from raising the issue. It
seems to me that a variety of answers can be made.
First and most important, I deny the premise,
since I would have thought that a demonstration
of limits to a methodology is itself a contribution, and since I never claimed that my delineation of those limits was original.

Moreover, I think it fair to say that the
paragraph on pages 260-261 both indicates the
sorts of studies I had in mind and the very
real possibility that such studies would be
incapable of providing any definitive answers.
Perhaps more to the point, in two separate
places (pages 252-53 and pages 254-55) I specifically adverted to the methodological difficulties raised by the "anticipated reaction" and
"community agenda" hypotheses.

Let me start with the second of those
passages on pages 254-55. I quote a passage
from Dahl's "A Critique of the Ruling Elite
Model" and then raise two objections. The
first, the insistence on attacking a model of
an actively manipulative rather than passive
elite, is the one you quoted, and your objections to which seem to me to be based on the
"Who Governs?"--"Who Benefits?" dichotomy to
which I have already addressed myself. I then
go on, however, to raise a second objection
having to do with time. To put the point in the
context of New Haven, what I am arguing is that
methodology capable of producing results which
are perfectly valid at a given time and place
(as those of Who Governs? seem to me to be valid
for the New Haven of the 1950s) may be unable
to account for events occurring in the same
place at a different time, as the methodology
of Who Governs? seems to me to be incapable of
accounting for much of what is happening in the
New Haven of the 1960s.

If you accept this line of reasoning, I
would suggest that the ultimate question concerning the Who Governs? methodology reduces to
one of the relevance of the results which it can
be expected to produce in any given context.
This, of course, ultimately reduces, as you
point out, to a question of what one is interested in studying; but I think it fair to say
that most of what most of us are interested in
finding out about the 1960s will require a
considerably more sophisticated method of
approach--more sophisticated, but not impossible!
As I point out in connection with the methodological difficulty I canvassed on pages 252-53,
historians have been making precisely the sort
of judgments I postulate as necessary for a very

long time indeed.

In this connection, I hope it is clear by now that I was trying to adumbrate a critique, not of Who Governs?, but of Dahl's concept of power in general.

III

There are two points at issue about the social and economic elites' interest in school and nomination politics. The immediate one is that contrary to what Bachrach and Baratz said, many members of both of these groups live in New Haven and all of the economic ones have important financial stakes in New Haven and therefore have objective reasons for caring about New Haven schools and New Haven municipal elections. The more important point is that irrespective of their interest in these issues, the outcomes in these issue areas are 1) important and 2) not determined by the elites. If one is interested in how policies are made, then, the elites are not very important.

Not important, that is, unless one entertains the proposition that the elite really do make the decisions in that the apparent decision-makers are their tame pets who know better than to do anything distasteful. I'm not sure whether you advance this as your own or mean only to say that other people believe it. I also am unsure whether this statement means only that "identification of those people [the formal decision-makers] does not answer the question which role they are playing." If you mean that politicians may take orders from other people and that therefore one must do more than identify the politicans, there is no argument, for Dahl has followed this precept in his research. But if you mean that the elite control is passive, that officials can do whatever they want as long as they don't offend the elite, then this proposition must take its chances in the face of the data, which do not support it. Moreover, rather than asking, how does group X benefit from the "agenda," concluding that it does OK, and then assuming that X really runs the town, one has to ask this question about all conceivable collectivities. As I think you will agree, trying to find out who really has the power by locating those people least dissatisfied with the party in City Hall has some fairly obvious deficiencies as a method of research. I don't see any way out of this dilemma that does not involve both a priori assumptions about whose power should be investigated (e.g., the stratification theory) and unverifiable propositions. I think your "so long as the agenda favors a group . . ." has both of these problems.

Furthermore, I do not see a single attempt in your article to address Dahl's methods, or for that matter any alternative methods. That is, you do not show how Dahl's methods may be faulted or improved upon. What you are doing

instead, I think, is offering alternative inferences and conclusions from statements contained in Who Governs? and insisting that these inferences are not conclusively excluded by anything in Who Governs?. You are of course correct; it is more than anything else the weight of evidence that makes Dahl's conclusions acceptable. And it is the lack of evidence that makes the alternatives you offer seem threadbare. Even so, the prior causes you postulate could exist. No non-experimental methodology escapes this problem. But Dahl discusses these problems with some subtlety and tenacity in his own work.

You say that the methods of Who Governs? permit an accurate description of New Haven in the 1950s, but that "the same methodology" is "incapable of accounting for much of what is happening . . . in the 1960s." By this, and by your remarks about "time scale" you must mean to tax Dahl for not predicting the course of future history, since you offer no alternative "methodology" nor hint at a reason why Dahl's eclectic methods aren't perfectly suitable for a contemporary study. Again I must inquire: if no method escapes the "time scale" objection—in the sense of failing to predict at least some historical events that seem important to later observers—in what sense is this objection a "methodological" objection?

I believe that the "time scale" objection if I understand it does lie against virtually any contemporary study, however conducted. So it is in my view a methodologically trivial, that is, inconsequential objection. The inconsistency here is in demanding of Dahl what we customarily demand of no other studies.

Your suggestion on pp. 252-53 that the "existence" of historians proves something strikes me as—to be charitable—a non sequitur. Surely in order to be consistent you would have to infer correspondingly from "the existence" of political scientists that books like Who Governs? are methodologically adequate.

Finally, given the difficulties of political socialization studies that you mention, it puzzles me that you should offer them as a way out for political scientists whose trained incapacity fails to give sufficient weight to internalized norms. It puzzles me especially, since you do not cite studies by legal scholars of the internalization of norms that would support your claim, that legal scholars have some understanding on this score denied to the rest of us.

Let me now briefly react to footnote 288. I am sorry that my use of the phrases "plausible answer" and "construct of the analyst" caused such difficulty. I think I should have been clearer that "real" interests as a possible determinant of a community agenda was a notion that many analysts had found plausible and would find plausible. I did not and do not find it very helpful, for reasons that I am sure are obvious. I merely wanted to indicate what a range of possible answers to the question "what determines the agenda?" might look like.

As for "construct of the analyst," I was much too cryptic. Obviously, there are "constructs" and "constructs." What I was trying to suggest about Mills' discussion was that he was offering a construct of his own as a representation of real world conditions that was palpably unfaithful to these conditions. I think that it is fairly obvious from context. The number of items discussed in my book that can be characterized as "analytic constructs" must be rather formidable; it surprises me that the "community agenda" was the only one that caught your eye. By agenda I think I meant the population of decisions in some sense up for settlement at any given time—not the underlying values of community members. I think your excursion into the discussion of community values misses my point. What you are doing is offering a prejudice of your own as an "insight" about the sources of community agendas. See Dahl's statement in his "Power" article about the train of power and causation. (What killed John Doe? Heart action stopped. Bullet in heart. Trajectory of bullet. Composition of bullet. Laws of ballistics. Aim of gun. Mechanism of gun. Finger on trigger. Easy availability of weapons in American society. Jealousy of Richard Roe. Adultery of Mrs. Richard Roe. Blondness of Mrs. Richard Roe. Preference of John Doe for blondes. And so on.) All of these answers are in some sense adequate and in some sense inadequate, depending on the purposes of the investigator—which, I am happy you concede, are up to the investigator to specify. All in some sense answer the questions "how" and "why" and so that distinction doesn't seem to help much. You may think of internalized norms as the bedrock of human experience, hence these norms are for you the ultimate answer, but I suggest that is a prejudice. You are merely insisting that "Preference of John Doe for blondes" and not (e.g.) "Easy availability of weapons" is the answer to the question "why." What you might have said was: we have a superb study of the availability of weapons. Let us now move to a related question—the preference of John Doe for blondes. But you did not do that. You—in my view—quite groundlessly dismissed Dahl's investigation as unimportant because it missed "the" point.

IV

To begin with, let me say that I am quite prepared to accept a construction of my argument as "Who Governs? does as good a job as exists in the literature of exploring one set of causes; let us now look at a set of causes it overlooks." On the other hand, it seems to me that you stress too strongly the notion that what I propose is wholly impossible. Again, perhaps I have been too terse, but I would want to reiterate that

historians have been doing the sort of thing I propose for a very long time indeed. Lawyers have not—and that is why I do not cite studies by legal scholars—but the volume of historical studies to this point surely needs no citation. It is, of course, true that many social scientists have leveled against history the charge of having no methodology at all, and if you agree with that charge, then we do indeed have a point to debate, although I doubt we could add much to a literature that has by now grown to absurd proportions.

This, of course, was also the meaning of my focus on "time scale" and I would reiterate my own intuition that a satisfactory account of the events of the 60s, unlike the 50s, seem to me to present the possibility that benefits long taken for granted by the economic and social elites are perceived as being threatened. I wholly agree with you, incidentally, that (even if I am right) to phrase the issue as one of whether or not an elite exists in the abstract, is simply to frame an unanswerable question. But it seems to me important (if I am right) to draw the distinction between a period in which certain groups did not see their interests as significantly threatened and one in which such threats were perceived.

Finally, if you will permit me to use "preferences" rather than "prejudices," I can say that I prefer my epistemology for the reason I gave in my last letter: that it seems to me to entail a methodology which—unlike that of Who Governs?—promises to make possible valid and meaningful statements about more than the particular set of decisions under study. You say that you are quite satisfied with a methodology that can produce valid statements only about the precise phenomena being studied; I am not, and I frankly cannot believe that you are either, since such a position seems to me to trivialize social science and to transform history into antiquarianism.

V

Let me tax your patience by discussing a few points you raise in your most recent letter. The first concerns "internalized norms" as an explanation of policy-making processes. I know of no social scientists, from Skinnerians to demographers, who would deny the relevance of "internalized norms" in human behavior. There are problems, however, of specification and operationalization in the use of such a variable in scientific or even in ordinary explanation. Many such explanations take the form "he did it because of internalized norms." That is, they are tautological and hence do not explain. A common cure for this problem can be experimentally produced—that is by stimulating one group of subjects while withholding or varying the learning experience for control groups.

Another type of cure is the use of nonreactive
measurement in the comparison of naturally occurring phenomena.  Thus Weber's speculation about
the internalized norms facilitating and retarding
economic development, and similar work by Tawney,
Bellah, and McClelland.  Or, perhaps closer to
home, consider the following quotation:

> The effective political elites, then, operate
> within limits often vague and broad, although
> occasionally narrow and well defined, set by
> their expectations as to the reactions of the
> group of politically active citizens who go
> to the polls

or:

> Each of the conditions of polyarchy increases
> with the extent of agreement (or consensus)
> on the relevant norm

or:

> Polyarchy is a function of the total social
> training in all the norms

These quotations are from a part of Dahl's
critique of Madisonian Constitutional theory in
A Preface to Democratic Theory, in which Dahl
attempts to specify the relative strength of
certain internalized norms and constitutional
checks in the maintenance of polyarchy (pages 72
ff.), and in which he argues that internalized
norms are the more important.  (Or see, e.g., the
last chapter of Who Governs?)

As your argument now strikes me, you are
insisting upon the power of an explanatory
variable whose strength is at present open to
question except in the most vacuous sense.  This
is what I mean when I say you are asserting a
mere prejudice.  A "preference" would entail--
would it not?--better empirical grounds than we
presently have for asserting the strength of your
preferred variable.

To move to the second point:  your contention
that somehow historians have solved this, or any
similar, methodological problem puzzles me.
Judgments as to "motivations" and "causes" in
historical writing are, of course, quite common.
Some are more convincing than others.  I would
agree with those who hold that historians have
no unique methodology, but also think it is
obvious that they have access to most of the
methods available to other students of human
behavior.  So your argument that we repair to
the historical literature for directions on how
to avoid the neglect of internalized norms is, in
my view, imprecise and puzzling.  As I read
historical writing, much of it is argued less
cogently by far than Who Governs? and much of
it--even the best of it--does neglect aspects of
the subject it covers that prove to be of interest
to those who come later.  Consider this passage
of commentary upon a work of historical writing:

> The omissions . . . are as striking as the

small scale of its subject.  Not a word about
surrounding empires . . . except so far as
they affect the midgets.  Nothing about
economics or social life; apart from an occasional allusion, nothing of . . . finance. . .
No social history; we do not hear how these
people were housed or lived.  No details
about industry or commerce.

This is from Livingstone's introduction to
Thucydides' History of the Peloponnesian War.  He
continues:

> The years from 480 B.C. to 400 B.C. are
> among the great ages of the world:  an age
> when a small people created some of the best
> literature, art, and thought of the world,
> when some of its greatest drama was written,
> some of its finest sculpture carved, its most
> beautiful building erected--the age of
> Herodotus, of Aeschylus, Sophocles, Euripides
> and Aristophanes, or Ictinus and Phidias, the
> age when Socrates lived and Plato was born.
> Thucydides does not even mention their names
> or their works.

I quote this at length only to dispute your
claim that "the existence" of historians, even
indisputably great ones, constitutes sufficient
introduction in the arts of inclusion and exclusion, in forecasting the future interests of
observers, or in the analysis of power.

VI

First, let me clarify my understanding of
where we are on Who Governs?  I'm not sure it
makes any difference to our discussion, but what
I have said is that my own assessment is that,
given its purposes, Who Governs? adequately
describes the decisions it canvasses and that
therefore the methods utilized were wholly adequate to the task undertaken.  Whether this
amounted to a satisfactory description of power
in New Haven depends on the purposes for which
power was being described.  If, as in Who
Governs?, the purpose was to determine who made
the decisions under review, then the description
was satisfactory.  But my point was precisely
that there are other purposes one might have in
mind in describing power for which that description would not be satisfactory.  Nor, finally, am
I always certain that Who Governs? shares your
modesty in claiming that what it is describing is
something whose meaning is limited to the
decisions under review.

As to Dahl, I must confess that I had up to
now excluded the Preface when I referred to
"Dahl's entire theory of power" and that, insofar
as that work is concerned, I think his recognition
of internalized norms more than adequate.  But
is it really fair to include the Preface in our
discussion?  There is, after all, a considerable
body of Dahl's writing explicitly on the problem

of elites, even aside from Who Governs?, and I
tried, in my piece, to comment on passages from
some of these articles, in an attempt to show
that the failure to grapple with internalized
norms which I thought I detected in Who Governs?,
ran through all of Dahl's work on the elite
issue. If I am right on that score, what is the
relevance of the fact that the Preface does
grapple with the issue? As to your citation to
the last chapter of Who Governs? in this connection, I can do no more than refer once again to
footnote 288, where I explicitly note that in
Book VI of Who Governs? it seems to me that Dahl
goes beyond the notion of internalized norms in a
most helpful and provocative way. So I guess my
response is that I agree, but since Book VI is
rather clearly delimited as a set of speculative
hypotheses springing from, but not an integral
part of, the descriptive part of Who Governs?,
remain at a loss as to the relevance of those
notions to our present discussion--apart from
that which I acknowledged in my footnote.

Moreover, I think I detect in your letter an
instance of the kind of simultaneous acceptance
and distrust of the notion of "internalized
norms" which, frankly, I share, but which inevitably leads to the kind of overstatement or nuance
which seems to me to account for many of the
illusory differences between us. At one point
you say "I know of no social scientists, from
Skinnerians to demographers, who would deny the
relevance of 'internalized norms' in human
behavior." Later you conclude, "As your argument
now strikes me, you are insisting upon the power
of an explanatory variable [i.e. "internalized
norms"] whose strength is at present open to
question except in the most vacuous sense."
Well, there, I think, we have it, and as I said
before, I agree with you, but it simply won't
do. If the damn thing is undoubtedly relevant,
it just won't do never to crank it in because
it's so hard to deal with, because a refusal to
crank it in (assuming its relevance) must
necessarily lead to a distorted set of conclusions.

As to historians, notice what Livingstone
finds remarkable about Thucydides: "the small
scale of its subject." Now compare that with
the scale of the subject dealt with in Who
Governs? And there you have the point I was
trying to make. Historians are constantly dealing with matters they cannot gather all relevant
data about. Consequently, they are constantly
writing against a background of what we are calling internalized norms; of what the Napoleonic
Age "stood for" or what impact the French Revolution had on ideas about politics. Many,
probably most, of these notions are vacuous if
not demonstrably false, but they are the very
stuff of a good deal of what historians do. And
the point is, historians do do something; little
by little, they refine those ideas and give them
more precise meaning, demonstrating at least that

their use of these notions does not destroy the
possibility of explaining events in terms of
myriads of other factors as well.

Once again, then, the methodological point
seems to me to be the one I made in my last
letter. The issue is that of generalization. If
you are content to say that of course Who Governs?
explains nothing beyond the decisions there being
canvassed, then I agree that none of what I have
said need be taken into account. If however, you
do not so agree, and--for the reasons I gave last
time, I can't really believe that you take this
position--then I think what I have said about
historians must be taken into account. Not that
they have a different methodology in the sense
that they would study the decisions in Who
Governs? differently, but that--because they are
constantly engaged with phenomena so much broader
in scope than those canvassed in Who Governs?--
they operate against a background in which given
sets of internalized norms play a major part.

Limits of space and time, inter alia, prevented publication of any continuation of this
exchange.

David B. Roe

I N T E R R O G A T I N G   T H E

L E G A L   P R O C E S S

The Moral Judge and Samuel Beckett

David B. Roe

A discussion of communication devices for
courts, in the context of corporate social
responsibility, assumes a great deal.  It
assumes that social responsibility is a moral
question and that courts have at least a partial
answer, that courts care about communicating the
content of that answer and not merely the results
of its application in specific cases; and that
successful communication will help to control
the social behavior of the intended recipients--
for example, corporations--in some way more comprehensive than a series of specific commands.
Finally, it assumes at least provisionally that
we want all this to happen.

None of these assumptions is necessarily
true.  Equally, the importance they place on
courts as instruments of social control may be
misplaced; even if we want to impose a moral
influence on corporate behavior, courts may not
be the appropriate agency, or even a possible
one.  The discussion below relies nonetheless on
all these assumptions and must be read with them
in mind.  The assumed model is of a judge or
panel of judges who can differentiate between
right and wrong corporate social behavior as he
is given examples, who feels the distinctions to
be moral ones, and who is willing to give legal
effect to his judgment.

Communication is at the heart of the judicial
process.  As has often been said, we are willing
to be ruled by the judgment of other men, but we
ask that the judgment be explained.  Moreover,
not every explanation will do.  In important
cases, and particularly in constitutional ones,
we ask that the explanation meet certain standards.  The harder the specific result is to
accept, the more we demand of the explanation, as
a condition of acceptance, that it meet those

standards.  And the more suspect the explanation,
the more likely we are to demand that its conformity to those standards be made explicit.
There is, therefore, a premium on standards which
can be communicated.

Perhaps the most commonly accepted method of
communicating decision-making standards is for
the decision maker to invoke for his audience
some shared experience as a starting point of
reference, an anchor from which the line of explanation tends.  And the most commonly chosen
experience, at least for lawyers, is a printed
text.  The written law consists of texts specialized to this purpose, both statutes and
constitutions.  Since all copies of printed laws
are identical we therefore believe that the experience of each man in reading those printed
laws has something in common with the experience
of all other men who read copies of the same
text.  And when a judge claims that he makes a
decision in accord with such a printed standard,
he is confident that his audience will understand both the standard and the claim.

Of course, any decision which can be
explained merely by reciting a printed legal
standard is a trivial one.  If, for example,
a corporation in this country fails to file an
income tax return, or if it pays its adult
employees $1.55 an hour, it hardly takes a court
to decide that the corporation's behavior should
change (though it may take a court to force the
changes).  The standard speaks for itself, which
is to say that anyone who shares the experience
of the statutes will share the belief that the
decision is justified.

The much more common decision involves an
explanation which is not self-evident from the
printed text.  It is more than trivial to decide
that a corporation which owns all the real
property in a town may not, by enforcing the
trespass laws, wholly prevent the distribution
of leaflets in that town.  The text--the shared
experience--is a prohibition of government
interference with freedom of expression; the
decision requires the further explanation that
a company which owns and operates a town bears
some of the obligations of a municipal government.  Here the printed standard--the First
Amendment--is only a starting point, but it is a
point from which, in Marsh v. Alabama, the
Supreme Court and its audience can start together.

A third category of familiar cases are those
which do not depend on the shared experience of
a text; an example is Griswold v. Connecticut.
Though the opinions cite provisions of the Constitution, the Court cannot be confident that it
shares its experience in reading those provisions
with its audience.  Mr. Justice Douglas finds
that five Amendments contain specific protections
of privacy, and thereby infers that a general
protection of privacy was the intention of the
document as a whole; but as John Hart Ely has

pointed out, other readers might take the same findings to an opposite inference. In fact, Douglas' explanation of his decision rests on a shared experience which is not a printed text. It is no accident that the opinion emphasizes privacy as something universally understood and desired: "the right most valued by civilized men." Douglas too can assume a common starting point with his audience.

In the two latter decision categories, the discussion of standards is obviously inadequate. Explanations of those kinds of decisions must be accessible to an audience not only at their starting points but also in the process of moving from start to finish. That process too must meet standards, and we recognize those standards as the chief concern of decision analysts like Wechsler and Bickel. In the real world, and particularly in the real world of the Supreme Court, those standards may seem to be the only important ones. After all, the texts are given; what counts is what the Court should do with those texts, and what it should not. Even in the Griswold-type case, where the Court starts from a nonconstitutional premise, what counts is how far the Court goes with it, how closely the Court hews to standards of argument. However, the apparently trivial first problem—meeting standards for a point of departure—may prove difficult in the context of social responsibility.

Part I of this essay briefly reviews some standards for the process of moving from constitutional premises to constitutional conclusions which have been developed, and suggests that those standards too depend on the communication of shared experience between the Court and its audience. Part II discusses, much too briefly, the moral problem which communication itself may raise, at least for one special kind of communicator. Part III takes the communication device worked out in Part II and tries to see whether any court could make use of it.

I

According to Deutsch, Mr. Justice Black flatly disagreed with the famous aphorism of Holmes; he believed instead, though he never put it in these words, that "the life of the law has been logic." That apocryphal statement is the subject of this section.

Of course, Black claimed to speak only for constitutional law, and he claimed that Holmes was speaking about only the common law. But Deutsch is right to see the two positions in conflict, since there is no clear distinction today between common law and constitutional adjudication, and since critics of judicial decisions would not be willing to accept wholly different standards for the two types of decisions, even if they could be neatly sepa-

rated. The decision that California recognizes a common-law right to privacy and the decision that the U.S. Constitution recognizes a constitutional right to privacy are reached in the same manner, and they are gauged as decisions by the same yardstick.

What, then, does it mean to say that the life of the law has been logic? Bickel suggests the beginning of an answer.

> Whatever it calls itself, and whether or not it actually proceeds from principle, a decision of the Court must be self-conscious; it must be intelligible, rational, candid. In no circumstances can it begin to be justifiable unless it meets the irreducible implications that the very words 'court' and 'judge' have for centuries conveyed in our tradition; unless, in short, it is disinterested. Self-conscious intellectual candor in finding and following a rational path to decision is one of the chief assurances of disinterestedness. . . . We consider it a crisis when we find rationality lacking. We exempt only, if at all, the most representative of political institutions. But never the judiciary, never above all, the Supreme Court.

The argument of the passage is less important than the emotive level on which it functions. Bickel demands standards for constitutional decision-making and gives as reasons the expectations of "centuries," the danger of "crisis" if those expectations are not met, and the importance "above all" of those expectations being met by the Supreme Court. His tone tells us better than his words that he believes the vitality, the "life" of courts depends on their meeting the demand for standards. Black makes the same link in Kingsley Pictures between "reasonably fixed and certain standards" and "the rule of Law."

Bickel's actual standard, "rationality," is thoroughly familiar, and so are its limitations. But his discussion hints at the reason so many have urged the standard of rationality. He asks that judicial decisions be self-conscious, candid, and intelligible, and each of these criteria go to the same point: that the standards of any given decision be communicable. Self-consciousness requires that a judge be aware of the relationship of his explanation to standards, candor requires that he explain the relationship, and intelligibility requires that whole be something which not only the judge but also his audience can perceive. If they cannot perceive the standard, they cannot tell whether the explanation meets it, and they must take the self-consciousness and candor of the judge on faith. Rationality is a favored standard because, rightly or wrongly, we assume that rationality constitutes a shared experience among us, and that therefore when it is invoked, something is

David B. Roe

communicated. It is this shared experience which is the life of the law. In Deutsch's words, "As is true of all common-law courts, much of the Supreme Court's prestige stems from the public's identification of the law with 'logic,' . . . it is this identification that ultimately accounts for the reservoir of public acceptance upon which courts draw."

Deutsch takes issue with the Black insistence on logic in every decision of the Supreme Court; he suggests instead the possibility that "experience" be used as a standard for decision-making.

> Black's system of constitutional 'logic' can successfully eliminate the element of discretion in constitutional adjudication only if it provides a totally coherent and comprehensive system, whose principles never conflict with each other in any conceivable set of circumstances....Under such a system . . . there would be no need for mediating devices and the avoidance of constitutional issues. Consequently, the Court, in each and every case, would be able to fulfill completely the requirement of 'candor' with regard to the basis for decision that Shapiro seeks to impose upon it.

His criticism, essentially, is that Black's "logic" does not adequately communicate a standard for decision-making unless the "logic" is in fact logic, a perfectly formal system. Otherwise the standards of decision will not be fully communicable, and the Court's audience will have to take on faith the self-consciousness and candor--the meeting of standards--of some part of its decisions. Deutsch calls this the area of discretion, but the term is slightly deceptive. The Court has no license in a discretionary decision to ignore the requirement that its decision meet standards; it has only the knowledge that its success in doing so will not be able to be measured by its audience. If discretion means freedom to decide in a number of different ways, the conscientious Justice may feel he has less discretion in cases where his standards for reaching the decision are not communicable to an audience, because he is the only one who can evaluate his own decision. Though the standards may be entirely within him, he may hold himself more highly to them.

Deutsch's common-law "experience" does not provide an alternative standard to "logic" which is equally communicable, nor is it intended to; he explicitly states that the decision-making mode he proposes is based on "the certainty, rather, . . . that words are inadequate, that even if a totally coherent and comprehensive system of law is theoretically possible, there is no warrant for believing that our judges are capable of finding and administering it." In other words, even if a full set of decision-making standards could exist within one person's consciousness, we are certain that he could not

successfully communicate it. But at the end of Deutsch's brief discussion of the logic-experience division, he includes an argument which claims to integrate the two through the medium of time. He argues that "over time, as the slow accretion of individual decisions works itself into a recognizable pattern," the decision-making standard of "experience" can achieve "the status of 'logic.'" If this means that standards of decision which are not communicable in a given decision become so over time, it is not necessarily true. If Deutsch means to say that a series of decisions may be a more effective communication device for a given standard than a single decision can be, the argument is unobjectionable. But if that is all it means, it assumes the communicability of the standard. In other words, it assumes the standard can be understood with reference to some experience shared between the judge and his audience. And in that case, it is a valid complaint from the audience of the first decision in the series that the judge should have tried harder to communicate the standard by which his decision was to be evaluated. However, if Deutsch means that time will eventually allow the communication of all standards used by judges to reach decisions, I cannot agree. Some standards, I claim, cannot be communicated, because they are based on elements of a judge's mind which are unique to him. He cannot communicate his standard because he cannot invoke any relevant shared experience with his audience. And these standards are just those we are most likely to call "moral."

## II

The struggle to communicate is not a problem only for judges or even primarily for them, since for the most part they define their sphere of competence as including only those decisions which can be measured against shared standards. Thayer's clear mistake rule, Wechsler's neutral principles, and Black's logic are all reminders to judges that their competence is so limited. The pressure to exceed those limits is strong: Bickel has complained of the inadequacy of Thayer's prescription, Deutsch of the inadequacy of Wechsler, and Black's own decisions belie his standard. But when the limits are exceeded, when judges hand down decisions which have been reached in accord with a standard which they cannot communicate, the process is likely to be furtive. Like Black, they are likely to claim that their standards are clear and clearly shared. This may be so even though the individual judges fully recognize their responsibility to explain the real standards of their decisions, because they also recognize that if they try and fail, they will damage the institution of law in more immediate ways. Judicial texts, therefore, are a poor starting point for a systematic inquiry into the problem of communicating moral standards.

A more useful text, I propose, is the work of a novelist, Samuel Beckett. The novelist also speaks to people in groups, he also depends on the possibility that his premises can be communicated to his audience through words, but unlike the judge he serves no other institution than that which allows him to communicate. I choose Beckett because, as I will try to show, he so clearly recognizes a responsibility not to mislead his audience about the reasons why he does what he does. His novels insist on the standards which the artist must meet and obsessively search out their failures to do so. Beckett's trilogy--Molloy, Malone Dies, The Unnamable--is a sustained and systematic inquiry into the possibility of communicating the experience of the self in words.

The trilogy consists of four narratives, each invented by a different narrator. In succession, each narrator becomes more self-conscious of his act of narration and more obsessed to discover his own purpose. And the more self-conscious the narrator, the less his narrative displays the conventional trappings of fiction--setting, characters, plot--and the more it focuses on the narrator himself and the motive for his existence. After a long and painstaking elimination of the devices of fiction, one by one, as each is shown to be only a distraction from some central meaning, what is left is a full book, The Unnamable, in which an unidentified consciousness speaks and in doing so tries to speak about itself.

From its opening lines, The Unnamable is a closed circuit, a narrator whose only subject and audience seem to be himself.

> Where now? Who now? When now?
> Unquestioning, I, say I. Unbelieving.
> Questions, hypotheses, call them that.
> Keep going, going on, call that going,
> call that on. . . . What am I to do,
> what shall I do, what should I do,
> in my situation, how proceed? By
> aporia pure and simple? Or by affirm-
> ations and negations invalidated as
> uttered, or sooner or later? Generally
> speaking. There must be other shifts.
> Otherwise it would be quite hopeless.
> But it is quite hopeless. (293)*

Molloy and Malone Dies showed the futility of affirmation or negation for their narrators. This speaker, if he is to go on speaking at all, must continually remind himself that he deals with paradoxes exclusively.

---

* All page references are to the one-volume Calder and Boyars edition of the trilogy, which is paged consecutively.

The fact would seem to be, if in my situation one may speak of facts, not only that I shall have to speak of things of which I cannot speak, but also, which is even more interesting, but also that I, which is if possible even more interesting, that I shall have to, I forget, no matter. And at the same time I am obliged to speak. I shall never be silent. Never. (294)

Briefly the speaker reviews the earlier characters of the trilogy, which he calls "my delegates" and "my creatures" (299, 302). The earlier narrators, Molloy, Malone, and Moran (who narrates Molloy Part II), refer to each other as companions; this narrator's attitude toward his fellow narrators suggest that he is something different, that his predecessors are only fictional avatars for some real, permanent being. This narrator claims to be that being, and tries desperately to explain. But he cannot use fictions.

> Perhaps it is time I paid a little attention
> to myself, for a change. I shall be reduced
> to it sooner or later. At first sight it
> seems impossible. Me, utter me, in the same
> foul breath as my creatures? Say of me that
> I see this, feel that, fear, hope, know and
> do not know? Yes, I will say it, and of me
> alone. Impassive, still and mute, Malone
> revolves, a stranger forever to my infirmi-
> ties, one who is not as I can never not
> be. (302)

His compulsion is to explain himself, to understand himself, not to be misled.

> All these Murphys, Molloys and Malones do
> not fool me. They have made me waste my
> time, suffer for nothing, speak of them,
> when, in order to stop speaking, I should
> have spoken of me and me alone. . . . It is
> now I shall speak of me, for the first time.
> I thought I was right in enlisting these
> sufferers of my pains. I was wrong. They
> never suffered my pains, their pains are
> nothing, compared to mine. . . . Let them
> be gone now. (305)

The narrator claims to have some idea of his real task, which he faintly perceived while narrating earlier fictions. He expects that by eliminating the confusion of those stories by refusing to go on with them, he should be able to get a clearer idea of his goal.

> For if I could hear such a music at such a
> time, I mean while floundering through a
> ponderous chronicle of moribunds in their
> courses, moving, clashing, writhing or
> fallen in short-lived swoons, with how much
> more reason should I not hear it now, when
> supposedly I am burdened with myself alone.
> But this is thinking again. And I see myself
> slipping, though not yet at the last extrem-
> ity, towards the resorts of fable. (310)

David B. Roe

He expected the discarding of the moribunds
Molloy, Moran, and Malone to make the music clearer, but it does not work.  And even by putting the
proposition in rational form he alters it in a way
which makes him suspicious; rationality has something in common with fable.  Not to be deceptive,
then,

> Would it not be better if I were simply
> to keep saying babababa, for example, while
> waiting to ascertain the true function of
> this venerable organ? (310)

These passages from The Unnamable come between long, vague pieces of narrative which are
self-consciously fable.  Only occasionally does
the narrator adopt the tone and theme illustrated
above; more of his energy is spent wrestling
with his own admitted creations, which are constantly getting out of hand.  In cycles he
returns to the familiar declaration: "It's of
me now I must speak, even if I have to do it
with their language" (326) but the topic never
lasts long, and fiction always returns.  "To
tell the truth--no, first the story" (329).  To
isolate them deprives them of much of their
power.  Yet they contain what for Beckett is
the central moral issue for the artist.  In the
first of his published dialogues with Georges
Duthuit, Beckett refers to "a certain order on
the plane of the feasible."

Duthuit:   What other plane can there be for
           the maker?
Beckett:   Logically none.  Yet I speak of an
           art turning from it in disgust,
           weary of its puny exploits, weary
           of pretending to be able, of being
           able, of doing a little better the
           same old thing, or going a little
           further along a dreary road.
Duthuit:   And preferring what?
Beckett:   The expression that there is
           nothing to express, nothing with
           which to express, no power to
           express, together with the obliga-
           tion to express.

The narrator of The Unnamable struggles with
that paradox, trying to describe the source of
the obligation in himself, yet aware that every
time he tries to speak, he is not the artist
but the artist's dummy, the equivalent of the
earlier characters of the trilogy.  "Murphy
spoke now and then, the others too perhaps, I
don't remember, but it was clumsily done, you
could see the ventriloquist" (351).  As the
novel goes on, the narrator ascribes more and
more of the ventriloquism, the "puny exploits"
of fiction, to a set of voices--a "they,"--who
interfere with his progress, distort his words,
make him say what he does not mean.  "They" are
a necessary invention for the narrator if he is

to preserve his own identity, separate from the
words which issue from him.

Molloy narrates Molloy, Malone narrates
Malone Dies; who can we say narrates The Unnamable?  Most critics have assumed that the speaker
in the last book of the trilogy who calls himself
"I" is the title figure, and have glibly referred to him as "The Unnamable."  But to do so
is to ignore the voices, the "they" who hover
over the text, not only of The Unnamable but of
the two earlier books as well.

> and so on, till I'm tempted, no, all lies,
> they know it well, I never understood, I
> haven't stirred, all I've said, said I've
> done, said I've been, it's they who said it,
> I've said nothing, I haven't stirred, they
> don't understand. (381) (emphasis added)

This claim, often repeated, makes it difficult
to label "I" as the narrator of The Unnamable.
It is even more difficult to call him the title
figure.  That title figure is the protagonist of
Beckett's book, but it does not appear in that
book.  Making the book's title into a name
violates that title; the protagonist of the book
is not merely unnamed but explicitly unnamable.

> Someone speaks, someone hears . . . the case
> is clear, it is not he, he who I know I am,
> that's all I know, who I cannot say I am, I
> can't say anything, I've tried, I'm trying,
> he knows nothing, knows of nothing, neither
> what it is to speak, nor what it is to hear,
> to know nothing, to be capable of nothing,
> and to have to try (405-06) (emphasis added)

The "he" of these lines is as close as Beckett
ever gets to his unnamable.  The "I" who speaks
is a false representation of the unnamable, false
just because it does speak and use words.

Beckett's unnamable is the mute unnamable
essence of the artist, the motive which forces
someone to try to explain himself and the standard against which the explanation is judged.
Necessarily it has no voice and no name, and
this is its frustration: "there is no name for
me, no pronoun for me" (408).  In his essay on
Proust, Beckett observed the "impenetrability of
the most vulgar and insignificant human creature"
The Unnamable focuses on that impenetrability,
located within the human creature who himself
tries to penetrate it--the artist.

The Unnamable's search is foredoomed, caught
in the paradox that its object cannot be expressed in words and yet words are its only means
of communication.  Nevertheless it makes a desperate effort to name the unnamable, to put words
to the source of words.  After a succession of
stories, an "I" emerges who seems to be the
protagonist giving voice.  "There is I, yet, I
feel it, I confess, I give in, there is I" (392).
Immediately, however, this new arrival separates
himself from his voice:

I and this noise, I see nothing else for the
moment, but I have only just taken over my
functions . . . I repeat, I and this noise,
on the subject of which, inverting the natural order, we would seem to know for certain
. . . with regard to the noise, that it has
not been possible up to date to determine
with certainty, or even approximately, what
it is, in the way of noise, or how it comes
to me, or by what organ it is emitted . . .
with regard to me, nice time we're going to
have now, that it has not yet been our good
fortune to establish with any degree of
accuracy what I am, where I am, whether I am
words among words, or silence in the midst
of silence . . . if it's I who speak, and it
may be assumed it is, as it may be suspected
it is not . . . if it's I what it is, and
if it's not I who it is, and what it is . . .
I conclude, not the good fortune to establish
. . . why I do it, if it's I who do it. (392-
93)

This long passage, sustained for two pages, is
perhaps the most dogged investigation in
The Unnamable into the identities of "I" and the
speaker. The beginning, "There is I, yes, I feel
it," is a dramatic turn in the novel, and we wait
eagerly for the promise to be fulfilled. But by
separating himself from his voice the "I"
promptly makes his words untrustworthy; who
knows how the voice, an other, is mediating
them? Then the investigation, though systematic
("I'm doing my best"), begins to disintegrate,
and as it turns to its real subject it falls
apart. The speaker recognizes his failure:
"Nice time we're going to have now" is his wry
comment on the impossibility of any inquiry
"with regard to me." As he realizes the impossibility of answers, he tries instead to identify
himself by exhorting the imagination of the
listener.

> But I really mustn't ask myself any more
> questions, if it's I, I really must not.
> More resolutions, while we're at it, that's
> right, resolutely, more resolutions. . . .
> Assume notably henceforward that the thing
> said and the thing heard have a common source,
> resisting for this purpose the temptation to
> call in question the possibility of assuming
> anything whatever. Situate this source in
> me, without specifying where exactly, no
> finicking (393)

In the same didactic tone the speaker suggests
that the visual image of "a vast cretinous
mouth" might help to sustain the listener's
imagination "when discouragement threatens to
raise its head," and he concludes boldly:

> Equate me, without pity or scruple, with him
> who exists, somehow, no matter how, no
> finicking, with him whose story this story
> had the brief ambition to be. Better,

ascribe to me a body. Better still, arro-
gate to me a mind. Speak of a world of my
own, sometimes referred to as the inner,
without choking. (394)

The subject of these self-confident sentences is
clearly the unnamable, whose story The Unnamable
tries to be. But the hortatory style of the
passage, with the repeated admonition "no fin-
icking," betrays the fact that the equation proposed between "I" and something which has
existence, body, mind, must be imperfect; it is
offered only as an approximation. Finally the
speaker concedes,

> can it be of me I'm speaking, is it possible,
> of course not . . . now I'll have to find a
> name for this latest surrogate, his head
> splitting with vile certainties. (396)

He decides, "Now it's I the orator," and in
giving him a name he concedes that this latest
"I" cannot be the unnamable.
      "I" is inevitably a surrogate; the genuine
unnamable commands no pronoun. Yet the passage
is noteworthy. It is the purest examination of
the central problem of the trilogy, the one
least encumbered with the trappings of fiction.
It presents itself as the examination of words
by words, a bodiless force pursuing itself. It
is also the last of the trilogy's episodes, the
last attempt by a narrator to communicate his
self, and it is the most disciplined.
      The novel continues for some twenty pages
more, but the text becomes a frantic recitation
of the paradoxes already established, a report
of pain without a search for the knife. The
compulsion to go on keeps the narrative alive,
but the hope of success is dead.

> I wanted myself, in my own land for a brief
> space, I didn't want to die a stranger in the
> midst of strangers, a stranger in my own
> midst . . . I must have wanted so many
> things . . . with longings and visions,
> mingling and merging in one another, I'd
> have been better employed minding what I was
> saying. But it didn't happen like that, it
> happened like this, the way it's happening
> now, that is to say, I don't know . . . I'm
> going on as best I can. (400-01)

We recognize Beckett's vision of the artist,
unable to explain the stranger of the creative
urge in his own midst. But the established
reaction to this dilemma has been revisionist,
the attempt to pull the mask of coherence and
logic over the absurdity. Here at last is no
revisionism: "But it didn't happen like that,
it happened like this, the way it's happening
now" (400). The narrative becomes only a going
on, not seeking sense but trying to avoid the
roadblocks which sense imposes.

> So long as one does not know what one is
> saying and can't stop to inquire, in tran-

David B. Roe

quillity, fortunately, fortunately, one would
like to stop, but unconditionally, I resume,
so long as, so long as, let me see, so long
as one, so long as he, ah fuck all that, so
long as this, then that, agreed, that's good
enough, I nearly got stuck. (402-03)

Fiction as a futile struggle for expression
is the image which Beckett's trilogy seems to want
to deposit with its readers.  The narrator who
most closely resembles the artist admits failure.

Notice, I notice nothing, I go on as best I
can, if it begins to mean something I can't
help it, I have passed by here, this has
passed by me, thousands of times, its turn
has come again (404)

But our response to this painstaking demonstration
of failure contradicts its judgment of fiction; we
do learn something of what Beckett is getting at,
through the processes of attenuation and extrap-
olation.  The more the words try to avoid misleading images and impressions, the smaller the
field which they can cover--but the greater their
chances of reflecting the only fact that is not
misleading.

A process of elimination can have only relative success, however, and at bottom the narrators
hold out for absolutes.  The dichotomy between
"they"--the voices--and "I"--the image of the
unnamable--is designed to reflect a dichotomy
between falsehood and truth, seen also as a
dichotomy between speech and silence.

That proves my innocence, he says it, or they
say it, yes, they who reason, they who believe, no, in the singular, he who lived, or
saw some who had, he speaks of me, as if I
were he . . . I am far, do you hear him, he
says I'm far, as if I were he . . . he seeks
me, I don't know why, he calls me, he wants
me to come out, he thinks I can come out, he
wants me to be he. (407)

"He" is the words, or the being who writes the
words in the illusion that the words can approximate truth.  But truth, what these narrators
really want to communicate, the real identity of
the unnamable, is silent.

I never spoke, I seem to speak, that's because
he says I as if he were I, I nearly believed
him, do you hear him, as if he were I (407)

The trilogy, and most clearly The Unnamable,
devotes itself to the paradox that what it wishes
to identify and communicate in words is distorted
and lost in words, that the act of speech destroys
the goal of speech.  Once the paradox is fully
developed and grasped, it leads inevitably to the
conclusion that the artist's goal is silence.
This concept is scattered in germinal form
throughout the trilogy, implicit in the many complaints about the difficulty of "going on."
Finally, The Unnamable faces it directly; the

three last long sentences of the book deal explicitly with "The silence" (411 ff.).  After
interminable rehearsals, the theme receives its
final formulation:

there I am the absentee again, it's his turn
again now, he who neither speaks nor listens,
who has neither body nor soul, it's something
else he has, he must have something, he must
be somewhere, he is made of silence, that's a
pretty analysis, he's in the silence, he's
the one to be sought, the one to be, the one
to be spoken of, the one to speak, but he
can't speak, then I could stop, I'd be he,
I'd be he, I'd be the silence, I'd be back in
the silence, we'd be reunited, his story the
story to be told, but he has no story . . .
he's in his own story, unimaginable, unspeak-
able (417) (emphasis added)

The plot of the book is the unnamable unnamed, and
so it ends.  As Beckett himself put it, "at the
end of my work there's nothing but dust--the
nameable."

Yet there is a final subsuming irony.  The
last words of the book are those which most surely
describe the stalemate of the artist--"I can't go
on, I'll go on."--and the white space, the
silence which follows them, can be read as the
last failure.  But at the same time, it is
silence which breaks the stalemate, which allows
the speaker to stop, to become reunited with himself.  Silence is the answer, the way to tell the
story which cannot be told.

III

Judges are not novelists, nor would they submit novels instead of opinions to explain their
decisions.  Even if they seek to communicate the
moral standard by which a decision is reached, of
what use to them is Beckett's rarified moral
exercise?  His morality, after all, is the
specialized morality of the artist, and the only
evidence we have that his topic is at all a moral
one is the otherwise inexplicable importance his
work places on it, the urgency to communicate the
origin and motive of art which eventually over-
whelms the art itself.  In communicating, the
artist has an intense responsibility to meet his
own standards, but none to meet the standards of
his audience.  That part of the judge's work which
is communication is performed precisely to allow
an audience to set up its own standards against
the judge's, an opportunity it demands as a condition of its continuing acceptance of the judge's
authority.  However, the cases we are concerned
with are those in which the judge has difficulty
communicating his standard and yet feels compelled to apply it to the decision before him.  We
call his compulsion moral, but is it moral in any
different way than the compulsion of The Unnamable?  In both there is a need to be understood
which struggles with the risk of being misunder-

stood, and in both the source of the struggle
is moral.

So far is not far enough.  Even if Beckett's
artist and the moral judge are theoretically
similar, it remains to be seen whether the communication tactics of the former can have any
application for the latter.  Does it mean anything to say that a judge might communicate the
moral basis for a decision through silence?

Judicial silence cannot be the same as
literary silence; the institutional demands on
judges prevent them from issuing blank sheets
of paper.  But there are various ways of fulfilling the judicial function of disposing
of cases in near silence, among them the summary
dismissal of an appeal, the denial of certiorari,
the per curiam decision, and most pointedly the
dismissal of certiorari as improvidently granted.
In each of these there is a minimum of written
explanation of a decision.

These devices, of course, are the passive
virtues of Professor Bickel.  For him, they
represent attempts by the Supreme Court to
protect "neutral principles" of decision by
avoiding the application of those principles
in awkward cases.  With Wechsler, Bickel assumes
that a neutral principle constitutes a common
standard for decision-making which the Court
shares with its audience.  Deutsch's discussion
of neutrality as the equivalent of adequate
generality illustrates the point; the importance of generality in the context of this
essay is that if a principle is sufficiently
general, each member of an audience will have
access in himself to an experience in which
he can recognize the presence of the principle.
If the Court invokes a neutral principle as
a standard for decision, therefore, it can be
confident that it has successfully communicated that standard to its audience.  When
the Court worries that the standard for a particular decision cannot successfully be communicated, it does least damage to the system
of expectation that its decisions will meet
standards if it does not even purport to
follow one.  At least such is Bickel's formulation.

Even if Bickel is right about the function of
the passivity devices, he must answer Deutsch's
complaint that the devices are devilishly hard to
keep empty.*

---

* Revealingly, Bickel appears at one point to
equate principles with morality, and to admit
that neither is susceptible of precise communication (Least Dangerous Branch at 199).  Yet
consistently he relies on the communicability of
his principles.  He does not meet the paradox
directly, but the attempt to solve it, to have it
both ways, is the necessary attempt for any explanation of morality in law.

Bickel's analysis . . . rests on the dubious
assumption that the society will always perceive the difference between 'doing nothing'
and 'legitimation.'  If, however, the Court
'does nothing' long enough, if it leaves
undisturbed--because the issue is unripe,
because further experimentation is needed,
or because it wants to 'give the electoral
institutions their head'--a sufficient
number of lower-court dispositions at variance with those of the Court would reach 'if
pushed to the wall of principled judgment,'
those decisions may well be perceived as
legitimated. . . . Conversely, a sufficiently
prolonged series of invalidations on nonconstitutional grounds might well be perceived
as an attempt to implement an unspoken
constitutional judgment.

If Bickel's interpretation of per curiams
and the rest is accepted, then the Court which
uses them must resist and fear this tendency of
the passivity devices to creep back into the most
carefully nonprincipled presentations of decisions.  But the foregoing discussion leads to
another interpretation.  Bickel claims these
devices are techniques of preventing communication of standards; but perhaps they are techniques
uniquely suited to allowing the communication of
standards in certain cases:  the communication of
morality through silence.  In other words, when
the Court reaches a decision on moral grounds and
seeks to communicate that fact to its audience,
it may choose to do so by its silence.  By refusing to invoke an experience shared with its
audience, the Court emphasizes that the standard
for its explanation--a moral one--cannot be
shared.  And yet at the same time, ironically,
the choice of silence may itself be a shared
experience, the common response of men forced
to articulate a moral standard.  To that extent
the Court, though it does not communicate the
standards by which it reaches its decision, may
communicate the point from which it starts.
Though the content of moral standards may be
uncommunicable, the sense that they are moral may
be an experience which men share, and hence if it
can be invoked that sense may be communicated.
Silence may be the only way for a Court to invoke
that sense, to bring the member of its audience
to its own starting point.

A reinterpretation of the devices which
Bickel calls passive calls for a look at their
use in real cases, where their passive or active
effect can be examined.  And the set of cases in
which they most commonly occur are the reviews of
convictions for obscenity.  Whatever the nature
of the decision standard in obscenity cases, it
has proved very difficult to put in words, and
for many the last word on the subject was
written in 1964 by Mr. Justice Stewart:

the Court [in these cases] was faced with the
task of defining what may be indefinable.  I

David B. Roe

have reached the conclusion, which I think is confirmed at least by negative implication in the Court's decisions since Roth and Alberts, that under the First and Fourteenth Amendments criminal laws in this area are constitutionally limited to hard-core pornography. I shall not today attempt further to define the kinds of material I understand to be embraced within that shorthand description; and perhaps I could never succeed in intelligibly doing so. But I know it when I see it. (Jacobellis v. Ohio, 378 U.S. 184, 197)

Stewart's concurrence, of which this is almost the whole, says both in its language and in its length that the standard is personal and that the attempt to write it down should be abandoned. The only logical sequel, and the one which actually took place, was a series of per curiam decisions, mostly without any opinion. As Deutsch points out, those decisions were not passive but active; they met the constitutional issue, albeit with silence. The most celebrated was the decision in Redrup v. New York, U.S. 767 (1967), in which the Court not only reached a per curiam decision without agreeing on its theory, but also forthrightly admitted that it had granted certiorari on the assumption that the obscenity vel non involved in the three situations before it could be determined, and had had to reject the assumption (386 U.S. at 769-70). The opinion was handed down seven months after argument was heard.

The Court's gravitation toward silence in explaining its obscenity decisions has produced a body of recent precedent which consists largely of per curiam affirmances and reversals and denials of certiorari, usually citing Redrup. According to the argument of suggested above, these devices of silence taken together can be seen as a successful communication by the Court of the ground from which it starts in deciding such cases. Normally this thesis would be hard to test, since the evidence of its truth would be a lack of attempted discussion of these very precedents. However, at least one unit of the Court's audience, a three-judge panel of the Court of Appeals for the District of Columbia, has undertaken to analyse and apply just these precedents.

Huffman v. United States was argued and decided in 1971 and a slip opinion by Judge Leventhal was issued and then withdrawn. A year later, after rehearing, the same opinion was formally issued (470 F. 2d 386), but the court deferred the issuance of its mandate in the case pending further decisions by the Supreme Court (470 F. 2d at 406). Though the case cannot be said to be decided, the opinion itself is a rare illustration of judicial construing of silence.*

The putative obscenity in Huffman consisted of "a collection of photographs of two females engaged in undressing, caressing, fondling and embracing the [sic] other." The lower court concluded that the photographs "intended to and did portray homosexual activities between two females." At trial one psychiatrist testified to the appeal to prurient interest of the pictures, and another psychiatrist contradicted him. In addition, an art critic testified without contradiction that the pictures "exceeded the national community standards for the depiction of nudity in art."

In his opinion, Leventhal finds the Huffman pictures obscene, and he claims to do so on the basis of Supreme Court precedents. "Our only proper function is to assess appellants' contentions in the light of the guidelines provided by the Supreme Court" (470 F. 2d at 394). He implies that he has produced at least a partial objective test:

Application of the obscenity standard involves a subjective element on the part of the tribunal . . . making the critical determination. With regard to the constitutional limits of this standard, however, our analysis of Supreme Court decisions makes possible some relevant conclusions for a working approach that aids us in our task in this case. (470 F. 2d at 397)

And he notes that judgments based on the subjective response of the judge are liable to Supreme Court reversal:

In I & M Amusements v. Ohio, 389 U.S. 573 . . . (1968), the Court reversed a criminal conviction based on the exhibition of a film featuring "pinups" and a series of scenes in which two women "at least nude to the waist" were "going through actions" which the trial judge said "could lead to no conclusion . . . except that they were behaving like lesbians." (470 F. 2d at 398)

Leventhal adds:

This description clearly states the judge's abhorrence . . .

---

* Since the reasons for deferring its mandate in 1972 were presumably the same as the reasons for holding back its opinion in 1971, the court's motive for issuing the opinion in 1972 makes interesting speculation. It could not simply have intended to communicate its uncertainty, for then it would have continued to withhold the opinion and would merely have announced the result of the rehearing.

law student paper

In other words, Leventhal will offer not his own standard but the standard of the Supreme Court.*

Of course, the precedents Leventhal analyses are the precedents of silence, and he lists 24 post-Redrup per curiams in a footnote (fn. 15). He thus puts himself squarely in a position to interpret the silence of the Court and to be guided by it. Nor does he simply accept the invitation of the convicted appellants to look only at results; he is sensitive to the fact that the Court's silence cannot be ignored. Yet he interprets that silence as a command to which he can put words.

> There is a tendency to dispose of cases like these with conclusory condemnations, often based on overdrawn descriptions. If we read the Supreme Court decisions aright, what is required is a factual description of contents and an analysis of what is being presented. (emphasis added) (470 F. 2d at 396)

The silent precedents mean to Leventhal that he should pay attention to the specifics of each case rather than try to apply a broad, generalizable standard. In other words, he sees the fact of silence as itself important, but he locates the importance in a meaningless distinction.

The Huffman pictures, Leventhal apparently concedes, are not hard-core pornography, since they do not depict actual "vaginal, anal, or oral penetration in the course of sexual intercourse."** He will have to draw his dividing line short of that, and he claims the authority to do so, despite Redrup, from a passage in United States v. Reidel, (402 U.S. 351, 357 (1971).*** That claim is uncertain, but at least it relies on uncertainty in the precedents. With-

out going further, Leventhal could have looked at the specific photographs in front of him and declared them to be obscene despite the absence of hard-core characteristics. In doing so he would have imitated the judicial behavior of the Court. Instead of ruling that in theory a line can be drawn and that a specific item falls on one side, however, Leventhal finds himself able actually to draw the line, to offer a definition of what is constitutionally obscene in terms which can be applied to test all cases.

Leventhal's line runs between pictures which show only one person ("singles") and those which show two or more ("duals"), and between pictures which show "imminent" sexual activity and those which do not. He cites several cases illustrating the permissible side of the line: photographs of every kind showing only one nude woman, and photographs of two or more nude people engaged in nonsexual activity, such as nudist colony photographs, cannot be prohibited (470 F. 2d at 399-400). But to indicate the far side of the line which he claims to find in the opinions of the Supreme Court, Leventhal cites only three cases, and each is a denial of certiorari on a conviction for sale of obscene photographs. In none of the three denials is there any text at all in explanation, not even a citation to Redrup.* Leventhal is thus construing judicial silence in its purest form.

To support the proposition that photographs depicting overt sexual activity between two people are constitutionally obscene, Leventhal analyses the specific contents of the photographs in each of his three precedents.** He

---

* I & M Amusements itself was a per curiam opinion and on its face offered no disapproval that the trial judge used a subjective standard; it merely reversed the conviction. Leventhal reads into the decision that disapproval, and the implication that an objective standard exists.
** Leventhal takes the definition from the Report of the Commission of Obscenity and Pornography (1970), which calls it the "market" definition. The only judicial definition he cites is from none other than Justice Stewart, dissenting in Ginzburg (two years after Jacobellis) and merely quoting from the government brief. 470 F. 2d at 393-94 n.9.
*** In Leventhal's opinion the Reidel passage appears only in a footnote, headed "See also . . . ." (470 F. 2d at 395 n.14). But in the court's per curiam opinion written after the 1972 rehearing--the opinion which defers the issuance of a mandate--the Reidel passage is said to have been relied on by Leventhal's opinion (470 F. 2d at 405).

---

* In only one, G.I. Distributors, was there any text at all, and it consisted of a dissent by Douglas citing Redrup, and a dissent by Brennan and Stewart stating the case was moot. Nothing in the last two dissents suggests an explanation of the outcome.
** The analysis appears at p. 400 of the opinion. Interestingly, though his approach depends on exactly what the photographs show, Leventhal does not consult the photographs directly; instead he relies on the descriptions of the lower courts in all three of the cases.

Even within the three carefully chosen fact situations, the existence of Leventhal's claimed standard is hard to demonstrate. By his own report, only the first case--Phelper v. Texas, 382 U.S. 943 (1965)--involves photos of what is clearly actual or imminent sexual activity between two or more people. In the second case-- Levin v. Maryland, 389 U.S. 1048 (1968)-- Leventhal says the photos in question each showed a single male with a "full erection," but alone. His explanation of the Court's action in denying certiorari on the conviction deserves to speak for itself:

David B. Roe

ignores the silence, and in the facts he finds
enough consistency to declare a legal standard.
In other words, he assumes that the Court disposes of obscenity cases according to a consistent standard, and that its method of disposition
in any case does not affect that standard or its
use. The Court may not articulate its standard,
but Leventhal is sure he can, because he is sure
it is there.

Judge Leventhal's analysis of cases in
Huffman may be taken as evidence against the
proposition of this essay: that courts can
successfully communicate through silence.
Phelper, Levin, and G.I. Distributors, along with
the other cases he cites, should have communicated
to him, through their silence, that the Court was
leaving him to his own resources to reach a moral
decision in obscenity cases. Instead of hearing
that message, Leventhal heard a contrary one.
But the current posture of Huffman may in fact
support this essay's claim. On the same day it
released the Leventhal opinion, the court in a
per curiam opinion refused to put the Leventhal
logic into effect. As its reason, the court
cites two more silent precedents of the Supreme
Court, decided since the writing of Leventhal's
opinion, which appear to contradict it. The
two decisions were per curiam reversals of con-

victions for obscene photographs, and in at least
one of the cases the photographs involved "simu-
lated sexual activity" (470 F. 2d at 404-05). If
he extrapolates from their silence as he did from
the silence of his own precedents, Leventhal is
at a dead end. As of now, the result for the
court in the District of Columbia must be to
abandon Leventhal's approach, and perhaps to
question the assumption which animates it: the
assumption that the Supreme Court is guiding its
actions by a standard which it can communicate,
but has chosen not to. If enough of its inquiries
conclude like Huffman, the court may be forced to
ask itself the obvious but disturbing question:
if the Supreme Court does have a standard which
it can communicate to us, why has it not done so?
And when it reaches that question, the D.C. court
will be in a position to understand the ironic
answer: it has.

The success of communication through silence
depends on exhaustive preparation, as Beckett
demonstrates. All alternative means must be
shown to be false, before an audience will accept
the means of silence; it will listen to anything
else first, and when it hears nothing it will
think it hears something. Each such illusion
must be disproved. A court, even the Supreme
Court, may never be able to focus the attention

This disposition is of particular signifi-
cance--even though normally denial of
certiorari is said to import no view as to
the merits. . . .In the case of the nude
male, photographs that show a full erection
may fairly be referred to as presenting the
kind of sexual response that typically
denotes imminent sexual activity. (470 F. 2d
at 400) (footnote omitted)

The "particular significance" of Levin appears
to be that not only is it a cert denial and hence
ambiguous, but that even if a resolution on the
merits is implied, the case requires even another
stage of rationalization before it can be used as
a demonstration of the proposed standard in
action. Using the same interpretive method, one
could easily claim that Levin undercuts Leventhal's standard. If Levin is one of the three
strongest cases he can come up with, one wonders
how difficult it would be to discover cases
which contradict his. Finally in the third
case--G.I. Distributors, Inc. v. New York, 389
U.S. 905 (1967)--the existence of sexual activity, actual or imminent, in the photographs was a
matter of debate even in the lower court; in a
dissent, Chief Justice Fuld of the New York Court
of Appeals objected to that majority's finding of
imminent sexual activity. See Huffman fn 44.
And as mentioned earlier, Justice Douglas dissented from the denial of certiorari in G.I. Distributors stating that he would accept cert and

reverse the conviction on the strength of Redrup.

When Leventhal goes to apply his derived
standard to the Huffman photos, he demonstrates
once again the ambiguity of his own standard,
even if one is willing to approve his methods in
obtaining it. The Huffman photos show women
undressing each other, nude women fondling each
other's breasts, and nude women lying in bed and
embracing. Leventhal singles out one picture in
particular, a photograph of "one nude lady on top
of the other, with their pubic areas about to
touch." He concludes that the Huffman photos
"represent explicit portrayal of lesbian sexual
activity, either ongoing or imminent, that bring
them within the decisions of refusing to upset obscenity convictions." (470 F. 2d at 402) But how
does he know what the models in still photographs
are "about to" do? In guessing, he provides
the subjective response for which he criticized
the trial judge in I & M Amusements. That
judge, looking at other pictures, said that
what they showed "could lead to no conclusions
except that they were behaving like lesbians,"
and he was reversed per curiam by the Supreme
Court. 389 U.S. 573. Leventhal cannot be any
more objective. Nor can he seriously claim that
the uncontradicted testimony of an art critic is
decisive, since if it becomes so it obviates the
need for Leventhal's standard. Also, of course,
if it becomes decisive it will be contradicted
testimony in all subsequent cases.

of its audience for long enough to complete the process, and therefore it may never be able to use silence confidently; the preparation may never be adequate.  But to the extent that it wishes to make decisions based on moral standards, and to communicate those standards to its audience, there may be no satisfactory substitute.

If the conclusion of this essay's argument is an absurdity, then the argument can be read as a reductio ad absurdum, and one or more of the premises set out on the first page is proved false.  That reading and that conclusion are both highly plausible.  But the argument on its face is also seriously intended, as is the concluding prescription.  That argument must be ironic because its point cannot be proved.  It is therefore entitled to claim its own failure as evidence of its moment.

Gian Carlo Menotti, *The New York Times*, Oct. 14, 1973

# The World as an Audience

## By Gian Carlo Menotti

It is difficult for an artist today not to feel that his contributions are marginal or superfluous to a social pattern that relegates his to the field of entertainment. The efforts of such artists as Picasso, Pound, Chaplin, Sartre and Mishima to concern themselves with world problems are greeted with suspicion if not derision. The many people who still believe that the artist should confine himself to esthetics seem to forget that Verdi's, Beethoven's and Mozart's operas made strong political statements just as Goya, Picasso and Titian did in their paintings and Dante, Voltaire and Tolstoy in their writings.

I do not agree with Sartre that the work of a contemporary artist must be politically committed. On the other hand, there's nothing more moving than an art which devotes itself to a noble human cause and nothing more challenging for an artist than to feel needed within a social structure. Perhaps it is true that more often than not an artist's political views are somewhat naive; but at least they generally state something. How is it that the press, so ironic toward the politically minded artist, doesn't make equal fun of the politician's speech, which can succeed in saying absolutely nothing?

In illuminating conversations with Margaret Mead, Sol Tax and other anthropologists, I discovered that we all share conclusions about man's inhumanity, intolerance and racial hatred. A certain emotional deadness makes man unable to share his enemy's feelings.

I've been accused of manipulating the guts of my audience. But doesn't most art do just that? Whether it is to evoke pity or pride or patriotism or indignation or religious feelings it is by disturbing the emotions of his audience that the artist delivers his message. Isn't that how the Trojan Women and Rigoletto and Tristan and Guernica achieve their aim? If any criticism can be made of contemporary art it is just this: that it is no longer able to reach its audience emotionally.

No moral judgment about our fellow man is really valid unless it is emotionally felt. Nothing is more hateful than cold self-righteousness. It is easier for a man to accept the desperate iconoclasm of the drunkard than the cool moralizing of the teacher. But, of course, the process of feeling is a very painful one. Because of the excess of today's horrors, there is a marked tendency in our generation, either through drugs or self-imposed indifference, to avoid it.

Should our Presidents and leaders really know what it is to bomb a village; could they witness the death of a napalmed child; could they be taught to read the sorrow in a mother's face—would we still have wars? A naive question, but what man who has lived through a war has not asked himself the very same question.

All this leads to the inevitable question: What can one do about it? I am an artist, not a philosopher or a moralist. I state the case without offering a solution. But it is perhaps at home where mankind should be taught to feel. Rather than simply tell our children about the humiliation of poverty and the force of despair, we should teach them to experience and not only observe. Let young men, now that it is possible, live with all sorts of races and civilizations rather than tell them that the French are selfish, Jews avaricious, Germans sadistic.

Nietzsche said that "never does man lie more than when he's indignant." What the phrase implies to me is that we all carry within us the seed of evil; that we condemn in others what we could commit ourselves; that our indignation is a way of hiding the frightening reflection of our own image. We like to identify ourselves with the persecuted, with the tortured, with the killed because we hate to think that we are also the executioners.

We are not too different from the gangster who weeps at soap operas. It is easy to say: "Oh, I would never do that." I, too, of course, like to think that about myself, but I also ask myself the haunting question: Would I not drop a bomb "somewhere" were I threatened with the death of my own child? "If they torture me I will admit anything," declared the Soviet historian, Piotr Yakir.

Perhaps only the saint can achieve an emotional identity with another human being. I cannot agree with T. S. Eliot that there are several ways of serving God and that the man who preaches at the cocktail party is equal in the eyes of God to the missionary who is eaten in Africa by a colony of ants. Most of us are too cowardly to seek martyrdom. But we do have our saints today and they are those who risk ridicule, if not their lives, by baring their true feelings.

An evil man is fundamentally a man in whom emotional atrophy is complete. Whether we like it or not we must learn to identify ourselves not only with the killed but also with the killer because, unfortunately, we are both.

*Gian Carlo Menotti has composed many operas. His newest in "Tamu-Tamu."*

THE EPISTEMOLOGY
OF POLITICAL ANALYSIS

L. T. Hobhouse and the Concept of the State

Jan G. Deutsch

I

A historian of political thought of the
stature of Sir Ernest Barker has recommended
Leonard Hobhouse's volume on The Metaphysical
Theory of the State to future generations.(1)   It
seems a work of supererogation, therefore, to
begin an essay on Hobhouse with an analysis of
factors which make a study of his political theory
peculiarly rewarding.

Hobhouse has, however, attracted relatively
little attention since his death in 1929.(2)   In
part, this is due to the large-scale changes in
the historical situation which have taken place
since Hobhouse wrote.  Neither the problem of
aggressive imperialistic expansion by Great
Britain nor the problem of labor's right to
organize, for example, are central issues in
today's world, and Hobhouse's writings on these
issues consequently seem today to be either self-
evident or beside the point.  In this sense,
Hobhouse was too much the product of his time.

Another difficulty evident in much of his
work--a difficulty explicitly recognized even by
some of his most ardent admirers(3)--is the extent
to which his epistemological speculations conditioned his work in other areas.  This, however,
is also one of the most valuable aspects of his
thought.  To a remarkable degree, The Metaphysical
Theory of the State represents merely one facet of
a system of thought embracing all aspects of the
social process.(4)  Based on an epistemology
explicitly developed in his Theory of Knowledge,
Hobhouse's political thought is solidly anchored
in a comprehensive theory of sociology based both
on historical surveys (such as the one contained
in Morals in Evolution) and studies in comparative
culture (such as the one in The Material Culture
and Social Institutions of the Simpler Peoples).
Consequently, an analysis of his political
thought is immeasurably aided by the fact that
the philosophical and sociological premises on
which it is based are explicitly presented.

Hobhouse's political thought is also representative of his age in the sense of embodying a
mean between more extreme schools.  Thus, one
contemporary history of political thought classi-
fied him as one of the philosophers of "compromise."(5)  In short, an analysis of Hobhouse's
conception of the state should provide an insight
into the struggle of his age to develop political
philosophies independent of the Hegelian principles criticized in The Metaphysical Theory of the
State.

An insight into this struggle is of peculiar
importance in terms of the present historical
situation.  Perhaps the most striking fact about
the difference between the present era and that
in which Hobhouse lived is that they are separated by so few years.  In many ways, furthermore,
events have altered the objective facts of our
world far more rapidly than our conceptions of
that world have changed.  To a striking degree,
Hobhouse's thought seems to be that of a contemporary, in spite of the fact that the problems
to which that thought was applied belong to an
earlier era.  If we face different problems, many
of the principles we apply are nevertheless based
on systems of thought very like that contained
in the works of Leonard Hobhouse.  That his work
is representative of the age in which it was
produced is important, then, because at least in
terms of the conceptions by which contemporary
events are analyzed and judged, that age is in
very many ways our own.

II

Hobhouse's method in The Metaphysical Theory
of the State is to reduce the Hegelian theory of
the state to three basic propositions and to
demonstrate the inadequacies inherent in each.
The first of these propositions is that true
individuality or freedom results from conformity
to one's own real will.  Hobhouse criticizes this
formulation as involving a confusion between an
ideal possibility and practical reality.  Granting for the sake of argument the premise that
there would be no conflict between social duty
and personal desire in a perfectly rational will,
Hobhouse insists that human nature is both richer
and more varied than the conscious and deliberate
will.  Consequently, human beings have desires
other than those which fit in with the plans of
the society in which they live and--waiving the
question as to whether or not such desires are in
their own best interests--frustration of such
desires is regarded as a lack of complete freedom.
Hegel's identification of true freedom with the
real will thus involves a will which is not real
in the sense that it exists in human beings as we

know them.

The second proposition which Hobhouse regards as central in the Hegelian conception of the state is the identity between the real and the general will. Such an identity entails the assertion of the existence of a common self, which wills that which is desired by all. This assertion Hobhouse attacks as involving a confusion between identity of character and identity of continuous existence. Hobhouse recognizes the existence in human beings of feelings which can be generalized to all of society. He denies, however, that sympathetic or even shared feelings or wills ever become identical. On the contrary, the knowledge that the I which is experiencing exists separately from other individuals, is itself a datum of experience which will always make a personal experience something different from the same events experienced by another person, or even from a second personality's awareness of what I am experiencing.

An individual, according to Hobhouse, is characterized by a sense of his own continuous existence, and no amount of experience shared with other individuals can result in the loss of the personal identity reflected in this sense of continuous existence. As Hobhouse puts it,

> The entire system of . . . subjective acts or states forms a continuum, constituting what I know within me as my individuality or myself. My consciousness of myself rests upon a distinction between this thread of enjoyment and suffering and the entire system of objects to which it relates, and my sense of personal identity is my recognition of the continuity of this thread.(6)

Consequently, there can exist no single common self willing that which all men in a society desire, but only a group of individuals, each of whom is considering the others in what he wills.

The impact of these two sets of criticisms upon Hegel's system is well illustrated by an analysis of the famous paradox of the criminal willing his own punishment. In terms of Idealist theory, a criminal, as a rational member of society, recognizes the need for certain general rules by which society must be governed if anarchy is to be avoided. Since such rules are by definition general, the criminal must have willed that they should apply to all men in the society, including himself. In this sense, then, he has willed his own punishment.

Hobhouse's first argument is directed towards the assumption that the criminal acts freely only when he acts as a rational member of society. Granting that even a criminal recognizes that society must be governed by a set of general rules, he also has certain desires which he is attempting to fulfill by means of his criminal acts. Nor is there any reason to conclude that these desires are less real for the criminal than his rational appreciation of the need for general rules. Quite the contrary, if the criminal has

considered the matter at all, he has concluded that he would rather attempt to fulfill those desires than abide by the necessary general rules. To punish him for such acts, therefore, is not to implement his freedom by helping him to realize that which he has freely willed but, on the contrary, to restrain him from doing what he desires.

If a man acts freely only when he acts as a rational member of society, however, the Idealists then attempt to demonstrate that there can no longer exist any difference between the individual and the social will. In terms of our example, the criminal's will can be identified by reference to the laws and customs of the society in which he lives. Hobhouse, however, denies that individual experience, or will, can ever merge into an objective general will embodied in law and custom, and he bases his argument on the analysis outlined above of the difference between individual and shared experience.

The third basic Hegelian proposition is the identification of the common self or general will with the state. Hobhouse has, of course, already denied the existence of a common self or general will. Consequently, he denies to the state the role of supreme arbiter of social affairs, and insists instead on regarding it as one association among many. Furthermore, writing as he did in the midst of World War I, he regarded this false view of the dignity and power of the state as one of the causes of that conflict. Continued adherence to such a theory could, he felt, end only in a world of militarized states, suppressing freedom in the name of the state internally, and continually engaged in aggressive war against one another. The alternative, he felt, lay not only in a different view of the end and role of the state, but also necessarily entailed a different view of philosophy and history than that espoused by Hegel—a system, in short, such as that represented by his own works.

III

In strikingly contemporary fashion, Hobhouse defines truth as correlation.(7) In other words, a statement is said to be true when several independent tests all point to its validity. In this way, knowledge is a continually self-correcting process.

This principle enabled Hobhouse to reconstruct a great deal of sensationalist psychology and epistemology which had been subjected to severe criticism. Thus, with Locke, Hobhouse believed that knowledge started with received sensations. The obvious difficulty with such a starting point is that there is no necessary connection between the simple sensation and what we know to be a varied and complex reality. The school of philosophers who attempted to develop

Locke's epistemology found it extremely difficult to explain the process by which a complex picture of reality was evolved from a series of simple received sensations. Kant offered one solution, by positing pre-existing categories in the mind into which reality was organized. This solution has the severe limitation, however, of making unmediated knowledge of reality impossible. In terms of Kant's epistemology, we know that reality which the structure of our minds imposes on received sensations, but not necessarily that which has caused those sensations.

Hobhouse, however, because of his principle of truth by correlation, was able to deny that the ideas which the mind derived from sensations were in any sense simple. He asserted that the datum received from outside was in itself real, but that its meaning was a complex matter, which would become increasingly clear as it was interpreted in a variety of ways in different situations. Thus, in place of Locke's sensations resulting in simple ideas representative of reality, there are data being received by our senses, interpreted in a variety of ways, and slowly developed into an integrated picture of reality. Reality, then, must no longer be imposed by the mind of man, since what is real is the datum itself.

The debt owed by this theory to scientific method is obvious. What Hobhouse is proposing is the application of scientific method to epistemology. In other words, the received data of experience are subjected to a variety of independent operations based on varying hypotheses. Each operation will reveal a new fact about the datum and true hypotheses or interpretations are those which serve to correlate the largest number of facts.

What was valuable in this theory was that it enabled Hobhouse to overcome many of the difficulties of sensationalist epistemology by postulating that the received data are in themselves as complex as the reality they describe. This he is able to do because his epistemology is itself a self-correcting one, in which ideas about the datum become more complex as new and independent operations produce more and more information about it. As a result, Hobhouse is further able to identify reality with the datum of the received sensation.

It is, of course, not the purpose of this essay to determine the validity of this particular theory. What is important, however, is that Hobhouse's work represents to a remarkable degree a unified system, and certain principles derived from this epistemology will be found in all of his sociological and political conceptions. As might be expected from an epistemology modeled so closely on the lines of scientific method, Hobhouse is a rationalist. By this is meant simply that he believes that reality is capable of being described in terms of objective, communicable, correlative statements. If truth is to be determined by the extent to which statements about given data are correlated by other statements about the same data in different situations, it is evident that such statements about facts discovered as a result of performing operations on these data must be capable of being communicated.

What is more important, however, is that Hobhouse's theory that our knowledge itself represents reality, rather than merely thoughts about reality, implies that reality itself is subject to the same laws of rationality in terms of which our minds operate. In that case, man as a rational being should be capable of controlling the reality in whose midst he exists. The extent to which Hobhouse accepted this view will be considered in connection with his views on evolution.

A theory which envisages reality as being continually revealed as hypotheses become correlated with one another in increasingly complex ways implies more, however, than a belief in rationality. It requires also the assumption that such correlations do in fact exist in nature. This belief Hobhouse referred to as the principle of harmony, and he held that it was present both in the natural and social worlds. Hobhouse realizes, of course, that not all elements in the social world do in fact exist in a relation of mutual helpfulness or harmony. In The Rational Good, however, he develops the conception of social harmony as the proper end for human action. What must be noted, then, is the relationship between this normative conception and the epistemological assumption of the existence of this harmony implied in Hobhouse's conception of reality as discoverable through a process of correlation.

Hobhouse's conception of correlation was, however, a sophisticated one. Thus, he realized the damage which was done to facts by an attempt to apply mechanistically a fruitful hypothesis developed in one field of research to questions in quite different contexts. Consequently, while the concept of evolution is central in Hobhouse's sytem, he does not follow Spencer in holding that evolution, even in social relations, is necessarily an automatic process which functions according to its own logic despite any attempt by man to turn it to his own uses. On the contrary, Hobhouse believed that evolution was an automatic process only until the emergence of rational beings. Thereafter, as beings developed who were capable of reasoning, and therefore of adapting to a wide variety of situations in terms of general principles--rather than responding to stimuli only in terms of predetermined reactions--evolution became increasingly a matter of purposive development, subject to control by rational beings. As man became increasingly rational, then, and learned to control his own environment, he, rather than any automatic process of natural selection, increasingly determined the conditions of his

future development, and in this way, that development itself.

Man, in Hobhouse's view, is a social animal.
Thus,

> Men need society not merely to protect them-
> selves, but as the field of their own
> lives. . . .[If] I would be any of the things
> that would make me a man I must for their com-
> pleteness live in a society. I must do so,
> not primarily for what I get from society but
> rather for what I give, not for what I receive
> but for what I spend, for my own impulses,
> cravings, capacities that I fulfil in social
> life.(8)

It is the acute awareness of the social side of
man's nature that caused Hobhouse to characterize
society as organic, although he was careful, in
Social Development, to indicate the extent to
which man as an individual is far less rigidly
determined by the society of which he is a part
than, for example, a single cell in a more complex animal.(9) Hobhouse's analysis of comparative ethnographical materials in The Material
Culture and Social Institutions of the Simpler
Peoples and his account of the historical
development of law, the position of women, and
interclass relations in Morals in Evolution, all
describe the increasing rationalization by man
of his social environment. Given Hobhouse's
view of harmony as the proper end of human action,
it is hardly surprising to find that this process
is described in terms of an increasingly complex
adjustment in society of individual needs and
desires.

Hobhouse's description of the development of
political institutions follows a similar pattern.
After an early stage in which man is organized on
the basis of kinship groups, a period of con-
solidation ensues which is characterized by the
emergence of some form of absolute authority.
This is followed by a third form of political
organization, based upon citizenship rather than
authority. At this stage, government is merely
the delegated agent of the people as a whole, and
exists to secure the recognition of personal
rights and the advancement of the common good.

The advancement of the common good, as
indicated above, involves a process of harmonizing increasingly greater amounts of individual
freedom. The possibility of this harmony is
based on man's social nature, on his awareness of
the extent to which he needs society in order to
live a full life. On the other hand, however,

> in so far as men's natures are out of
> harmony, restraints are required. They are
> required by freedom as much as by harmony,
> for . . . the uncharted freedom of one would
> be the unconditional servitude of all but that
> one, and conversely a freedom to be enjoyed
> by all must impose some restraint upon all.
> If I am free to do this, take that, or go

this way, that means that neither you nor
anyone else must prevent me. The respect in
which I am free places a limiting restraint
upon everyone else. The guaranteed system
of liberties is, therefore, the obverse of
an enforceable system of restraints.(10)

The function of the state, therefore, is to
impose those restraints which will secure the
greatest freedom for the greatest number, by
limiting rights at the point at which they
threaten to impinge upon the rights of others.
In this way, the state fulfills its function of
enforcing a set of rules designed to create that
harmony which is the end of human action.

At this point, however, it might well be
asked how far Hobhouse is from the Hegelian concepts which he criticized in The Metaphysical
Theory of the State. The harmony which it is
the state's function to enforce is the product of
man's increasing application of rationality to
his social environment. Man uses the state in
order to legislate those restraints for the
community, which will ensure the greatest freedom
for the greatest number. Presumably, as man
becomes increasingly rational, he will legislate
more restraints in order to implement greater
freedom in terms of an increasingly complex
adjustment or harmonization of individual interests. Is this however, saying something other
than that man will increasingly recognize his
own real will, and, in Hegel's terms, that he
will find real freedom only by following that
will? The answer to this question requires a
more extended analysis of Hobhouse's conception
of the nature and role of the state in society.

IV

In a system whose premises are as explicit as
those in Hobhouse's works, it is surprising to
find relatively few definitions of key terms.
There is, for example, no attempt formally to
define the concept of sovereignty. Given this
lack of definition, it is perhaps not surprising
to find Hobhouse confusing the state as an
organization with its support in the governed
society in his definition of the state system as
including "along with the machinery of law and
administration the constituent authority on which
the government rests."(11) A similar confusion
exists in his later definition of the state as
"the community, organized for certain purposes."(12)

Both definitions inevitably obscure the
problem of legitimacy. Any state which includes,
by definition, the constituent authority on which
the government rests, is by definition legitimate.
The problem of political obligation cannot be
analyzed in these terms, because the definition
of the state given by Hobhouse already includes
the assumption that the state is itself the
community, organized for certain purposes.

This constituent authority must be that aspect of the community which is fulfilling its purposes by means of the state. In Hobhouse's terms, this refers to that aspect of man's rationality which is imposing harmony upon the social environment. Insofar as man, as a social animal, exercises his rationality, then, he organizes a harmonious community, employing the state for the purpose of enforcing the necessary system of restraints. By postulating a state which includes its own constituent authority, however, Hobhouse comes perilously near to holding that the state itself includes this rational aspect of man's nature, which Hegel would identify as the common self.

Hobhouse, however, is attempting to make quite a different point. Admittedly, his definition assumes the answer to any inquiry concerning the grounds of political obligation. By defining the state as the community organized for certain purposes, however, he emphasizes that it is only one association among many, fulfilling only certain social functions. Other, equally important functions are fulfilled by the family, the trade association, and even the social club. Consequently, Hobhouse is opposing a pluralistic society to the Idealist conception of the state as the final arbiter of society.

Furthermore, based on his theory of purposive evolution, Hobhouse regards rationality as the standard to which the state must conform. As man has evolved, he has utilized the state as a means of imposing rationality upon his social environment. Consequently, the success or failure of the state must be judged in terms of man's rationality. This standard Hobhouse opposes to the Idealist standard of a general will embodied in the society's laws and customs, which is ultimately self-validating in that it refers for its standards only to itself.

Finally, in place of the Hegelian proposition that the purpose of the individual is to advance the general will embodied in the state, Hobhouse regards the state as existing only for the purpose of ensuring the greatest freedom for the greatest number. In his words, "the more developed the conception of the common good the more completely will a society guarantee the natural rights of its individual members."(13)

Thus, Hobhouse was enabled to formulate the difference between his and the Idealist conception of the state in the following terms:

> In the democratic or humanitarian view it is a means. In the metaphysical view it is an end. In the democratic view it is the servant of humanity in the double sense that it is to be judged by what it does for the lives of its members and by the part that it plays in the society of humankind. In the metaphysical view it is itself the sole guardian of moral worth. In the democratic view the sovereign state is already doomed, destined to subordination in a community of the world. In the metaphysical view it is the supreme achievement of human organization.(14)

In order to define precisely the nature of the opposition between these two conceptions of the state, however, it is necessary to analyze Hobhouse's conception of the common good and the nature of the rights which its development creates. Hobhouse was a professor of sociology. As might be expected, therefore, his awareness of the social nature of man is supplemented by a definition of rights in basically sociological terms. Thus, to say that A has a right to something means that the members of A's society have agreed to do nothing to interfere with A's right. This is not, of course, a theory of natural rights in the sense in which Locke used that term, a distinction which is drawn by Hobhouse himself when he points out that

> The older thinkers spoke of . . . "natural rights," but to this phrase, if uncritically used, there is the grave objection that it suggests that such rights are independent of society, whereas, if our arguments hold, there is no moral order independent of society and therefore no rights which, apart from social consciousness, would be recognized at all.(15)

Rights exist, therefore, because they are enforced by the state, and the state is successful when it succeeds in harmonizing the greatest possible number of rights. Hobhouse is thus able to adopt the utilitarian standard of measuring happiness in terms of the greatest good for the greatest number. His view of the function of the state, furthermore, enabled him to respond to the social needs of his age by advocating state action--as opposed to the Benthamite policy of laissez-faire--as the means in terms of which this good was to be attained.

In order to enforce these rights, however, the state must have the power to coerce individuals. It has, moreover, a duty to utilize this ultimate right of coercion in the interests of society. "The state," as Hobhouse puts it,

> a fallible organization of fallible man, has nevertheless to act according to its lights for the safety of the whole. . . . [W]hen by disobeying A would in its judgment do a wrong to B, there in the end it has to exercise constraint, and there seems to be no appeal.(16)

Hobhouse recognizes that the state is fallible, and that its judgment as to whether A's act would do a wrong to B may in retrospect prove to have been incorrect. Beyond admonishing against cruelty and irresponsible use of power, however, there seems, as Hobhouse puts it, "to be no appeal." Since the state has the power to

coerce the individual, therefore, it is, in
practice, the final arbiter of its own actions.
It has, furthermore, a duty to impose any constraint which it finds to be necessary.  Thus,
though fallible, Hobhouse's state, within its
own sphere of action, seems to be as unchallengeable as the metaphysical state.  The difference
between the two conceptions, then, must be accounted for in terms of the difference between
the sphere of action which is granted to the
state in each of the theories.

Hobhouse's state exists in order to realize
the common good, by providing the means for increasing harmony in society.  It accomplishes
this by enforcing necessary restraints upon
individual action, and thus harmonizing the conflicting rights of members of society.  What sets
limits to its sphere of action is, therefore, the
fact that it is justified in imposing a restraint
only when the exercise of one man's right
threatens to conflict with the rights of a different individual.  It may, being fallible, overstep these bounds, but it is, in such a case,
acting beyond the bounds of its legitimate
authority.

In terms of this limitation upon the
sphere of action of the state, Hobhouse is able,
in a passage crucial to an understanding of his
conception of the state, to re-introduce a
theory of natural rights.

> If [an individual] maintains as a right a
> general principle of action incompatible
> with the good of the community, he must hold
> that what is right is one thing and what is
> good another, and that not merely by the
> accidental circumstances of a peculiar case
> but as a matter of principle.  Unless then
> we are to suppose such deep-seated conflict
> in the ethical order we must regard the
> common good as the foundation of all personal
> rights.  If that is so, the rights of man
> are those expectations which the common good
> justify him in entertaining, and we may even
> admit that there are natural rights of man
> if we conceive the common good as resting
> upon certain elementary conditions affect-
> ing the life of society, which hold good
> whether people recognize them or not.
> Natural rights, in that case, are those
> expectations which it would be well for a
> society to guarantee to its members,
> whether it does or does not actually guar-
> antee them.(17)

At least three propositions are implicit in
this attempt to re-establish a modified doctrine
of natural rights.  First, the impossibility of
a "deep-seated conflict in the ethical order"
such as that which would be entailed by an
individual right impossible of harmonization with
the common good represents, on Hobhouse's part,
what is ultimately an act of faith.  He recognizes, of course, that such disharmonies and

examples of selfishness exist and are, in fact,
deeply rooted in human nature.  As an analysis
of his epistemology indicated, however, his
definition of truth as a function of correlation
implied the assumption that reality is ultimately
harmonious.

To the extent that man is rational, he
shares in this harmony.  Furthermore, based on
his view of purposive evolution, Hobhouse believed that man, as he becomes increasingly
rational, more and more shapes his environment
according to this principle of harmony.  The
state, then, is for Hobhouse the instrument which
a community of men employ in order to develop
society in accordance with the principle of
harmony.  It is this development, finally, which
results in the continual expansion of personal
rights.  Man's increasing freedom, therefore, is
the product of his increasing rationality.  Consequently, although Hobhouse may insist that man
does not become free by conforming to his real
will, he is himself implying at least that man is
free only insofar as he in fact participates in
the principle of harmony.

The second proposition implicit in Hobhouse's
attempt to re-establish a form of the natural
rights doctrine concerns the nature of those
rights themselves.  There can be no "deep-seated
conflict" between personal rights and the common
good precisely because those rights are themselves social in nature and exist only because
society has organized a state whose function it
is to enforce such rights.  Consequently,
although Hobhouse denies the identity between
the real and the general will (as well as that
between the individual and the common self), he
is holding at least that an identity exists between the individual's personal rights and the
common good.  He holds, furthermore, that man
participates in this common good precisely to
the extent that he is rational.

The third proposition which Hobhouse
attacked in The Metaphysical Theory of the State
concerns the identification of the state with
the common self or general will.  His own theory,
however, leads to a very similar conclusion.
Practically speaking, Hobhouse's state is the
final arbiter of its own actions, and it has the
duty of imposing restraints upon individuals in
the best interests of society.  In so doing,
however, it is inevitably defining its own
proper sphere of action and, in the process,
increasing or contracting the scope of the
common good, and with it, the concomitant system
of personal rights.  In at least this practical
sense, then, the state itself defines the common
good, and is, to that extent, identical with it.

Hobhouse argues, however, that the state,
though in terms of power the final arbiter of its
own actions, is nevertheless fallible, and may
therefore act wrongly and overstep the bounds
of its legitimate authority.  Insofar as man's
rationality has successfully resulted in an

expansion of the common good and the concomitant system of personal rights, this has been done, according to Hobhouse, by utilizing the state to impose a greater and more complex body of restraints in order to create a wider range of individual rights. Whatever the common good may be at a particular point in history, therefore, it exists concretely in the form of a series of restraints imposed upon individuals by the state. Once again, then, the common good is identified with the state.

A change in the system of restraints imposed by the state indicates that a new stage of harmony has been achieved. On the basis of this new common good, certain prior decisions on the part of the state may be seen to have been erroneous. In a sense, of course, this implies that the state is self-correcting. It does not, however, support Hobhouse's assertion that the state may exceed its legitimate authority. On the contrary, if the identification of the common good involves a reference to the complex of restraints enforced by the state, it then appears that any restraint imposed by the state is by definition a part of that common good. The state is thus by definition always acting in the interests of the common good.

Upon analysis, then, the system contained in Hobhouse's writings strikingly resembles the metaphysical theory of the state. Any attempt to limit the state, in terms of either system, seems by definition to involve opposition to the common good. It is safe to say, on the basis of The Metaphysical Theory of the State, that Hobhouse intended to reach no such conclusions.(18) His system, in fact, represented an attempt to provide an alternative to Hegelian theories. That system must be examined, therefore, in order to determine the defect in it which makes possible the deduction of Hegelian conclusions from Hobhouse's conception of the state.

V

As indicated by the fact that Hobhouse defined the state as including within it the constituent authority on which it rests, the problem which he failed to take into account was that of creating enforceable limits on state action. Thus, in describing the difference between democracy and absolute monarchy, Hobhouse states that once the people

> could look upon the Government as their servant and the acts of the Government as their acts, it followed necessarily that the antagonism between democracy and governmental action fell to the ground.(19)

In one sense, this conception of the state can be explained in terms of Hobhouse's historical setting. Hobhouse wrote at a time when the shortcomings of laissez-faire as a social and

political doctrine were becoming increasingly obvious. The economic problems of democracy--in particular those involved with labor's right to organize for purposes of collective bargaining--were becoming increasingly acute. A good deal of Hobhouse's work, such as Liberalism, was devoted to justifying state intervention for the purpose of guaranteeing that measure of equality in terms of economic power which is necessary if the conception of political equality is to be a meaningful one.(20) Similarly, his doctrine of purposive evolution may be understood as a philosophical justification for state intervention, in opposition to Spencer, whose theory of social evolution as an automatic process, incapable of being modified by human intervention, involved the advocacy of a policy of laissez-faire in order to allow this evolutionary process to function with maximum efficiency.

The problem of establishing enforceable limits on state action is, of course, an acutely practical one. Hobhouse's failure to deal with it is, then, in one sense due to the fact that his practical aim was to justify an increase in the scope of such action. What Hobhouse failed to realize, however, was that as the sphere of legitimate state action expanded, the increasing power necessary to fulfill the state's new functions made it increasingly difficult, as a practical matter, to check even unwarranted usurpations.

On this point, Hobhouse was not only a careless philosopher, but also a bad sociologist. He realized, of course, that

> Any association of people involves some modification, temporary or permanent, superficial or far-reaching, in the people themselves.(21)

What he neglected to do, however, was to examine the logical consequences of this fact. Thus, his view that the democratic state was destined to be subordinated in a community of the world is based on his belief that

> In reality there is no such thing as a unity of experience as between the members of a state contrasted with the lack of unity as between members of different states . . . and for many purposes the relations between corresponding classes of different states are closer than the relations between very different classes within the same state.(22)

What he neglected to consider, however, was that a unity of national experience would be increased precisely to the extent that the state more actively intervened in a broader range of individual activites.

The results of this unity of experience in terms of national loyalty are apparent in a recent study of the social attitudes of the populations of several states.(23) Even in his own day, however, the phenomenon of German Social

Democrats voting war credits for a conflict which
they had, in terms of class, specifically dis-
avowed, should at least have given Hobhouse
pause.

Institutions, furthermore, at a certain point
in their development, do develop purposes of
their own, at least to the extent of preserving
the conditions necessary to their own continued
existence. While these purposes are not necessarily congruent with the best interests,
objectively determined, of the members of any
given institution, a good sociologist should have
been aware of the extent to which a powerful
institution is capable of moulding its members'
preferences to the point that, at least in
the individual's mind, his own interests do
coincide with those of the institution. It
was this insight, albeit in an exaggerated form,
that the Idealist theory of the state erected
into a complete philosophical system, and
Hobhouse's own opposing system is a faulty one
to the extent that it denies the validity of
this phenomenon.

Insofar as the Idealist theory tends to make
the state supreme, however, it fails completely,
as Hobhouse was acutely aware, to provide any
justification for imposing limits on state
actions. The most important criticism of Hobhouse's sytem, then, is that it, too, fails to
provide any such justification. This is, of
course, far more serious than the absence of a
practical formula for imposing such limits.
That, it could be argued, is not the task of
political theory. What Hobhouse has failed to
provide, however, is a justification for the
imposition of limits, and this is a task which
only political theory can fulfill.

Hobhouse rightly insists upon the social
nature of rights, and thus identifies rights
with restraints upon individual conduct. The
identification of such rights with the common
good, however, results in the common good itself
becoming identical with the system of restraints
imposed upon individuals by the existing state.
The degree to which the common good has been
realized, is also, for Hobhouse, a measure of
the extent to which man has succeeded in imposing
his rationality upon the social environment. In
this way, the existing state also becomes identified with man's developing rationality. The
state is, then, in theory as well as in practice,
the final arbiter of the limits of its own
action. In Hobhouse's theory, therefore, no less
than in the Idealist conception, state action is
ultimately self-validating.

The natural rights theory, as presented in
the works of a political philosopher such as
Locke, provided a theoretical justification for
the imposition of limits on state action. Due
to his insistence upon the social nature of
rights, Hobhouse is forced to deny the validity
of this natural rights doctrine. In so doing,
he is destroying one possible justification for

limiting state action. Because of his failure
to provide any alternative theoretical justifications on the basis of which such limits
could be imposed, however, his own conception of
the state ends in the Hegelian paradox of self-
validating action.

As indicated above, the paradox involved in
Hobhouse's conception of the state stems from
his insistence upon identifying personal rights
with the common good. This identity was justified in terms of his principle of harmony. This
principle, as an analysis of Hobhouse's epistemology demonstrates, is implicit in the definition of rationality as a means of making valid
and increasingly complex statements about
reality. The validity of such statements, and
therefore the basis of our knowledge of reality,
Hobhouse identified with the process of constructing a system of mutually supporting correlations. By identifying the results of this
process with reality, however, Hobhouse is
assuming that such correlations do, in fact,
exist, or, in other words, that reality is
ultimately harmonious.

Such correlations are, moreover, by definition social in nature. What they represent are
those aspects of experience about which men
agree. This area of common agreement is not,
however, identical with the whole of experience.
Some truths--perhaps some very important ones--
are individual and ultimately incommunicable.
Such truths are, of course, uncorrelateable, but
they are not for that reason any the less real.
That Hobhouse was aware of this is suggested by
the careful distinction he made between shared
and identical experience in his refutation of the
Hegelian proposition that the real will is
identical with the general will. Without
attempting to offer either an alternative epistemology or an original political theory, it is
suggested that Hobhouse ignored this irreducible
element of disharmony in formulating his own
epistemology, and that the failure of his
political theory is due to this defect in his
theory of knowledge.

Needless to say, the problem of justifying
the imposition of limits upon state action is
still with us. It is, in fact, one of the
paramount problems facing contemporary political
theory. At least in democratic societies, this
is in large part due to the success which
theories like that of Hobhouse had in justifying
an increasing amount of state intervention in
the life of the individual. That theory represents a valid response to the problems of the
age in which Hobhouse lived. It remains
important for our own age, however, in that an
analysis of its defects serves to delineate the
terms of the questions which contemporary
political theory is called upon to answer.

1. Sir Ernest Barker, "Leonard Trelawny Hobhouse" in Proceedings of the British Academy, Volume XV (1931), p. 11.

For a similar view, see H. E. Barnes, "Some Typical Contributions to Political Theory. Part II: Leonard T. Hobhouse and the Neo-Liberal Theory of the State" in The American Journal of Sociology, Vol. 27 (1922), p. 442.

2. But CF. Herbert Marcuse, Reason and Revolution (1954) pp. 390, 395-398.

3. See e.g., Hugh Carter, The Social Theories of L. T. Hobhouse (1927), p. 3.

4. The Metaphysical Theory of the State (1918) is itself but the first part of a larger work on the Principles of Sociology. The remaining three volumes in this composite work are The Rational Good (1921), The Elements of Social Justice (1922), and Social Development (1924).

5. Lewis Rockow, Contemporary Political Thought in England (1925), p. 199.

6. The Metaphysical Theory of the State (1918), p. 53.

7. Hobhouse's epistemology is contained in his volume on Theory of Knowledge (1896). For a more complete account than can be given here, see J. A. Nicholson, "Some Aspects of the Philosophy of L. T. Hobhouse" in University of Illinois Studies in Social Sciences, Vol. XIV, no. 4 (1926), pp. 9-52.

8. Social Development (1924), p. 61.

9. See, e.g., Id., p. 67.

10. The Elements of Social Justice (1922), p. 59.

11. Social Development (1924), p. 50.

12. Id., pp. 50-51.

13. Social Evolution and Political Theory (1913), p. 198.

14. The Metaphysical Theory of the State (1918), p. 137.

15. Social Evolution and Political Theory (1913), p. 197.

16. The Metaphysical Theory of the State (1918), p. 93.

17. Social Evolution and Political Theory (1913), pp. 197-98.

18. As Sir Ernest Barker pointed out at page 16 of the address cited in note 1, there were, of course, Hegelian elements in Hobhouse's philosophy. In an early work on the philosophy of evolution, Development and Purpose (1913), at pp. 154-55, Hobhouse pays tribute to the contribution made by Hegelian philosophy. It is interesting to note that this passage was omitted from a later edition (1927) of the same work, published after Hobhouse wrote The Metaphysical Theory of the State (1918).

19. Democracy and Reaction (1904), p. 221.

20. For an outline of Hobhouse's economic program, see The Elements of Social Justice (1922), pp. 130-84. Sir Ernest Barker characterizes these ideas as an "approximation to Collectivist ideas" in Political Thought in England (1915), p. 254

21. The Metaphysical Theory of the State (1918), p. 28.

22. Id., p. 103.

23. Buchanan and Cantril, How Nations See Each Other (1953), pp. 17-22.

Irving Kristol, *The Wall Street Journal*, Oct. 18, 1973

# Notes on the Yom Kippur War

**By Irving Kristol**

Since the outbreak of war in the Middle East, I have been getting up at dawn to listen anxiously to the radio reports. I sit there, in a silent city, glued to the transistor radio, cursing the inane ads as they jangle my raw nerves, then listening glumly to the news bulletins when they do come. Things have not been going so well for Israel, as in my bones I had always feared might be the case. No prescience on my part, just a Jewish instinct for impending disaster, an instinct that has been grotesquely overdeveloped in the course of generations by a kind of "natural selection," you might say. I am one of those Jews who has never been able to take Jewish good fortune seriously, but rather suspect it as a deception. Only misfortune is real. . . .

I find that I am irritated, too, with almost everyone. Irritated at those of my friends who ring me up for one reason or another, and somehow never get around to mentioning what is happening in the Middle East. It's like having major surgery in the family and discovering that the world would prefer to take no notice of it. I am annoyed, too, at Israel for having been so smug, and for having failed to confront the realities of her situation. I am most annoyed at those urbane Jewish liberals who claim to see "both sides" of this conflict and apportion blame and responsibility with academic detachment. Oddly enough, I cannot work up any real feelings against the Arabs, who are behaving—well, like Arabs. I'll explain that remark in a moment.

## Decisive for the Future

Why am I so deeply affected? I am not an Orthodox Jew, and only a barely observant one. I am not a Zionist and I did not find my two visits to Israel to be particularly exhilarating experiences. Truth to tell, I found Israeli society, on the whole, quite exasperating, and none of the Israeli ways of life—there are several to choose from—had any great appeal for me. Still, I care desperately. I think it is because I sense, deep down, that what happens to Israel will be decisive for Jewish history, and for the kinds of lives my grandchildren and great-grandchildren will be leading.

Should Israel be extinguished in a blood bath, it could be the end of 3,000 years of Jewish history. In the course of World War II, two out of every five Jews on this earth were slaughtered for no other reason than that they were Jews. But that holocaust was in part redeemed—was given some meaning—by the astonishing emergence of the State of Israel, a sudden and unanticipated answer to 2,000 years of daily prayer. If that fantastic dream, now realized, should turn into just another Jewish nightmare, a great many Jews are going to conclude—reluctantly but inevitably—that the burden of Jewish history is just too grievous to bequeath to one's descendants, and they will opt out.

It is not likely they'll be converted to Christianity—there is, alas, so little of it left

to be converted to. It is more probable that they will simply drift into that spiritual void which so many educated and "sophisticated" people inhabit these days, and which is destroying the very soul of Western civilization. There are enough Jews there already—so far as I am concerned, and I'd rather not see the rest of us propelled into that ghastly, identity-less existence where all you can pass on to your children is a life insurance policy.

I suppose what it comes down to is that, though you don't have to be religious to be Jewish, being Jewish may eventually tend to make you—in some mysterious way—religious, at least minimally. When I find myself reciting a Jewish prayer, in which I avow that we are worthy of God's grace because of the virtue of "our fathers"—Abraham, Isaac, Jacob—and despite our own sinfulness, I find myself taking the prayer literally. They are my "fathers," after all—I *am* the distant seed of their loins. And this being true, perhaps the rest is true too.

So any war in which the existence of Israel may be at stake becomes for me a spe-

## Board of Contributors

cial kind of war, not a conventional crisis in "international relations." In such a war, not only is the whole of the Jewish past at stake, but also the whole of the Jewish future. If that past and that future, and the meaning which unites them, is to be killed in dubious battle—this is to think the truly unthinkable, in Jewish terms.

I have said that I find it hard to be angry at the Arabs, and that is the truth. Unfortunately, when I try to explain what I mean, people think I am being frivolous. That is because we in the West—most of us anyway—have so little sense of history, cannot take religious beliefs seriously, and are so resolutely inattentive to the ways in which history and religion shape national character. Indeed, the use of that term, "national character," is distinctly frowned upon these days. There isn't supposed to be any such thing, every one of us presumably being born into "one world." What nonsense.

The Arabs are an extraordinarily proud people—in some ways a quite noble people—whose religion assures them that they have been chosen for a superior destiny. The Jews, too, of course, have a notion of themselves as "a chosen people"—but the Jewish idea is moral, not political in nature. The Arabs, in contrast, believe that it is unnatural for them to be politically or militarily inferior to any other people. Centuries of subordination, even of foreign occupation, have made only a small impression on this profound conviction. For Arabs, the glories of medieval empire are like yesterday; the intervening centuries are a lamentable hiatus of no intrinsic significance or even of much interest, and, "soon" to be annulled by foredestined triumph.

But, surely, it will be argued, this Arab vision of history and of the world is bound to be dissipated by industrialization, and oil royalties, and urbanization, and television, and what we call "modernization"? The only reason we can even entertain such a thesis is that we, the moderns of the Western world, are so smugly certain that our "progressive" view of history is the absolutely true one, and that to become modern must mean a gradual conversion to our own liberal-secular materialism. The Nazi experience should have suggested to us that there are other possibilities, but we won that war and therefore concluded that we had refuted and foreclosed these other possibilities. We are now, once again, learning otherwise. The Arabs, simply because they are becoming more "modernized," are not going to become "just like us." (Nor are the Chinese, or the Africans, I am confident.) True, their "national character" might indeed change in the course of future generations—everything changes, sooner or later—but a centuries-old way of life, and a way of looking at life, is not going to be transformed overnight, just to suit our convenience.

What this means, in actual political terms, is that it is wishful thinking to expect, in our lifetime, that the Arabs are going to be "reasonable" *vis a vis* Israel, or foreign oil companies, or anything else which they regard as an infringement of their historic rights over the areas settled by the Arab people (or assimilated—by conquest or conversion—into the Arab world). Their idea of "reasonableness" is utterly different from ours. They are less interested in making money or in the world's good opinion than in reviving a lost grandeur. In short, they are behaving exactly as they have always behaved, and as they said they would behave. True, they speak a different tongue at the United Nations Assembly, and therefore appear hypocritical. But they are not really hypocritical at all—they are merely talking the kind of diplomatic jargon which they know we regard as proper and suitable for intercourse among nations. They don't talk that way at home—in their newspapers, in their magazines, on their radio and television. One might almost say their rhetoric at the United Nations is a form of politeness; they understand how painful we would find candor.

## Arab Realities

One of the things that most exasperated me in Israel was the unwillingness to face up to Arab realities. Many of my Israeli friends could not confront the fact that the Arab nations do not accept, and will not in the foreseeable future accept, the existence of a non-Arab nation in "their" Middle East. The most they will concede is the survival of a limited Jewish community in a bi-national Palestine which would be part of the Arab world. They may agree to cease fires, or truces, or armistices, and they may even temporarily recog-

Irving Kristol, *The Wall Street Journal*, Oct. 18, 1973

nize demilitarized zones if it is to their advantage to do so. But they will not sign any treaty giving *de jure* recognition to a Jewish state—no Arab leader has ever hinted at such a possibility—and it is utopian to think otherwise.

Utopianism, however, is a kind of political orthodoxy in Israel. The dominant political tradition of Israel is democratic-socialist, and the original Jewish settlers in Palestine, in the first decades of this century, envisioned the creation of a "cooperative commonwealth": egalitarian, fraternal, pacific. Just where the Arabs would fit into this lovely picture they never clearly said, but they seemed to think that the sheer perfection of Israeli society would so enchant the Arab masses as to transform them, too, into secular, humanitarian Socialists. They also took it for granted that, as the Arabs of the Middle East became more prosperous and better-schooled, they would be only too happy to join Israel in the task of "making the desert bloom."

Incredibly enough, this is still the basic Israeli outlook—despite the evident fact that it is the better-educated, middle-class Arabs, and most especially the college students, who are most rabidly anti-Israel. The Israelis actually feel (or at least think) that time—in the form of the economic development of the Arab nations—is inevitably on their side. It might be; but there is no obvious inevitability about it. When I was in Jerusalem 15 months ago, at a conference of intellectuals, I timidly questioned this thesis. I was promptly accused of lacking all appreciation of the idealism which was the essence of the Zionist movement and which was the moving spirit behind this Jewish state.

## A Profound Confusion

At that same conference, I discovered that *the* big problem under discussion in Israel was the way in which this original idealism of the founders was being corrupted by commercial-industrial growth and, above all, by the needs of military defense. Time and again I was told that Israel had not been conceived as a rich and strong nation, let alone as a "garrison state," but as a uniquely just social order that would be a "light unto the nations." Being myself a warmer admirer of the Old Testament than of modern social democracy, and preferring the patriarchs to the prophets, I felt no inhibitions about insisting that Israel, if it were to survive under contemporary circumstances, *must* be to a considerable degree a "garrison state"—hopefully more on the model of Athens than of Sparta, but a state in which the priority of military needs was beyond all challenge.

There is nothing inherently un-Jewish about such a state, I pointed out, nor did I see that the world was exactly looking to Israel for lessons in political economy or social science. But all to no avail. The confusion between Jewish ideals and Socialist messianism has been so profound in Israel that even the government never seems quite sure which hat it is wearing.

And so, a week before the Yom Kippur attack, one could read eloquent articles in the Israeli press, articles brimming over with pathos and self-criticism, about the dangers of —Israeli militarism. For a country whose ethos is about as militaristic as Switzerland's, this is a rather far-fetched anxiety I'd feel much better if the Israelis let *me* worry about the flaws in their social order, while they took the business of survival more seriously.

---

*Mr. Kristol is Henry Luce Professor of Urban Values at the New York University and co-editor of the quarterly The Public Interest. He is also a member of the Journal's Board of Contributors, four distinguished professors who contribute periodic articles reflecting a broad range of views.*

LAW  AND  EPISTEMOLOGY

Leninism as the Ideology of the Technostructure

Jan G. Deutsch

The problem of establishing enforceable limits
on governmental action is acutely practical in
that it delineates the contexts in terms of which
different persons are permitted to exercise
power.  Since an interpersonal context by definition requires agreement by more than one person to
its existence, the problem also invokes significant epistemological components.  It is a problem
that both Hegel and Wechsler faced, and the latter
solved it by postulating two sets of connections
that defined antitheses: reason, courts of law,
and neutral principles; and will, power organs,
and ad hoc political decisions.(A)  To some extent, the coalescence between the views of
Justice Black and the "modest" can be accounted
for in terms of the parallel between these antitheses and Black's commitment to "logic" as
opposed to "experience."  Black's motive for a
commitment strikingly parallel to that of
Wechsler can also be characterized as a desire to
achieve certainty in the implementation of constitutional rights, to avoid the uncertainty inherent in a need to trust that the Justices will
strike the correct balance between the disputing
claims presented to them in the course of arriving at decisions concerning the content to be
given to the guarantees embodied in constitutional provisions.

It is important to stress, however, that such
a position is consistent only in terms of an
epistemology such as that espoused by Hobhouse.
To dispense with the necessity of trusting the
judgement of given individuals serving as judges,
in other words, we must postulate that truth concerning the law is capable of correlation.  Only
if an objective reality exists in the sense that
agreement can be reached concerning all of its
properties rather than some aspects of that

reality remaining a matter of subjective inter-
pretation--and only if the law is part of this
objective reality--then and only then could the
law be sufficiently certain to obviate the need
for trusting that the court (or the individual
judge) will make the correct choice between the
disputing parties.

Thus, it seems important that "[w]hat Hobhouse
is proposing is the application of scientific
method to epistemology."  If the law as an expression of reality is this certain, however; if
there are no such things as personal and incommunicable aspects of experience or uncorrelatable
objections to social views of reality (whether or
not formally embodied as laws) for which protection can justifiably be demanded; if, in other
words, law is in this sense truly a science, then
it is precisely at this point that the person
before the bar of justice (accepting as he must
the view of reality which correlates with his own
experience) wills his own punishment or the imposition of the appropriate legal penalty.  Thus,
even if the law is not a wholly deterministic
science, one which could be applied by a computer
utilizing only logic rather than reason, even if
law represents a body of knowledge accessible only
to a group of individuals expert in the manipulation of the data on which it is based, the fact
remains that its application can be justified as
the result of correlatable knowledge accessible
to the transgressor, and therefore perceived as
fiat rather than reason--in Wechsler's terms--
only because of lack of such knowledge.

So long as reality (including the law) is
wholly objective, in other words, and so long
as we postulate that all of society participates
in the correlations that establish reality, an
erroneous judicial decision must represent a
willful refusal on the part of the court to apply
the law to the situation before it.  If we
assume only that the court is acting in good
faith--that it is attempting to apply the law
as it knows it--then reason and fiat can no
longer be distinguished.  It is, in short, only
the possibility of personal, incommunicable, and
uncorrelatable truths that makes the possibility of erroneous decisions--of a perception of
law as fiat rather than an absence of good faith
on the part of the court--a real one.  The
important point, therefore, is to accept the
possibility that there are aspects of reality
that may be uncorrelatable and that the rendering of judicial decisions may therefore well
require varying combinations of reason and will,
of certainty and subjectivity.  If we do not
accept these propositions, in other words, all
judicial decisions rendered in good faith
involve punishments and penalties willed by the
transgressor on whom they are imposed, unless
the law in question involves an aspect of
reality which is not capable of correlation,
in which event the punishment or penalty represents fiat alone.

It should be noted, finally, that Marxism as a political and social theory embraces both of the possibilities delineated above, with the choice of characterization depending on the question of whether the legal decision is rendered before or after the proletarian revolution. Thus, if the decision occurs after the revolution, then the law being applied is an aspect of objective social reality(B); if before the revolution, then the decision rendered can be understood only in terms of the location in the social structure of those who rendered it.(C)

For John Kenneth Galbraith the key to understanding the rendering of decisions crucial to the society is the location of the individual, not in the social structure, but in the corporate organization and, in particular, his participation in the processes carried on by the technostructure. That Galbraith's theory defines power in these terms, and the basis for that definition, is summarized as follows:

In the industrial enterprise, power rests with those who make decisions. In the mature enterprise, this power has passed, inevitably and irrevocably, from the individual to the group. That is because only the group has the information that decision requires. Though the constitution of the corporation places power in the hands of the owners, the imperatives of technology and planning remove it to the technostructure.(1)

In Leninist theory, it is the party that performs a function parallel to that fulfilled by the technostructure:

Lenin held that centrally directed, co-ordinated action was the secret of success for a revolutionary party. He had the utmost respect for organization, so much so that we might say he made a fetish of it. Organization, to him, not only meant strength--this was but one of the axioms on which the Marxian theory of revolution was based--it also meant rationality. Somehow, Lenin seems to have believed that the party, as organized consciousness, consciousness as a decision-making machinery, had superior reasoning power. Indeed, in time this collective body took on an aura of infallibility, which was later elevated to a dogma, and a member's loyalty was tested, in part, by his acceptance of it. It became part of the communist confession of faith to proclaim that the party was never wrong. Nor could it be inefficient, for there is no inefficiency in rational organization. Mistakes of judgment or bungling in executing orders can only be made by individuals, and the presumption is always strong that these individuals by making mistakes have shown themselves lacking in consciousness. This is tantamount to disloyalty. Hence ineffi-

ciency is seen as the result of ill intent. Bureaucratic mistakes are seen as rebellions against the party by criminals, wreckers, saboteurs, or counter-revolutionaries. The party itself never makes mistakes.(2)

Furthermore, although Lenin's political experience in the revolution of 1905 was instrumental in ensuring that Leninist theory accepts the proposition that antitheses define a spectrum of possible combinations, it is striking that--in addition to accepting an inevitable correlation between organization and power, as Galbraith does--the Leninist conception of the party embodies many of those aspects of logic and predictability that seem to account for Black and Wechsler's commitment to "reason" as opposed to "will":

Marxism in its original form maintained that the spontaneous unfolding of historical events produces progress and, finally, a rationally acceptable form of human relations. Leninism is more pessimistic and therefore became a manipulative theory of history. Its aim is to subject the most irrational, spontaneous forces to reason (consciousness) by means of organization; even revolution is made the object of science and rational organization. Yet the irrational forces are recognized as given, and they receive their place in the rationalized scheme of revolution. Their specific function is to help determine the moment of action. They dictate the "irrational hic et nunc," as Mannheim calls it. Hence Lenin, with all his stress on consciousness, and his demand that it must gain and maintain the initiative over spontaneity, could during World War I write with confidence that the next Russian revolution would, like that of 1905, start spontaneously, unexpectedly, and locally. He did not consider this an ideal situation; he would have preferred a nationwide revolution carefully planned in advance by the party. But he warned that the party must be prepared to take advantage of any unique opportunities provided by spontaneous outbursts, because only such outbursts would ensure the mass basis necessary for the establishment of a proletarian dictatorship.(3)

The Leninist conception of the party is derived from this acknowledged superiority of socialist theory (consciousness) over the spontaneous movement of the working class. The party is conceived as the organization, incarnation, or institutionalization of class consciousness. In it, historical will and purposiveness are to acquire domination over unguided and irrational instinct and drift. The party

is therefore to be composed of those intellectuals, whatever their background, who
have acquired consciousness and, prompted
by ideas and convictions, have turned into
revolutionaries by profession, men whose
vocation it is to conspire against the existing order and to prepare a proletarian
dictatorship.  The task of the party is "to
make the proletariat capable of fulfilling
its historical mission."  It should not
"adapt itself to . . . the backward sections
of the working class, but raise the entire
working class to the level of its communist
vanguard. . . .  The party exists for the
very purpose of going ahead of the masses
and showing the masses the way."  Or, to
use the military terminology of which Lenin
was so fond, the party was to be the general
staff of the proletarian revolution, con-
ceiving the strategy of class war, revolutionary attacks, and strategic retreats,
training the cadres, organizing shock
troops, collecting and digesting intelligence, and building up the fighting spirit
of the rank and file.  It was to be a
military hierarchy, functioning with
strictest discipline and according to the
command principle.(4)

In personal terms, moreover, the extent to
which it was precisely the "scientific" aspects
of Marxism that attracted Lenin is indicated in
a psycho-historical analysis of Lenin's conversion to that doctrine:

The tense and agitated Lenin who in 1891
was still enquiring about the value of his
late brother's scientific investigations
relived, apart from his relationship to
Alexander, his own inner struggle about
the meaning and value of the revolutionary
path.

Within the context of such doubts and of the
mixed attraction and revulsion felt by him
toward the previous generation of the
revolutionaries, Marxism must have appeared
as an ideal answer and solution.  Within
Marxian socialism are found the elements of
ambivalence and yet of orderliness
characteristic of Lenin's own mind.  The
emotions and the language of Marxism breathe
violence and defiance of all the nineteenth
century conventions, and yet its conclusions
are coldly rational and practical.  Revolution is presented not only as an act of will
but of scientific necessity.  There is a
pleasing vision of the final holocaust of
capitalism, of "the expropriation of the
expropriators," but no utopian and lyrical
evocation of the Socialist world of the
future:  the entrance to the world of freedom is through an increased productivity
and better organization of labor.  After

the intense emotionalism of Populism, its
infatuation with the mythical peasant, its
denial of the reality of the all-too-visible
and growing "Europeanization" and industrialization of Russia, Marxism must have
represented a model of sobriety and realism.
By following it one did not cut oneself off
from the revolutionary tradition, only from
its illusions.(5)

Finally, in describing "The Years of
Waiting: 1908-1917," this same analysis stresses
the extent to which Lenin in power was to be
concerned with precisely those aspects of
industrial reality that for Galbraith confirm
the crucial role of the technostructure in
The New Industrial State:

It is curious how the problems of the
future crowded upon Lenin in this prewar
period.  To the contemporaries, whether
the Mensheviks, Trotsky, or the Tsarist
police, he was still the arch intriguer,
the man who kept the Russian Socialists
from reuniting and leading the working
class.  But in some ways he already looked
beyond the Mensheviks and even beyond the
revolution.  He had for long had a great
if somewhat dilettantish interest in
problems of productivity and industrial
organization.  From Siberia he used to
write asking for the latest books on new
mechanical inventions, especially those
distant ancestors of today's mechanical and
electronic computers.  Now his interest
quickened in such devices and techniques
apparently far removed from a revolutionary's immediate concerns.  The speed-up
system devised by Taylor, he wrote, was
obviously a capitalist's device to exploit
the worker.  But the Socialist state would
be able to put Taylor's system to its own
use to increase the productivity of labor.
The news of Sir William Ramsay's technique
of extracting gas from coal made Lenin
forget for a moment Martov, Trotsky, and
the others.  This invention opened splendid
perspectives for socialism.  With it and
with similar scientific devices, they
should be able to reduce the working day
from eight to seven hours.  Nothing refutes
more fully the thesis that Lenin is another
Nechaev or Tkachev, merely a man obsessed
with the revolution, than this very
practical, very Marxist concern with labor-
saving devices, with productivity and
applied science.  His Russia would not be
like Chernyshevsky's, one vast choral
society dedicated to healthful and innocent
amusements.  It would be, first of all a
country of hard work, of strict industrial
discipline and organization, where socialism
would turn into a cult of production unmatched by the most exacting capitalism.(6)

The opposition to this view of reality within the Marxist revolutionary movement was expressed by Rosa Luxemburg in two articles published in 1904 under the title "Organizational Questions of the Russian Social Democracy," one version of which was published in Glasgow in 1935 under the title, "Leninism or Marxism?". Utilizing Freudian terminology, this pamphlet concludes with an attack on the Leninist conception of the party:

> In Lenin's overanxious desire to establish the guardianship of an omniscient and omnipotent Central Committee in order to protect so promising and vigorous a labor movement against any misstep, we recognize the symptoms of the same subjectivism that has already played more than one trick on socialist thinking in Russia.
>
> It is amusing to note the strange somersaults that the respectable human "ego" has had to perform in recent Russian history. Knocked to the ground, almost reduced to dust, by Russian absolutism, the "ego" takes revenge by turning to revolutionary activity. In the shape of a committee of conspirators, in the name of a nonexistent Will of the People, it seats itself on a kind of throne and proclaims it is all-powerful. [The reference is to the conspiratorial circle which attacked tsarism from 1879 to 1883 by means of terrorist acts and finally assassinated Alexander II.--Translator.] But the "object" proves to be the stronger. The knout is triumphant, for tsarist might seems to be the "legitimate" expression of history.
>
> In time we see appear on the scene an even more "legitimate" child of history--the Russian labor movement. For the first time, bases for the formation of a real "people's will" are laid in Russian soil.
>
> But here is the "ego" of the Russian revolutionary again! Pirouetting on its head, it once more proclaims itself to be the all-powerful director of history--this time with the title of His Excellency the Central Committee of the Social Democratic Party of Russia.
>
> The nimble acrobat fails to perceive that the only "subject" which merits today the role of director is the collective "ego" of the working class. The working class demands the right to make its mistakes and learn in the dialectic of history.
>
> Let us speak plainly. Historically, the errors committed by a truly revolutionary movement are infinitely more fruitful than the infallibility of the cleverest Central Committee.

The view of reality shared by Lenin and Galbraith can be characterized as an emphasis on organization as opposed to the individual: faith that the technostructure leads the consumer, as the party leads the worker. It is this faith that is challenged by the Edsel event.

In terms of law, moreover, it is only a commitment to this challenge--a belief in the possibility that the individual can act in other than organizational terms--that makes it realistic to speak of the necessity of trusting that an individual judge will render a correct decision. Given the jurisprudential need for the epistemological postulates that underlie that commitment, it is striking that, even in power:

> It was not within Lenin's power to conquer bureaucratism, for the only means of restraining this monster, a government of laws, was to him equally hateful as a bourgeois and philistine concept. Always sensitive to official brutality, rudeness, or red tape, he could not quite admit that there was one way of combating them: legal procedures. On May 17, 1922, when the Civil War was already over, the candidate of laws, former member of the bars of Samara and St. Petersburg, Vladimir Ulyanov-Lenin wrote to his Commissar of Justice: "Courts cannot dispense with terror, to promise that would be a self-deception or lie." One cannot see sadism in that or a delight in terror for terror's sake, but again his recurrent irritation at anything reminiscent of the ideology of the vanished world of the liberal intelligentsia, at the "philistine" notions of impartial justice and independent judiciary that had been the aspirations of the Russia of his youth.(7)

In terms of the extent to which this state of affairs can be traced to a "scientific" view of reality, however, it is even more striking that Marx had developed a doctrine that attempted to deny the possibility of an antithesis between science and morality, and that Engels introduced explicitly normative judgements even into the economic doctrine of the labor theory of value:

> Marx repudiated all notions of universal morality. Here, too, his stand seems to be close to the pragmatic one: our aims must be derived from reality, if socialism is to become scientific. "We do not want to anticipate the world dogmatically, but want to find the new world only in our criticism of the old one." This position does not take into account the problem, already alluded to, that no moral conclusions can be drawn from a mere description of reality, unless at least one moral premise be given. We cannot criticize reality scientifically, we can criticize it only on the basis of preconceptions as to what is to be approved and what is to be

J. G. D.

condemned. Marx would brush this objection aside, however, and would thereby imply that the moral preconceptions underlying his criticism are either common-sense notions and therefore unchallengeable, or, that they are the generally accepted moral notions of the Western-Christian-Humanist tradition. More specifically, he would identify himself as the spiritual heir of the Jacobins, and claim that in his criticism of social reality he was carrying on their revolutionary tradition. But once the claim has been made that the value judgments of Marxism are scientific, moralizing arguments are used with great abandon. More than that, the doctrine of the unity of theory and practice implies that even morality is a material force, an indispensable element in revolutionary development.

In short, the doctrine of the unity of theory and practice obliterates all differences between science and ethics, and tries to unite both in an all-embracing world outlook, in which ethics is derived scientifically, but social science is scientific only when it is ethical.

An interesting illustration is the importance which Engels attributed to the labor theory of value as a moral rallying cry for the proletariat. Both the so-called Utopian Socialists and Marx took as point of departure Ricardo's propositions, (1) that the value of any commodity is solely determined by the quantity of labor required for its production; and (2) that the product of all social labor is divided amont three classes: (a) landowners get rent; (b) capitalists get profit; and (c) workers get wages. Socialism, writes Marx, draws the following conclusion from this.

And Engels quotes from the Critique of Political Economy: "If the exchange value of a product is equal to the labor time which it contains, the exchange value of a labor day is equal to its product. Or the wage must be equal to the product of labor. But the contrary is the case."

But he adds the following note: "The theoretical correctness of the formula being presupposed, practice was blamed for contradiction with theory, and bourgeois society was invited to draw in practice the supposed conclusions from its theoretical principle. In this way at least, English socialists turned the Ricardian formula of exchange value against political economy.

Engels later commented on this in a very interesting fashion: "The above application of the Ricardian theory . . . leads directly to communism. But, as Marx

indicates . . . formally it is economically incorrect, for it is simply an application of morality to economics. According to the laws of bourgeois economics, the greatest part of the product does not belong to the workers who have produced it. If we now say: that is unjust, that ought not to be so, then that has nothing immediately to do with economics. We are merely saying that this economic fact is in contradiction to our moral sentiment. Marx . . . never based his communist demands upon this, but upon the inevitable collapse of the capitalist mode of production which is taking place daily before our eyes to an increasing degree; he says only that surplus value consists of unpaid labor, which is a simple fact.

"But what formally may be economically incorrect may all the same be correct from the point of view of world history. If the moral consciousness of the masses declares an economic fact to be unjust, as it has done in the cases of slavery or serf labor, that is proof that the fact itself has been out-lived, that other economic facts have made their appearance, owing to which the former has become unbearable and untenable. Therefore, a very true economic content may be concealed behind the formal economic incorrectness." Engels, Preface to the first German edition of Das Elend der Philosophie (The Poverty of Philosophy), p. 10. (Italics added.)(8)

1. John Kenneth Galbraith, The New Industrial State (rev. ed., 1971), p. 98.
2. Alfred G. Meyer, Leninism (1962) [hereinafter cited as Leninism] pp. 97-98 (footnote omitted).
3. Leninism at 41-42 (footnotes omitted).
4. Leninism at 32-33 (footnotes omitted).
5. Adam B. Ulam, The Bolsheviks: The Intellectual and Political History of the Triumph of Communism in Russia (1965) [hereinafter cited as Ulam] p. 99.
6. Ulam at 293-294 (footnote omitted).
7. Ulam at 452 (footnote omitted).
8. Alfred G. Meyer, Marxism: The Unity of Theory and Practice (1963) [hereinafter cited as Marxism] p. 105, including n.4.

Extended Analyses of Some Definitional Concepts

## A.

### Literary Devices as Legal Tools

The final difficulty with deriving the need for neutral principles from a contrast between ad hoc political decisions and principled judicial processes goes to the heart of the contrast itself. Far from describing reality, that contrast, like the use of rhetorical questions, is ultimately no more than a literary device. Wechsler himself believes that a society governed by political institutions whose decisions were always and entirely unprincipled could not long survive; his catalog of contemporary ad hoc judicial decisions is preceded by an historical survey of constitutional positions taken by a President and in Congress--positions he deems unprincipled. And the implied judgment is not an approving one.

Unfortunately, this commendable recognition of an obligation to principle on the part of the political branches dissolves the very contrast from which Wechsler derives the judicial need for neutral principles. Once it is admitted that political decisions are only sometimes or partially ad hoc, the literary device of a contrast can no longer serve to justify the demand that constitutional adjudications be always and absolutely principled. Yet that is precisely the demand that Wechsler makes. (J.G.D., The Meaning of the Legal Process)

## B.

### The Law as Objective Social Reality

Whether we call it materialism or realism, this assertion that the world exists objectively is, in the last analysis, no more than a faith. Attempts to refute the claims of idealism and subjectivism rest either on circular reasoning or on silent assumptions which, when examined, leave the dispute unresolved. Someone tells of Lenin trying, in a heated argument, to prove the correctness of this materialism to a neo-Kantian opponent; he is said to have battered his fist against a wall and to have cried, "Look at this stone wall! You see it, you can feel it, and here I am knocking my hand bloody against it. And you want to deny or doubt its objective reality?" Philosophically, Lenin's argument begged the question. Yet, the fact that we can all repeat this act, the fact that we all shall bloody our fists if we knock them against brick walls, is a cogent argument for the adoption of the materialist faith as a working hypothesis. Whatever the philosophical inadequacies of this position, it is no more than good common sense to assume the material reality of things against which we constantly knock ourselves sore. Just as the refinements of the modern theories of indeterminacy and relativity do not affect the validity of fundamental mechanical laws while we are dealing with common-sense magnitudes, so some of the refinements of philosophy are wasted on the social scientist. The philosophical error of Marxism does not consist in accepting the materialist hypothesis, but in accepting this common-sense notion dogmatically, unquestioningly, and without qualifications. Or, we might say, the error of Marx's followers consists in elevating Marx's common sense into a philosophical statement. (Marxism, p. 76, footnote omitted)

## C.

### The Judicial Decision as a Function of the Judge's Location in the Social Structure

Marxism constitutes a curious synthesis of determinism and voluntarism. It holds that history is made by man, but that man makes history not as he wishes, but as circumstances, particularly his position in the social structure, force him to make it. Moreover, the Marxist believes that history is made not by individuals but by classes, for even great individuals act only as exponents or representatives of specific social classes. History is thus manmade, but men's actions are determined by circumstances. Men may labor under the illusion that they have ideas and a will of their own; they may consider themselves the sovereign masters of their fate, and exalt the history-making power of the human mind. The Marxist, indeed, would admit that men's ideas and will do play a role, but he relegates this role to a position of minor importance. According to his view, the ideas and the intentions of men are not prime movers of history, because they are themselves determined; they are instead but transmission belts of historical forces.

Here we have a paradox: man makes history, but he does not master it. Underlying this ambiguous view is the double, and contradictory, conception of human nature that characterizes Marxism. On the one hand, Marxism accepts what we might call a Promethean image of man as a "conscious and purposive" animal, that is, as an intelligent being who through reason can understand himself and his environment, and, again through reason, devise means by which to make himself the master of his environment. This is the most basic Marxist definition of human nature. An opposite conception is revealed, however, in the Marxist theory of history. The development of mankind from primitive to higher stages is seen as cumulative progress in man's mastery over the forces of nature. This mastery

is achieved through improvements in the means of
production.  Cumulative technological progress is
intimately tied with the development of a more
and more complex social structure.  This structure not only entails the development of the class
struggle, including the growth of ruling classes
and the appearance of exploitation; it also
brings with it the alienation of man both from
his natural environment and from his own human
nature.  Modern civilization, despite its
progressive character, includes cumulative evil,
in that it deprives the individual of the full-
ness of life.  As the division of labor is
perfected, men turn into specialized cogs within
a vast social machinery that defies their understanding and control.  Stuck in the idiocy of
specialization, they cannot develop their innate
physical and rational faculties.  Harried and
frightened by the class struggle, overawed by
the social leviathan of which they are but a
tiny part, they fashion themselves consoling
and reassuring images of benign forces working
in their favor.  Their reason turns into false
ideology, their knowledge into self-deception,
their purpose into utopia.  Promethean man
becomes a pitiful caricature of his real self.
(Leninism, pp. 21-22)


D.

The Theory of Marxism

     The sheer intellectual brilliance of the
Marxian system has always attracted to it
individuals who live by and for intellectual
pursuits.  In comparison other Socialist
systems appear, as indeed Marx condescendingly
characterized them, as moralizing or utopian
dreams.  In a very science-conscious age, when
economics and politics were thought susceptible
of being analyzed by rigid laws, Marxism was
bound to shine with theoretical profundity and
elegance.  But not only for the intellectuals.
Underneath the mass of statistics and mathematical formulas, and yet plainly visible,
there is this stern moral judgment and doom
pronounced upon the rich and powerful of this
world, all the more satisfying, for it cannot
be avoided or softened.  It is no wonder that
for all its materialistic and free-thinking
base Marxism has always held a secret attraction
for some religious-minded: it promises, and
considerably sooner than in the next world,
certain chastisement for those who have
succumbed to the false idols of worldly success.
(Ulam at 140)

## U.S. Communist Suggests C.I.A. Held Soviet Art Show

The leader of the American Communist party said yesterday that the nonconformist art show broken up in Moscow last Sunday might have been staged by the Central Intelligence Agency and that "local Soviet citizens seemingly overreacted."

The assessment was given by Gus Hall, general secretary of the Communist Party, U.S.A., in The Daily World, the party's newspaper.

"One would have to be totally naive indeed not to see the fine hand of the C.I.A. in this affair," Mr. Hall said, expressing regret that the Russians had reacted so strongly Vigilantes broke up the show and assaulted some Soviet citizens and American newsmen.

Five participants in the show who were sentenced to workhouse terms and fines after the incident have since been released, apparently as a result of widespread criticism abroad.  Soviet authorities reportedly have given permission for another show to be held.

## No More Joy and Laughter

# Soviet Art: They Know What They Dislike

### By JOHN RUSSELL

The Russians just don't know what to do about art, as last week's goings-on attest. They believe what Plato believed: When the laws of art are altered society alters with them. So the laws of art must not alter, and the masterpieces of even 60 years ago, Vasily Kandinsky's monumental "Composition VI," for instance, must never be put on view. "It is too soon to show them," an inquiring visitor will be told.

It was not always so. When Lenin formed his first government in October, 1917, A. V. Lunacharsky, poet, philosopher and playwright, was put in charge of the arts. "Lunacharsky is drawn towards the future with his whole being," Lenin said; "that is why there is such joy and laughter in him."

Nothing in the world is more tenacious than Russian patriotism, and Lunacharsky was able to call upon Russian artists who had been living in the West, Kandinsky, Marc Chagall, Naum Gabo, all now securely placed in the canons of modern art. Other avant-garde artists, Kasimir Malevich for one, Vladimir Tatlin for another, were already in full ebullition in Russia itself. In art, as in poetry, drama and architecture, the formidable energies of the new Russia were wholeheartedly on the side of the new.

Lunacharsky had, in all this, a free hand. And he used it. In ways that would still pass as innovatory, he put the whole weight of authority behind artists who had, as he said, "been outlawed while bourgeois taste ruled the day." Lunacharsky gave the men and women he had to work with, and many of them were of genius, their heads.

People still talk of the symphony of factory sirens, of the way in which whole towns were painted over on special occasions, of the inter-disciplinary experiments in street theater, of the 62 museums which Lunacharsky planned to open in record time and of the new system of art education which Kandinsky was asked to devise for anyone who cared to enroll for it. "Bourgeois taste" has made progress since then, by the way. But the West still has catching up to do, with what went on in Russia at that time.

It was too good to last. Lunacharsky's "joy and laughter" went out of style, and within five years the unsmiling standardizers had taken over. In times of famine and civil war it was difficult to argue the case for artists who wanted to paint the trees blue and yellow"outside the Kremlin walls. (Lenin let them do it, but he was not amused.) Kandinsky, Chagall and Gabo went back to the West. Malevich and Tatlin ended their days somewhere on the margins of life. Advanced art as it had been practiced in Russia was exported once and once only: to Berlin and Amsterdam, in 1922. Advanced architecture stayed on the drawing board. The advanced theater was shut down, and advanced literature went private.

In 1932 socialist realism was promulgated under Stalin as the only acceptable form of art. While this remains in force, the subject matter of art must be drawn from proletarian life; and that life must be shown in terms of heroic effort and ultimate success.

In the Artists' Union, as in the Writers' Union, power goes to men of small and careful nature. Even so, there are differences between the two. The continuity of Russian literature was preserved, single-handedly, by

Tvardovsky when he was editor of the magazine Novy Mir. This was at the time when Khrushchev had decided that the shut mind might in the long run be injurious to Russia. Khrushchev was willing to try something of the kind in art also. But when he saw the result, at a famous and shortlived exhibition at the former Riding School beside the Kremlin, he blew his stack. How was it possible that a man like the sculptor Ernst Neizvestny, with a war record second to none, should make such peculiar work?

Khrushchev never got over his first experience of Neizvestny's vigorous but undeniably eccentric handling of the human form. But at least he wanted to understand; as an old man living in retirement he would sometimes call up the dissidents for whom he had once made life so difficult and say, "I do so miss our talks. Why don't you drop by one day next week?"

There is no one like Khrushchev today, and advanced art in Russia remains a clandestine activity. It is made for the love of it, and for an audience of five or six friends. Inevitably it is awkward and provincial: The continuity of the written word in Russia has no parallel in art. Without first-hand knowledge and without free discussion, art cannot develop. If Alfred Barr's classic "Cubism and Abstract Art" [1936] can be found in a second-hand bookshop in Russia it is likely to cost $250.

Among dissident artists in Russia the quality of human endeavor is very high, movingly so, but the quality of achievement is not. Conceivably the unsmiling standardizers know this. Perhaps it has got through to them that for someone who wants to make new art the real punishment is not a nominal fine or a few days in jail. It is a lifelong severance from the things that make new art possible.

# Values

If the issue raised by the *New Industrial State* is how the technostructure is to be controlled, the answer must be phrased in terms of political as well as economic reality. Whether or not his scholarly peers approve of the techniques he has employed, in short, the argument being made is that Galbraith has given an inadequate answer to the questions he has posed. The answer argued for in this section is phrased in terms of law.

# THE RESPONSIBILTY OF A CORPORATION: AN ATTEMPT AT IMPLEMENTATION

## Editors' Preface

The case of *Medical Committee for Human Rights v. SEC*[a] raised some interesting questions. Why did the directors of the corporation act as they did? How should society judge these actions? Resolution of these issues involves consideration of psychological and legal doctrines, as well as an assessment of the social and individual meaning of the professional roles of psychoanalyst and lawyer.

While these questions are relevant to any discussion of corporate social responsibility, this article does not claim to provide definitive answers; it is merely an attempt to demonstrate that the various strands of thought, doctrine and argument examined herein provide insights into the specific questions raised by the *Medical Committee* litigation. If the board of directors of the corporation cannot be psychoanalyzed to determine why they acted as they did, an attempt can at least be made to determine the relevance of Freudian thought to formulation of a system for evaluating those actions. Similarly, the thought of Herbert Marcuse — who is widely regarded as having provided the philosophical basis for much of the contemporary protest against industralized society — will be examined insofar as it is relevant to a resolution of the questions discussed herein. Finally, the author will attempt to delineate what is meant by denominating corporate social responsibility as a legal question.

— *The Editors*

## I. Prologue

IMPLEMENTATION OF A DUTY is a process which occurs over time, and the factual patterns which form the basis for that implementation also change over time. Investigation of specific instances of such implementation, however, is the way in which the nature of the duty is defined.

---

a. 432 F.2d 659 (D.C. Cir. 1970), *vacated as moot,* 404 U.S. 403 (1972).

The case of *Medical Committee for Human Rights v. SEC*[1] is a period piece — yet it is not *merely* a period piece, defined by the proposition embodied in its holding.

> Thinking of a description as a word-picture of the facts has something misleading about it: one tends to think only of such pictures as hang on our walls: which seem simply to portray how a thing looks, what it is like. (These pictures are as it were idle.)[2]

## II. THE STATEMENT

### *A.*

Since the argument for the necessity of concrete factual detail is presented herein, it seems appropriate to begin by laying down factual assumptions which structure the problem to be considered.

We are concerned with a corporation which manufactured a product sold exclusively to the United States Department of Defense.[3] There was considerable public protest against the manufacture of this product,[4] because it was instrumental in producing massive, permanent and painful personal injuries, and because the nature of the conflict in which it was utilized made it difficult to distinguish civilians from combatants. Such protest was prompted also by the fact that the purposes for which that war was being fought were unclear — and their validity and legitimacy were widely disputed. The board of directors of the corporation recognized that its continued manufacture might well adversely affect the corporation's long-range future.[5] In addition,

---

1. 432 F.2d 659 (D.C. Cir. 1970), *vacated as moot*, 404 U.S. 403 (1972).
   [Editors' Note] The case involved a petition for review of an order of the Securities and Exchange Commission (SEC) refusing to require the corporation to include in a proxy statement a resolution that it discontinue the manufacture of napalm. The United States Court of Appeals for the District of Columbia Circuit held that the SEC action was reviewable, and remanded the case to the SEC so that it might "reconsider petitioner's claim within the proper limits of its jurisdiction." 432 F.2d at 682.
2. L. WITTGENSTEIN, PHILOSOPHICAL INVESTIGATIONS ¶ 291, at 99 (1953).
3. Brief for Petitioner at 2, Medical Comm. for Human Rights v. SEC, 432 F.2d 659 (D.C. Cir. 1970), *vacated as moot*, 404 U.S. 403 (1972) [hereinafter cited as Brief]. The brief stated:
   > Dow Chemical Company manufactures a chemical product known as "napalm" which is sold exclusively to the United States Department of Defense.

   *Id.*
4. Petitioner's brief stated:
   > It is common knowledge that many American citizens are deeply concerned about the destructive use of napalm, and there has been a considerable degree of public protest against Dow's napalm production.

   *Id.*
5. The following corporate statement appears in the record: "There may be outstanding businessmen or scientists of the future who have been lost to Dow because of deep personal feelings on this matter . . . . From a long-range viewpoint we could be hurt in many ways."
   *Id.* at 3 n.2.

the contract under which the corporation manufactured the product had a negligible impact on the corporation's sales and profits.[6]

The board of directors decided to continue manufacture of the product on the basis of a sense of patriotic duty to the Government of the United States.[7] The chairman of the board publicly characterized that action as a "moral decision,"[8] and the president referred to it as a matter of individual "conscience."[9]

To the extent that the question of corporate social responsibility is a legal one, that question can in general be explored by queries such as whether the board of directors must be guided by the long- or short-term interest of the corporation in order to avoid liability in a shareholder's derivative suit. In the case we are considering, however, the outcome of that inquiry apparently makes no significant difference.[10]

As a result, a more promising inquiry concerning corporate responsibility in this instance would delineate the extent to which "consciences . . . should be . . . part of the [corporate] decision-making process."[11] This inquiry surfaces the issue of whether the relevant legal question is the nature of the conscience possessed by the individual (the implicit basis of the argument being made by the president of the corporation),[12] or whether there are aspects of "conscience"

---

6. The management of Dow was aware of this fact.

Dow's President stated in 1967: "The contract has little economic significance to Dow. It amounted to less than one-half of one percent of total sales last year — in the range of $5,000,000 — and an even smaller percentage of total profits. This year it will be in the range of one-fourth of one percent and again a smaller percentage in profits."

*Id.* at 25 n.1.

7. *Id.* at 2–3.

Dow's management has made the "moral" decision to continue to produce the product out of a sense of patriotism. According to Dow's President, "We as a company have made a moral judgment on the long-range goals of our government and we support these."

*Id.* (emphasis added).

8. *Id.* at 3 n.1. In a report to its shareholders, the corporation stated:

At the May 1969 annual meeting Dow's Chairman of the Board said, in answer to persons who criticized during the question and answer period the company's production of napalm: "Last year you said Dow should make a *moral decision.* We've made one."

Dow Chemical Company, Shareholders Q. 2 (July, 1969) (emphasis in original).

9. Brief at 3 n.1. The following statement was made by the president of the corporation:

We, as individuals, are personally concerned with the world and its problems. We have sons and daughters in the armed forces, in the Peace Corps, and in the universities. A corporation is a collection of individuals, and the *use of our consciences is, as it should be, a part of the decision-making process.*

Address by President Doan, Dow Chemical Company 1967 Annual Shareholder Meeting, May, 1967, *quoted in* L. Lasser, Dow Chemical Company, 20, 1968 (case study on file at Harvard Business School) (emphasis added).

10. *See* notes 3 & 4 and accompanying text *supra.*

11. *See* note 9 *supra.*

12. *Id.*

which the law imposes on the role of the corporate director; aspects which, if unexercised, will sustain a shareholder's derivative action.

### B.

#### 1.

In Freudian terms, the agency of "conscience" is designated "superego."[13] Freud described the genesis of the superego as:

> [A] successful instance of identification with the parental agency . . . . With his abandonment of the Oedipus complex a child must . . . renounce the intense object cathexes which he has deposited with his parents which have probably long been present in his ego.[14]

This superego represents the locus of the connections between the individual and tradition, between humans and society, between existence and morality. Freud's characterization, indeed the very postulation of this mental agency, implicitly asserts its critical significance to the framing of theories of social behavior.

He seems to have been fully aware of the extent to which his concept of the superego sharply diverges from Marxist views of reality. Immediately after describing the superego as "the representative . . . of every moral restriction . . . the vehicle of tradition and of all the time-resisting judgments of value which have propogated themselves . . . from generation to generation,"[15] Freud argues:

> It seems likely that what are known as materialistic views of history sin in underestimating this factor. They brush it aside with the remark that human "ideologies" are nothing other than

---

13. Sigmund Freud stated:
   There is scarcely anything else in us that we so regularly separate from our ego and so easily set over against it as precisely as our conscience. I feel an inclination to do something that I think will give me pleasure, but I abandon it on the ground that my conscience does not allow it. Or I have let myself be persuaded by too great an expectation of pleasure into doing something to which the voice of conscience has objected and after the deed my conscience punishes me with distressing reproaches and causes me to feel remorse for the deed. I might simply say that the special agency which I am beginning to distinguish in the ego is conscience. But it is more prudent to keep the agency as something independent and to suppose that conscience is one of its functions and that self-observation, which is an essential preliminary to the judging activity of conscience, is another of them. And since when we recognize that something has a separate existence we give it a name of its own, from this time forward I will describe this agency in the ego as the *"superego."*
S. Freud, *New Introductory Lectures on Psychoanalysis,* in 22 The Standard Edition of the Complete Psychological Works of Sigmund Freud 60 (J. Strachey ed. 1964) (emphasis in original) [hereinafter cited as Freud].
   14. *Id.* at 63–64.
   15. *Id.* at 66–67.

the product and superstructure of their contemporary economic conditions. That is true, but very probably not the whole truth. Mankind never lives entirely in the present. The past, the tradition of the race and of the people, lives on in the ideologies of the superego, and yields only slowly to the influences of the present and to new changes; and so long as it operates through the superego it plays a powerful part in human life, independently of economic conditions.[16]

At this point, we have confronted the division of views, Freudian and Marxist, on the social role of the term "conscience." In the record of the case we are considering, we have only the testimony of the directors from which a position on this issue can be inferred.[17] Of course they believed, with Freud, that "conscience" both existed and was not susceptible to reductionism; most of us act as though we do. It is ironic, but explicable, that the plaintiffs in *Medical Committee for Human Rights v. SEC,* no doubt widely viewed as having mounted a moral effort, were careful *not* to rely on an explicitly moral perspective. To understand the source of this extraordinary juxtaposition is to undertake an examination of social forces in American society that were uncontemplated by either Marx or Freud.

I turn, therefore, to the most influential commentator who has sought to reconcile Freudian and Marxist viewpoints and whose ideas enjoyed wide recognition during the period which produced the *Medical Committee* litigation. Herbert Marcuse propounded many of the ideas that underlay opposition to contemporary society, characteristic of student protests and lifestyles during the 1960's.[18] Marcuse's concept of the historical impact of technology, which diverges dramatically from Marxist views, accounts in great measure for the popularity of his opinions during that period. Marx maintained that technology was a neutral factor, in that it was determined by the social and economic organization of the society which developed it; Marcuse, however, viewed technology as one of the factors determining that organization.

In defining the impact of technology on society, Marcuse focused upon elements of Freudian theory other than the superego, and redefined those insights in ways less divergent from Marxist views of reality. Thus, Marcuse accepted Freud's correlation of civilization with repression, of the triumph of the reality principle over the unrepressed behavior comprising the pleasure principle. He argued, that the affluence produced by the capitalist economic system based upon

16. *Id.* at 67.
17. *See* text accompanying note 12 *supra.*
18. *See generally* H. Marcuse, Eros and Civilization: A Philosophical Inquiry Into Freud (1955).

such repression had created a situation in which the technology required for such affluence imposed upon individuals more repression
than was necessary. This historical variant of the reality principle, which
Marcuse designated as the "performance principle," functions within
his theory in ways analogous to Marx's use of the concept of surplus
value in that it embodies a moral condemnation of the society which
imposes such demands upon the individual.[19]

A theoretical description of this conduct is useful to us, in a legal
context, only if its insights are functional (and therefore ultimately
procedural); therefore this description will be derived from an analysis
of the functional implementation of Freudian theory — psychoanalysis.
Specifically, since the concept of the superego represents, in Freudian
terms, the basis for any description of why the board of directors in
our problem acted as they did, it seems appropriate to attempt to ascertain whether Marcuse's reformulation of Freudian insights ought to
be accepted.[20]

---

19. *See* P. Robinson, The Freudian Left 204–05 (1969), where the author
stated:

> Like surplus repression, which could be correlated with Marx's essentially
> quantitative notion of surplus value, the performance principle, Marcuse implied,
> corresponded to Marx's *qualitative* characterization of existence under capitalism,
> namely the notions of alienation and reification . . . . To be sure, Marcuse's per-
> formance principle was a more inclusive concept than either alienation or reifica-
> tion. It incorporated elements of Weber's Protestant ethic (the irrational psycho-
> logical need to perform, to work for work's own sake) as well as the salient
> features of modern mass society analysis (the technique of mass manipulation and
> the organization of leisure by the communications and entertainment industries).
> But at the heart of the concept was Marx's notion of the transformation of men
> into things, alienated from the products of their labor, from the labor process itself,
> and from their fellowmen.

*Id.* (footnotes omitted). *See also* T. Roszak, The Making of a Counter Culture,
Reflections on the Technocratic Society and Its Youthful Opposition 110–11
(1969). Roszak observed:

> [I]n *Eros and Civilization,* . . . Marcuse offers us the idea of "repressive de-
> sublimation" as his explanation of the technocracy's ingenious assimilation of the
> "erotic danger zone." Repressive desublimation is the "release of sexuality in
> modes and forms which reduce and weaken erotic energy." . . . Just as Marx,
> in his analysis of capitalism during the period of primitive accumulation, found
> the secret of gross physical exploitation in the notion of "surplus value," so
> Marcuse, in his study of technocracy under the regime of affluence, finds the secret
> of psychic exploitation in repressive desublimation. It is an excellent example of
> psychological categories replacing sociological economic categories in social
> theory — and in this case Marcuse's analysis leads to a much solider [sic] idea
> than Marx's rather foggy use of the labor theory of value. It also leads to a
> distinctly non-Marxist conclusion, namely, that technology exerts an influence
> upon society *in its own right* and independent of the social form under which it
> is organized.

*Id.* (emphasis in original).

20. The individuals whose work is the subject of Marcuse's analysis are identified
in H. Marcuse, *supra* note 18, at 248 (footnote omitted):

> The discussion will neglect the differences among the various revisionist
> groups and concentrate on the theoretical attitude common to all of them. It is

*2.*

Marcuse defines the historical relationships between psychoanalysis and the societies in which it has existed as follows:

> Psychoanalysis has changed its function in the culture of our time, in accordance with fundamental social changes that occurred during the first half of the century. The collapse of the liberal era and of its promises, the spreading totalitarian trend and the efforts to counteract this trend, are reflected in the position of psychoanalysis . . . . [W]hen Central and Eastern Europe were in revolutionary upheaval, it became clear to what extent psychoanalysis was still committed to the society whose secrets it revealed. The psychoanalytic conception of man, with its belief in the basic unchangeability of human nature, appeared as "reactionary"; Freudian theory seemed to imply that the humanitarian ideals of socialism were humanly unattainable. Then the revisions of psychoanalysis began to gain momentum.[21]

Marcuse then makes it clear that the argument which underlies *Eros and Civilization* is that his views are faithful to the revolutionary insights of Freudian *theory* as opposed to the socially defined ends of Freudian *therapy* (stressed by the Neo-Freudians) which represent the demands of the civilization in which psychoanalysis takes place:

> Freud was fully aware of this discrepancy [between theory and therapy] . . . while psychoanalytic theory recognizes that the sickness of the individual is ultimately caused and sustained by the sickness of his civilization, psychoanalytic therapy aims at curing the individual so that he can continue to function as part of a sick civilization without surrendering to it altogether. The acceptance of the reality principle, with which psychoanalytic therapy ends, means the individual's acceptance of the civilized regimentation of his instinctual needs, especially sexuality. In Freud's theory, civilization appears as established in contradiction to the primary instincts and to the pleasure principle. But the latter survives in the id and the civilized ego must permanently fight its own timeless past and forbidden future. Theoretically, the difference between mental health and neurosis lies only in the degree and effectiveness of resignation: mental health is successful, efficient resignation — normally so efficient that it shows forth as moderately happy satisfaction. . . . Consequently, the critical insights of psychoanalysis gain their full force only in the field of theory, and perhaps particularly where theory is farthest removed from therapy — in Freud's "metapsychology."

distilled from the representative works of Erich Fromm, Karen Horney, and Henry Stack Sullivan. Clara Thompson is taken as a representative historian of the revisionists. *Id.*

21. This passage was contained in the Epilogue of *Eros and Civilization*. *Id.* at 238–39.

J. G. D., *Villanova Law Review*, June 1975

The revisionist schools obliterated this discrepancy between theory and therapy by assimilating the former to the latter. This assimilation took place in two ways. First, the speculative and "metaphysical" concepts not subject to any clinical verification (such as the death instinct, the hypothesis of the primal horde, the killing of the primal father and its consequences) were minimized or discarded altogether. Moreover, in this process some of Freud's most decisive concepts (the relation between id and ego, the function of the unconscious, the scope and significance of sexuality) were redefined in such a way that their explosive connotations were all but eliminated. The depth dimension of the conflict between the individual and his society, between the instinctual structure and the realm of consciousness, was flattened out. Psychoanalysis was reoriented on the traditional consciousness psychology of pre-Freudian texture. The right to such reorientations in the interest of successful therapy and practice is not questioned here; but the revisionists have converted the weakening of Freudian theory into a new theory, and the significance of this theory alone will be discussed presently.[22]

Marcuse then reviews what he perceives to be the significant differences between Neo-Freudian views and those of Freud:

The chief objections of the revisionists to Freud may be summed up as follows: Freud grossly underrated the extent to which the individual and his neurosis are determined by conflicts with his environment. Freud's "biological orientation" led him to concentrate on the phylogenetic and ontogenetic *past* of the individual: he considered the character as essentially fixed with the fifth or sixth year (if not earlier), and he interpreted the fate of the individual in terms of primary instincts and their vicissitudes, especially sexuality. In contrast, the revisionists shift the emphasis "from the past to the present," from the biological to the cultural level, from the "constitution" of the individual to his environment. . . . Freud saw society as "static" and thought that society had developed as a "mechanism for controlling men's instincts," whereas the revisionists know "from the study of comparative cultures" that "man is not biologically endowed with dangerous fixed animal drives and that the only function of society is to control these." They insist that society "is not a static set of laws instituted in the past at the time of the murder of the primal father, but is rather a growing, changing, developing network of interpersonal experiences and behavior." To this, the following insights are added [by the Neo-Freudians]:

"One cannot become a human being except through cultural experience. Society creates new needs . . . Of such a nature are the ideas of justice, equality and cooperation. [But] [s]ome of the new needs lead in a destructive direction

22. *Id.* at 245–48 (footnotes omitted).

and are not good for man. . . . When the destructive elements predominate, we have a situation which fosters war."

This passage may serve as a starting point to show the decline of theory in the revisionist schools. There is first the laboring of the obvious, of everyday wisdom. Then there is the adduction of sociological aspects. In Freud they are included in and developed by the basic concepts themselves; here they appear as incomprehended, external factors.[23]

As to the second of these charges, "the adduction of sociological aspects," the fact is that the Neo-Freudians, in stressing the influence of the cultural environment (the society) upon the psychological development of the individual, were engaging in something strongly resembling Marxist analysis, which takes the socioeconomic environment as its starting point. Unless the "adduction of sociological aspects" is worthless (or otherwise illegitimate) we might conclude that, in this specific instance, Marcuse was rejecting Marxist analysis altogether.[24]

It is significant that Freud himself pleaded guilty to the first of these charges, which is "the laboring of the obvious, of everyday wisdom":[25]

I am now prepared to hear you ask me scornfully whether our ego-psychology comes down to nothing more than taking commonly used abstractions literally and in a crude sense, and transforming them from concepts into things — by which not much would be gained. To this I would reply that in ego-psychology it will be difficult to escape what is universally known; it will rather be a question of new ways of looking at things and new ways of arranging them than of new discoveries.[26]

Similarly, given Freud's emphasis upon the Oedipus complex in that description, it seems significant that Marcuse barely refers to it, except to deny its importance.[27] Marcuse maintained that the Neo-

23. *Id.* at 248–50, *quoting* C. THOMPSON, PSYCHOANALYSIS: EVOLUTION AND DEVELOPMENT 143 (1951) (footnotes omitted).

24. The more precise charge was that the difficulty resided in the fact that the sociological aspects were "incomprehended, external factors" rather than "included in and developed by the basic concepts themselves." *See* text accompanying note 23 *supra*.

25. Marcuse leveled a similar charge at Charles Reich in a review of THE GREENING OF AMERICA:
Consciousness III is of course that of the young generation in rebellion against the Establishment. What are the new revolutionary values of the rebels? The author formulates them in three "commandments" . . . The astonished reader might ask: "What is revolutionary about these commandments which from the Bible to Kant and beyond have graced the sermons of the moralists?"
Marcuse, *Charles Reich — A Negative View*, N.Y. Times, Nov. 6, 1970, at 41, col. 3.

26. FREUD, *supra* note 13, at 60.

27. *See* P. ROBINSON, *supra* note 19, at 211 & n.142.

J. G. D., *Villanova Law Review*, June 1975

Freudian revisionists had "minimized or discarded altogether" those "most speculative and 'metaphysical' [Freudian] concepts not subject to any clinical verification"; it was on this basis that he accused them of "hav[ing] converted the weakening of Freudian theory into a new theory."[28] Given this charge, what seems important is that Marcuse's treatment of "the killing of the primal father"[29] uses Marxist themes to make the implicit question posed the *moral* one of the legitimacy of power rather than the *existential* one of the meaning of revolt.

> In Marcuse's hands the primal crime became a kind of capitalist allegory. Although he did not state so explicitly, he obviously transformed Freud's primal father into the capitalist entrepreneur, and the band of brothers into the European proletariat. The most significant result of this transmutation of Freud's theory was that it moved the focal point of the drama away from the revolt of the brothers, which marked the beginning of civilization for Freud, and back to the establishment of the paternal dictatorship. For Marcuse civilization began not with the revolt against paternal tyranny, but with the founding of the father's rule over his sons. This was the historical moment at which the reality principle (or more accurately, the performance principle) replaced the pleasure principle.[30]

### 3.

The goal which Marcuse both prescribes and defines is a society in which "Eros, the life instincts, would be released to an unprecedented degree."[31] Utilizing Freudian terminology, Marcuse delineates the difference between his views and those of Freud on the question of whether such a society can be realized:

> The development of the ego is development "away from primary narcissism"; at this early stage, reality is not outside, but is contained in the pre-ego of primary narcissism. It is not hostile and alien to the ego, but "intimately connected with, originally not even distinguished from it." This reality is first (and last?) experienced in the child's libidinal relation to the mother — a relation which is at the beginning within the "pre-ego" and only subsequently divorced from it. . . . The Narcissistic phase of individual pre-genitality "recalls" the maternal phase of the history of the human race. Both constitute a reality to which the ego responds with an attitude, not of defense and submission, but of integral identification with the "environment." But in the light of the paternal reality principle, the "maternal concept" of reality

---

28. *See* text accompanying note 22 *supra*.
29. This is one of the specific instances offered by Marcuse of the concepts which the Neo-Freudian revisionists ignored. *See* text accompanying note 22 *supra*.
30. P. Robinson, *supra* note 19, at 208 (footnotes omitted).
31. H. Marcuse, *supra* note 18, at 154.

here emerging is immediately turned into something negative, dreadful. The impulse to reestablish the lost Narcissistic-maternal unity is interpreted as a "threat," namely, the threat of "maternal engulfment" by the overpowering womb. The hostile father is exonerated and reappears as savior who, in punishing the incest wish, protects the ego from its annihilation in the mother. . . . The patriarchal reality principle holds sway over the psycho-analytic interpretation. It is only beyond this reality principle that the "maternal" images of the super ego convey promises rather than memory traces — images of a free future rather than of a dark past.[32]

Accepting the proposition that Freudian terminology may be functional, permitting us to assess the validity of competing attitudes towards reality, what should be noted is that Marcuse's reference to "[t]he hostile father . . . reappear[ing] as savior . . . in punishing the incest wish" may refer to precisely the Oedipus complex.[33] The difference between Marcuse's views and those of Freud apparently rest upon the importance to be attached to the fact that the child is separated from its mother at birth in assessing the psychological make-up and progress of the individual. The divergence between the two views may also be related to Marcuse's emphasis upon the fact that the "sociological aspects" adduced by the Neo-Freudian revisionists were "incomprehended, external factors," rather than "included in and developed by the basic concepts themselves."[34]

Marcuse also notes the extent to which the Freudian concept of the death instinct functions as an obstacle to the attainment of the society which Marcuse delineated:

[O]ne innermost obstacle seems to defy all prospect of a non-repressive development — namely, the bond that binds Eros to the death instinct. The brute fact of death denies once and for all the reality of a non-repressive existence. . . . The mere anticipation of the inevitable end, present in every instant, introduces a repressive element into all libidinal relations and renders pleasure itself painful. . . . The flux of time is society's most natural ally in maintaining law and order, conformity, and the institutions that relegate freedom to a perpetual utopia; the flux of time helps men

---

32. *Id.* at 229–31 (footnotes omitted). In this connection, Marcuse observed:
   In other words, narcissism may contain the germ of a different reality principle: the libidinal cathexis of the ego (one's own body) may become the source and reservoir for a new libidinal cathexis of the objective world — transforming this world into a new mode of being.
*Id.* at 169.

33. *See* note 27 and accompanying text *supra.*

34. *See* text accompanying note 23 *supra.*

to forget what was and what can be: it makes them oblivious to the better past and the better future.[35]

Marcuse overcomes this obstacle by defining a "Nirvana principle" that, in converging with the pleasure principle and becoming reconciled with the reality principle, makes possible the acceptance of death:

> The striving for the preservation of time in time, for the arrest of time, for conquest of death, seems unreasonable by any standard, and outright impossible under the hypothesis of the death instinct that we have accepted. Or does this very hypothesis make it more reasonable? The death instinct operates under the Nirvana principle: it tends toward that state of "constant gratification" where no tension is felt — a state without want. This trend of the instinct implies that its *destructive* manifestations would be minimized as it approached such a state. If the instinct's basic objective is not the termination of life but of pain — the absence of tension — then paradoxically, in terms of the instinct, the conflict between life and death is the more reduced, the closer life approximates the state of gratification. Pleasure principle and Nirvana principle then converge. . . . As suffering and want recede, the Nirvana principle may become reconciled with the reality principle. The unconscious attraction that draws the instincts back to an "earlier state" would be effectively counteracted by the desirability of the attained state of life. The "conservative nature" of the instincts would come to rest in a fulfilled present. Death would cease to be an instinctual goal. It remains a fact, perhaps even an ultimate necessity — but a necessity against which the unrepressed energy of mankind will protest, against which it will wage its greatest struggle.

> In this struggle, reason and instinct could unite. Under conditions of a truly human existence, the difference between succumbing to disease at the age of ten, thirty, fifty, or seventy, and dying a "natural" death after a fulfilled life, may well be a difference worth fighting for with all instinctual energy. Not those who die, but those who die before they must and want to die, those who die in agony and pain, are the great indictment against civilization.[36]

Given Marcuse's attack on the Neo-Freudian revisionists for "the laboring of the obvious, of everyday wisdom,"[37] it seems appropriate

---

35. H. Marcuse, *supra* note 18, at 231. Additionally, Marcuse stated:
It is the alliance between time and the order of repression that motivates the efforts to halt the flux of time, and it is this alliance that makes time the deadly enemy of Eros.
*Id.* at 233.

36. *Id.* at 234–36 (emphasis in original).

37. *See* text accompanying note 23 *supra*.

to note that very much the same charge can be leveled at his treatment of the death instinct.[38] Perhaps even more important for our purposes, given the connection Marcuse draws between the death instinct and the "flux of time,"[39] is the fact that Freud defined the difference between his views and "materialistic views of history" precisely in terms of time:[40]

> Mankind never lives entirely in the present. The past, the tradition of the race and of the people, lives on in the ideologies of the superego, and yields only slowly to the influence of the present and to new changes.[41]

If the reader is by now satisfied that Marcuse's views will not serve society as effectively as Freudian insights — because Marcuse takes insufficient account of "time" — there still remains the issues raised by the picture of reality contained in the views of Freud himself. If this picture is accepted as an accurate portrayal, it would require that the problems posed by corporate responsibility be treated, at least in part, as psychoanalytic problems.

---

38. Roszak stated:
To protest, to refuse, to struggle against death. . . . What Marcuse's version of non-repressiveness promises us, then, is the capacity to continue this futile opposition with the prospect of marginal gains like greater longevity and consolations for the dying. By no means empty ideals — but very traditional ideas that scarcely need repetition from Marcuse.
T. Roszak, *supra* note 19, at 113.

39. *See* text accompanying note 35 *supra.*

40. *See* text accompanying note 16 *supra.*

41. *See* text accompanying note 36 *supra,* delineating Marcuse's formulation of the "Nirvana principle." One contemporary observer has noted a phenomenon similar to that described by Marcuse:
Radicals often object that liberal programs generate an illusory feeling of movement when in fact little is changing. Their assumption is always that such an illusion slows down movement, but it is just as likely that the reverse is true. Radicals are so absorbed with the difficulties they have in overcoming inertia that they tend to assume that motionlessness is a comfortable state that everyone will seek with the slightest excuse. But even an illusory sense of progress is invigorating, and whets the desire for further advances. Absolute stagnation is enervating, and creates a feeling of helplessness and impotence. The "war on poverty" may have done very little to alleviate poverty and nothing at all to remove its causes, but it raised a lot of expectations, created many visions of the possibilities for change, alerted a large number of people to existing inadequacies in the system and to the relative efficacy of various strategies for eliminating them. One factor that radicals overlook, in other words, is the educative value of liberal reform, however insignificant that reform may be in terms of institutional change.
P. Slater, The Pursuit of Loneliness: American Culture at the Breaking Point 123–24 (1970).

## C.

### 1.

Joseph Goldstein, trained in both law and psychoanalysis, has described the basis upon which one could assume that the two disciplines are relevant to each other:

> Psychoanalysis endeavors to provide a systematic theory of human behavior. Law, both as a body of substantive decisions and as a process for decision-making, has been created by man to regulate the behavior of man. Psychoanalysis seems to understand the workings of the mind. Law is mind-of-man-made. There is in law, as psychoanalysis teaches that there is in individual man, a rich residue which each generation preserves from the past, modifies for the present, and leaves for the future. An initial, though tentative assumption that one discipline is relevant to the other seems therefore warranted.[42]

If that relevance rests on the success of the endeavor "to provide a systematic theory of human behavior," however, it seems quite clear "that the student of law who turns to psychoanalysis for a finished theory offering a complete explanation of any and all human activity will be either duped or disappointed."[43] Freud himself has described the factors which made success at "developing a systematic theory of human behavior" unlikely:

> Psycho-analysis is not, like philosophies, a system starting out from a few sharply defined basic concepts, seeking to grasp the whole universe with the help of these and, once it is completed, having no room for fresh discoveries or better understanding. On the contrary, it keeps close to the facts in its field of study, seeks to solve the immediate problems of observation, gropes its way forward by the help of experience, is always incomplete and always ready to correct or modify its theories.[44]

---

42. Goldstein, *Psychoanalysis and Jurisprudence,* 77 YALE L.J. 1053 (1968).
43. *Id.* at 1077.
44. S. FREUD, *Psycho-Analysis,* in 18 FREUD, *supra* note 13, at 253. Freud further commented:

> I must confess that I am not at all partial to the fabrication of *Weltanschauungen.* Such activities may be left to philosophers, who avowedly find it impossible to make their journey through life without a Baedeker of that kind to give them information on every subject. Let us humbly accept the contempt with which they look down on us from the vantage-ground of their superior needs. But since we cannot forgo our narcissistic pride either we will draw comfort from the reflection that such "Handbooks to Life" soon grow out of date and that it is precisely our shortsighted, narrow and finicky work which obliges them to appear in new editions, and that even the most up-to-date of them are nothing but attempts to find a substitute for the ancient, useful and all-sufficient church catechism.

S. FREUD, *Inhibitions, Symptoms and Anxiety,* in 20 FREUD, *supra* note 13, at 96.

It is remarkable that despite these views, Marcuse insists that he deals with psychoanalysis strictly as a theory or philosophy. He focused precisely on the "most speculative and 'metaphysical' [Freudian] concepts not subject to any clinical verification,"[45] and stressed that "[t]he purpose of [*Eros and Civilization*] is to contribute to the philosophy of psychoanalysis — not to psychoanalysis itself. It moves exclusively in the field of theory, and it keeps outside the technical discipline which psychoanalysis has become."[46]

Marcuse argues, moreover, that the reasons for believing that the society, which he believes to be optimal, can be attained are based upon

> Freud's own theory [which] provides reasons for rejecting his identification of civilization with repression. On the ground of his own theoretical achievements, the discussion of the problem must be reopened. Does the interrelation between freedom and repression, productivity and destruction, domination and progress, really constitute the principle of civilization? Or does this interrelation result only from a specific historical organization of human existence? . . .
>
> The notion of a non-repressive civilization will be discussed not as an abstract and utopian speculation. We believe that the discussion is justified on two concrete and realistic grounds: first, Freud's theoretical conception itself seems to refute his consistent denial of the historical possibility of a non-repressive civilization, and second, the very achievements of repressive civilization seems to create the preconditions for the gradual abolition of repression.[47]

The second ground upon which Marcuse seeks to refute the charge of "abstract and utopian speculation, . . . the very achievements of repressive civilization," is apparently based on the view that

> [t]he more complete the alienation of labor, the greater the potential of freedom: total automation would be the optimum. It is the sphere outside labor which defines freedom and fulfillment, and it is the definition of human existence in terms of this sphere which constitutes the negation of the performance principle.[48]

45. H. MARCUSE, *supra* note 18, at 7. *See* text accompanying note 22 *supra*.
46. H. MARCUSE, *supra* note 18, at 7. One commentator, in an assessment of Marcusian thought, said:
> With Freud's own writings it is continually necessary for the reader to turn back from the theorizing to the case histories, from the inflated conceptual schemes to the revealing clinical detail or other shrewd empirical observations; and it is in such observations that in the end the evidence for the truth or falsity of psychoanalytic claims must be found.

A. MACINTYRE, HERBERT MARCUSE: AN EXPOSITION AND A POLEMIC 44 (1970).
47. H. MARCUSE, *supra* note 18, at 4–5.
48. *Id.* at 156.

This view is politically significant insofar as it depends on some remarkable assumptions about the world. It is not clear whether the world possesses sufficient material resources, and the technology to exploit those resources, such that a political reorganization would universally eliminate poverty and scarcity, while reducing labor. It is clear, however, that "total automation" postulates a world in which work is not needed. One need only deny *that* possibility to conclude that Marcuse's lack of analysis of either empirical problems[49] or political obstacles in connection with the question whether such a world *could* in fact be achieved means that he is himself engaging in "abstract and utopian speculation."

Even if Marcuse appears unsuccessful in utilizing Freud's "own theoretical achievements" to demonstrate the possibility of a non-repressive civilization, however, the question nevertheless remains whether Freud's own views — which stress the relationship between civilization and repression — are entitled to a significantly greater degree of acceptance. The first point to be made is that Marcuse seems correct in stressing the importance to the evaluation of any human concept of the "specific historical organization of human existence" from which it emerges. Thus, as Erik Erikson has noted:

> [I]t is important to concede that there is a hidden ideological connotation to all theories concerning man's nature: even the most carefully verified observations will prove to have been subject to the ideological polarizations of their historical period. This certainly has been the case with the theory of psychosexuality.[50]

And Erich Fromm — one of the Neo-Freudian revisionists attacked in *Eros and Civilization* — himself identified the "ideological connotation" of psychoanalysis with the "specific historical organization of human existence" that gave rise to Marxist analysis:

> Freud's concept of man was the same which underlies most anthropological speculation in the nineteenth century. Man, as he is molded by capitalism, is supposed to be the natural man, hence capitalism the form of society which corresponds to the needs of human nature. This nature is competitive, aggressive, egotistical. It seeks its fulfillment in victory over one's competitors. In the sphere of biology this was demonstrated by Darwin

---

49. *See* H. ARENDT, THE HUMAN CONDITION 132 (1958):
The progress ([in] the gradual decrease of working hours) has been rather overrated, because it was measured against the quite exceptionally inhuman conditions of exploitation prevailing during the early stages of capitalism. If we think in somewhat longer periods, the total yearly amount of individual free time enjoyed at present appears less an achievement of modernity than a belated approximation to normality.

50. Erikson, *Reflections on the Dissent of Contemporary Youth,* 51 INT'L J. OF PSYCHOANALYSIS 11, 12 (1970).

in his concept of the survival of the fittest; in the sphere of economics in the concept of *homo economicus,* held by the classical economists. In the sphere of psychology Freud expressed the same idea about man, based on the competitiveness resulting from the nature of the sexual instinct.[51]

To a considerable extent, therefore, Marcuse's views on the psychology of human nature may simply be an example of one of those "new ways of looking at things and new ways of arranging them" that Freud himself accepted as characteristic of "ego-psychology":[52] a "new way," accounted for in Marxist terms, by the fact that it originates from a "specific historical organization of human existence" different from that in which Freud lived.

It is equally true, however, that the language in which Freud expressed much of his own "new way of looking at things" served to hide the connection between his views and those of Marx described immediately above. As Erik Erikson has noted:

> To express the fact that libidinization withdrawn from the genitals thus manifests itself elsewhere, Freud used the thermodynamic language of his day, the language of preservation and transformation of energy. The result was that much that was meant to be a working hypothesis appeared to be making concrete claims which neither observation nor experiment could even attempt to substantiate.[53]

Thus "way[s] of looking at things" represented by the physical sciences — such things as atomic theory and relativity theory, for example—may themselves be subject to the same sort of Marxist analysis in terms of relationships to a "specific historical organization of human existence" which has been adumbrated immediately above in connection with the views of Freud.[54] In terms of the problem we are

---

51. Fromm, *The Human Implications of Instinctivistic "Radicalism": A Reply to Herbert Marcuse,* 2 Dissent 342, 343 (1955).

52. *See* text accompanying note 26 *supra.*

53. E. Erikson, Childhood and Society 59 (1950). *See* R. Rhees, Wittgenstein Lectures and Conversations on Aesthetics, Psychology & Religious Belief (1966), where the author stated:

> Or suppose you want to speak of causality in the operation of feelings. "Determinism applies to the mind as truly as to physical things." This is obscure because when we think of causal laws in physical things we think of *experiments.* We have nothing like this in connexion with feelings and motivation. And yet psychologists want to say: "There *must* be some law" — although no law has been found. (Freud: "Do you want to say, gentlemen, that changes in mental phenomena are guided by *chance*?") Whereas to me the fact that there *aren't* actually any such laws seems important.

*Id.* at 42 (emphasis in original).

54. *See generally* A. Whitehead, Science and the Modern World (1925), for a delineation of many of the implications of a view of the physical sciences such as

considering, however, what seems more important is that both law and the social sciences — at least for the present and foreseeable future — will "be making concrete claims which neither observation nor experiment could even attempt to substantiate":

> [T]he meaning of an actual experience in giving direction to a person's life rests on countless internal and external variables. Not only may what appears to be a similar event have different significance for the same person at different stages in his development, but it may also have different implications for different people at similar stages of development. Implicit in this observation is an insight of substantial significance to anyone seeking to predict or to evaluate the consequences of decisions in law. It points to a limitation, frequently obscured in assumptions, on empirical studies about the impact or likely impact of a statute, judgment, or administrative ruling. Unless such decisions are perceived as external events in the lives of many people — events which have different meanings for different people — statistical evidence of success may include, without recognizing a distinction, a number of people upon whom the decision had no impact and, even more significant, may include in the failure column a number upon whom the decision had not just no impact, but an impact contrary to that sought. For example, in evaluating a decision to impose a criminal sanction against a specific offender for purposes both of satisfying the punitive demands of the community and of deterring others from engaging in the offensive conduct, the student of law must recognize that the decision may satisfy some demands for vengeance, exacerbate some, and have no effect at all on others; and may for some restrain, for some provoke, or for some have no impact on the urge to engage in the prohibited conduct. Recognition of the multiple consequences of every law-created event makes comprehensible the never-ending search for multiple resolutions of what is perceived to be a single problem in law and the resulting need to find an ensemble of official and unofficial responses which on balance come closest to achieving the social control sought.[55]

The answers social scientists have evolved is to focus not upon the individual person, but upon the person's role or institutional capacity, or to define explanation in terms of prediction and often to utilize statistical techniques to describe the responses of a given sample of

that suggested in the text. For a detailing of the extent to which development of a "new way of looking at things" in the physical sciences can be regarded as following a process strikingly similar to the one adumbrated in the text concerning Freud's development of his views on "ego-psychology", *see* T. KUHN, THE STRUCTURE OF SCIENTIFIC REVOLUTIONS (1962). *See also* J. YOUNG, DOUBT AND CERTAINTY IN SCIENCE: A BIOLOGIST'S REFLECTIONS ON THE BRAIN (1960), where the author suggests that certain aspects of human "ways of looking at things" may be correlated with the nature and structure of human brain components.

55. Goldstein, *supra* note 42, at 1071–72 (footnotes omitted).

the population. The environment in which human behavior takes place (because it includes other human beings) is, however, sufficiently complex that the problems involved in selecting and adequately analyzing a sufficient number of factors in choosing the population sample may frequently be insuperable, especially since awareness of being part of the sample may change the behavior of the population being surveyed.[56]

Since another possible way of addressing the issue of corporate social responsibility is in terms of the *legal* "way of looking at things," however, it must also be noted that — at least as embodied in judicial decisions — the law, too "appears to be making concrete claims which neither observation nor experiment could even attempt to substantiate." As in the case of the other sciences, much of the difficulty results from a failure to distinguish between the results reached, *i.e.,* the particular scientific theory or judgment, and the process utilized to achieve those results. The use of "logic" that is deductive in form — reasoning from premises contained in legislative enactments or judicial precedents — permits judicial decisions to give the appearance of having been dictated by the facts recited in the opinion, although the results reached may in many of the important cases be determined by a combination of the judge's individual personality and the "specific historical organization of human existence." As Judge Jerome Frank observed:

> Generally, it is only after a man makes up his mind, that he attempts, and then artificially, to separate [the determination of the facts and the determination of what rules are to be applied to those facts].

> This must be as true of the judge as of other men. It is sometimes said that part of the judge's function is to pick out the relevant facts. Not infrequently this means that in writing his opinion he stresses (to himself as well as to those who will read the opinion) those facts which are relevant to his conclusion — in other words, he unconsciously selects those facts which, in combination with the rules of law which he considers to be pertinent, will make "logical" his decision. A judge, eager to give a decision which will square with his sense of what is fair, but unwilling to break with the traditional rules, will often view the evidence in such a way that the "facts" reported by him, combined with those traditional rules, will justify the result which he announces.[57]

---

56. *See generally* C. ARGYRIS, INTERVENTION THEORY AND METHOD: A BEHAVIORAL SCIENCE VIEW 97–102 (1970).

57. J. FRANK, LAW AND THE MODERN MIND 134–35 (1936). *See also* M. COHEN, REASON AND LAW 73–74 (1950):

[I]n any intellectual enterprise . . . there must always be a certain difference between theory and practice or experience. A theory must certainly be simpler than the factual complexity or chaos that faces us when we lack the guidance which a general chart of the field affords us. A chart or map would be altogether

J. G. D., *Villanova Law Review*, June 1975

It is therefore necessary to seek criteria which will form the basis for determining which "way of looking at things" is to be preferred. The resolution of that problem may well depend on which facts are perceived as relevant to any given situation. There are two bases for the belief that this is likely to be the case: first, the multiplicity of things that can be denominated "facts" which are related to any events or process of importance to human being; second, the fact that, even if a science could persuade us that it described *all* facts relevant to a given event or process, it remains true that any persuasive attempt at explanation necessitates a demonstration of *which* of the relevant facts are to be stressed. A conflict between a Marxist and Freudian view of a given historical event or process, for example, can fairly be summarized as a dispute over whether socioeconomic or individual psychological facts provide more powerful analytic or explanatory tools.

The criterion applied here for the purpose of determining which "way of looking at things" to prefer is that of *purpose,* the function fulfilled by stressing or seeking one rather than another fact. Given this criterion, it seems significant that Marcuse explicitly gave as a ground for preferring his "way of looking at things" to that adopted by the Neo-Freudian revisionists his preference for the theoretical rather than therapeutic purpose of psychoanalysis:

> Our concern is not with a correlated or improved interpretation of Freudian concepts but with their philosophical and sociological implications. Freud conscientiously distinguished his philosophy from his science; the Neo-Freudians have denied most of the former. On therapeutic grounds, such a denial may be perfectly justified. However, no therapeutic argument should hamper the development of a theoretical construction which aims, not at curing individual sickness, but at diagnosing the general disorder.[58]

Even if we accept the purpose of psychoanalysis as therapeutic,[59] however, it cannot serve to answer many of the specific questions raised by the factual assumptions previously discussed. Thus, what-

---

useless if it did not simplify the actual contours and topography which it describes. . . . No science offers us an absolutely complete account of its subject matter. It is sufficient if it indicates some general pattern to which the phenomena approximate more or less. For practical purposes any degree of approximation will do if it will lead to a greater control over nature than we should have without our ideal pattern. But for theoretic purposes we need the postulate that all divergences between the ideal and the actual will be progressively minimized by the discovery of subsidiary principles deduced from, or at least consistent with, the principles of our science.

58. H. Marcuse, *supra* note 18, at 7–8.

59. *See generally* P. Rieff, The Triumph of the Therapeutic: Uses of Faith After Freud (1966).

ever psychoanalytic therapy may do for the individuals whose "moral decision[s]" and "conscience[s]" produced the actions of the corporation's board of directors, neither psychoanalytic therapy nor theory claim to be able to provide answers to the question as to how to judge those actions.

2.

Goldstein has formulated a general description of the purpose of law:

> Law is at the same time the guardian of a powerful substantive heritage, as well as a generator and regenerator of fundamental societal values. It is a concrete and continuous process for meeting both man's need for stability by providing authority, rule, and precedent, and his need for flexibility by providing for each authority a counter-authority, for each rule a counter-rule and for each precedent a counter-precedent. In deciding between available alternatives and among oft-conflicting goals, law ideally allows, encourages, and secures an environment conducive to man's growth and development. . . . Thus the study of law focuses or should focus, upon the ways in which this process meets or fails to meet these needs.[60]

This description may be utilized as a description of law as "applied" social science. As noted above, however, one technique social scientists have developed to meet the problems presented by the fact that they deal with conscious beings rather than inanimate objects is "to define explanation in terms of prediction." When one attempts to intervene in disputes among human beings, however, this technique inevitably raises such questions as: how much probability justifies an intervention directed towards this given end, or any intervention at all. At least in terms of those interventions known as judicial decisions, it is the attempts to answer questions such as these that make a lawyer's "way of looking at things" stress so heavily such tools as presumptions, burdens of proof, and other evidentiary requirements.

Furthermore, in systemic terms, there are four characteristics that mark the lawyer's "way of looking at things": reliance upon facts rather than theoretical generalizations; emphasis upon concrete, existing situations and their interrelationships rather than hypothetical possibilities; a stress on an adversary process that presupposes that purposes may conflict, *i.e.,* that "ways of looking at things" may differ; and a characteristic attempt, when dealing with institutions (which play so large a role as employer, beneficiary and target of legal talents), to hold these institutions to their stated goals or ideals.

---

60. Goldstein, *supra* note 42, at 1056 (footnote omitted).

The first two characteristics, the emphasis upon facts and upon the particular situation being addressed, are most valuable because of the precision they make possible: it is probable that a larger proportion of the total possible factors and the interrelationships between them can be studied and understood as the specificity with which the issues are defined is increased.[61]

This stress on concreteness and complexity, on facts in terms of the specific situation being addressed, also implicates the third characteristic of a lawyer's "way of looking at things": an adversary process that presupposes that purposes may conflict, that "ways of looking at things" may differ.[62] The ideological basis for this characteristic is our society's insistence on the treatment of another human being — another "way of looking at things" — as a subject rather than an object, an entity at whose disposal legal talents are to be put. Strict adherence to this characteristic will in almost all cases entail a loss in efficiency, since the operation of the adversary system results in a significant expenditure of resources. Social "waste" in these terms, therefore, can be measured by the costs incurred in terms of efficiency resulting from the treatment of human beings as subjects rather than objects. Insofar as a society is willing to accept this "waste," however, the purpose of law can be defined as a process for establishing communication, agreement, or common language[63] among disputing

61. *Compare* this proposition *with* the problems raised in the text accompanying note 56 *supra*.

62. *See* P. FREUND, ON UNDERSTANDING THE SUPREME COURT 90–91 (1949):
    One final objection to the so-called Brandeis brief is that it places an inappropriate task on counsel. Is the adversary method the most suitable one for dealing with economic data? Someone has said that there are three sides to every lawsuit — my side, your side, and the truth. Should the responsibility for developing the background facts be placed on counsel, or should it be borne by some disinterested source? Should there be established for the courts something equivalent to the legislative reference service organized in a number of states for the benefit of the legislature? This would perhaps be a more radical innovation than the Brandeis brief itself, and yet it is not altogether fanciful. We owe much of our commercial law to the boldness of Lord Mansfield in seeking advice from experienced merchants regarding mercantile practices. The English admiralty courts have utilized the services of retired mariners drawn from the Royal Navy and the Merchant Marines — the celebrated "elder brethren of Trinity House." Some of our courts are beginning to employ disinterested medical and psychiatric advisers. The great difficulty with this idea in constitutional litigation is that the experts would be tempted to intrude their views on the merits of the legislation instead of helping the court to understand other people's views.
*See also* Karst, *Legislative Facts in Constitutional Litigation.* 1960 SUP. CT. REV. 75.

63. In discussing the role of the Supreme Court in this process, one commentator has stated:
    In setting the verbal formulas that define phrases like "ordinary and necessary business expenditure," "auxiliary and supplementary," "rail-trucking services," "reserve gate picketing," and "public service" broadcasting, which are the common coin of administrative decision making, the Supreme Court helps to set the terms of debate and trade in the bargaining that constantly goes on between those

"ways of looking at things";[64] a purpose whose significance resides in the fact that

> [t]here may be truths beyond speech, and they may be of great relevance to man in the singular, that is, to man in so far as he is not a political being, whatever else he may be. Men in the plural, that is, men in so far as they live and move and act in this world, can experience meaningfulness, only because they can talk with and make sense to each other and to themselves.[65]

### 3.

Since this article represents an attempt to apply legal analysis to the institution known as the corporation, much that will be indicated about the role of corporate director is also relevant to the role of lawyer insofar as any given legal system is itself an institution.

Reference to the provisions of the Constitution of the United States as they have historically been interpreted by the United States Supreme Court seems sufficient to establish the relevance of the fourth characteristic of a lawyer's "way of looking at things," the proposition that the content given institutional goals or ideals can vary significantly over time; and a reference to the Warren Court seems sufficient to establish that reasonably rapid changes can be brought about through utilization of legal processes. In terms of this characteristic, however, it seems clear that the institutional structure of the legal profession ought to operate so as to counteract the dangers involved in excessive adherence to professional values.

The basis for the privileges and respect society has accorded those fulfilling a professional role has presumably been the assumption that professionals were sufficiently experienced in the area of their concern and sufficiently in control of their talents, so that they could be relied upon in any given concrete situation to evaluate the meaning and

---

> who administer and those who are administered. . . . It is in these terms that judicial legitimation should be thought of — judicial doctrines become the legitimate bases for discourse and negotiation in the administrative process.

M. SHAPIRO, THE SUPREME COURT AND ADMINISTRATIVE AGENCIES 270 (1968).
    64. *See* Gilmore, *The Truth About Harvard and Yale,* 1964 YALE L. REP. 9, where the author stated:

> No lawyer worthy of the name can ever be either truly a conservative or truly a radical: at one and the same time we must somehow devote ourselves to the preservation of tradition, which we do not greatly respect, and to the promotion of change, in which we do not greatly believe.

*Id.*

I would argue that the legal profession's "way of looking at things," *i.e.,* that pattern of organizing concepts that is legal analysis as contrasted with mathematical or theological or another mode, has its own requirement. This helps to explain why psychoanalytic testimony, originating in a different "way of looking at things," presents such substantial evidentiary difficulties. *See* note 77 and accompanying text *infra.*
    65. H. ARENDT, *supra* note 49, at 4.

relevance of their own "way of looking at things." However, in terms of personal responsibility for the environment in which one lives and which one therefore, to some extent, creates, too narrow a focus upon a specific situation runs the substantial risk of abdicating that very responsibility. Thus, the extent to which the status quo (the "specific historical organization of human existence") remains in being is a function of the extent to which the need for change, for new "ways of looking at things," is accepted by those in a position (or playing a role) in society such that their acceptance of this need will bring about such a change. Insofar as too narrow a focus on concrete and specific situations impedes this acceptance, therefore, it runs the substantial risk of delaying necessary societal changes.[66]

Given the very substantial privileges that surround the attorney-client relationship, therefore, one possible application of the characteristic of holding institutions to their stated goals or ideals would be a willingness by bar association grievance committees to recommend disbarment of lawyers who assist clients in achieving acts violative of conscience in the sense that the lawyers themselves regard the acts as immoral.

The basis for demanding this personal moral responsibility is the fact that institutional decisionmaking increasingly affects the daily lives of individuals. Thus, the privileges accorded to the status of director by the society, like those accorded lawyers, ought to be matched by an effort on the part of directors and the organizations they control to prevent a director's "way of looking at things" from impeding the exercise of the director's personal moral responsibility. In these terms, however, the role of the director differs significantly from that of the lawyer, in the sense that, in our society, the task of representation asso-

---

66. The following is an excerpt from an address by Mr. Justice Stone delivered on June 15, 1934:

I venture to assert that when the history of the financial era which has just drawn to a close comes to be written, most of its mistakes and its major faults will be ascribed to the failure to observe the fiduciary principle, the precept as old as holy writ, that "a man cannot serve two masters." . . . The loss and suffering inflicted on individuals, the harm done to a social order founded upon business and dependent upon its integrity, are incalculable. There is little to suggest that the Bar has yet recognized that it must bear some burden of responsibility for these evils. But when we know and face the facts we shall have to acknowledge that such departures from the fiduciary principle do not usually occur without the active assistance of some member of our profession, and that their increasing recurrence would have been impossible but for the complaisance of a Bar, too absorbed in the workaday care of private interest to take account of these events of profound import or to sound the warning that the profession looks askance upon these, as things that "are not done."

Address by Justice Stone, Dedication of Law Quadrangle, Univ. of Michigan, June 15, 1934, in Stone, *The Public Influence of the Bar,* 48 HARV. L. REV. 1, 8–9 (1934).

ciated with the former role has historically been perceived in terms of a more specific purpose: that of profit maximization.

Analogous to the effect that the use of "the thermo-dynamic language of his day" had in the development of Freudian theory,[67] the use of the language of economics — especially when expressed in mathematical form — gives to decisions justified in terms of profit maximization an aura of certainty, objectivity, and an aura of not having been influenced by any given "way of looking at things." There exist, however, three different objections — which may be three different expressions of the same objection — to a justification of directors' decisions in this manner.

First, while it may be true that money is socially utilized simply as a measure of exchange and is therefore totally fungible, recognition of that fact does not make it impossible to recognize and act upon the realization that different uses of wealth resulting in the same profit, and different ways in which any such use of wealth is implemented, may well have different meanings for different human beings. Second, given the mathematical language, the terms of which appear to justify the "objectivity" of profit-maximization decisions, it should be noted that the difficulties which are raised by the possibility that the "new way of looking at things" represented by the physical sciences could be analyzed in terms of relationships to a "specific historical organization of human existence,"[68] may well also be true of the "way of looking at things" represented by mathematics.[69]

---

67. *See* text accompanying note 53 *supra.*

68. *See* note 54 and accompanying text *supra.*

69. *See* W. QUINE, *Two Dogmas of Empiricism,* in FROM A LOGICAL POINT OF VIEW (1961), where the author noted:

Physical objects are conceptually imported into the situation as convenient intermediaries — not by definition in terms of experience, but simply as irreducible posits comparable, epistemologically, to the gods of Homer. . . . I do, qua lay physicist, believe in physical objects and not in Homer's gods; and I consider it a scientific error to believe otherwise. But in point of epistemological footing the physical objects and the gods differ only in degrees and not in kind. Both sorts of entities enter our conception only as cultural posits. The myth of physical objects is epistemologically superior to most in that it has proved more efficacious than other myths as a device for working a manageable structure into the flux of experience. . . . Moreover, the abstract entities which are the substance of mathematics — ultimately classes and classes of classes and so on up — are another posit in the same spirit. Epistemologically these are myths on the same footing with physical objects and gods, neither better nor worse except for differences in the degree to which they expedite our dealings with sense experiences.

The over-all algebra of rational and irrational numbers is underdetermined by the algebra of rational numbers, but is smoother and more convenient; and it includes the algebra of rational numbers as a jagged or gerrymandered part. Total science, mathematical and natural and human, is similarly but more extremely underdetermined by experience. The edge of the system must be kept squared

Finally, in terms of the problems we are considering, however, it seems most significant that our society's legal system has already refused to accept immediately measurable maximization of profits as the exclusive standard in terms of which a board of directors' fidelity to its responsibilities would be assessed. Thus, *A.P. Smith Manufacturing Co. v. Barlow*[70] involved a claim by shareholders that directors had both exceeded corporate powers and misappropriated corporate funds in making a contribution of corporate funds to a privately supported, educational institution.[71] Corporate officers testified in support of the directors:

> Mr. Hubert F. O'Brien, the president of the company, testified that he considered the contribution to be a sound investment, that the public expects corporations to aid philanthropic and benevolent institutions, that they obtain goodwill in the community by so doing, and that their charitable donations create favorable environment for their business operations. In addition, he expressed the thought that in contributing to liberal arts institutions, corporations were furthering their self-interest in assuring the free flow of properly trained personnel for administrative and other corporate employment. Mr. Frank W. Abrams, chairman of the board of the Standard Oil Company of New Jersey, testified that corporations are expected to acknowledge their public responsibilities in support of the essential elements of our free enterprise system. He indicated that it was not "good business" to disappoint "this reasonable and justified public expectation," nor was it good business for corporations "to take substantial benefits from their membership in the economic community while avoiding the normally accepted obligations of citizenship in the social community." Mr. Irving S. Olds, former chairman of the board of the United States Steel Corporation, pointed out corporations have a self-interest in the maintenance of liberal education as the bulwark of good government. He stated that "Capitalism and free enterprise owe their survival in no small degree to the existence of our private, independent universities" and that if American business does not aid in their maintenance it

---

with experience; the rest, with all of its elaborate myths or fictions, has as its objective the simplicity of laws.

*Id.* at 44–45. *See also* Tribe, *Policy Science: Analysis or Ideology?*, 2 PHIL. & PUB. AFFAIRS 66 (1972); Tribe, *Technology Assessment and the Fourth Discontinuity: The Limits of Instrumental Rationality*, 46 S. CAL. L. REV. 617 (1973).

70. 13 N.J. 145, 98 A.2d 581 (1953).

71. Such a use of corporate funds was expressly authorized by a state statute. N.J. STAT. ANN. § 14A:3–4 (1969). The court noted, moreover, that

since in our view the corporate power to make reasonable charitable contributions exists under modern conditions, even apart from express statutory provision, [the State's] enactments simply constitute helpful and confirmatory declarations of such power, accompanied by limiting safeguards.

13 N.J. at 160, 98 A.2d at 590.

is not "properly protecting the long-range interest of its stock-holders, its employees and its customers."[72]

The Supreme. Court of New Jersey, relying on a plethora of precedents (largely from other jurisdictions), upheld the conduct of the directors, on, *inter alia,* the following grounds:

> As has been indicated [in this opinion], there is now wide-spread belief throughout the nation that free and vigorous non-governmental institutions of learning are vital to our democracy and the system of free enterprise and that withdrawal of corporate authority to make such contributions within reasonable limits would seriously threaten their continuance. Corporations have come to recognize this and with their enlightenment have sought in varying measures, as has the plaintiff by its contribution, to insure and strengthen the society which gives them existence and the means of aiding themselves and their fellow citizens. Clearly then, the appellants, as individual stockholders whose private interests rest entirely upon the well-being of the plaintiff corporation, ought not be permitted to close their eyes to present-day realities and thwart the long-visioned corporate action in recognizing and voluntarily discharging its high obligations as a constituent of our modern social structure.[73]

In the case we are considering, therefore, the issue presented can be framed in terms of the extent to which the directors' individual consciences should be permitted — in shareholder derivative suits — to serve as justifications for decisions as to which a corporate statement admits that "[f]rom a long-range viewpoint we could be hurt in many ways."[74] An attempt will therefore be made to sketch several different (although hopefully not inconsistent) lines of argument, directed towards resolving such a suit.[75]

First, relying on the doctrine that the standard by which actions of the board of directors is judged is that of profit maximization, and stressing heavily the negligible impact on the corporation's profits of the contract at issue, facts could be developed concerning the extent to which *this* corporation's performance of *this* contract was of relevance to the United States Department of Defense: facts concerning the extent to which the product was necessary to the conduct of the conflict at hand and the ease with which other business enterprises could have filled any urgent Defense Department need for the product.

72. 13 N.J. at 147–48, 98 A.2d at 583. *See* text accompanying note 10 *supra.*
73. 13 N.J. at 161, 98 A.2d at 590.
74. *See* note 5 *supra.*
75. What follows are not briefs or trial strategies, but suggested outlines. *See generally* Douglas, *Directors Who Do Not Direct,* 47 HARV. L. REV. 1305 (1934).

In addition, if psychiatric testimony is available and the court can be persuaded that it is admissible, it may be possible to utilize the psychoanalytic "way of looking at things" to persuade the court that the operation of personal, rather than corporate, purposes played so large a role in the reaching of the "moral decision[s]" relied on as justifications here that the directors were not adequately performing their representative function.[76] An analogous argument, utilizing conflict-of-interest terminology, might also be based on psychiatric testimony detailing the effects on individual directors of service in, or close personal contact with, officials of the Defense Department.[77]

Finally, if there is division on the board of directors concerning the contract in question, it may be relevant to attempt to disqualify certain directors on the basis either that commitments of their time to other enterprises or to personal interests are such that they are devoting insufficient time to the function of directing this corporation, or that — on the basis of testimony or corporate minutes — the time devoted to this decision was insufficient to meet the high standard with which corporate directors must comply in reaching decisions as difficult as the one at issue here.[78]

One hopes, moreover, that there will be within our society, individuals and institutions willing and able to expend the resources required to obtain the number of lawsuits (successful either in terms of results or deterrence or both) sufficient to produce practices among corporate directors that more fully comport with the theoretical ideal in terms of which their function is legally defined.[79]

## III. Epilogue

Events have taken place, subsequent to the decision by the court below, and some subsequent to our decision to grant certiorari, that require that we dismiss this case on the ground that

---

76. *See* A.P. Smith Mfg. Co. v. Barlow, 13 N.J. 145, 98 A.2d 581 (1953), where the court stated:

> There is no suggestion that [the charitable contribution at issue] was made indiscriminately or to a pet charity of the corporate directors in furtherance of personal rather than corporate ends.

*Id.* at 161, 98 A.2d at 590.

77. Assuming, that the psychiatrist would be testifying in terms of Freudian doctrine and that he would be qualified as an expert in the course of persuading the court to admit his testimony, this trial strategy runs a substantial risk that the psychiatrist's opinion will have an undue impact on the judge or jury's determination. In this connection, *see* text accompanying notes 62 & 64 *supra*.

78. The doctrinal legal basis for this line of argument is summarized in H. Ballantine, Corporations 156–67 (rev. ed. 1946).

79. *Id. Cf.* Rohrlich & Rohrlich, *Psychological Foundations for the Fiduciary Concept in Corporation Law*, 38 Colum. L. Rev. 432 (1938).

it has now become moot. In January 1971, the Medical Committee again submitted its napalm resolution for inclusion in Dow's 1971 proxy statement. This time Dow acquiesced in the Committee's request and included the proposal. At the annual stockholder's meeting in May 1971, Dow's shareholders voted on the Committee's proposal. Less than 3% of all voting shareholders supported it . . . . We find that this series of events has mooted the controversy.[80]

80. SEC v. Medical Comm. for Human Rights, 404 U.S. 403, 405–06 (1972). *But cf.* Deutsch, *Perlman v. Feldman: A Case Study in Contemporary Corporate Legal History,* 8 U. MICH. J.L. REFORM 1, 58–59 (1974).

John Warwick Montgomery, *History and Christianity*

The earliest records we have of the life and ministry of Jesus give the overwhelming impression that this man went around not so much "doing good" but making a decided nuisance of himself.

The parallel with Socrates in this regard is strong: Both men infuriated their contemporaries to such an extent that they were eventually put to death. But where Socrates played the gadfly on the collective Athenian rump by demanding that his hearers "know themselves"—examine their unexamined lives—Jesus alienated his contemporaries by continually forcing them to think through their attitude to him personally. "Who do men say that I the Son of man am? . . . Who do you say that I am?" "What do you think of Christ? whose son is he?" These were the questions Jesus asked.

And it seems patently clear that the questioner was not asking because he really didn't know who Jesus was and needed help in finding out. Unlike the "sick" characters in Jules Feiffer's Greenwich Village cartoons, when Jesus asked, "Who am I?" he was evidently fully aware of his own character; what he sought to achieve by his questions was a similar awareness of his nature by others.

Even as some given pathology can exert a powerful destructive influence on a writer's style, however, there may be selected disorders that actually heighten his expressive powers—as witness the case of Uspensky's far greater contemporary, Fyodor Dostoevsky. Dostoevsky clearly suffered from severe epilepsy, which appears to have implicated his temporal lobes. Such a pathology has been known in many instances to exert a dramatic effect on an individual's personality and emotional life. Irrespective of his earlier cosmology (if any), the patient may become deeply concerned about religious issues, highly conscious of good and evil, prone to favor mystical views and to invoke God or Fate as the cause of unusual circumstances, including his own weird behavior. This profound alteration in outlook seems explicable by the fact that, with little prior warning, the patient undergoes a powerful sensory experience (the "aura" of the epileptic fit) which lasts a few moments, immediately thereafter experiences rapid jolting of his musculature and frame, and then goes into convulsions and loses consciousness. This rapid sequence—a brief interval of exquisite rapture, followed by a traumatic fit and a subsequent amnestic period—seems sufficient to convince the individual that he is a "chosen" person; the laws governing the world require reformulation in the light of his experience.